The Arab-Israeli Accords: Legal Perspectives

CIMEL Book Series

1. *The Arab Israeli-Accords: Legal Perspectives* (Eugene Cotran and Chibli Mallat, eds.), 1996.
   ISBN: 90-411-0902-1

Also published by CIMEL and Kluwer Law International

1. *Yearbook of Islamic and Middle Eastern Law: Volume 1 1994* (Eugene Cotran and Chibli Mallat, eds.), 1995.
   ISBN: 90-411-0883-1
   ISSN: 1384-2935

The Arab-Israeli Accords: Legal Perspectives

edited by

Eugene Cotran, LL.D.
Circuit Judge, Visiting Professor of Law, SOAS
Chairman, CIMEL

and

Chibli Mallat, Ph.D.
Director, CIMEL

with assistance from

David Stott, LL.B.

Foreword by

The Right Honourable Lord Slynn of Hadley

CIMEL Book Series No. 1

CIMEL
SOAS

KLUWER LAW INTERNATIONAL
LONDON – THE HAGUE – BOSTON

Published for CIMEL
by Kluwer Law International
Sterling House
66 Wilton Road
London SW1V 1DE
United Kingdom

Sold and distributed in the USA and Canada
by Kluwer Law International
675 Massachusetts Avenue
Cambridge MA 02139
USA

Kluwer Law International incorporates
the publishing programmes of
Graham & Trotman Ltd,
Kluwer Law & Taxation Publishers
and Martinus Nijhoff Publishers.

In all other countries, sold and distributed
by Kluwer Law International
P.O. Box 85889
2508 CN The Hague
The Netherlands

First published in 1996

ISBN 90-411-0902-1
CIMEL Book Series ISBN 90-411-0903-X

British Library Cataloguing in Publication Data and Library of Congress Cataloging-in-Publication Data is available

Proceedings, in part, of a conference convened by the Centre of Islamic and Middle Eastern Law (CIMEL), School of Oriental and African Studies (SOAS), University of London, held in London in December 1994.

The publishers, the convenors of the conference and officials of the University of London (where the sessions, were held) do not necessarily share the views expressed in this publication.

Printed and bound in Great Britain by Hartnolls Ltd., Bodmin, Cornwall

CIMEL

Contents

Note on the Contributors

Eyal Benvenisti is Senior Lecturer of Law at the Hebrew University of Jerusalem, where he teaches public international law and public law. His publications include *International Law of Occupation* (Princeton, 1993). He is currently conducting research on water resources law.

Eugene Cotran was appointed one of Her Majesty's Circuit judges in 1992. He has been Chairman of the Centre of Islamic and Middle Eastern Law since 1990 and Visiting Professor of Law with reference to Africa and the Middle East at the School of Oriental and African Studies since 1988. He has published and edited several books and series on the laws of Africa, the Middle East and immigration law. He is a Board Member of the Palestinian Independent Commission for Citizens Rights.

Sharif Elmusa is currently a research fellow at the Institute for Palestine Studies in Washington, D.C. and an independant consultant. He is writing a book on the Israeli-Palestinian water conflict. He has worked as a consultant/author with World Resources Institute and the Library of Congress. His book *A Harvest of Technology: The Super-Green Revolution in the Jordan Valley* has just been published by the Center for Contemporary Arab Studies, Georgetown University, where, as an adjunct professor, he also taught courses on technology and agrarian development in the Arab World.

Celia Fassberg is Professor of Law at the Hebrew University of Jerusalem where she teaches private international law and international trade. She is currently working on a book on the recognition and enforcement of foreign judgments.

Eran Feitelson is Senior Lecturer in Geography at the Hebrew University of Jerusalem. He has published extensively on environmental aspects of land use, water issues and environmental aspects of immigration absorption. He is currently conducting research with the Truman Institute for the Advancement of Peace on the joint management of shared aquifers and has conducted several international workshops on the subject. He is also working on a waste water management project for the Jerusalem region.

Ruth Gavison is Haim Cohn Professor of Human Rights at the Faculty of Law of the Hebrew University of Jerusalem, where she teaches legal theory and human rights. She is the former Chair of the

Association for Civil Rights in Israel, and is presently working on a collection of essays on feminism and state, church, law and politics.

Mahmud El-Jaafari is associate professor of economics at the Islamic University of Gaza.

David Kretzmer is Professor of Law at the Hebrew University of Jerusalem where he teaches public law and human rights. He is Director of the Human Rights Centre of the Hebrew University and former Chair of the Association for Civil Rights in Israel. His recent publications include *Legal Status of the Arabs in Israel* (1990) and he is completing a book on the Israeli Supreme Court and the Occupied Territories.

Ruth Levush is Senior Legal Specialist of the Near Eastern and African Law Division, Law Library of Congress, Washington D.C. She recently coordinated a project on campaign financing of national elections in foreign countries for the US Congress. Recent publications include "Absorption and implementation of foreign legal systems in the Israeli legal system" in *Implementation of Foreign Legal Systems and Destiny*. The Law Library of Congress recently granted her an award for excellence in research in foreign law.

Chibli Mallat, from the Beirut bar, is the Director of the Centre of Islamic and Middle Eastern Law at SOAS, and an international legal consultant. He is the author of *The Renewal of Islamic Law* (Cambridge University Press, 1993) which received the Albert Hourani award in 1994, and of *The Middle East into the 21st Century* (in press at Garnet). His *Introduction to Middle Eastern Law* should also appear in 1996.

Anis al-Qasem is a barrister at Lincoln's Inn. He is Chairman of the Legal Committee of the Palestine National Council and has prepared the draft of the Basic Law for the Palestinian National Authority. He is Secretary General of the International Organization for the Elimination of All Forms of Racial Discrimination (EAFORD) which has consultative status with the United Nations. He has written several books and articles in Arabic on related topics.

Mona Rishmawi is a Palestinian lawyer and Director of the Centre for the Independence of Judges and Lawyers of the International Commission of Jurists (Geneva). She is former director of Al-Haq: Law in the Service of Man, the West Bank affiliate of the International

Commission of Jurists. She has written on a number of issues including legal systems, independence of the judiciary, women's issues and human rights. She is also editor of the ICJ's Yearbook on Judicial Independence.

Raja Shehadeh is a Palestinian lawyer practising in Ramallah since 1979 and is a barrister at Lincoln's Inn. He is one of the founders of Al-Haq, and was its co-director from 1979 to 1991. He has written a number of books and articles on law and life in the Occupied Territories and on the Palestinian-Israeli Accords, including most recently *The Sealed Room*, *The Law of the Land*, and *Declaration of Principles and Legal System* (1994). He is the 1986 recipient of the Rothco Chapel award for commitment to truth and freedom.

Lord Slynn of Hadley is a Lord of Appeal in Ordinary.

David Stott studied law at Bristol Polytechnic and the College of Law and is currently completing a Masters degree in International Law and Relations focusing on the Arab-Israeli Accords.

Acknowledgements

The production of this book is owed to the dedicated efforts of several individuals who offered a lot of their unpaid time for the success of the conference on which it is based. The effort sustained from the spring of 1994 to December 1994, when the conference was held, needed to be complemented for the production in record time of the present volume. Again, the generosity of key individuals needs to be acknowledged.

For the conference, we would like to thank first and foremost Nathalie Blezard, who offered her leadership and knowledge of the field to cater for all the details needed by the unusual group of jurists who met for two intensive and exciting days on the eve of Christmas. The atmosphere and the quality of the conference were a high point for all of us, and the meeting was enhanced by the dedication of chairs and discussants of an exceptional calibre: Lord Slynn of Hadley, Professor Henry Steiner, Sir William Dale, Professor Camille Mansour, Emma Playfair, Greg Shapland and Raji Sourani; we also benefited from the sympathetic support of our colleagues in the law department, especially Michael Anderson and the head of the department at the time, Michael Palmer. We should like to also thank the many collaborators and researchers at CIMEL who made certain that no detail was disregarded before and during the conference: Shai Wade, Judge Ghayth Mosmar, Kathleen Lawand, Cathy Green, Ibrahim al-Jazy, Andrew Allen, Rukhsana Kiani, Sadaf Ijaz, Shereen Ma'sum, Peter Van den Auweraert and Mai Yamani.

Immediately after the conference, the efforts to produce the book began, and all the contributors were remarkably responsible for the careful transformation of their papers into the chapters which follow. There is no better reward for editors than the efficient commitment of contributors to deadlines. We were also lucky to see several of the aforementioned helpers at the conference dedicate themselves again for the next stage. It is thanks to them, and the coordination of Susan Faidi, that the book was so rapidly brought to the press.

On the production side, we would like to thank Cécile Insinger and Sarah Magarey from Kluwer Law International for their enthusiasm and support, and Professor Tony Allan and the Geography department at SOAS for the map. The conference and the book were helped by donations from Basil Eastwood and Andrew Green at the Foreign and Commonwealth Office and from Matthew Tuler at the US Embassy, as well as from the Research Committee of the School of Oriental and African Studies. In addition, CIMEL is grateful for the continued and generous support of Salah al-Hejailan and Nemir Kirdar, who have allowed us to pursue our work in adverse financial conditions. To all, our heartfelt thanks.

Transliteration

We have used a simplified transliteration of non-European words and names. Many such names are of household celebrity, and we preferred not to alter them for the sake of the professional transliteration of specialised journals. We have also kept the system of citation in the various contributions as generally provided by their authors.

CIMEL Book Series

This book is the first title in the CIMEL Book Series, a new publication venture between the Centre of Islamic & Middle Eastern Law at SOAS and Kluwer Law International. The Series Editors are His Honour Judge Eugene Cotran and Dr Chibli Mallat, though each title will have its own author or authors or editors in suitable cases.

Foreword

The assassination of Prime Minister Yitzhak Rabin adds considerable poignancy to this publication.

By analysing past and present problems and future possibilities this book makes a serious contribution to an understanding of relations between Arabs and Israelis. It is a sequel to a Conference at the School of Oriental and African Studies on the legal aspects of the Arab-Israeli agreement. Attended by many lawyers on each side of the discussion the Conference was organised by His Honour Judge Eugene Cotran and the Director of the Centre of Islamic and Middle Eastern Law at the School, Dr Chibli Mallat. I had the privilege of opening the Conference and hearing some of the speeches and I am very glad that it has proved possible to publish them more widely.

The Conference was sub-titled "Legal Perspectives" but the papers do not just deal with legal issues. They give an extensive explanation of the history of the conflict, indeed in general terms of the history of the area from the Ottoman Caliphate through the British Mandate to the Israeli occupation. They concentrate more particularly on the period of "transition from conflict to reconciliation" in 1992 to 1994. They analyse the difference in attitude of the Israelis and the Palestinians in the approach to a solution, the importance of the Declaration of Principles and the inter-action of politics and law. And some very practical human problems are revealed – who is to be responsible for the enforcement of human rights particularly in the area under the Palestine Authority's control? How far, if at all, can one distinguish between Jewish settlers on the West Bank, for example, those who went there as a religious duty or a national requirement and those who went there for other reasons? How far can those Palestinians who collaborated with the Israeli occupation be protected not just from physical violence but also from social ostracism? How far should terrorists be punished for the past?

Above all, however, it is the analysis of the legal issues which forms the core of the book. Some interesting legal issues are considered. What is the legal definition of "occupation" in the present context? Who in law, if anyone, is entitled to the territory of the West Bank? What is the status of and who is responsible internationally for the acts of the Palestinian Authority? The extraordinarily delicate and difficult task of the Supreme Court of Israel in some of the cases which come before it is well shown as is the no less difficult task of producing an acceptable draft basic law for the national authority in the transitional period.

The opening words of the Declaration of Principles read:

> The Government of the State of Israel and the Palestine Liberation Organization team (in the Jordanian-Palestinian delegation to the Middle East Peace Conference) (the "Palestinian Delegation"), representing the Palestinian people, agree that it is time to put an end to decades of confrontation and conflict, recognize their mutual legitimate and political rights, and strive to live in peaceful coexistence and mutual dignity and security and achieve a just, lasting and comprehensive peace settlement and historic reconciliation through the agreed political process.

It is tempting – maybe premature, maybe naive, on the other hand perhaps constructive – to ask whether the regional integration in Europe has any lessons for the region with which these papers are concerned. Regional co-operation is being explored in so many parts of the world – in the Far East, in South Asia, in South America, in NAFTA, that if the agreements and the peace in the Middle East hold, it is not unreal to think for the region in terms of economic co-operation, of social and environmental improvements jointly planned and executed, of common commercial policies towards third nations. If the long-standing enemies of three terrible wars could subscribe to the preamble and the aims of the Treaty of Rome, it is not impossible that the political will can come about to produce perhaps more limited aims and more limited co-operation but nonetheless a meaningful and a real joint endeavour. The Protocol on Economic Relations attached to the Cairo Agreement and the proposal for a Regional Development Bank for the Middle East provide a start. There are indications in the book of the way in which this might go.

It is here that the role of the courts and the importance of the rule of law have something to show. Without the Court of Justice the European Community would not have advanced as far as it has; without the unwritten principles defined by the Court to ensure the protection of fundamental rights, to control the abuse of power and to prevent back-sliding by the States in Treaty obligations, the citizen could not have benefited from the foresight of the founding fathers in the years following 1945. In the present book the stress on the importance of the rule of law and on the definition of legal rules is firm. The role of the courts in the context of the Arab-Israeli agreement is considered. These matters indicate that there is to some extent a common basis and that there are some common problems.

There are, of course, more fundamental differences, deeper seated antagonisms, historically longer roots to the problem here than those which had to be faced by Europe. Yet the exploration and the study of what Europe has done, of what mistakes it has made, of what it has achieved, must be worthwhile in the present context and may have something to teach. Even the history of the association agreements between Israel and the Community may point the way to the basis of a new grouping in the Eastern Mediterranean. On a non-political level there may be some analogies to be drawn with the problems which Europe faced. Raja Shehadeh notes:

> There were also fundamental differences between the Israeli and Palestinian legal thinking which became evident in the course of the negotiations. The Israeli legal community follows the English common law tradition of gradual development from decision to decision. The Palestinian legal community thinks abstractly in terms of codes and first principles, not concretely in terms of cases. This is partly because the Palestinian jurists acquired their education in such law faculties as Egypt, Syria and Lebanon where the civil law system is used.

It is unnecessary to make the obvious comparison in Europe of a difference which had to be, and to a significant degree has been, accommodated.

This is perhaps a slight matter in comparison with the other political, economic and military questions. But it has relevance.

For those with a detailed knowledge of the problem this book will be of considerable interest; it is of no less value to those like me who have only a broad background awareness of the history and the problems.

Slynn of Hadley

Preface

Eugene Cotran and Chibli Mallat

The book brings together, for the first time ever, independent and well-established lawyers and jurists from both sides of the century-old conflict, to reflect over matters of common interest. As violence recedes before negotiation and compromise, the issues covered by the ongoing negotiations will be increasingly determined by the emerging rule of law. Part of the originality of the book comes from the professional and experienced legal contributions of the best authors in the field over strategic issues: reflections on history and law, on key international treaties, on the domestic dimensions in the process, on water arrangements, on economic issues, and on the legal institutions which are being created and must adapt to the new scene. Another feature of the book is that, as an end result, it succeeds in showing that the old legal apposition of Israeli and Arab views is giving way to a common informed reflection and endeavour on modes of coexistence primarily determined by law.

Difficult as keeping pace with momentous developments may be on the political level, taking account of the hundreds of pages of legal agreements is a task even more difficult to contemplate. At the same time, there is no escaping the fact that, in the same way as force has dictated the efforts of four generations to cope with the new realities which the Zionist project had created in the late nineteenth century, once violence is shunned for the benefit of institutionalised processes, the only guide out of the persisting conflicts must be the law. The Peace Treaty with Jordan, the Palestinian-Israeli Declaration of Principles and the several agreements and protocols which followed it, the latest being the Interim Agreement[1] which was signed in Washington as this book was going to press: all these detailed texts and their appendices offer an inescapable point of reference for generations to come. The latest Interim Agreement, which comes in 31 long articles and appendices running into dozens of pages, serves perhaps as another reminder that in the Palestinian-Israeli search for accommodation, there will never perhaps be a final text. The Interim Agreement itself, together with its antecedents discussed in the present book by the most eminent authorities in the field, is testimony to a legal opening up onto several other agreements to come.

First, we should venture a word on the impulse behind the conference which led to this book, itself an unprecedented event in the legal history

---

[1] Israeli-Palestinian Interim Agreement on the West Bank and the Gaza Strip, Washington, September 28, 1995. For full text (without Annexes), see Appendix, p. 271.

of the region. Back in December 1992, the Centre of Islamic and Middle Eastern Law had organised a conference on water in the Middle East,[2] which was attended by several Israeli scholars, including a jurist from the Hebrew University, Dr Eyal Benvenisti. It was already clear, even though the agreements between the PLO and the Israeli government were still in the making, that the experience of lawyers would be crucial in the process, including the potential conflicts over water in the area. Since many other issues alongside water were under discussion since the international conference had been convened in Madrid in October 1991, a more sustained and comprehensive reflective effort was needed. The sense that a more serious attention to the importance of law was required prompted CIMEL to start planning a conference on the legal frameworks in the region soon afterwards. Eyal Benvenisti was the main facilitator, on the Israeli side, as was Raja Shehadeh on the Palestinian side, for the set-up of the delicate arrangements leading to the conference which resulted in the present book. The signing of the Declaration of Principles in September 1993 encouraged us in our efforts, and the slow process of a scholarly enterprise was undertaken, with particular insistence on the long-range academic value of a proper thinking on law. The conference came together in December 1994 in London, with a unique atmosphere of measured discussions, which will also be evident in the chapters in this book. The strongest indicator of the quality of the proceedings is the necessity to look carefully into the texts to discover, perhaps, the national provenance of their authors.

An ongoing process like the present negotiations is not conducive to long-term reflection. As agreement follows agreement, eyes are fixed on the practical results: as this book goes to press, the foremost issues are elections, withdrawals, redeployment and the release of prisoners. This does not mean that other texts were superseded, and the insistence in the recent Interim Agreement on building upon the founding accords means that the trail will get even more complex. Indeed, new texts are informed by the old, themselves opening the door to the vaster field of international law and UN decisions such as the famous 1967 Security Council Resolution 242. In the maelstrom of technical documents, only a clear legal vision offers adequate appreciation of what is primary in a text and what has become secondary because of time and new realities on the ground. In many ways, the chapters in this book help illustrate the phenomenon of the existing priorities, as well as those priorities which will force themselves onto the agenda in the future.

As an illustration, both Raja Shehadeh and Ruth Gavison open up the negotiating process into avenues, the importance of which the negotiators might have failed to realise. How the philosophy of

---

2 Proceedings are now published in J.A. Allan and C. Mallat, eds., *Water in the Middle East: Legal, Political and Commercial Implications*, (1995, London, I.B. Tauris Publishers).

conducting legal negotiations failed the Palestinian team appears, in Shehadeh's analysis, in the poor treatment of the laws of occupation by the Declaration of Principles, and the contradictions it forced onto the earliest emanations of Palestinian legal sovereignty. More fundamentally perhaps, he points out the deficiencies of the legal philosophy of the Palestinian national movement over generations, which the leading negotiators may still be unaware of. Part of the problem, of course, is the nature of occupation, and before it, the difficulty for the Palestinians in being educated in a dynamic system of law or for the production of judges and courts in the absence of territorial autonomy or stable living conditions. The reflections of Ruth Levush on the strengths of the domestic legal system in Israel over the past decades, and the criticism of Mona Rishmawi of the fledgling rule of law in the freed Gaza strip reinforce that importance at the close of the book. In the section History and Law, Professor Gavison's view has a different slant. She pays attention to those whom the process finds difficult to accommodate: how is it possible to address the difficult moral and legal arrangements confronting Jewish settlers, Palestinian 'collaborators', and the Palestinian 'heroes' of the national movements who ended up in prison for their sometimes violent resistance? Dealing with this eminently legal problem is not simple, nor are there easy recipes which could be transplanted from South African or European experiments. Only a legal reflection informed by the excruciating moral problems entailed in this particular historical set-up of interlocked peoples and individuals can help smooth the transition to peace with all the legal 'rejects' it produces. Thus the several overlapping layers of history and law.

More immediate attention is accorded in the next two chapters to the Declaration of Principles and the subsequent Palestinian-Israeli agreements: whilst Judge Eugene Cotran questions the spirit in which the agreement was made and the view of its chief draftsman, and points to the protracted process of its application, the delays and the deadlocks occasioned, and the resulting frustrations over repeatedly missed deadlines, Eyal Benvenisti observes in the transitional process hallmarks of a new legal configuration taken by the Palestinian Authority. Both studies are situated in an early transitional context. Since the signing of the Interim Agreement in Washington on 28 September 1995, the deadlines originally intended appear to have been revived. This may be especially the case with regard to the withdrawal of the Israeli army from heavily populated Palestinian sites to allow for the first Palestinian national elections to take place since the Majlis-e Mab'uthan of 1908, the Ottoman Parliament of the Emissaries which saw several deputies elected in Jerusalem to represent Palestine in the Ottoman capital. The scene at the time of writing this introduction (October 1995) is dominated by these momentous and defining events, as elections[3] can only be within the process opened up four years ago in Madrid.

The structures of domestic developments are addressed by two of the most eminent jurists of the area: David Kretzmer, who has authored one of the most thorough studies on the patterns of legal inequality between the Jewish and Arab citizens of Israel, and Anis Al-Qasem, who, as Chairman of the Palestine National Council Legal Committee, has accompanied the difficult production of legal texts by the Palestinian movement since before the formation of the PLO in 1964. The subjects addressed here might seem, in classic legal categories, separate from the Arab-Israeli accords proper. As international law moves away from the patterns of the non-intervention in domestic affairs principle, perhaps the most remarkable illustration of the undermining of this principle appears in the agreements between Israelis and Palestinians, and between Israelis and Jordanians. In the first case indeed, Professor Kretzmer shows how the domestic definition of the rule of law and human rights in Israel is affecting the process, and is in turn affected by it. Dr Anis Al-Qasem addresses an eminently domestic Palestinian issue: that of defining the Constitution or Basic Law of the Palestinian state. In the absence of a Palestinian state with full attributes of sovereignty for the present, this might sound an ambitious exercise. This domestic dimension, however, is the essence in the present process, not only for Palestinians, but also for the Israeli government, which has insisted from early on that the so-called Palestinian Covenant of 1968 be changed as early as possible. Already in his first letter to the Israeli Prime Minister, and as part of the package deal of mutual recognition and the Declaration of Principles, the PLO Chairman had written that:

> the PLO affirms that those articles of the Palestinian Covenant which deny Israel's right to exist, and the provisions of the Covenant which are inconsistent with the commitments of this letter are now inoperative and no longer valid. Consequently, the PLO undertakes to submit to the Palestinian National Council for formal approval the necessary changes in regard to the Palestinian Covenant.[4]

With the Interim Agreement, the process of change appears more pressing, as Article XXXI.9 stipulates that:

> the PLO undertakes that, within two months of the date of the inauguration of the Council, the Palestinian National Council will convene and formally approve the necessary changes in regard to the Palestinian Covenant...[5]

---

3 The elections for the Council and the President are expected to take place on 20 January 1996.

4 Letter from Y. Arafat to Y. Rabin, 9 September 1993, in E. Cotran and C. Mallat eds., *Yearbook of Islamic and Middle Eastern Law 1994*, (London and the Hague, 1995, Kluwer Law International). This book includes the main agreements between Palestinians, Israelis and Jordanians.

5 See Appendix containing full text, and Article XXXI.9 at p. 295.

Since the Palestinian National Council remains the most representative institution for Palestinians inside and outside Palestine, and the Covenant requires, under its own terms, modification by two thirds of its members, the legal intersection between the draft constitution or Basic Law and the historic charter now appears significant. Even if, as noted in the chapter, the draft remains a project, the internal structure of the Palestinian Authority introduced in 1994, and the Palestinian Council which should, after the electoral process, now emerge, will have to be governed by Palestinian-made institutions against the background of the Covenant. Conflicting rights and duties will no doubt emerge, as will, perhaps even more significantly, issues of identity. A serious reflection at this level, as started perhaps for the first time in the present book, has become all the more necessary for the next final stage of the peace process.

This interlocking of domestic and regional structure might be inevitable because of the interlocking of populations. The section of the book on water shows how the geographic imperative makes the fluidity between domestic and regional inevitable in the case of water, which both Israelis and Jordanians have officially recognised as a problem in the Treaty signed in October 1994. The legal consequence of this reality also defies the classical system of the impermeability of frontiers, and the concept of joint management might be another model which the Middle East is constructing with some success. The principle of exchange of water as established in the Treaty, and the reality of this exchange in the summer of 1995 between the two countries, reinforces the unusual premise taken by both Sharif Elmusa and Eran Feitelson in their chapters: that the structure of joint management in an area of particular scarcity and importance, such as water, should be the focus of discussion, rather than a classical division of water according to fixed percentages.

Like water, economy tends to defy boundaries. Economic issues are obscure to non-economists, and the two studies in the book should help foster an understanding of the more practical side of the new arrangements in terms of trade and labour flows, even if the picture at the end tends to be discouraging both from the point of view of a ravaged Palestinian economy to which the agreements have not proved particularly generous (Elmusa and Jaafari), or from the absence of a joint approach where common ventures could create common stakes beyond the division of spoils tailored to two different entities (Fassberg).

The book closes with separate reflections on the process of creating legal institutions on the two sides of the divide. Whilst the conclusions of Mona Rishmawi clearly show the amount of effort needed to overcome the problems faced by new Palestinian rule, it is clear in the remarkable overview of Ruth Levush that the construction of the rule of law in Israel has required a considerable investment of time and effort since before the creation of the Israeli state in 1948, and much more effort since. Whilst this reality could cause some to be disheartened before the task to be accomplished, almost from scratch, there is no escaping the fact that the rule of law does not come all-equipped like the Greek Goddess of war. It is a patient and protracted process, and a never ending one. This is a book, no doubt, on the *first* Arab-Israeli accords. The new chapter opened up by the Interim Agreement already requires a similar effort to be undertaken anew.

I. History and Law

1. The Weight of Legal History: Constraints and Hopes in the Search for a Sovereign Legal Language

Raja Shehadeh

The confrontation between the Israeli and the Palestinian national movements has taken many forms throughout the years. With the commencement of the Madrid peace conference and the Palestinian Israeli bilateral negotiations, it has passed on to a new stage, i.e. one where the legal narrative of each side regarding the territories occupied by Israel in 1967 had to necessarily confront the other.

This paper will review these two narratives with special regard to the question of land and Jewish settlement, and offer some thoughts as to their difference, extent of development and the way they have manifested themselves in the course of the negotiations.

I. The Palestinian Narrative

Elements of the narrative of the new period, characterised by acceptance of negotiations with Israel, can be traced to the meeting of the Palestinian National Council in Algiers on 15 November 1988. In this meeting "the necessity of convening the effective international conference on the issue of the Middle East and its core, the question of Palestine", was recognised. Amongst the main aims which this conference was to achieve were:

> The annulment of all measures of annexation and appropriation and the removal of settlements established by Israel in the Palestinian and Arab territories since 1967.[1]

Three years after this meeting, the PLO accepted the letter of invitation to the International Peace Conference in Madrid. In this letter the aim of the conference was expressed as follows:

> With respect to negotiations between Israel and the Palestinians... negotiations will be conducted in phases, beginning with the talks on interim self-government arrangements. These talks will be conducted with the objective of reaching agreement within one year. Once agreed, the interim self-government arrangements will last for a period of five years. Beginning the third year of the

[1] For the text of the Communiqué see *Journal of Palestine Studies*, Vol. XVIII, No. 2, Winter, 1989, pp. 216-223.

> period of interim self-government arrangements, negotiations will take place on permanent status. These permanent status negotiations, and the negotiations between Israel and the Arab states, will take place on the basis of resolutions 242 and 338.

The acceptance by the Palestinians of a phased resolution of the Israeli Palestinian conflict gave prominence to the questions as to which arrangements were going to determine the interim phase and constitute "the self-government arrangements". Were they to be those arrangements which had been instituted by the Israeli military government over the course of the Israeli occupation of the Palestinian territory, or were new arrangements to be negotiated between the two sides? Clearly, no commitment was made by the Palestinians when they accepted to negotiate "self-government arrangements" that these arrangements were going to be merely and exclusively the arrangements unilaterally imposed by Israel over the years preceding the negotiations.

Obviously, for the Palestinian side to achieve arrangements for self-government other than those which had been imposed by the Israeli side prior to the negotiations, the first prerequisite was to have an alternative to propose.

I was involved in the first year of bilateral negotiations which took place in Washington DC and will base this section of my paper on my personal experience and knowledge of what took place then as well as the documents produced by both sides. I will argue that, despite the efforts of the original negotiation team to the Washington talks, the position of the Palestinian leadership in the negotiations that followed the Washington talks and which resulted in the Agreements between the two sides, can be characterised by the absence of a legal strategy and I will propose some possible reasons as to why.

At the outset, it is important to point out that during this first phase of the negotiations, the Palestinian team was composed of delegates from the Occupied Territories, who were appointed by the PLO and openly proclaimed on more than one occasion that they were acting on behalf of their leadership, the PLO. This position, however, was rejected by the Israeli side who religiously held on to the fiction that they were not directly negotiating with the PLO. Despite this Israeli position, the fact of the matter remained that the positions of the Palestinian team were closely co-ordinated with the leadership in Tunis and the team bound themselves to the leadership's directives.

My own involvement in the negotiations began when I was asked by the head of the Palestinian team, Dr. Haidar 'Abdel Shafi, to advise on how the question of the Israeli settlements could be brought into the negotiations given the terms of reference which had been agreed upon.

Considering this question, I immediately became aware of the fact that the Israeli strategy was based on the formulation of the objective of the negotiations for the interim phase. As long as the two sides were expected only to negotiate interim self-government arrangements for the Palestinians, the Israeli response to any attempt to bring the Israeli settlements into these negotiations would be that these matters were outside the scope of the negotiations. It was clear that any successful Palestinian strategy would have to bring those settlements within the frame of discussions. It was my belief therefore that the first objective of the Palestinian side should be to force certain fundamental issues that primarily relate to land and water as well as to the administration of the settlements to be brought into the negotiations as preliminary matters which would be justified as a necessary first steps in any negotiations over self-government. The response to the expected Israeli refusal to have these placed on the agenda would be that it is impossible to negotiate arrangements for self-government before going through the first preliminary step of examining the prevailing arrangements that are now in place.

The proposed preliminary matters included for example access to information. It was argued that it cannot be expected that the Palestinian side would negotiate new arrangements for self-government while being ignorant of public information, such as the population register, government budget, areas and location of land registered as state land etc., which is held solely by the Israeli side. The legitimacy for full exposure of the facts about which the two sides were engaged in negotiating surely was a legitimate first step. Other proposals were for a review of existing arrangements, including extra territorial legislation. The Israeli settlements were governed by Israeli laws which by an act of the Israeli legislature had come to apply to the Occupied Territories. Now that these territories will be under the self-government of the Palestinians they were entitled to review these extra territorial legislation with a view of abolishing them. They were also entitled to insist as a preliminary matter that Israel undertake not to pass any more laws that apply to the area that is the subject of negotiations.

Another of the preliminary matters proposed was the cessation by the military commander of the Occupied Territories of issuing any more military orders as long as the negotiations are continuing. Otherwise whatever is negotiated can be annulled or altered by the unilateral changes in the law carried out by the Israeli side.

Another was the request that the military order which suspended land registrations issued in 1968, be revoked in order to allow the process of land registration to resume so that the disputes between the two sides about the status of the land in the Occupied Territories could be resolved through a neutral judicial process. Once this happens then the law of the land which requires the government to conduct land registration would be allowed to resume. Then the unilateral actions by Israel declaring large areas of Palestinian land as public land over which the Jewish settlements were built, would be subject to scrutiny. The basis for the appropriation of the land on which the settlements were built would itself become once again open for review.

These were some of the proposals made then. As is evident, the approach was primarily legal. It was intended to bring about through indirect means the issue of the Jewish settlements into the negotiations which were defined as negotiations over Palestinian self-government arrangements.

The Palestinian delegation had only one jurist amongst its members, and he had been more involved in his professional life in politics than in law.[2] None of the other members had been involved in the legal struggle against the occupation. While the team supporting the delegates included several legal personnel, the constraints imposed by the Israeli side against Palestinians from outside the Occupied Territories or those holding Jerusalem identity cards, meant that none of these legal experts could enter the negotiation room. The Israeli ban continued until the last round of the Washington talks. In contrast, the Israeli delegation was headed by a jurist and had a number of delegates who had direct experience of forging the structures that the negotiations had come to consolidate, and of implementing them during a number of years of service in the military and civilian government of the Occupied Territories. The team included for example the former legal advisor to the Israeli Civilian Administration in the West Bank.

Long meetings were held with the delegation to discuss these questions and forge a strategy for the negotiations. At the same time, co-ordination with the leadership in Tunis was also taking place. After many hesitations and difficult discussions, a unified Palestinian position was formulated. It was called: "An Expanded Outline: Palestinian Interim Self-Government Agreement: Concepts, Preliminary Measures and Election Modalities". It was dated 3 March 1992 and was approved by the PLO in Tunis.[3]

Following Article 2 of Part Two "Preliminary for the Interim Phase" in the expanded Outline, "the preliminary phase" was defined as "the period between the commencement of the peace process on 29 October 1991 and the elections for the Palestine Interim Self-Government Authority (PISGA) and its subsequent inauguration on a date no later than 29 October 1992, during which these preliminary measures are to be implemented". Article 4 went into further detail:

> During its prolonged occupation of the Palestinian Territory, the Israeli military government and the Israeli government have diverged increasingly since 1967 from the principles laid down in the Hague Regulations of 1907, the Fourth

---

2 This was Frieh Abu Meddien. The guidance committee which included people from outside the Occupied Territories but was not accepted by Israel as part of the delegation, included Anis al-Qasem, an international law expert. The present author was never a member of the delegation. As legal advisor to the delegation he was refused any form of participation in the negotiations by the Israeli side – including participation in the working committees – on the basis of his residence in Jerusalem.

3 The full text of the Palestinian position can be found in *The Journal of Palestinian Studies*, Vol. XXI, No 3, Spring 1992, pp. 135-141.

Geneva Convention of 1949, United National Security Council Resolutions 242 and 338, and other international conventions and standards.

To rectify these violations it was proposed that:

6. Discriminatory and extra-territorial legislation must therefore be rescinded and the issue of new military orders, whether in the guise of primary or secondary legislation, must cease.
8. ...the Israeli authorities should immediately implement the following measures with regard to land and natural resources:

d. Revoke military order 291 which suspended the land registration process, thus allowing land registration to continue according to law.

The raison d'être of the process was explained in the following terms:

7. Dismantling the legal basis of this discriminatory system in the Occupied Palestinian Territory is necessary for the successful transition into the interim phase and for the ultimate success of the peace process as a whole.

As the negotiations proceeded hopeful developments took place with more and more of the members of the Negotiating Team and the Palestinian leadership in Tunis coming to see the point of insisting on the preliminary issues. The team now proceeded utilising at times a clear legal strategy. It saw as one of its objectives the necessity to conduct the negotiations so that the Israeli strategy (taking the legal arrangements imposed unilaterally by Israel in the course of the occupation, as the starting point) would not be accepted as constituting the basis of the negotiated arrangements to apply for the five year interim period.

My own participation in the negotiations as legal advisor continued until September 1992. After struggling for a whole year to impress upon the leadership the importance of finding a way to insist on a review of some of the detrimental military orders, instructions arrived from Tunis on the 13 September 1992 that there was no meaning for the review of the military orders since this can only give these orders recognition and legitimacy. I gave the leadership the benefit of the doubt and assumed that perhaps they were aware of the danger of building the interim arrangements on the military orders in force but had a different strategy which they were keeping secret. But I no longer returned to advise the delegation in Washington.[4]

Exactly a year later, on 13 September 1993 the PLO signed the Declaration of Principles which was followed on 4 May 1994 by The Agreement on the Gaza Strip and the Jericho Area. The Israeli success in bringing the PLO to agree to implement the occupier's law is more clearly stated in the later agreement. Article VII.9 declares that "(L)aws

---

4 With the exception of April 1993, when I was called to advice specifically on the land and water issues for which a special committee was constituted.

and military orders in effect in the Gaza Strip or the Jericho Area prior to the signing of this Agreement shall remain in force, unless amended or abrogated in accordance with this Agreement".[5]

The safeguards that the Palestinian leadership seemed satisfied with were such general provisions as appear in almost all the agreements signed between the two sides, such as that the "the outcome of the permanent status negotiations should not be prejudiced or preempted by agreements reached for the interim period" (DOP Article V(4));[6] that "the two sides view the West Bank and the Gaza Strip as a single territorial unit" (DOP Article IV);[7] and that the "the permanent status will lead to the implementation of Security Council Resolutions 242 and 338" (DOP Article 1).[8]

It was as though one side was negotiating a contract which was going to create entirely new relations between the sides and yet insisted on the provision that the entire contract is made without prejudice to all the alterations that the agreed changes were going to bring about.

When the leadership assumed authority in the Gaza Strip and the Jericho area, it attempted to correct all its previous legal omissions by one formal legal action which was adopted almost immediately upon taking charge. It is revealing of the leadership's attitude to legal matters to examine this first decree. PLO Chairman, Mr. Yasser Arafat, declared that "the laws, regulations and orders in force before 5 June 1967 in the West Bank and the Gaza Strip shall remain in force until unified", thus implicitly cancelling the military orders as this declaration was interpreted in the press.[9]

The casualness of such a legal decision with potentially tremendous consequences is the first matter that strikes the observer. The decree

---

5 I have reviewed the Gaza-Jericho Agreement in 'Questions of Jurisdiction: A Legal Analysis of the Gaza-Jericho Agreement', *The Journal of Palestine Studies*, Vol. XXIII, No. 4, Summer 1994, pp. 18-25.

6 Article XXIII.5 of The Agreement on the Gaza Strip and the Jericho Area (Gaza-Jericho): "Nothing in this Agreement shall prejudice or preempt the outcome of the negotiations on the interim agreement or on the permanent status to be conducted pursuant to the Declaration of Principles ...". Article XIII.3 of The Agreement on the Preparatory Transfer of Powers and Responsibilities (Transfer Agreement): "Nothing in this Agreement shall prejudice or preempt the outcome of the negotiations on the Interim Agreement or on the permanent status to be conducted pursuant to the Declaration of Principles...".

7 Gaza-Jericho Article XXIII.6: "The two sides view the West Bank and the Gaza Strip as a single territorial unit, the integrity of which will be preserved during the interim period", and in the Transfer Agreement Article XIII.4: "The two parties view the West Bank and the Gaza Strip as a single territorial unit, the integrity of which will be preserved during the interim period".

8 Gaza-Jericho preamble: "...the negotiations on the permanent status will lead to the implementation of Security Council Resolutions 242 and 338", and the Transfer Agreement preamble: "....the negotiations on the permanent status will lead to the implementation of Security Council Resolutions 242 and 338."

9 This decree was published in the Palestinian Official Gazette, Vol. 1, 20 November 1994, at p. 10. The Palestinian Official Gazette is published by the Ministry of Justice.

made no mention of the legal changes that occurred after 5 June 1967, allowing for the interpretation that these are not recognised as part of the law and therefore are annulled. This was done without any attempt to reconcile this decree with Article VII.9 of the Gaza-Jericho agreement where there is an explicit confirmation of the laws and military orders in force at the time of signing the agreement. Nor did the leadership consider either the prospect of being able to implement such a draconian measure, nor the consequences of such a measure on the lives of the people in the self-rule areas if the measure were to be implemented. The decree was more likely intended as a political statement to appease critics of the Gaza-Jericho Agreement and raise the morale of the people who, the politicians felt, wanted to be assured that the agreement would lead to an end to the occupier's law under which they had suffered for almost three decades. The casualness itself of using a legal decree solely to serve political ends, after which the legal decree is forgotten and discarded, is itself indicative of the attitude of the leadership to legal matters.

Despite this first declaration by the Palestinian Authority, the law applicable in the Gaza Strip was and continues to be the dual system of law imposed by the Israeli occupier. One law to the Palestinian Gazans, another to the Israeli settlers living in Gaza. As to how the Palestinian leadership has realised or plans in the future to realise the objective of the 1988 Palestinian National Council decision to annul "all measures of annexation and appropriation and the removal of settlements established by Israel", is simply unclear to this observer and perhaps also not to the leadership itself.

To be relevant, a legal narrative must emanate from the lived reality of the people to whom it purports to speak. The attempt of the Palestinian delegation during the Washington phase of the negotiations to develop such a narrative was a unique event in the history of the Palestinian national movement although individual Palestinian legal experts and non governmental human rights organisations had previously undertaken such an effort. As it turned out, the Palestinian leadership was unable to appreciate the potential in such a strategy nor was it apparent that it saw the need to formulate an alternative legal strategy. But that failure went beyond the negotiations themselves. Assuming the political forces as they existed at the time of the secret negotiations in Oslo did not enable the leadership to impose any strategy of its own, when the agreements were signed no attempt was made to provide any indication as to how the leadership proposed to bridge the gap between the reality as experienced by Palestinians in the Occupied Territories and the proclaimed national objective of achieving an independent Palestinian state. The discourse remained at the level of generalities, abstractions and slogans while the people were expected to continue to have blind faith that despite the restrictive terms agreed upon and the confirmation which took place through the agreement of the occupier's law which they had resisted at great cost, the leadership would somehow deliver them safely to where they had struggled to get. But the slogans are nowhere close to constituting the sovereign legal language which the Palestinian people desperately need.

Throughout the course of the negotiations, the Palestinian leadership placed continual stress on UN resolution 242 which was repeated in all the main agreements signed so far with Israel. The resolution was treated as absolute, as capable of only one interpretation, namely that of the Palestinian side. This attitude to a UN resolution characterised by deliberate ambiguity, coupled with the leadership's failure to prepare a legal case to support its position and incorporate in the Agreement safeguards to ensure that its interpretation of the resolution will be implemented, can be taken as indicative of another of the leadership's prevalent ways of thinking on legal matters. It is characterised by a search for absolutes; it is abstract; it fails to consider the changing legal reality and shifting ground over which it is conducting the negotiations, and it fails to anticipate the legal case of the other side to be able to respond adequately to it. In almost all these ways the legal thinking of the Palestinian establishment stands in direct opposition to the way of thinking on legal matters of the Israeli establishment. The Israeli legal discourse avoids generalities and is characterised by being deductive, positivist and lays strong emphasis on the details. It is to the Israeli legal narrative that I shall now turn.

II. The Israeli Narrative

When the Israeli army occupied the Palestinian territories in 1967, they had, on the face of it, an altogether weak legal case. They were occupiers. This was how most of the world saw their status in these territories. This status was even recognised by the commander of the West Bank in Military Proclamation Number 3 when he recognised the applicability of the Fourth Geneva Convention in the area. Not much later strange formulations and distinctions were made by Israeli academic pundits whose positions gained currency amongst official circles. One of these was Yehuda Blum who later became the Israeli Ambassador to the UN.[10] His conclusion regarding the status of the Occupied West Bank was as follows:

> ...whenever, for one reasons or another, there is no concurrence of a normal 'legitimate sovereign', with that of a 'belligerent occupant' of the territory, only that part of the law of occupation applies which is intended to safeguard the humanitarian rights of the population. Conversely, as already stated, the rules

---

10 Y. Blum, 'The Missing Reversioner' *Israel Law Review*, Vol. 3, No. 2, 1968, p.294.

> protecting the reversionary rights of the legitimate sovereign find no application, there being no such sovereign. The legal standing of Israel in the territories in question is thus that of a state which is lawfully in control of territory in respect of which no other states can show a better title. Or, if it is preferred to state the matter in terms of belligerent occupation, then the legal standing of Israel in the territories in question is at the very least, that of a belligerent occupant of territory in respect of which Jordan is NOT entitled to the reversionary rights of a legitimate sovereign.

In short, in the course of one article, Mr. Blum had found in effect that occupation is sometimes legitimate under international law and that the specific area which the Israeli army has legitimately occupied is a free-for-all. If the Israeli government wished to violate all other "non-humanitarian" provisions of the international conventions which protect inhabitants of Occupied Territories (whatever these undefined provisions are) it will not be in violation of international law. And if it settled its own people in the land it occupied it will not be depriving anyone else of the land, since the land is basically up for grabs.

It is important to note here that throughout the occupation, the Israeli government did not formally annex the Occupied Territories with the exception of East Jerusalem and its environs. At the same time it went about dealing with the territories as de facto its own even when it did not change its status. It is in this way of relating to law that the Israeli legal mind differs from the Palestinian. Rather than bother with abstractions, with having to argue for and defend a position of annexation (whether or not it felt it had the right to do so) it went about relating to the area and achieving physical and legal changes as though the area were in fact annexed. The outcome was that for a large proportion of the land occupied in 1967 a full annexation in all but name was achieved. Israelis live in these areas. They apply Israeli law and are subject to the jurisdiction of Israeli courts and are considered by many Israeli laws as living inside Israel. This annexation without annexation was done without having to admit or suffer the full consequence of committing the fundamental breach of international law of the occupier annexing occupied land.

This is not the place to describe the legal manoeuvres utilised by the Israeli occupier to acquire Palestinian lands in the occupied areas. But a brief summary of the general positions on which the process rested may be helpful to reveal the Israeli legal thinking and approach to colonisation:

In the first place, no time was lost arguing that the land acquisition should take place according to Israeli municipal law. It was consistently the position of the Israeli High Court that the applicable law in the West Bank was Jordanian law. Therefore the process had to find its justification from within that law. When the settlers in the *Elon Moreh* case refused to rely on the argument that their settlement was being made on grounds of military security and they sought to claim the right to settle on the land on ideological and religious grounds, the court rejected their arguments.

Secondly, however, it was not going to be Jordanian law as interpreted by Jordanian jurisprudence, precedents and practice, but rather Israeli courts which also relied on the amendments made to this law by the military area commander without accepting to examine the legality of these amendments. Jordanian law requires the Authority to carry on land registration. The Israeli commander suspended this process by a military order. He then proceeded to amend the law making it possible to register unregistered land as public land by a mere declaration. Any claimant of that land could only resort to a military tribunal. However, only exceptional cases have been successful in proving that a declaration of land as public land issued by the military authorities was in error.

Much was written in defence of this particular process of land theft. It was argued that it was consistent with the local Jordanian law, with international law and most shockingly with the principles of the rule of law since it allowed for an appeal.[11] But the interesting feature of the practice is how meticulous it was. Although the government had the means to do it otherwise, they took care to go through all the steps of making a declaration and serving it on the village Mukhtar; and if an appeal was lodged to hear it to the full. It was as though going through all the formalities would render what is basically faulty and violative of the principles of both local Jordanian and international law appear as legal, proper and correct.

It is also interesting to observe how the Israeli legal thinking goes. In the Israeli High Court of Justice, Justice Landau observed in the *Elon Moreh* case that the view concerning the right of the Jewish people to settle in the West Bank was based on the fundamentals of the Zionist doctrine.[12] Others go farther and insist that the Jews have the right to settle anywhere in the "land of Israel". If one keeps in mind this principle then everything falls into place. It goes something like this: in the interim between the time when Jews inhabited the land and the present, non-Jews came to inhabit the West Bank. The rights of these to the land is recognised as long as they are in actual possession. Once they leave for any reason including the outbreak of war, they lose their right to their land and their land reverts to its original owners, the Jews. Thus the term used to refer to the property of those who left during the war of 1967 is "abandoned property".[13] Land which is declared by the military as public land is given to the Jewish public, the settlers. To

---

11 See for example D. Yahav, *Israel, the Intifada and the Rule of Law*, (Israel Ministry of Defence Publications, 1993).

12 *Izat Mohammad Mustafa Dwaikat and Others v Government of Israel et al,* HCJ 390/79 (34 P.D.(l) 1 (1980)).

13 This is the term used in Military Order Number 58 published by the area commander in the West Bank. See Proclamations Orders and Appointments, Vol. 3, p. 158.

rebut the claim that such land is the public land of the Jews, the non-Jew has to prove continuous actual use of a sort acceptable to the Israeli military tribunal for a period of ten consecutive years, otherwise his land will be taken away from him and made available to the Jewish settler.

Using such methods the Israeli occupier acquired large areas of Palestinian land and used it to build settlements which applied Israeli law. From the beginning of the negotiations with the Palestinians, the Israeli side presented proposals which attempted to consolidate the gains made during the occupation and preserve the arrangements regarding legal and administrative matters which had been put in place and which had achieved a physical and functional separation between the Jewish community in the Occupied Territories and the Palestinian community living there. These proposals changed very little in the course of the negotiations. Thus the "Ideas for Peaceful Coexistence in the Territories during the Interim Period", submitted to the Palestinian Delegation on 20 February 1992 included Provision B.5.c. which states that "the laws and orders in force in Judea, Samaria, and Gaza District, and all powers vested by virtue of them shall remain in force". In the "Informal Compilation of Israeli Ideas on the Concept of the Interim Self-Government Arrangements" submitted almost a year later (10 December 1992), it was stated that "the prevailing laws in the territories will remain in force during the Interim Arrangements period, subject to modifications which will be agreed upon following a review process..., conducted by a joint legal working group...". In every respect all the agreements signed between the Israeli and Palestinian sides – the Declaration of Principles, the Agreement on the Gaza Strip and the Jericho Area or the Agreement on Preparatory Transfer of Powers and Responsibilities – confirmed the initial positions on which the Israeli side based its strategy in these negotiations from the beginning of the process.

One of these principles related to the issue of land. It was expressed in a proposal submitted by the Israeli negotiating team to the Palestinian team in Washington D.C. dated 14 September 1992 in the following manner:

> The overall territorial – geographical issue, should be dealt with in the permanent status negotiations. The concept of Jurisdiction during the interim period of self-government arrangements should be powers and responsibilities orientated.

This means that from the point of the view of the Israeli side, the issue of the Jewish settlement was outside the scope of the negotiations which are merely reduced to negotiating powers and responsibilities over people and not over territory.

Both the fact that the Israeli delegation included some of the a rchitects, defenders and implementers of the legal and administrative structures that had been established in the Occupied Territories and the fact that the delegation head, along with a substantial number of the members, were not changed throughout the negotiations, were contributing factors to the team's ability to pursue the same strategy. It is worth noting here that the substantive Israeli strategy in the negotiations seemed to undergo no modification with the change of government from the right wing Likud to the Labour government under the leadership of Yitzhak Rabin. The head of the delegation also remained the same.

Having consolidated through the agreements signed with the PLO the gains made during the years of the occupation, the Israeli government proceeded to develop its legal narrative through issuing further military orders and proclamations applicable to the Palestinian areas (which were the subject of the negotiations) and at the same time to legislate Israeli laws to implement the agreements.

The first of these was Proclamation Number 4 signed thirteen days after the Gaza-Jericho Agreement was signed.[14] The Proclamation dissolved the Israeli Civil Administration in the Gaza Strip and transferred its powers to the Palestinian Authority. In this way it was confirmed that the source of the authorities transferred to the Palestinian Authority was the Israeli Military Administration. At the same time the military government was preserved. This was consistent with the original Israeli conception of the function of the negotiations as expressed in the above mentioned Israeli "Ideas for Peaceful Coexistence" of 20 February 1992, in which it was stated that, "the established links between Judea, Samaria, Gaza district and Israel will be kept intact". It was also made clear then that any powers and responsibilities which the Palestinian Authority will come to enjoy will be "delegated to the designated administrative organs" (Part B section 4).[15] As to the Jewish settlements in the Occupied Territories, a number of military orders were issued in August and September 1994 amending Orders 783 and 892 regarding the local and regional councils of the Jewish settlements in the West Bank, increasing the powers of these councils and consolidating their administrative separateness from the Palestinian local government.

---

14 For the text, see Proclamations, Orders, and Appointments, Vol. 154, May 1994, p. 1563 (issued by the Military Legal Advisor of Judea and Samaria).

15 The Commander of the Israeli army transferred powers in the spheres of education, health, social welfare, tourism, direct taxation and value added tax as agreed upon between Israel and the PLO to the Palestinian Authority by virtue of Proclamation no. 5 dated 11 December, 1994 entitled Proclamation Regarding the Implementation of the Agreement on Preparatory Transfer of Powers and Responsibilities (published in Proclamations, Orders and Appointments, Vol. 159, pp. 1750-1751, issued by the Military Legal Advisor to the area of Judea and Samaria). Military Order No. 1430 entitled Amendment No. 6 to the Interpretation Order No.130 (published in *ibid.*, Vol. 159, p.1751) defined "The Palestinian Authority" as "the Palestinian Authority established by virtue of the Agreement regarding the Gaza strip and the Jericho Area".

Then on 25 July 1994, the government submitted a bill to the Knesset entitled Bill on Implementing the Agreement Concerning the Gaza Strip and Jericho Area (Amendment of Legislation) 1994. In many of its articles the Bill distinguishes between "the Gaza and Jericho areas" and the "Areas" which are defined as "Judea and Samaria and the Gaza Strip, except for the Gaza and Jericho Areas". Whereas some provisions apply to both areas, most apply only to the Gaza and Jericho Areas. The authority proposed to be given to a police officer by an amendment to the Law on Entrance to Israel, to remove visitors who remain in the Palestinian territory without permit or beyond the terms of their permit, applies to both areas (Article 5 of the proposed bill); whereas according to the proposed Article 55 prohibiting transport and possession of agricultural produce applies only to the Gaza and Jericho Areas and not to the West Bank. In all, fifteen Israeli laws will indirectly be amended by the proposed bill. In the explanatory notes to Chapter B of the Bill it is indicated that the extension of the validity of some of the Emergency Regulations which the bill proposes to amend shall be until 3 May 1999 the date on which the interim period should end. It is as though it is not expected by the Israeli side that the Interim Agreement which according to the Declaration of Principles remains to be negotiated and signed will come about and that if it did, that agreement would not differ substantially from the Gaza Jericho Agreement of 4 May 1994.

As shown above in all three major agreements signed between Israel and the PLO the article preserving the integrity of the Gaza Strip and the West Bank which shall be "viewed ... as a single territorial unit", appears. Although the proposed Israeli bill seems in violation of this principle, there was no Palestinian objection to it and no attempt to point out that if it passes as law Israel will be violating the agreement it has signed.

What the Israeli side has achieved then, is the victory and supremacy of its own legal narrative. The Palestinian side neither developed nor succeeded in asserting a narrative that expresses the aspirations of its people. It has not established a position that can explain how it views its movement from where it now finds itself to where it wants to get in five years time. The Israeli narrative dictated and continues to dictate the overall fate of the Palestinians living in the Occupied Territories. If one of the attributes of law is a symbolic language, then a language of peace and reconciliation has not been achieved through the long and painful process of negotiations. Instead what the process has brought about is a re-statement of relationship. Israel, the more powerful side, dictated its terms on the other side. The Israeli military has transferred to the Palestinian authority those legal arrangements which it had put in place to ensure the fulfilment of the overall objectives of the occupation which include the effective annexation of large parts of the Occupied Territories and all the restrictions on the civil life of the Palestinians ensuring that it cannot develop in any way that is not to Israel's liking and its long-term policies.

III. General Reflections on the Two Narratives

It is clear then that the main difference between the two sides, the Israeli and the Palestinian, is that one has a legal strategy and appreciation of the use of law to achieve political ends, while the other minimises the significance of law. The legal strategy of the Israeli side guided it in all its actions throughout the negotiations and enabled it to formulate positions which found their expression in the agreements which Israel signed and in the legislative actions that were carried out or proposed since the signing. The Palestinian side failed to adopt a consistent legal strategy and ended up by signing an agreement which reveals no vision of how this leadership intends to proceed to achieve its political objectives.

It must be taken into consideration in analysing the large gap between the two sides regarding their respective abilities to develop and implement a legal strategy that the two sides are in no way equal. One is a state, the other is not. However this difference should not excuse the PLO for failing to live up to its promises and pursue them as effectively as possible in all ways including through conducting effective negotiations.

The Palestinian failure in this regard can be related to the break in the legal tradition that occurred in the Palestinian community as a result of the disasters of 1948 and 1967. The first meant that the Palestinian legal community became scattered in all parts of the world. The continuity with the legal traditions established by the British Mandate was severed. The Jerusalem Law Classes, for example, from which many able Palestinian jurists had graduated were not continued. Unlike the case on the Israeli side, there was no school of law in Jordan throughout the period from 1948 to 1967 nor in the Palestinian Occupied Territories after 1967 to carry out legal research or educate future jurists. After 1967 the entire Bar Association went on strike and the legal profession became politicised and was never able to assume its responsibilities and play any effective role in the legal life of the community. Whatever legal traditions developed during the Jordanian period in the West Bank and in the Gaza Strip were severely disrupted under the Israeli rule which appointed judges, deprived the judiciary of any semblance of independence, and interfered in the work of the judges whenever Israeli interests were perceived to be at stake.

Other than the difference in standards and the lack of a continuous tradition in the case of the Palestinian legal tradition, there were also fundamental differences between the Israeli and Palestinian legal thinking which became evident in the course of the negotiations. The Israeli legal community follows the English common law tradition of gradual development from decision to decision.[16] The Palestinian legal community thinks abstractly in terms of codes and first principles, not concretely in terms of cases. This is partly because the Palestinian jurists acquired their education in such law faculties as Egypt, Syria and Lebanon where the civil law system is used. The Palestinian politicians who are effected by the principles of that tradition, were concerned for example that Palestinian side should insist in the negotiations on the application by Israel of the Fourth Geneva Convention. While it cannot be underestimated that the applicability of the Convention is a key issue for the status of the Occupied Territories, this insistence was done at the expense of appreciating the concrete changes on the ground carried out by Israel throughout the 27 years of occupation which had to be taken into consideration in formulating the negotiation strategy. When faced with the prospect of having to deal with a bottom up strategy because any discussion of the status of the territory was not going to be possible at the stage of the negotiations for the interim phase, there was a constant repetition by the leadership of the need to insist upon the applicability of the Fourth Geneva Convention. But this Israel was able to avoid simply by stating that it was outside the scope of the negotiations. There was great difficulty in facing the Israeli legal challenges because the legal thinking of most of the people involved followed the civil law tradition of dealing with abstractions and first principles not concrete incremental changes which needed to be approached in an entirely different manner.

It cannot be said that the absence amongst the Palestinian leadership of a legal strategy and appreciation of law as a means for change and development is an Israeli problem. It is a Palestinian problem. And yet the two sides are searching for a new relationship between them, one that is based on the resolution of disputes through negotiations and not through violence. Since 1991 it has been the position of both sides that this relationship will be determined through negotiations. The outcome of negotiations are agreements. Agreements can be characterised in many ways, one of these is as legal documents. For agreements to have durability without the necessity of enforcement through force, they must be acceptable to the two sides who made them. If they are perceived as being the imposition of the powerful side over the weaker side they will be resisted and the anticipated peace will not be achieved.

---

16 Israeli case-law remains typical of that in countries following the common law tradition. The manner of discussion, the mode of reasoning and the general approach are all characteristics of the common law system. This is also true of the attitude of judges, jurists and attorneys to precedent, to the role of the courts and to their contribution to the development of the law. Friedmann, *The Effect of Foreign Law on the Law of Israel* (1975), quoted in K. Zweigert and H. Kötz, *An Introduction to Comparative Law*, (2nd edn, Oxford, 1994), p. 245.

Perhaps for this reason the status of law and the dependence on the legal process as a means for resolving disputes in the Palestinian side should also be an Israeli concern.

A legal narrative is how a people tell the story of their right to a land using the symbolic language of law. It is by necessity a constructed narrative. For it to stand it must have consistency and its own internal logic. It must relate to reference points outside of it which others can relate to and understand. It must be communicable. During the occupation and prior to the signing of the DOP, the Palestinian human rights community in the Occupied Territories developed a Palestinian legal narrative. This enabled a common language to develop to evaluate and describe Israeli actions and other developments that were taking place in the territories. It was shared with others inside and outside Palestine. It was also shared with progressive Israelis. As such, it proved an important common link between Palestinians and Israelis.

With the signing of the DOP the Palestinian legal narrative was given a severe and possibly fatal blow while the Israeli narrative was confirmed and promoted into the only official narrative. The common language for progressives from both sides was lost. The DOP was hailed as marking a new phase in the relationship between the two sides. While all the features of the occupation and all the spoils of war remained, peace was proclaimed.

The Israeli government was over a number of years in a position to influence the course of the development of the legal standards of the Palestinians living under its control, who are now the main subject of the interim arrangements on which the present situation is based. Whatever influence it exerted was in the negative. It weakened the courts and robbed the judiciary of any semblance of independence. It closed schools and universities for a number of years, it constantly claimed that those working in human rights had affiliations with the most extreme of Palestinian political factions outside.[17] The wisdom of such an Israeli position which affects not only the area of the law but all other areas of the life of the Palestinian community, was never seriously debated in Israel. The establishment view was allowed to prevail. Rather than assume that by allowing the Palestinian society to develop they

---

[17] Over the years, I have written extensively about the deteriorating situation of the legal system under Israeli rule. Through numerous articles and interviews, I tried to bring this home to the Israeli public through the Israeli press. See for example: *The West Bank and the Rule of Law*, (1980) (with Jonathan Kuttab, which was responded to by the Israeli section of the International Commission of Jurists in *The Rule of Law in the Areas Under Israeli Rule*, (1982)); *Occupiers Law, Israel and The West Bank*, (2nd edn, 1988); and 'The Myth of Law and Order', *The Jerusalem Post*, 23 March 1988. The most recent Israeli apologia for the occupation was D. Yahav, *Israel, The Intifada and the Rule of Law*, mentioned above. I am only concerned here with the publications from the Israeli side supporting the Israeli colonial efforts. There were many Israelis who throughout the years of the occupation warned against the policies of successive governments and wrote critically about their short-sighted policies.

would have to deal with a better neighbour, they chose to tear that society apart taking the classic colonial view that a divided, under-developed society is easier to control and dominate. Such a view does not seem to have undergone any transformation since the agreements have been signed between the two sides.

The Israeli establishment now calls upon the Palestinian leadership to abide by the agreement signed between them. When in a speech in Gaza marking the Declaration of Palestinian Independence, Mr Arafat called the Israelis the enemy, he was reminded that the agreement he signed with Israel forbade him from using this language.[18] Israeli officials now call the PLO their partners in the peace process.

The test for the success of the peace treaty is whether it marks the genuine end of a relationship between the two sides characterised by violence and ushers a period of peace when differences are settled through negotiations. Those committed to reconciliation between the two sides whether from Israel, Palestine or other parts of the world spent many years trying to bring the two sides to the negotiating table. The agreements that resulted did not meet the test of their intentions. These were agreements dictated by the strong on the weak. What should be obvious is the limit of power. A relationship between the two sides based solely on the power relationship between them, is but a continuation of the old relationship when violence was the common language whatever the ways in which it was exhibited and expressed. For that to really change the majority of the Palestinians have to truly believe that peaceful negotiations can change matters fundamentally. The agreements have not proven this to be the case. This only weakens those calling for a negotiated settlement and strengthens the rejectionists and proponents of violence.

In a recent article on peace with Syria, Abba Eban proposes that "the effectiveness of a treaty should be judged by the three criteria that go beyond its text: Does it contain advantages that a country would lose by violating it? Would the violation be worth the risk of countermeasures that could be taken by the aggrieved party? Would failure to honour the treaty weaken the defaulting country's international position to such a

---

18 The Israeli Minister of Police on the Israeli Arab News on Israeli Television (15 November 1994). Perhaps the best indicator of how Israeli officials regard their partner in peace came in the report of the address of Major-General Danny Rothschild, co-ordinator of government activities in the Palestinian territories. He was reported as saying: "The economic situation in Gaza affects the ability of the Palestinian Authority to manage affairs and helps strengthen Hamas." The report continues: "He noted that countries which have promised to contribute to the PA will not transfer promised funding to Palestinian officials, especially police, who have not been approved by Israel. Therefore, the economic difficulties in Gaza will continue unless the PA co-operates with Israel... He said Israel has demanded that Yasser Arafat treat Hamas as a political rival and deal with it in the political arena, except for its military wing which should be taken care of." See 'Hamas Seeks Control of Services in Autonomy', *Jerusalem Post*, 18 November 1994.

degree that other countries would refuse to make agreements with it?"[19] Using these criteria, the Agreements signed with the PLO will ultimately not prove effective. Amongst a large number of Palestinians in the Occupied Territories now, it is not felt that much can be lost if the Agreement with Israel is violated because it is felt that little has been gained.

For a long time, the relationship between the two sides was characterised as a zero sum game where the losses of the one side where the gains of the other. It was hoped that this characterisation would be changed once the two sides sat together to negotiate peace. When this happened it turned out that the Israeli side exercised its greater power and imposed its own legal narrative and silenced that of the Palestinians. The sounding of the narrative of the one side, it seemed, had to be on account of the narrative of the other. The zero sum game had not been abandoned. A new language of reconciliation was not found and has not been given the chance to develop. The much coveted peace was formally proclaimed before it was truly established.

---

19 'Victorious Climax for Zionism', *The Jerusalem Post,* 18 November 1994.

2. Legal Systems and Public Attitudes During Negotiations Towards Transition from Conflict to Reconciliation: The Middle East, 1992–1994

Ruth Gavison

Legal theorists know that the enforcement and the stability of legal orders depend to a large extent on an extensive 'infrastructure' of community, beliefs and attitudes among the population subject to the law.[1] Law cannot rely exclusively on the imposition of sanctions, despite the Austinian attempt to define it in these terms.[2] Law that depends only on sanctions for its operation cannot last. Any stable legal regime is based, primarily, on the legitimacy of its underlying authority, and on the acceptance of this legitimacy by most people subject to it.

In societies in deep and prolonged conflict, stability is threatened by the absence of this feeling of legitimacy shared by all the individuals subject to the law. Where societies are in a prolonged state of conflict, especially societies under siege or occupation or a tyrannical rule, there are groups that see law and law enforcement agencies as their protectors, and groups which see them as their oppressors.[3]

This disparate perception of law is only one of the differences separating the groups participating in the struggle. Within each of these groups, the conflict generates perceptions of the other groups and their representatives that facilitate life within the conflict. There is among both groups a combination of anger, hatred, fear, suspiciousness and contempt. These emotions colour most interactions between representatives of the groups, and they are in turn used to aid in the acts of war and cruelty that the conflict seems to require, especially when it reaches a violent stage.

---

[1] In *The Concept of Law,* (Oxford, 1961), H.L.A. Hart emphasized these elements of legal stability when he claimed that law (as distinguished from regimes of terror) presupposed acceptance on the part of the population.

[2] Austin defines law as a command accompanied by a sanction. In justice to Austin one must recall that he defines the sovereign as the entity which does not obey anyone, and to whom the population has a 'habit of obedience'. This habit may in fact be based on more than fear alone.

[3] In terms of legal theory, this fact creates a problem for all sophisticated theories which build on the perspectives of 'participants' rather than 'observers'. O.W. Holmes was faulted because he proposed a 'Bad Man Theory of Law' while not all individuals were 'bad'. Similarly, if one's sole point of view is that of segments of the population subject to law, one's theory of law must be distorted. The very same legal system will be seen as a tool of oppression by its victims, and as a source of legitimacy by those using it. This may be an argument for observers' theories of law, or for an acknowledgement that, on some levels, a unitary description of a legal system may be impossible.

It is thus not surprising that advocates of peace or conciliation among the groups are not only concerned with the real parameters of the conflict and possible resolutions thereof. They must also be concerned with more subtle aspects of the conflict, such as a tendency to distance the enemy and to demonize and de-humanize its representatives. In addition, they must be concerned with the conditions which may make the process of negotiation, reconciliation and compromise possible.[4] The identification of these conditions may suggest which are the conditions necessary for stability and legitimacy of legal orders and arrangements.

In democracies, legal regulation of the expression of opinions and the encouragement of demonized perceptions of the enemy is not easy to justify. The valid reasons for not prosecuting individuals who contribute to such attitudes should not blind us to the importance and the seriousness of this kind of activity. History proves that ideas should be taken extremely seriously. While an idea alone cannot hurt one, actions that can hurt are facilitated and triggered by an atmosphere of ideas and attitudes. Peace often cannot replace conflict if leaders, groups and individuals are not freed from their (mis)perceptions of the enemy, his actions and his motives. The transition from violent conflict to peace thus requires an accompanying change in the mutual perceptions and attitudes of the parties. They must be willing, at least, to accept a shared system of norms that will govern their relations and be viewed as legitimate by both.[5]

However, the political process initiated in Madrid, with the Oslo and Cairo agreements, the peace treaty between Jordan and Israel and negotiations with Syria are hotly debated in all the affected communities. Groups objecting to these processes are fighting against them, each within its own constraints and possibilities. While signatories persist in re-affirming the agreements as binding upon them, the populations do not seem to be united behind them. Part of the intensity of the struggle against the agreements stems from the fact that they radically challenge the system of perceptions, expectations and evaluations that informed and governed the existence of many of the affected individuals and groups before them. In other words, the agreements are themselves a major transition from the period preceding them. Nonetheless, this transition has not been consolidated. The agreements are, in fact, a step in a process of transition. The prospects of this attempted transition depend on the ability and the willingness of the parties to accept a shared normative system within which they will pursue their interests.

---

4 One of the great attractions of a military victory is that it may seem to make this long and complex process redundant. But this may be an illusion: A stable peace usually requires more than a (temporary) military superiority.

5 It should be noted that this requirement is minimalistic. It does not contain as a condition the requirement that parties agree on the history of the conflict, or even on their goals within the negotiations.

Political transitions often create the need to decide about the treatment of those who acted on the basis of 'old' norms, perceptions or power structures, and whose activities may now have to be re-assessed and re-evaluated. There is extensive literature, on a variety of levels, on the treatment of the past in situations of political transitions.[6] The post-war trials in Germany and Japan are still an important focus of such debates.[7] Other aspects of the same set of problems are disclosed by the periods of 'popular justice' against 'collaborators' or agents of a defeated and hated regime.

These situations raise a variety of difficult questions. First is the problem of legality: the justification of imposing liability on individuals who acted in obedience to norms that were legal (or were even deemed desirable and mandatory) when they acted under them.[8] There is also the issue of political prudence. The need to strike the right balance between the backward-looking interests and values of justice and desert and the forward-looking aspect of building a future without spending too much energy on a painful past. This consideration is made more weighty by the questions raised concerning the feasibility and justice of condemning today those who were on all levels of the administration of one's country before the 'transition'.[9] There is also the question of the rights of the 'collaborators' to due process and public trial.

Transitions may be very different. While some of them are located in a dramatic point in history (the end of the war, the withdrawal of an army), others are the result of a long process of gradual reconciliation and negotiation (e.g. the transition in South Africa). Yet most of the transitions discussed in the literature share a structural similarity. The 'good guys' come to power (usually in the form of a freely elected democratic government) after a period in which power was held by the 'bad guys'. The bad guys committed crimes against humanity and terrible violations of human rights. The old regime left a large number of people dead, tortured and injured in various ways, often relying on terror and humiliation. The new regime now faces the question of how to deal with the people responsible for these crimes.

---

6 See the comprehensive discussion in S. Cohen, 'State Crimes of Previous Regimes: Knowledge, Accountability, and the Policing of the Past', *Law and Social Enquiry*, (March 1995).

7 See e.g. the analysis of J. Sklar, *Legalism: Law, Morals and Political Trials*, (Harvard U.P., enlarged edn, 1986).

8 In the case of the Nuremberg trials there were those who sought to avoid this difficulty by denying the legality of German laws during the Third Reich. Others who justified the trials argued that it is better to concede the legality of the norms, to acknowledge the retroactivity of imposing liability in such cases, and to justify it by the nature of the atrocities committed by the Nazis. Cf. The Hart-Fuller debate, *Harv. L. Rev* (1958).

9 For a discussion of these problems in the context of East Germany see 'The Past is Another Country', *The Economist*, 4 February 1995.

However, the simplicity and clarity of this description may be misleading. The period before the transition was a period of an oppressive dictatorship. While relatively small groups actually participated in executions and torture, large groups of people knew and were involved in the 'civil service', or belonged to the 'silent majority'. They lived under and with the dictatorial regime. Mostly they were not its victims, and did not participate in the active struggle against it. Mostly, they saw law-enforcement agencies as either neutral or as guards of safety and order. Many of them accepted the official declarations that the opposition were dangerous enemies of the people. Thus, before the transition, this was a society in conflict, with disparate and clashing visions of the law. After the transition, when all is presumably set right, the conflicts may well persist. A dramatic illustration is the situation in Chile, where the army negotiated its status before the transition, so that all those responsible for the atrocities are still holding the positions they held before democratization. Many societies after transitions have to deal with a combination of the issues raised by the transition and the need to deal with the past and with internal conflicts in the society.

The situation in the Middle East is unique in that it contains additional complicating factors which are usually missing from other transition situations. In most transitions, there is no serious attempt to reverse the change, because all parties accept the results of the process;[10] similarly, there is no lively and open debate, during the process, of who are (or were) the victims and who are (or were) the oppressors or aggressors. The new phase is one in which the change is completed and accepted as justified by those who now have the power to mete out justice. The problem is how to deal with the past, but the present is relatively secure.[11] Moreover, the public norm is a condemnation of the previous atrocities, even if there is a reluctance to impose liability on their perpetrators for a variety of complex reasons. The 'good guys' now in power do not have to take into account the possibility that someone else sees the past differently. The transition means that power changed hands, but it does not require a change in perceptions of the winning side about the justness of its cause.

The situation is very different when leaders of two groups who have been in a prolonged and bloody conflict try to take a non-violent route towards resolving it. The leaders share some important short-term interests and perceptions, notably the fact that the route of negotiations is better than the continuation of violence. However, they also have

10 More accurately, the factors that created the transition and made it inevitable are very much there, so there is no real option of reversing the change.

11 In some of the situations (e.g. Chile), the newly elected democratic regime is not powerful enough, and depends on an army that was involved in the human rights violations that preceded it. In such situations, the new government may fear that too much retroactive law enforcement may undermine its stability and the chances of democracy.

readings of the past and hopes for the future, and these are often very different. Moreover, these readings of the past include evaluations of the conduct of the other party itself. Often, these histories breed anger, resentment and suspiciousness which may be fatal to the process of negotiation and peace. People who are interested in the success of the process should attend, therefore, not only to deeds but also to underlying sentiments. Moreover, the deeds often reflect not only rational negotiations but the ambivalence that even the leaders committed to the change experience. This ambivalence is obviously strengthened by the fact that people within their communities continue, at the same time, to try and undermine the budding agreement. It is hard enough to start seeing your one-time enemy as an ally. It is even harder to do that when you are not sure that the functionality of seeing that person as an enemy has indeed been removed. It is easy to see these difficulties and ambiguities when the parties seek to agree about dealing with issues generated by the period before the transition.

To make this discussion less abstract, let me take four groups of individuals in the Israeli-Palestinian context, whose status is clearly affected by the transition. The Israel-Palestinian conflict is singled out even among Middle East conflicts. The peace with Jordan (and Egypt before it) was relatively easy, because Israel and Israelis were not so attached to the land they had to give up for peace. Moreover, hostility and competitiveness were limited. The situation is very different concerning the conflict between the Jews of Israel and the Palestinian Arabs. Since 1967, Israel controlled both its own territory and the occupied territories. The Israeli Arabs belong to the same people, often to the same families, as the Palestinian population of the territories. Israel, the West Bank and the Gaza Strip formed one economic unit. While there are important differences between the legal regimes governing Israelis (especially Israeli Jews) and Palestinians, there are also many similarities in both law and practices. The settlements created a situation where the ethnic communities are interwoven and cannot be easily separated. Finally, the hopes and the aspirations of Jews and Arabs in Palestine are simply contradictory. Both want the whole of Palestine and Jerusalem as a capital. If one adds the fact that the respective histories written and taught by the two groups are almost as contradictory, one can sense how complicated it is to negotiate for a reconciliation under these conditions. The fact that Israel enjoys much greater strength and status just adds to the complexity of the situation. Obviously, no serious political change operates in a vacuum. The 'new' norms were simmering under the ground for some time; the 'old' beliefs and faiths are still very much there. In the Middle East situation, many do not accept yet that the change is irreversible, and they are trying to maintain the norms of the 'past' and re-make them valid and applicable to the present and the future. This combination of facts is what makes the decisions so delicate and so painful, and this is why we should be extremely cautious and creative in our use of legal tools.

The first group I want to look at is that of Palestinians who committed acts of violence against Israelis as part of the Jewish-Palestinian conflict. The second group is that of Israelis who committed acts of violence against Palestinians for similar reasons. The third group is that of Palestinians who 'cooperated' with the Israeli authorities during the occupation – the so-called 'collaborators'. The fourth is that of Jewish settlers, who built their homes in the occupied territories, in part with the encouragement and financial help of Israeli governments, on the assumption that Israel will never relinquish its hold over them. For all these groups, many of the background assumptions that they made, and that governed their activities, are now changing. To some of them, this change may be welcome, but to many it is devastating. The way they see the process, and the way they are perceived and treated by both parties to the process, are an important part thereof.[12]

In principle, the decision concerning the right way to treat the past, the period before the transition, must seek to avoid two dangers. One is that of a total loss of continuity and a sense of justice, of right desert. The other is that of letting the past rule us so that all chances for a real change are jeopardized. The need to maintain this delicate balance affects the attitude towards change of perceptions. While these must change if conflict is to become a stable compromise, the change cannot be so radical as to threaten one's sense of self-identity and purpose. We are bound to have temporary tensions between actions, agreements and perceptions. If the process is successful, these tensions lessen. If the process is stagnated, the tensions may intensify and threaten the process itself.[13]

One could have expected that negotiating the balance between popular support under present perceptions and a change that presupposes and requires a significant change in these perceptions might be hard in a democracy, which is known to make unpopular moves very hard to pass. Interestingly enough, a similar problem manifests itself among the Palestinians as well. The fight over changes of perceptions, as well as for a new political approach, is being conducted both within each community, and in the inter-community relationships.

[12] I thank Eyal Benvenisti for drawing my attention to the fact that many other groups are affected. An example is IDF soldiers, who were used to a certain way of treating both Jewish settlers and Palestinians, and are now requested to change their attitudes. Their reported anxiety suggests the importance of our theme here.

[13] I must confess I am writing this paper not as an academic. Rather, I am writing it as an individual who believes that a negotiated compromise is the only hope for the region. I was becoming more apprehensive as I was writing the paper. Unfortunately, it now seems (May 1995) as if the process is indeed stagnating to an extent which is threatening to its prospects.

I. Amnesty for Ideological Users of Violence?

I take it that the right to life is a prime human right, and that intentionally taking the life of another human being is the ultimate violation of this right. It is always difficult to compromise and thus give up something that is very important to one. It is much harder to negotiate and reach reconciliation with people who are responsible for killing members of one's group. It is even harder to agree, as part of such negotiations, to let those responsible for the killings go unpunished and 'get away with it'. Between Israeli Jews and Palestinians there is a blood account. It is not surprising that one of the most charged issues for the negotiating parties is that of the release of prisoners, especially those with 'blood on their hands'.

The account above sounded symmetrical, and in some ways it is: Palestinians were killed by Jews, Jews were killed by Palestinians as part of the conflict between the two peoples. But there are many important sources of asymmetry. They are dramatized by the fact that at this stage (before the implementation of the agreements and with regard only to prisoners held for actions done before the agreements were signed), only Israel holds prisoners. It holds many Palestinians, and a very small number of Jews (all civilians) convicted of killing Palestinians.[14] Israelis who use 'official' violence, as members of the security services or army units, are rarely disciplined in any way. There have been serious problems of enforcing the law against Jewish settlers who use violence, including occasional killings.[15] So the disparity in numbers of prisoners does not attest to the fact that only Jews were killed by Palestinians. Rather, it reflects the fact that only Israel had the political power to pass judgement on those among the Palestinians who killed (just as – after 1967 – only Israel had the political power to commit 'official' killings or to subject Jewish violence to the law or to deport and evacuate and confiscate land). This asymmetry also explains why Palestinian killing of Jews is primarily intentional murder, while many of the Palestinians killed by the security forces were killed during attempts to disperse demonstrations and in similar circumstances.

In thinking about the way to handle users of violence in a process of negotiation there are at least two distinct issues. One is the question of evaluating the conduct of users of violence from the two camps. The other is the question of what should be done with them now, once the

14 The complexity is highlighted by remarking that some of the Palestinians are held for killing Palestinian collaborators, and the group of the Jews discussed in this context includes, for example, the man who threw the hand grenade that killed a man and injured a few in a 1982 Peace Now demonstration demanding that someone be held accountable for the Sabra and Shatila massacres.

15 The complexity of the issues may be exemplified by the fact that it is very difficult to say anything factual on these issues without being challenged. These statements are based on the findings of the Shamgar Commission of Inquiry Report.

political process has started. It is important to see that the two are interconnected in important ways, but they are nonetheless independent. Part of the difficulty is internal tensions, in parts of both communities, between answers to the two questions.

On the first question, the two societies do not have a serious internal debate, and their visions are conflicting. For the Palestinians, all their prisoners are heroes, people who paid a serious price for participating (or being suspected of participating) in their people's struggle for liberation. While there are important political divisions among the Palestinians, Israel and the occupation clearly were – until the agreements – the enemy of all. It was widely felt among Palestinians of all affiliations that Israel will only leave if it hurts. Making Israel hurt seemed to many a legitimate way of achieving national liberation. While some groups were willing to limit violence to the security forces, seen as the paradigm of the hated occupation, and the settlers, others saw Israel as a whole (and at times Jews in general) as the target.[16]

The Israelis, on the other hand, see the people who actually used violence as 'terrorists' – people who are a serious threat to life and order. Those who participated in killings are regarded as murderers. Even those sympathetic to the predicament of the Palestinians and who acknowledge that they did not have many non-violent tools at their disposal for changing their situation condemn these activities. There has never been a serious voice in Israel speaking against the use of the harshest legal measures against Palestinians who murdered Jews for ideological reasons. Israel's approach to the killing of Palestinians by the security forces and by Jewish civilians is more divided and much more nuanced and ambivalent. A majority of Israelis see a person like Goldstein, the man who committed the Hebron massacre, as a fanatic murderer. However, when Jewish settlers were arrested for murder and for conspiracy to murder – their terrorist activities involving the blowing up of a number of Arab buses – it took some courage and determination to indict them. The then Prime Minister Shamir was quite reluctant to condemn their actions and those who were not convicted for murder (which requires a mandatory life imprisonment) got light sentences. The murderers themselves were all pardoned by the President and released after relatively short periods. Most of the investigations against soldiers who kill Palestinians are concluded without indictment.

For the Palestinians, therefore, there is no tension between their moral evaluation and their practical stand in the negotiations. They think the Palestinians should not have been in prison to begin with, but there is no question in their eyes that they should be released now that a process towards peace has started. Their continuing imprisonment is,

---

16 It is interesting to note that it was Hamas, the more radical and fundamentalist group, with a clear religious-political aspiration to the whole of Palestine, that at the first stage limited themselves to violence against Israel in the territories and against the security forces.

therefore, a persistent reminder of the fact that Israel is still the controlling power, and that nothing has 'really' changed. More than that, some of these prisoners are the natural leaders of the new Palestinian entity. They were involved in the Palestinian struggle, and 'earned' their leadership status by hard work, charisma and determination. It seems strange that the people now move towards self-determination without acknowledging their debt to these leaders and soldiers, and without recruiting them into the new emerging governing elites. In the Palestinian context, their absence may also be a serious factor in tensions between 'local' and 'Tunis' leadership. Last but not least, the release of the prisoners is a tangible benefit of the change that the Palestinian leadership can present to their people. As popular support for the agreements dwindles, and as economic benefits take longer to materialize than the parties hoped and expected, the need to show progress on the release of the prisoners grows.[17]

For the Israelis who support the peace process, there is a tension between heart and head. They understand that peace negotiations and continued imprisonment of those who fought to achieve independence for their people are incompatible. On the other hand, it is not easy to let convicted prisoners, especially killers, go. There is a strong sentiment which sees their release as an offence to the victims, as a serious additional violation of the victims' right to life.[18] There is something very upsetting in seeing those who wilfully took the life of one's dear ones leave their prisons as welcome heroes.

The release of killers presents more than a psychological difficulty. Within the realm of principles, such action creates a tension between the idea of right desert and accountability for one's deeds, and the understanding that a radical change requires the willingness and the ability to look forward and let bygones be bygones.[19] It is interesting to note that there are situations of transition in which people who used

---

17 In the beginning of January 1995, after some lull in terrorist activity against Israel, the issue of release of prisoners got very high visibility. Nabil Sha'th announced that he would not participate in negotiations unless more prisoners were released. He declared that the peace process was incompatible with the fact that 6000 Palestinian prisoners, sent by their people to various missions, were still prisoners. It seemed as if negotiations were indeed leading towards the release of more prisoners when the Beit-Lid suicide-murder changed the situation once again.

18 The problem may be highlighted by the fact that Israel has already agreed to release Palestinians who were convicted of murdering other Palestinians. The group hardest to release are not 'murderers' but those who killed Jews in terrorist activities.

19 Both elements of internal tension exist in many situations of political transition. The Middle East situation has the complexities of negotiated transitions, in which the old regime has the power to ensure some degree of amnesty for its own officials. But it has the additional complexity that the political process itself requires impunity to be bestowed upon convicted Palestinians who committed murders. Those tortured and killed by the military juntas were victimized because they protested and seemed to be a threat. They did not use violence themselves.

violence against the dictatorship are not released after the democratization.[20]

Clearly, no such tensions exist for those Israelis opposing the process.

The Israeli picture is made even more complex by the fact that many are not sure that the agreements will be effective. Release of prisoners, especially those committed to violent action and having the competence and the know-how to perform it, may lead to more murders committed by these people themselves. This fear is strengthened by the fact that the Palestinian demand for release covers members of all groups, including those – like Hamas and The Islamic Jihad – who voice a political objection to the political process and are not willing to condemn terrorism or even to declare that they will give it up. On the contrary – as we have seen – they well know that terrorism is an effective tool in democracies, and Israel's vulnerability on this score creates a serious incentive to use terror to defeat the political process.

Israel's dilemma is highlighted by the fact that the 'transition' may take some time. When Palestinians are killed during terrorist activity now, they are referred to as '*shahids*' by many of their compatriots. Palestinian change in relation to Palestinian terrorism is slow and incomplete. To many of them, there is a continuity between those who killed before the agreements and the 'new' terrorists. But some change is visible; Palestinian leaders now openly condemn acts such as the blowing up of the bus in Tel-Aviv and the shooting in Jerusalem in November 1994. In the aftermath of the murder in Beit Lid in January 1995, Arafat publicly affirmed that there will be a Palestinian effort to curb Palestinian terrorism. These moves may well reflect political constraints rather than changed moral perceptions. If condemnation and some efforts to fight terrorism are not demonstrated, the process may come to a complete halt. Nonetheless, acting against organizations committed to terrorism will probably create within Palestinian society a more nuanced attitude towards violence as a political tool.

Within Israel, approaches to violence against Palestinians already vary. However, with the intensification of Palestinian terror, the responses from the Jewish street are far from re-assuring. There are open calls for counter-terrorism, and the voices saying that this conflict is unlikely to be won by force are not much stronger than they were before the agreements.

Some Israelis resent the fact that there is no parallel on the Palestinian side to the massive release of prisoners by Israel. They see this as yet another proof of the weakness and irresponsibility of Rabin's government. Release of prisoners is indeed an area where most of the burden – political and emotional – lies with Israel. However, this is because of the asymmetry between Israel and the Palestinians which the political process is aimed at changing. It is true that the Palestinians do

---

20 This is the case, for example, in Chile.

not have prisoners they can release. But the process involves a change of perspectives on their part which is no less radical than that required from the Israelis and which makes the release of Palestinian prisoners necessary, almost inevitable.

Moreover, Israelis cannot expect Palestinians to be harsher on their terrorists than we were on 'ours'.[21] As mentioned above, many Israelis are quite ambivalent about Jewish terrorism. Many Jews regard Goldstein as a hero and a saint.[22] How is that different from seeing Palestinian 'terrorists' who die in action as *shahids*?[23] At present, there is much more Arab terrorism than Jewish terrorism.[24] Throughout the occupation, more Jews were murdered in terrorist attacks than Palestinians in Jewish terrorist attacks. However, the number of Palestinians killed by Jews in 'non-terrorist situations' during the occupation is much larger than the number of Jews killed by Palestinians in the same period.

This, in fact, is one of the changes introduced by the process. It creates a symmetry where until now there was total asymmetry, and it highlights an inner tension that now exists for both communities. Policing violence committed by members of your own group against members of the other group is extremely hard. There are strong incentives to either do nothing or to treat these people very leniently. The peace process has created an independent incentive to fight one's own terrorists where before there was none or a weak one. Goldstein and Hamas do not want merely to hurt and kill Arabs and Jews respectively. They want to kill the political process itself. The leaders of the two peoples who have made a commitment to the political process now have to negotiate the very delicate line between undermining the effort to de-rail the process without losing the support of too large a part of their community. Moreover, the peace process creates, for both parties, an internal ambiguity within the security forces. Until now only Israel had security forces, and they had a relatively simple task; their role was to fight the enemy. And the enemy usually came from the other

21 In fact, before some legitimate rule is established among the Palestinians, Arafat's ability to deal with Palestinian terrorists must be weaker than Israel's ability to deal with its own offenders.

22 In a ceremony to commemorate a year since the massacre, a few hundred persons gathered to pay Goldstein their respects. On his stone he is described as the 'saint', some of the participants openly endorsed what he did.

23 There is also a symmetry between the Palestinians' seeing their victims of the conflict at large as *shahids*, and the Jewish habit to affix '*hashem yikkom dammo*' to the names of Jewish victims of the conflict.

24 This is the reason given by the court to justify its upholding the decision of the military authorities to blow up the family house of the man who exploded himself aboard the Dizengoff bus. When people asked that Goldstein's house be blown up, the State replied that it did not ordinarily blow up the houses of terrorists who died, so as not to impose punishment on the family of the offender. When asked why the Arab family was 'discriminated' against, the court responded that the needs of deterrence were not as powerful among Jews.

group. They enjoyed support and respect in their group for fighting that enemy. They usually got away with violating the rights of innocent Arabs, who were all seen as 'others' and 'potential enemies'. They did not use harsh measures against violent Jewish groups. It was a bad situation, with an attractive simplicity. The simplicity is gone now not because of a moral conversion, but because it has become the interest of both parties to control the excesses of their own people.[25]

Clearly, the attitudes described above affect law enforcement and the protection of human rights. In addition, a few legal questions emerge. All concede that the issue of release of prisoners is primarily political, and is determined in political negotiations by the government. Once a political decision of release is made, the meted sentence must be mitigated so that it is legal for prison authorities to actually let the people go. This may seem as a mere formality, but it may not be. The large majority of prisoners are held by the military and those charged and convicted were tried in the military courts. The military commander has the power to mitigate punishments and the Israeli High Court of Justice (HCJ) is unlikely to intervene.[26] In the rare cases in which Palestinians were charged and tried by Israeli courts, the presidential power of pardon will be invoked. It is unlikely that the president will refuse to pardon in such circumstances, or that the HCJ will intervene.[27] The political authorities can thus ensure that whatever they decide to do on this issue will indeed be done, and they are unlikely to encounter opposition from either the President or the Court.[28]

Is this situation right? Shouldn't there be a more serious involvement of the administration of justice system in such decisions? Are the effectiveness and respectability of the judicial system not hurt if its decisions can be set aside by political negotiators? Should prisoners,

---

25 This effect exists not only for Palestinian security forces but for their human rights organizations as well. Gone are the days in which it was easy to concentrate all efforts in documenting and fighting the violation of rights of all Palestinians by Israel. The new era means that some of the energy has to be directed against human rights violations by the Palestinian Authority. At the moment this may be an all-Palestinian affair, with its own complexities. Soon it may become a question of protecting the human rights of Jews as well.

26 See HCJ 1414/91, *Federman v. Minister of Defence* PD 45 (2) 774, where the court indicated that it will not intervene in a decision to release prisoners.

27 The presidential power was invoked in some of the cases included in the Gibril exchange transaction. There was an attempt to stop the release (see note 26 *supra*), but the court refused to intervene. Israel's current President supports the peace process. It might be interesting to think what would have happened had the President been committed to positions and visions inconsistent with it.

28 This paper was initially written in October 1994. In the meantime, in the wake of terrorism against individuals in Tel-Aviv and Beit Lid, the President issued a call to stop the process and re-think it. On the other hand, Palestinians present the issue of release of prisoners as urgent and critical. The present President, Mr. Ezer Weizmann, has already expressed an independent position about the use of his pardoning power. What seemed a far-fetched theoretical possibility three months ago may seem now a plausible development.

especially murderers, be released without any public input or debate? In the past, the HCJ has protested when the President used his pardoning power, for political reasons, to mitigate a punishment imposed by the court soon after the court's judgement. The current president has voiced misgivings about some aspects of the pardoning power, especially the power to mitigate life imprisonment for murder to a term sentence (which entitles the prisoner to leave and to a deduction of a third for good behaviour). Why should ideological offenders be released through pardons that are mere rubber stamps to political negotiations?

Indeed, a group of right-wing academics has called upon senior members of the judiciary in Israel to do all in their power, including resignation, to prevent release of Palestinians convicted of murder. The rhetoric is apolitical and professional. While it seems clear that the move is politically motivated, the plea does attest to a real problem.

Israel sometimes makes the release of prisoners dependent on their signing a statement declaring support of the peace process or an undertaking not to use violence. One may question the wisdom of this decision. But is it legal? Does it violate the human rights of the prisoners? A lawyer within ACRI (The Association for Civil Rights in Israel) argued that the practice was not legal, since it violated the prisoners' right to freedom of conscience and belief. I beg to differ. Prisoners whose freedom was attained through a political process do not have a human right to be set free. Presumably, the court that judged them operated lawfully, and the punishment is legal. Nothing in the political decision to release the prisoners casts doubt on that. If one does not have a right to be set free, the power granting freedom may demand that some prior conditions are met. However, I think there is a difference between requiring a declaration of support of the process, and requiring an undertaking of non-violence. People should have the political freedom to express their political opinions and to change them. I do not think it is legitimate to ask a person to make a commitment to have a certain attitude towards the process even if it is the process that obtained his release. On the other hand, I see no problem (although I see also no great gain) with asking prisoners to sign a declaration of non-violence as a condition of release.[29] However, it is not clear how one can check these observations. A prisoner may refuse to sign. Israel may refuse to let him go. The issue can then be discussed politically. But it seems that the prisoner cannot demand in court that he be released despite his refusal to sign (or that he can demand to be released even if he did sign, for that matter). Similarly, I doubt that he can challenge the requirement to sign as a violation of his rights.

Which leads me directly to a related question: Once Israel has released all (or some) of the Palestinians who took the lives of innocent, helpless

29 It is interesting to note that the Israeli authorities did just that in the case of Uddi Adiv. In his case it worked, Udi Adiv left the country and all political activity.

others, what should it do with the small number of Jews who were convicted of murdering Arabs and are now still in its prisons? All but marginal groups in Israel condemned these acts of violence.[30] In the past, attempts to enact legislation designed to pardon these prisoners were defeated. Even after the exchange with Gibril's group, in which thousands of Palestinian prisoners were released to obtain the return of a few Israeli soldiers, pressures to pardon these prisoners were refused. The reason always was that an amnesty might send the message that taking the life of Palestinians is something we treat as different from any 'regular' murder.[31] Should the beginning of the political process and the release of Palestinian murderers change this approach?

On the one hand, the answer seems negative. Why should these individuals benefit from the fact that a process of reconciliation and appeasement has started? Clearly, we are concerned with those whose actions contributed to the violence and the desperation of the conflict. On the other hand, the release of Palestinian prisoners as a part of the process reflects more than the acceptance that the political process cannot move forward unless this is done. It reflects a deeper willingness to 'open a new page' on the violent phase of the conflict. It seems permissible to open this new page symmetrically. When those left in prison are anyway the more marginal elements of Jewish violence against Palestinians, their release despite the fact that they have no lobby fighting for them might, in fact, be an act of public decency.

We should recall that due to the specific structure of the negotiations here, Palestinians do not have the power over those who allegedly violated their human rights before the transition, be they settlers or security forces, whereas Jews have no new incentive to police and punish the past. Thus a problem that often exists in periods of transitions is muted here by the unique structure of the process.[32]

---

30 The cases which were more controversial, e.g. the murders by the 'Jewish Underground', were treated differently. All those convicted as members of that group, including the murderers, have been released a long time ago.

31 One may point out, however, that this message was indeed sent by the early pardons of those convicted in the Kfar Kassem killing and those of the Jewish Underground convicted of murders. Those who are still in prison are individuals, who do not enjoy the support of respectable groups in the Israeli political scene. This is just another example of the fact that there are legal constraints that determine political results. An open, high-visibility legislation giving amnesty was rejected. Low visibility amnesty was given to the more powerful of the killers. The insult of discrimination was thus added to the injury of the leniency towards the murder of Palestinians. A similar message was sent by the different treatment of Palestinians who killed Palestinians suspected of collaboration – who were released – and those who killed Jews – who are still in prison.

32 This uniqueness was important enough at the early stages of negotiations, which seemed geared towards close cooperation between the two ethnic entities. It is even more true now, when the solution appears to be a disengagement between them. In most of the contemporary transitions to democracy, we are talking about a change of regime within the same state and the same community.

II. Moral and Legal Aspects of 'Collaboration'

People seen by Israel as terrorists were seen by many Palestinians as freedom fighters. People seen by many Israelis as heroes, fighting in special army and Security Service units, were seen by Palestinians as the paradigm of humiliation and occupation. The political process does not require a change of these perceptions (although it may require some willingness to see the other side's perspective), but it requires their disregard in some actions, e.g. the willingness to release prisoners, or the willingness to cooperate now with those regarded until very recently as bitter enemies.

There is no similar tension between changing perceptions and action concerning collaborators, although the moral and legal challenge they present is serious and urgent. Occupation, especially a prolonged one requiring a very close monitoring of elements within the population under occupation, must rely on collaborators. However, neither party likes collaborators or respects them.[33] For the Palestinians they are traitors, motivated either by fear, by greed or by political naivete. For the Israelis they are an indispensable source of information, or an opportunity to manipulate the population politically by using Palestinians to promote their own goals.

Some of the violence in the territories has always been an inter-Palestinian matter. People suspected of being collaborators were often attacked and sometimes brutally killed. There was some debate about the human rights aspects of these exercises of field justice. Clearly, there was a denial of due process. Some argued that the punishment was anyway not proportional to the deeds, and that the principle of legality was offended. There have been claims that at least in some cases, the absence of due process did result in violence being used against the 'wrong' people.[34] Israel, of course, tried to protect 'its' collaborators. Such protection, however, proved impossible in many cases. And often the collaborator's effectiveness required that they remain in their homes at least until they were 'burnt'.

What will happen to the collaborators once Israel withdraws from the territories? Should Israel guarantee their life and rights against 'popular justice'? Can it do it? How should Israel seek to do it?

Some of the collaborators want to stay where they are. They either hope their actions are unknown, or that with time they will be reintegrated into their society. Possibly, there could be an agreement regarding their security and a guarantee by the Palestinian Authority not

---

33 I do not think this truth should be distorted by the fact that some Israelis seek to present the collaborators as courageous individuals who helped them in the holy task of saving human life. There is a semantic edge to this emphasis. Until now both sides called them 'collaborators' (*meshatfei pe-ulah*). Now they are called 'helpers' or 'accessories' (*say-anim*).

34 See the report of B'tselem on this issue.

to harm them, and to protect them against attempts to take revenge by individuals.[35] The tendency to 'purge' and to punish those seen as collaborators with the enemy is universal.[36] It is well known that the process claims innocent victims,[37] and that even those who were indeed collaborators are often punished, sometimes killed, despite the fact that they could not have been convicted of any offence. Seeing to it that people suspected of collaboration enjoy due process is a serious problem for the Palestinians to deal with.[38]

Other collaborators are too afraid to stay among the Palestinians. Israel grudgingly accepts responsibility.[39] Many of them were given Israeli citizenship or at least are allowed to reside in Israel. However, since this is a rather large group of people, who are despised and feared by Israelis, both Jews and Arabs, relocating them has become a serious problem.[40]

This is not only a serious practical problem. It creates a different kind of tension between past and present. These people (someone mentioned a figure between twenty and fifty thousand once the West Bank is evacuated) live in a nowhere land, outside their old community and with no welcome into another.[41]

---

35 Such agreements were not included in the Gaza-Jericho agreements. The Cairo agreement only specifies in general that the parties make a commitment to protect human rights. It is not clear what this absence means. It may indicate that there are unwritten 'understandings' concerning the issue, or that all known collaborators have left with the IDF.

36 Cf. the series of 'trials' and in some cases executions of French people suspected of collaborating with the Nazis. French leaders were never proud of these episodes, but it was felt that they were understandable. The number of individuals 'purged' in this way is estimated at around 11,000. In 1947 and again in 1953, laws granted amnesty and rehabilitation to those harmed in the purges. The legitimacy of the purges is still controversial in France.

37 Innocent victims include individuals who did not have anything to do with the enemy and are suspected by mistake (or due to baseless accusations made by interested others), and individuals who had contact with the enemy that did not amount to collaboration, e.g. women who fell in love with enemy soldiers.

38 See e.g. *Ha-aretz*, 29 November 1994, reporting that complaints were made to the Palestinian authorities concerning allegations of killings and torture of collaborators in the Gaza strip.

39 At least one collaborator who escaped into Israel received an injunction against attempts to deport him back into the Gaza strip. He requested Israeli citizenship, or an adequate arrangement in the collaborators' 'village' in Dahanieh, *Ha-aretz*, 21 November 1994.

40 See *Ha-aretz*, 11 November 1994, reporting on the complexity of the attempt to relocate the collaborators within the Israeli Arab community. There seems to be a move by that community to take measures against this process, and to ask the government to find alternative solutions (e.g. persuading the collaborators to stay in the territories, or building for them a special settlement in Israel).

41 For one case see *Ha-aretz*, 30 December 1994, which tells the story of a collaborator who lived in the West Bank and was harassed, and later killed, by Palestinians. His widow, an Israel-born Arab, has been trying in vain to get the Israeli authorities to admit that the burning of their shop was a hostile act against Israel so that they can be compensated. This widow is fortunate, because her family in Israel is willing to help

In other historical situations, collaborators usually stayed within their community, hoping for consideration and mercy. They could not hope for protection from the now defeated regime they had served.[42] In the Palestinian-Israeli situation there is no defeated power, the territories are very close, and there is within Israel a large Arab population. The solution of moving the collaborators to Israel thus seems natural and simple. For the Israeli Arabs, however, these 'newcomers' are offensive. They see them as traitors, and do not want to welcome them. In addition, Israeli Arabs resent the fact that the collaborators seem rich and well connected. The Israeli Arabs fear that the collaborators may well continue to work for the security services, this time spying on the local community.

In simple terms of accountability, the collaborators pose a very serious problem. Unlike some of the people they served, mostly they themselves did not commit serious human rights violations of any sort. They worked for the occupier. Sometimes they gave the occupier information, sometimes they merely legitimated the occupation by their conduct. They clearly offended against the social and moral norm requiring a struggle against the enemy. Persecuting collaborators stems from a wish to keep one's ranks clean, and the frustration of not being able to really hurt those responsible for the human rights violations or the occupation itself.

Collaboration, by its very nature, is not illegal while it is done. Often, what most collaborators did would not be illegal had there been a Palestinian criminal code in action. Consequently, the principle of legality suggests that collaborators cannot be punished after the transition took place. Retroactive liability was justified in the trials following World War II only because the activities with which the defendants were charged were seen as against 'the law of nature' or as 'crimes against humanity', gross violations of basic human rights shared by all human societies. Punishment of collaborators cannot be justified under any of these rationales. Nonetheless, as we have seen, it is a very common phenomenon.

Treatment of collaborators illustrates very poignantly the tension between principles of justified punishment and basic human sentiments. It is not surprising that punishment of collaborators is not usually done by legal systems granting individuals full due process. Rather, it is done in the twilight of periods of transition, by individuals working in the aftermath of a period of great violence, and the new power often chooses to close its eyes for some period, and accept that the needs for

---

her. But in her community, it is said, her daughters will never be able to marry, and they will always be seen as traitors.

42 This was the case, for example, with the French accused of collaboration with the Nazis. In Algiers, some collaborators stayed, but a large group moved to France, where they are still a segregated, unhappy community.

this kind of justice are too deep. Collaborators are the victims of the transition because they are seen as people who violated the only norms left to victims – that of dignity and the duty to struggle actively for liberation, or at least to remain true to one's people. It is significant, both morally and as a statement about human nature, that the 'punished' collaborators are often the ones low in the echelons of power. Some of the factors working against punishment of your own people even if they erred (even if they erred terribly) seem to be less present for these people. For some reason, it is much harder to turn one's heroes and leaders of yesterday into traitors, despite the fact that they were in positions that could have mattered. In addition, the people at the top are often well connected with the heroes of the new regime. Punishing them may be too difficult or dangerous to the fragile transition. Consequently, popular justice against collaborators is often scapegoating at its worst.

In terms of human rights, collaborators (as all people) should be protected against lynching or unofficial risk of life and limb. Of course, no one can (or should) protect collaborators from natural social reactions like social ostracism or public condemnation. These should enable the alleged collaborators to correct the facts, but brutal scenes of humiliation should always be avoided.[43] History shows that collaborators cannot be effectively protected during the occupation or immediately after it. In the Middle East situation, with the unique 'solution' of relocation, the problem may become of longer duration. The Israeli Arabs now use legitimate ways of fighting collaborators – social ostracism. They demand that Israel finds a solution that will not force the collaborators on their communities. Naturally, they accuse the collaborators of being 'morally bad' in ways having nothing to do with the alleged collaboration. Allegedly, collaborators are involved with drugs and prostitution, and are generally corrupt and thus dangerous to the moral fabric of Arab society in Israel. The newcomers themselves are naturally quite terrified, and many of them do not hesitate to invoke their good connections with the security services, itself a doubtful recommendation within Arab society.

Israel is right to think that it is its task to protect individuals who collaborated with it. One cannot rely on agreements made on this score with the Palestinian Authority during this period of the twilight of the occupation. The collaborators who chose to leave in a way 'admitted' their guilt. Imposing them in large numbers on the Israeli Arab community, when their life styles are so different and when the background to their being in Israel is so obvious, is a bad idea. It can be done as an interim solution, but Israel has to face the problem now in a creative way, basing the solution on an understanding of the sentiments

---

43 Such as the notorious head-shaving of women accused of having intimate relations with members of the enemy group.

underlying and causing the intensity of the problem: that there is no natural home for these people and no community that is willing to accept them. No one has real sympathy with their predicament. The solution will have to build on a reasonably long period of limited friction between them and the general population in the hope of a possibility of slow re-integration on a small-scale basis.

III. The Jewish Settlers

The way the Jewish settlers are seen and treated may be an important factor in the prospects of this process.[44] Palestinians regard all of them as the essential enemy. Many of them are seen by the Palestinian population as arrogant and violent. They are the symbol of Israel's wish to expand and to uproot the local inhabitants. They are also perceived as a source of danger, since many of them are regarded as 'trigger-happy'.

Some people on the Israeli left share this vision of the settlers. In fact, there is a tendency on the Israeli left to see all settlers as ultra-religious Jews carrying guns and terrorizing the local population. They are seen as fanatics and as believers in a messianic vision of Israel and of Zionism, which are seen by Israel's left as the approach which prevented the acceptance of the necessity of dialogue and negotiation with the Palestinians.[45] Others in Israel see the settlers, especially the ideological variety, as the dynamic and dedicated carriers of the modern Zionist movement.

Quite naturally, the settlers themselves are rather anxious. Three different issues emerge for them. The first, which applies to all the settlers, is the painful prospect of being forced to leave their homes. Many of them have lived in the territories all their lives. It is much more than a financial matter. They love their homes, the landscapes. Their children were born there and this is for them home in all deep senses of the word. To be forced to move is a huge trauma. They see themselves as the victims of the process, those who are required to pay a heavy price for what is perceived by the present leaders as in the interests of Israel and its people. There are great differences between those among the settlers who share the government's assessment and those who do not. There are also obvious differences between locations. It is easy to see that the settlements based in the midst of the Palestinian

---

44 I do not include as 'settlers' the Jews living in suburbs of Jerusalem beyond the green line, despite the fact that it may well be that in legal terms there is no distinction between their status and that of the Jews living in Hebron.

45 See e.g. S. Yizhar's depiction of the ideological core of the settlers in *Ha-aretz*, 6 January 1995. The portrait triggered a host of responses, indicating the depth of the controversy on this subject within Israel.

population, and who thus need constant protection, create a problem that needs to be solved. It is less clear with regard to the Golan where settling does not involve the daily ruling of another people and where the security situation – in the short term – is quite satisfactory.

For a large number of settlers, however, the anxiety is not limited to the trauma of having to leave one's home. Many of them went there with the blessing and support of the government, and with the respect of their fellow-citizens. They often went to places that were deserted and developed them. They reflect a very basic element in Israel's self-image as those who make deserts blossom. They see themselves – and were seen by many others – not as people motivated by self-interest, people seeking a better quality of life, whose materialistic efforts have now collapsed. Rather, they were told, and believed, that they were *halutzim*, people who made a contribution to Zionism and to the security needs of Israel. From members of the Israeli aristocracy they have become a burden to peace. This is a very hard transition, and these people feel wronged, hurt and betrayed by their own government.

Finally, the settlers who see the settlement as a religious duty or a national requirement are devastated. The idea of leaving the West Bank, especially places considered holy, is to them much more than a personal disaster. They feel the political process is based on a total misunderstanding of the relationship between the Jewish people and *Eretz Yisrael*. A minority of these settlers rejects the legitimacy of Israel's government and denies its authority to undertake the process. A very small minority is even willing to use force against it. A somewhat different group may be willing to use violence against the Arabs in order to undermine the process by triggering more hate, suspicion and revenge.

Unfortunately, many Israelis committed to the peace process, and many government spokespersons (including the Prime Minister himself) seem to disregard the distinctions between settlers and to treat them all as enemies. Consequently, they do not respond to the fact that the transition does affect important and legitimate interests of the settlers, and that most of them are relatively innocent victims of this change.[46]

Needless to say, these very different perceptions affect the range of possible solutions considered by the parties for both the interim and the final agreements. For some time after the Oslo Declaration, the Left in Israel asked only whether the settlers should be compensated, and whether Israel should seek to negotiate permission to stay for its citizens who may wish to live under Palestinian, Jordanian or Syrian authority. There was no willingness to acknowledge that the question whether Israel should withdraw was real and urgent.

---

[46] All of the settlers knew or should have known that the territories were occupied, and that their fate will be determined by some settlement. Most of the settlers did not see themselves as helping to 'create' the parameters of this future settlement.

If there had been a very quick implementation of an agreement to withdraw, it might have been possible to 'create facts' before the opposition was consolidated, so that these questions could have been pre-empted. However, this was not done, and probably could not have been done. When the population is truly divided, it is not enough that leaders reach the conclusion that Israel should indeed return more or less to the 1967 borders if it can get peace and recognition. Even a majority in the Knesset is not sufficient (though clearly it is necessary for the move). The process needs a majority of the people. It had it in the initial stages because the alternative policy failed and the new route offered hope. The weakening of support in the public rests on a doubt whether what is gained (personal security) is credible. As a result, the question of the settlers' fate is returning to centre-stage.

Similarly, the question of the settlements and the settlers regains centrality with the Palestinians. The equivocation of the promise not to extend the settlements, and the delays in the implementation of the second stage of re-deployment and elections, make more Palestinians believe that the Israelis meant to start and end with Gaza and Jericho. What initially seemed a bad agreement that will start the dynamics of an acceptable arrangement now becomes a fig leaf to perpetuate and even intensify Israeli control and occupation. Consequently, the support which is crucial for progress is dwindling on both sides.

The settlers themselves are a minority in Israel. However, they are seen among both Israelis and Palestinians as representing much more than their numbers. It is unlikely that much progress in the process can be made without a determined decision on this issue and an implementation of it. To reach this point, the issue has to be debated and decided, without ignoring or belittling the cost to the settlers of a decision to evacuate the settlements.

Maybe it is not too late. There are limits to the gains from constructive ambiguities. The question whether Israel should withdraw is a serious political question. It needs to be debated and decided. If Israel decides to withdraw (as I hope it will), there should be no question of the settlers not being compensated. Even if they were subsidized by the Israeli government, so that their own personal investment was not great, the price they are asked to pay now is real and heavy. Some Israelis may resent the fact that the settlers are going to make financial gain from the fact that they created difficulties that now have to be removed. They may end up better off financially than those who, due to moral or political reasons, never considered settling behind the green line. To them, this may be a version of the situation of murdering and inheriting. But such an approach is neither just nor wise.

The question of Israelis living under Palestinian (or Jordanian, or Syrian) sovereignty is a complex one. In principle, there should be a symmetry between Israel and its neighbours. Israel has a large Arab minority which enjoys civil rights within it. Why shouldn't Jews be allowed to live in neighbouring Arab countries? The argument for symmetry may be strengthened by the issue of the collaborators mentioned above. If Israel will now absorb some tens of thousands of Palestinian collaborators, why shouldn't Palestine and Syria take a similar number of Israeli Jews?[47]

The agreement with Jordan provides yet more proof that what determines the content of legal decisions or agreements is the background situation rather than legal principles. There is nothing in logic or law to prevent Jewish settlements from remaining in the Palestinian entity. The important factors are social and political, not logical or legal. It is quite possible to divide sovereignty and use with Jordan. It might be possible to do the same with Syria on the Golan. It seems utterly impossible, at this stage, to devise a similar arrangement with the Palestinian entity.

IV. A Note on Processes

At periods such as these, there are likely to be many discrepancies between legal situations and realities. At times, these are just oddities of a change that is too quick to make the required legislative or administrative changes. More importantly, this discrepancy may itself be a sign of the process of transition.

A few examples may illustrate this point. The PLO is still defined in Israel's law as a terrorist organization. As a result, many PLO-related activities are still regarded as illegal in Israel, including the public expression of support for the PLO. When Arafat first returned to Gaza, a group of individuals petitioned the HCJ to ask the police and the Attorney-General to capture him so he could be charged for his part in the many terrorist murders performed by the PLO.[48] The prospect of Arafat's visit to Jerusalem provided the occasion for a huge demonstration which sought to prevent him from doing so – despite Israel's clear obligation to let him come to the holy places. Rabin's credibility is being attacked because he said that he would never talk to the PLO and would not return the Golan heights, just as Dayan was accused for changing his mind on the relative worth of peace and *Shar'm-a-S'heich.*

---

47 I am not suggesting that the analogy is complete or very powerful. There are, of course, many differences between Israel's obligation to 'its' collaborators and the attitudes of Palestinians to the Jewish settlers.

48 The HCJ did not allow the petition, saying the subject was too political. In a rare move, the court imposed costs on petitioners, signifying that it saw the petition as vexatious.

Ambivalence and conflicting sentiments towards the legitimacy of Israeli rule existed in 'Greater Israel' since 1967, and has intensified since the beginning of the *Intifada*. It is this ambivalence that made the beginning of the political process possible. Many Palestinians, and a growing number of the Jews, felt that the present situation was unacceptable and unsustainable. The move towards a political process was not the fruit of love, but the fruit of a realization that it was in the urgent interest of both Israel and the PLO to work together towards an agreement. The Jewish opposition, on the other hand, believes that with more perseverance, and with an intelligent use of force, Israel could force the Palestinians and the world to legitimate an agreement that will permit Israel, the Jewish State, to keep most of the occupied territories. Finally, the Palestinian opposition believes that with perseverance, and with the use of force, they would not have to give up their right to return to their villages within Israel proper and their dream of founding a Palestinian (now it is less clear that it would be secular and democratic) state in the whole of Palestine.

Both oppositions concede that the *status quo* before the Oslo agreement was not satisfactory, but both think that it is wrong to pay a painful price in order to change it in the direction taken by the present political process. This is why both oppositions take the route of de-legitimating the leaders of the process as traitors to the national (or religious) cause.[49] What they have in their favour is not only, and not mainly, the strength of their arguments. They are mainly assisted by the huge force of people's inclination to inertia, the great difficulty in changing one's perceptions and values as if by order. It is often easier to stay in the familiar scene of misery and struggle and revenge than to give these up and step into the unknown with its promises. This is why so many attempted transitions fail. Fears like that, when supported by strong opposition, tend to make prophecies of doom and failure come true. Therefore, I regard the Oslo agreements as a courageous move. This judgement is not affected by the knowledge that consideration of personal political survival helped. Both oppositions would like to continue the struggle until their side is able to claim material and historical victory by denying the truth and the statehood of the other. The Oslo framework opened a hope for a different conclusion.

The political process may indeed develop in the way expected by representatives of the opposition on both sides. It is crucial to remember that this would have been the probable result of a decision not to undertake the political process. The political process is unique in creating the chance that the vicious circle of violence will be broken, and that the long process of healing and changing attitudes and sentiments that is required if Jews

49 It should not be surprising that the rhetoric against Arafat and Rabin is sometimes similar to that used against collaborators. They are both accused of sacrificing the good of their people to their personal needs to survive politically.

and Arabs are to live together in the Middle East can begin. The process is far from perfect. Inevitably, it reflects the disparity in power between Israel and the Palestinians at this point. It is an extremely vulnerable process. But nonetheless only such a process can bring about with it the kind of changes that will ultimately be necessary if any political solution is to last.

II. The First Palestinian-Israeli Accords and their Implementation

3. The Status of the Palestinian Authority

Eyal Benvenisti

Introduction

The Israeli-Palestinian Declaration of Principles of 13 September 1993 (the "DOP")[1] provides the framework for the settlement of the conflict between the parties, by delineating a process of gradual transition towards peace, or "permanent status" as referred to in the DOP. The transitional arrangements include gradual assumption of responsibilities by Palestinians in the West Bank and the Gaza Strip. The DOP is followed by the Agreement on the Gaza Strip and the Jericho Area, signed in Cairo on 4 May 1994[2] ("the Cairo Agreement"), which establishes the first phase of the interim arrangements. During this phase, the Gaza Strip (excluding Israeli settlements and military locations) and the "Jericho Area" are to be administered by a "Palestinian Authority" (the "PA"), a body established under the Cairo Agreement, which is distinct from the PLO. Further steps delineated by the DOP were taken by the preparatory transfer of certain responsibilities to the PA, acting in the West Bank, excluding Jerusalem, the Israeli settlements, military locations, and Israelis.[3]

The subsequent steps, which are, at the time of writing, subject to further negotiations, include, *inter alia*, an agreement over the withdrawal of Israeli forces from population centres in the West Bank, elections to the Palestinian elected Council that is to be established in the West Bank and Gaza, and lastly, the permanent status agreement. The arrangements for the transitional period are to be replaced with a permanent status agreement by 4 May 1999.[4]

The DOP sets out a rather tight timetable for the various stages of its implementation. However, as experience has already shown, the parties

---

1 32 *I.L.M.* 1525 (1993). For analyses of various aspects of the DOP, see E. Benvenisti, 'The Israeli-Palestine Declaration of Principles: A Framework for Future Settlement', 4 *E.J.I.L.* 542, (1993); R. Shehadeh, 'Can the Declaration of Principles Bring About a 'Just and Lasting' Peace?', 4 *E.J.I.L.* 555 (1993); A. Cassese, 'The Israel-PLO Agreement and Self-Determination', 4 *E.J.I.L.* 564 (1993); J. Singer, 'The Declaration of Principles on Interim Self-Government Arrangements', 1 *Justice* (published by the Int'l Assoc. of Jewish Lawyers and Jurists) 4 (1994). See also *Israel Law Review*, Vol. 28 (1994).

2 33 *I.L.M.* 622 (1994).

3 Agreement on the Preparatory Transfer of Powers and Responsibilities, concluded in Erez, 29 August 1994. The powers are in the areas of education, culture, health, social welfare, tourism, direct taxation and value added tax on local production. The PA replaces the authorized Palestinians referred to in Article VI of the DOP (Article II.2).

4 See Article V.1 of the DOP and Article XXIII.3 of the Cairo Agreement.

have so far regarded the dates more as suggestions rather than as mandatory deadlines. While the dates for events during the course of the interim arrangements, such as the elections in the West Bank (no later than 13 July 1994), have long passed, it remains to be seen whether the date for commencing the permanent status negotiations (4 May 1996) or the date of implementation of the ensuing agreement, will be treated with similar flexibility.

The DOP, and the letters which preceded it, bring to an end a century-old ideological and legal controversy over the rights of the two sides regarding Palestine/*Eretz-Israel* (the Land of Israel), territory that both communities regard as their homeland. While both sides expressed in the past their readiness to negotiate a settlement of the conflict on the basis of U.N. Security Council Resolutions 242 and 338, neither side explicitly recognized the other's existence and rights.[5] The DOP does not contain an agreement as to the future nature of the Palestinian entity in the territories, or as to its future territorial jurisdiction. However, the DOP and the letters contain the first unequivocal mutual recognition by the parties of the other's existence and of its right to live side by side on this land.[6] Explicit Palestinian recognition of Israel appears in Chairman Arafat's letter, dated 9 September 1993;[7] Israeli recognition of the Palestinian people and of the PLO as its representative appears in

---

[5] Israel has always insisted on relating to the Palestinians as a community of individuals, consisting of the Arab residents of Judea, Samaria and Gaza, and at no time did it formally recognize the existence of a Palestinian people, certainly not with the PLO as its representative. Indeed, in the English version of the Camp David Accord (A Framework for Peace in the Middle East agreed at Camp David, 17 September 1978, 1138 UNTS no. 17853, p. 39) the term "Palestinian people" is mentioned, as are "the legitimate rights of the Palestinian people and their just requirements", but an accompanying letter to the Accord clarified that Israel understands this term as describing the "Palestinian Arabs" (see letter from President Carter to Prime-Minister Begin of 22 September 1978, 78 U.S. Dep't State Bulletin No. 2019 (October 1978), p. 10, in R. Lapidoth and M. Hirsch, *The Arab-Israeli Conflict and Its Resolution: Selected Documents*, (1992), p. 206; J.N. Moore, *The Arab Israeli Conflict, Vol. IV:, The Difficult Search For Peace (1975–1988)*, (Part 1, 1991), p. 320. The Israeli government's offer of 1989 referred to the Palestinians as "the Arabs of Judea, Samaria, and the Gaza district", (see article 1 of decision no. 453 of 14 May 1989: translated and reported in Lapidoth & Hirsch, *ibid*, p. 357), or "the Palestinian Arab inhabitants of Judea, Samaria, and the Gaza district" (*ibid* Arts. 4(d), 9 *et seq.*). The closest the PLO got to a recognition of Israel was in the Political Communique (Section 2(c)), which accompanied the Palestinian Declaration of Independence (reprinted in 27 I.L.M. 1664). It called, *inter alia*, for "the Security Council's establishment and assurance of arrangements for security and peace among all the concerned States in the region, including the Palestinian State".

[6] On this point see also Cassese, *The Israel-PLO Agreement*, p. 569; P. De Waart, *Dynamics Of Self-Determination In Palestine*, 1994, p. 185: "The legal and political significance of the [DOP] lies not in the interim self-government but in the unambiguous recognition of each other ..." Note that the exchange of letters conveys this idea in a much more straightforward way than the DOP does.

[7] "The PLO recognizes the right of the State of Israel to exist in peace and security."

Prime Minister Yitzhak Rabin's response of the same date.[8] This mutual recognition is also reiterated in the DOP.[9]

The clear mutual recognition was not reflected in the following legal arrangements that characterized the post-DOP instruments. While initially the DOP and the letters of recognition could have been seen as reflecting a bold political decision to shy away from symbolic impediments on the road to conciliation, subsequent negotiations revealed hesitations in both camps concerning the value of symbols of sovereignty. The concern for these symbols of sovereignty were highlighted in the complex arrangements established by the Cairo Agreement concerning the control of the border crossings between The Gaza Strip and Egypt, and between the Jericho Area and Jordan (Cairo Agreement, Annex I, Art. X). The deferment of these and other issues to the permanent status negotiations necessitated a blurring of the legal foundations and nature of the interim PA established under the Cairo agreement. This in turn raises the question dealt with in this paper regarding the nature of the PA, its international personality and responsibilities.

I. The Status of the Gaza Strip and the Jericho Area

The search for the definition of the status of the Gaza Strip and the Jericho Area involves sorting through the dissonance between the contents of the legal texts accepted by the parties and the actual interaction which develops between the parties. As I explain below, the DOP, and especially the Cairo Agreement, provide a characterisation of the PA that is quite different from real life. While the Cairo Agreement describes Israel as the source of authority in these areas, actual Israeli practice shows very little Israeli involvement in the affairs of the PA, and a failure to exercise control over it. Confronted with such a divergence between the positive law of the accords and actual conduct, it is necessary to turn to international law to serve as our guide. As I argue in this paper, according to the law of occupation, it is the actual facts that define the status of an area as "occupied" or not. But before examining the factual situation, it is necessary to analyze the relevant texts that provide the framework of the relationships between the PA and Israel.

8 "[T]he government of Israel has decided to recognize the PLO as the representative of the Palestinian people..."

9 From the introduction to the DOP: "[The two sides] agree that it is time to put an end to decades of confrontation and conflict, recognize their mutual legitimate and political rights, and strive to live in peaceful coexistence and mutual dignity and security".

A. Gaza and Jericho in the Texts

Mr. Joel Singer, the Legal Adviser to the Israeli Ministry of Foreign Affairs, and one of the drafters of the DOP, has argued that the Accords have not changed the status of the Gaza Strip and the Jericho Area. In his view:

> During the interim period, the status of the Gaza Strip and Jericho area will be identical to that of the West Bank. ...[Their status] will continue to be that of areas subject to military government, with Israel remaining the source of authority therein.[10]

This argument is based primarily on Article IV of the DOP, which regards the West Bank and the Gaza Strip as "a single territorial unit, whose integrity will be preserved during the interim period", and on Article 6 of Annex II, which specifies that the status of the Gaza Strip and Jericho Area will "not be changed in the interim period". The Cairo Agreement, in Articles XXIII.6 and XXIII.7, restates these principles. Article XXIII.7 adds that "[n]othing in this Agreement shall be considered to change this status". The claim that the status of the Gaza Strip and Jericho Area was not changed is further emphasized in other Articles which underline the continuity in the administration of these areas. Thus, Article III.1 states that:

> Israel shall transfer authority as specified in this Agreement from the Israeli military government and its Civil Administration to the Palestinian Authority ... except for the authority that Israel shall *continue* to exercise as specified in the agreement. (my emphasis)

In addition, Article V.3.b. provides that:

> Israel shall exercise its authority through its military government, which, for that end, shall continue to have the necessary legislative, judicial and executive powers and responsibilities, in accordance with international law.

This reference to international law as a source of powers must be understood as a reference to the international law of occupation, which may complement, and arguably supersede,[11] the Accords.

---

[10] Singer, *The Declaration of Principles*, pp. 12-13.

[11] Note that the law of occupation does not relieve an occupant from the duty to cater for the interests of the occupying population by the mere fact of signing an agreement to transfer power to local groups. Article 47 of the Fourth Geneva Convention of 1949 states: "Inviolability of Rights: Protected persons who are in occupied territory shall not be deprived, in any case or in any manner whatsoever, of the benefits of the present Convention by any change introduced, as a result of the occupation of a territory, into the institutions or government of the said territory, nor by any agreement concluded between the authorities of the occupied territories and the Occupying Power, nor by any annexation by the latter of the whole or part of the occupied territory."

Other provisions of the Cairo Agreement which provide Israel with an opportunity to impede initiatives of the PA, such as changes of membership in the PA (Article IV.3), legislation, including amendments to existing military orders (Article VII), and planning and zoning schemes (Annex II, Article II.B.32),[12] also support the conclusion that the parties agreed to accept the continuation of the Israeli military administration in the Gaza Strip and the Jericho Area, despite the establishment of the PA.

From this point of view, the signing of the Cairo Agreement and the establishment of the PA should have been implemented through the local law of the territories. And indeed, both the commander of the IDF in the West Bank and the commander of the IDF in the Gaza Strip issued "Proclamation[s] concerning the Implementation of the Agreement regarding the Gaza Strip and Jericho Area (Proclamation No. 4), 5754–1994".[13] By these two proclamations, using the powers of the commander of the IDF in the area, the Cairo Agreement was formally implemented. This promulgation may be viewed as purely formal transformation of the Agreement to the laws of the territories, but it may also hint that Israel does not view the Accords as international instruments, and therefore as having in themselves no effect on the occupant's authority under international law.[14]

This formal outlook enabled the Israeli officials to dismiss out of hand Chairman Arafat's official declaration published on 24 May 1994 in the daily newspaper *al-Quds* of East Jerusalem. Issued under his authority as the head of the PA and Chairman of the Palestinian National Council, Mr. Arafat declared that as of 20 May 1994, "the laws, regulations and orders in force before 5 June 1967 in the West Bank and the Gaza Strip shall remain in force until unified."[15]

This declaration, which by now has apparently been published also by an official gazette issued by the PA, was not promulgated according to the procedure for legislative amendments specified in the Cairo

---

12 Such schemes must be published in the form of law, and therefore are subject to Israel's approval, as described in Article VII of the Cairo Agreement.

13 The Promulgation concerning the Jericho Area was issued on 15 May 1994, effective from 13 May, while the Promulgation concerning the Gaza Strip was issued on 17 May 1994, effective from the date of the signature of the Cairo Agreement.

14 If the accords are international agreements, these promulgations are redundant. The accords affect the powers of the Israeli occupation administration, and for this matter they become part of the international norms that bind the occupant. For the same reason, those human rights instruments that Israel has ratified did not require transformation. For the status of this occupation as "armistice occupation", see Benvenisti, *The Israeli-Palestine Declaration*, p. 551. On the definition of this term, see M. Bothe, 'Occupation after Armistice' in R. Bernhart (ed.), *Encyclopedia of Public International Law*, (instalment 4, 1982), p. 63; A. Roberts, 'What is a Military Occupation?', 55 *B.Y.I.L.* 249 (1984), pp. 265-267.

15 For translation of the declaration and criticism, see R. Shehadeh, 'Questions of Jurisdiction: A Legal Analysis of the Gaza-Jericho Agreement', 23 (4) *Journal of Palestine Studies* 18 (1994), p. 23.

Agreement. The declaration was widely understood at the time by both the Israeli and the Palestinian communities as purporting to abolish all the military orders issued by the Israeli authorities since the beginning of the occupation.[16] As such, the declaration was clearly in violation of the Accords.[17]

Thus, this declaration was interpreted as an attempt to challenge the complex arrangements concerning legislative amendments, and thereby, the entire regime of the Cairo Agreement. Israel did not submit a formal complaint, probably relying on the limited legal significance of that declaration.

It was later argued that Mr. Arafat's declaration might be interpreted to be only a formal declaration, which did not intend to question the validity of the military orders whose continued force was taken for granted. Notwithstanding this explanation, a different Palestinian interpretation of the Accords cannot be overlooked. Indeed, two draft documents debated in PLO circles regarding the nature and powers of the PA seem to reject the view that the PA's powers stem either from the Israeli administration or from the Accords. A draft "Basic Law for the National Authority in the Transitional Period" states in Article 1:

> The Palestinian people are the source of all authority which shall be exercised, during the transitional period, through the legislative, executive and judicial authorities in the manner provided for in this Basic Law.[18]

A draft policy statement in the name of the PA, issued in Tunis on 28 May 1994 and published by the Jordanian daily *al-Dustur* the day after, states:

> The Authority [i.e. the PA] shall be formed by a decision from the PLO, the Palestinian people's sole legitimate representative. The Authority shall be considered an extension of the PLO and derives its legitimacy from the PLO, which also serves as the Authority's political and legal terms of reference.[19]

These Israeli and Palestinian statements point to a potential discrepancy between interpretations as to the status of the PA and the nature of its administration in the Gaza Strip and the Jericho Area. To analyze the merit of the possible claims, we should turn from the texts

---

16 See e.g. 'Arafat Declared the Return of the Pre-1967 Law, and the Abolition of the Israeli Military Law', *Ha-aretz,* A/4, 26 May 1994 (in Hebrew). See also Shehadeh, *ibid.*

17 Under Article VII.9 of the Cairo Agreement, and Article 6 of the IDF Proclamation "[l]aws and military orders in effect in the Gaza Strip and the Jericho Area prior to the signing of this Agreement shall remain in force unless amended or abrogated in accordance with this Agreement".

18 The third draft of this Basic Law, April 1994, reproduced in 23(4) *Journal of Palestine Studies* 137 (1994) and *infra*, p. 137. By the end of 1994, this Basic Law has still been not promulgated.

19 Translated and reproduced *ibid.*, 23(4) *Journal of Palestine Studies*, pp. 145, 146.

to the real experience of the PA and its actual rule in the areas under its jurisdiction.

B. Gaza and Jericho in Real Life

Despite the myth of continuity of the Israeli military administration of the Gaza Strip and the Jericho Area through the PA, a myth both parties, each for its own reasons, sought to maintain, the division of powers delineated in the Annexes of the Cairo Agreement and practised in real life, reveals a different picture. In effect, Israel no longer maintains public order nor controls civil life in the Gaza Strip (outside the Israeli settlements and military locations) and in the Jericho Area.

In order to analyze the claim that the status of the Gaza Strip and the Jericho Area has not changed and thus continues to be subject to occupation, two questions must be addressed. First, does the law of occupation – initially designed to address wartime occupations – apply to an area administered under an interim agreement in which the parties set the stage for the peaceful settlement of their outstanding differences? Second, assuming this body of laws applies, how does it define an occupied area? Beyond these questions, there remains the issue of responsibility for respecting human rights in the area under the PA's jurisdiction. In this context questions arise as to the applicability of humanitarian law, especially the Fourth Geneva Convention of 1949, or of international human rights law.

1. The Relevance of the Law of Occupation to Gaza and Jericho

The international law of occupation is recognized more by the title the law of "belligerent occupation" or "military occupation", due to the previously prevalent method of establishing control over enemy territory. Recent history, however, has shown that occupants rarely admit the existence of war or their formal role as occupants. Because of many occupants' reluctance to admit the existence of a state of "war" or of an international armed conflict, or their failure to acknowledge the true nature of their activities on foreign soil, the utility of retaining the adjectives "belligerent" or "wartime" has become rather limited.[20] It is therefore widely accepted that the law of occupation is applicable also to other forms of occupation, unless the parties agreed otherwise,[21] and to

20 E. Benvenisti, *The International Law of Occupation*, (1993), p. 4.

21 E. Feilchenfeld, *The International Economic Law of Belligerent Occupation*, 1942, p. 6: "Belligerent occupation, possibly but not necessarily preceded by a phase of invasion, may be followed by a phase in which the occupation continues during an armistice. The rules of Section III [of the Hague Regulations] will then apply with modifications. [...] Following a war or an armistice, a belligerent may continue to hold the same territory as an occupant under the terms of a peace treaty, or else may occupy new territory. This will no longer be belligerent occupation in the strict sense, although

the extent that they may derogate from the law.[22] In fact, it is quite irrelevant how the area was captured, the focus being on the very fact of effective control by foreign troops. As succinctly put by Adam Roberts:[23]

> One might hazard as a fair rule of thumb that every time the armed forces of a country are in control of foreign territory, and find themselves face to face with the inhabitants, some or all of the provisions of the law on occupations are applicable.

The law of occupation is expected to regulate the conflict of interest that potentially exists between the occupant and the local population:

> Occupation can be described as the effective control of a power ... over a territory to which that power has no sovereign title, without the volition of the sovereign of that territory ... The rationale for this inclusive definition of occupation is that in the heart of all occupations exists a potential – if not an inherent – conflict of interest between occupant and occupied.[24]

Accordingly, despite the peace agreement between Egypt and Israel that ended the war in which Israel captured the Gaza Strip, the Israeli High Court of Justice acknowledged the continued applicability of the law of occupation to the Gaza Strip.[25] Similarly, there is no theoretical

---

even then Section III remains important as a set of minimum standards". M. Bothe, *Occupation after Armistice*, pp. 63-64: "The rights and duties of an occupying power after armistice may thus be determined by two different sources. On the one hand, occupation after armistice is the result of an armed conflict and thus constitutes belligerent occupation, peaceful relations not having been restored among the parties. On the other hand, the armistice agreement or, where relevant, the armistice or cease-fire resolution may create a new legal basis for the occupation and may modify the applicable legal regime"; A. Roberts, *What is Military Occupation?*, p. 267: "It is widely accepted that the Hague Regulations apply to armistice occupations. Some modifications might be included in the armistice agreement, but the Hague Regulations remain important, at the very least, as a set of minimum standards". See also G. Von Glahn, *The Occupation of Enemy Territory*, (1957), pp. 27-28. For a description of the armistice and peaceful occupation of the Rhineland after World War I, see E. Fraenkel, *Military Occupation and The Rule Of Law*, (1944).

22 See Article 47 of the Fourth Geneva Convention of 1949, note 11 *supra* , which requires adherence to its provisions notwithstanding agreements between the occupant and local authorities. Human rights provisions which may be applicable in occupied territories may also be non-derogable. On the question of the applicability of human rights norms to occupied territories, see Benvenisti, 'The Applicability of Human Rights Conventions to Occupied Territories', 26 *Israel Law Review* 24 (1992).

23 Roberts, *What is Military Occupation?*, p. 250.

24 Benvenisti, *The International Law of Occupation.*

25 *Affu v. The Commander of the IDF in the West Bank et al.* 42 P.D. (2) 4 (1988), p. 50: "Despite the signature of a peace treaty, as long as the military administration has not withdrawn from the area of the Gaza Strip, and as long as the relevant parties have not agreed otherwise, the Area Commander continues to hold the area under belligerent occupation, and to be subjected to the customary international norms applicable during wartime". See also to the same effect, *Tsemel v. The Minister of Defence* 37 (2) P.D. 365 (1982); *Al-Nawar v. The Minister of Defence* 39 (3) P.D. 449 (1982).

impediment in applying the law of occupation to the Gaza Strip and the Jericho Area during the transitional period. This law could include the Fourth Geneva Convention.[26] This would be the case if indeed, under international law, these areas are to be considered as occupied. The next section examines this last question.

2. The Applicability of the Law of Occupation in Gaza and Jericho

The question whether an area is occupied or not is usually raised either when it is not sufficiently clear whether the foreign army is capable of maintaining control over an area, or when the foreign army shares power with local administering bodies *vis-à-vis* the local population.

The law of occupation applies to areas in which foreign forces are present, and in which they can maintain effective control over the life of the local population. As Article 42 of the Hague Regulations states:

> Territory is considered occupied when it is actually placed under the authority of the hostile army. The occupation extends only to the territory where such authority has been established and can be exercised.[27]

Article 43 prescribes the powers of the occupant, defined as the one into whose hands "the authority of the legitimate power ha[s] in fact passed". The emphasis is on effective control, and the ability to exercise the authority of the legitimate power. Accordingly, the British Military Manual[28] defines in Section 502 occupation as:

> actual and effective, that is, there must be more than a mere declaration or proclamation that possession has been taken, or that there is the intention to take possession ... It is sufficient that the national forces should not be in possession, that the inhabitants have been disarmed, that measures have been taken to protect life and property and to secure order, and that, if necessary, troops can within a reasonable time be sent to make the authority of the occupying army felt. It does not matter by what means and in what ways the authority is exercised, whether by military enclaves or mobile columns, by large forces or small. The manner of occupation will usually vary with the density of the population – a thinly populated country requiring, as a rule, a smaller number of centres to be garrisoned than one which is thickly populated.

And the United States Military Manual follows suit:[29]

---

26 On the conditions for the applicability of this convention in general and in particular to the West Bank and Gaza, see e.g. Benvenisti, *The International Law of Occupation,* pp. 109-112; A. Roberts, 'Prolonged Military Occupation: The Israeli-Occupied Territories since 1967', 84 *A.J.I.L.* 44 (1990).

27 Regulations Respecting the Laws and Customs of War on Land, annex to the Convention (IV) Respecting the Laws and Customs of War on Land, signed at The Hague, 18 October 1907 ("The Hague Regulations").

28 *The Law of War in Land*, (1958), p. 141.

29 'The Law of Land Warfare', *FM* 27-10 (1956).

> 355. Military occupation is a question of fact. It presupposes a hostile invasion, resisted or unresisted, as a result of which the invader has rendered the invaded government incapable of publicly exercising its authority, and that the invader has successfully substituted its own authority for that of the legitimate government in the territory invaded.
> 356. ...The number of troops necessary to maintain effective occupation will depend on various considerations such as the disposition of the inhabitants, the number and density of the population, the nature of the terrain, and similar factors ...

The recently published German Military Manual also emphasizes actual exercise of authority:[30]

> 526. ...The occupying power must be able to actually exercise its *authority*.
> 527. A force invading hostile territory will not be able to substantiate its occupational authority unless it is capable of enforcing directions issued to the civilian population.

This point is also emphasized by scholars. Julius Stone, for example, is of the opinion that "[o]ccupation of an area begins when there is a sufficient force to retain command of the situation, following cessation of substantial local resistance".[31] Morris Greenspan concludes that "[t]he prerequisite is that [the occupying troops] can make their authority felt when and where it is required".[32]

Note that the law of occupation is also applicable to occupations in which the occupant shares power with local administering agencies. From the point of view of the law of occupation it applies regardless of the modalities of administration chosen by the occupant.[33] As McDougal and Feliciano state:[34]

> The particular institutional modalities through which the occupant's authority is to be exercised are not specified in international law. The occupant may be regarded as free, within certain general limitations, to establish such governmental structures as it deems necessary or convenient.

Therefore, the test for effective control is not the military strength of the foreign army which is situated outside the borders that surround the foreign area. What matters is the extent of that power's effective control

---

30 Federal Ministry of Defence, *Humanitarian Law in Armed Conflict – Manual*, (1992) (emphasis in original).

31 J. Stone, *Legal Controls of International Conflict*, (1954), p. 696.

32 M. Greenspan, *The Modern Law of Land Warfare*, (1959), p. 214. For similar emphases on effectiveness, see Feilchenfeld, *The International Economic Law*, p. 6; Bothe, *Occupation after Armistice*, p. 65, and Roberts, *What is Military Occupation?*, p. 256.

33 Although it requires the establishment of distinct administration (see Benvenisti, *The International Law of Occupation*, p. 4), it applies as well to occupations in which such administrations have not been set up.

34 M. McDougal And F. Feliciano, *Law and Minimum World Public Order*, (1961), p. 747.

of civilian life *within* the occupied area;[35] their ability, in the words of Article 43 of the Hague Regulations, to "restore and ensure public order and civil life".

C. The Israeli Powers in Gaza and Jericho

The preceding discussion leads us to explore the ways in which the Israeli Military Administration controls, or is capable of controlling, the life of the civilian population in the Gaza Strip and the Jericho Area. Actual practice, the first and foremost important consideration, shows that neither Israel nor its military administration attempt to control the civilian life in those areas. Nor do they seem to be legally and practically capable of doing so. Indeed, if they did attempt to do so, this might have conflicted with the provisions of the Cairo Agreement. Annex II, concerning Civil Affairs, and Annex III, concerning Economic Relations, delineate the transfer of powers and responsibilities to the PA in all spheres of civil life. The PA is backed by its strong police force. Article II.6 of the Agreement specifies that "[t]he Palestinian Police shall be deployed and shall assume responsibility for public order and internal security of Palestinians ...". Indeed, the Agreement permits Israelis, including Israeli military forces, "to use roads freely within the Gaza Strip and the Jericho Area" (Article II.5), but this right does not include the right to use these roads to capture criminals, unless under defined conditions of "hot pursuit".[36]

Israel enjoys considerable powers *vis-à-vis* the PA, with respect to the nomination of members of the PA, to amendments to local legislation, and to planning schemes.[37] Yet these powers do not grant the Israeli authorities powers *vis-à-vis* the local population. They relate to the bilateral relations between the two sides, rather than to the relations with the inhabitants. These powers are not used unless the PA initiates the procedure that enables an Israeli response. And indeed, so far, these procedures have not been initiated by the PA.[38]

In short, Israel does not control civil life in the Gaza Strip and the Jericho Area. These areas are therefore not "occupied" in the sense of the international law of occupation.

35 See also *Tsemel v. The Minister of Defence* 37 (2) P.D. 365 (1982), p. 373 (discussing Israel's position in Lebanon during that period).

36 See Annex I, Article VII.9 concerning "hot pursuit"; Annex III, concerning the extradition of criminals in the Gaza Strip and the Jericho Area to Israel.

37 See note 12 *supra*.

38 On the uncertainties concerning the prevailing law in Gaza and Jericho, see M. Rishmawi, 'Judicial Independence under Palestinian Rule', *infra*, p. 259; G. Bindman and B. Bowering, 'Human Rights in A Period of Transition', *the British Law Society* (1994).

D. "Occupied"? "Not Occupied"? And If Not, What Else Can The Status Be?

One conclusion may be drawn from the discussion so far. There is a discrepancy between the objective status of the Gaza Strip and the Jericho Area and its characterisation in the Cairo Agreement. While Israel and the PLO agreed to continue to recognize Israel's authority in those areas as stemming from international law, impliedly the international law of occupation, this understanding does not seem to be congruent with an objective analysis, under the law of occupation, of the arrangements implemented under the Agreement.

There is nothing wrong *per se* in an agreement treating an unoccupied area as occupied. International law does not limit the parties' capacity to make such an agreement. This agreement does not derogate from the parties' responsibility to protect human rights in regions commonly referred to as "occupied". Indeed, it may be assumed that the parties' decision to refer to the Gaza Strip and Jericho Area as occupied was deemed a convenient solution to both parties' political constraints. For the PLO, the continuation of the military administration could explain the powers of the Israeli authorities, and the existence of Israeli settlements, without an implied recognition of Israeli sovereignty, or of any other Israeli right to retain the settlements and powers. For Israel, the prolongation of the military regime precluded claims concerning the establishment of a Palestinian State, and provided grounds for asserting the revocability of the arrangement.

Yet, as we saw earlier, there is a dissonance between the legal texts that bind the two sides, and the actual life under the PA's rule in Gaza and Jericho. In view of this dissonance, third parties, states and international organisations, who are not bound by the Israeli-Palestinian accords, cannot rely on the textual definition of these areas as occupied. Hence, the question of definition under international law remains: what legal creature has been established in the Gaza Strip and the Jericho Area?

1. The PA is not a State

The Cairo Agreement went to some length to describe the lack of competence of the PA in the sphere of foreign relations (Article VI.2).[39] This corresponds with the Israeli government position, namely

[39] This restriction is aimed at divesting the PA of at least the fourth conventional indicator of statehood as provided in Article 1 of the Montevideo Convention on Rights and Duties of States of 1933, 165 L.N.T.S. 19. The fourth criterion for statehood in this Article is the "capacity to enter into relations with other States". *The Restatement (Third) on the Foreign Relations Law of the United States* (1987) follows this formula by requiring that the entity "engages in, or has the capacity to engage in formal relations with other such entities" (Section 201). On the Montevideo formula see J. Crawford, *The Creation of States in International Law*, (1979), pp. 36-48. See especially the criticism of the fourth criterion at pp. 47-48, and the emphasis on the better criterion of

that the essence of the phased implementation of the DOP is its revocability, at any but the final stage.[40] Thus, the Legal Adviser of the Israel Ministry of Foreign Affairs has noted that any attempt to change unilaterally the status of the Gaza Strip and the Jericho Area during the interim period "would be a clear breach of the terms of the DOP, which may be considered a material breach and a ground for terminating the agreement".[41] To make this commitment even more explicit, Mr. Arafat, in the name of the PLO, confirmed in a letter dated 4 May 1994, attached to the Cairo Agreement, *inter alia* that "[w]hen Chairman Arafat enters the Gaza Strip and the Jericho Area, he will use the title "Chairman (*Ra'is* in Arabic) of the Palestinian Authority" or "Chairman of the PLO", and will not use the title "President of Palestine".[42]

For the time being, the PLO does not claim to have established statehood in these regions. The legal personality of the PA, which is in charge in the Gaza Strip and Jericho Area, is different from that of the PLO, the organ with the capability to implement the 1988 Algiers Declaration of Independence.[43] Thus, by accepting the elimination of the powers of the PA in the sphere of international relations, the PLO impliedly acknowledged that the question of the establishment of the Palestinian State in the territories would be deferred to the permanent stage.

2. The PA is an Autonomous Entity

Since Gaza and Jericho are not in fact occupied, and they are not part of a state either, the conclusion must be that the DOP and the Cairo Agreement established an autonomous regime. The powers of this autonomy seem to derive from the Accords, or from Israel's occupation. Thus, they are subject to the Israeli military administration's residual powers and overriding duties, as recognised in the Cairo Agreement (which refers also to the law of occupation).[44] By this arrangement the parties succeeded in neutralizing what is usually

independence, which is "the central criterion of statehood", (pp. 48 *et seq.*). See also Benvenisti, *The Israeli-Palestine Declaration*, p. 548.

40 On the revocability of the DOP, see Benvenisti, *The Israeli-Palestine Declaration*, p. 545-546.

41 Singer, *The Declaration of Principles*, p. 13.

42 Section 4 of Mr. Arafat's letter to Prime Minister Rabin, 4 May 1994.

43 See the Palestinian National Council's Declaration of Independence of 15 November 1988, and its Political Communique, 27 *I.L.M.* 1664, p. 1665; Lapidoth and Hirsch, *The Arab-Israeli Conflict*, p. 348. On the status of "the Palestinian State" following the Algiers Declaration, see e.g. F. Boyle, 'The Creation of the State of Palestine', 1 *E.J.I.L.* 301 (1990); J. Crawford, 'The Creation of the State of Palestine: Too Much Too Soon?', 1 *E.J.I.L.* 307 (1990).

44 On these residual powers, see note 11 *supra*.

the key issue in establishing autonomy regimes, the question of sovereignty over such areas.[45]

In fact, if this analysis is correct, the regime in the Gaza Strip and the Jericho Area represents a novel form of autonomy. So far, two types of autonomies existed or were suggested. Most of the autonomies are internally-based, i.e. having been established within existing states through the laws of that state, such as the arrangements concerning South Tirol in Italy.[46] The other type of autonomies, which may be called internationally-based, have so far been suggested in international instruments that envisioned the active participation of the United Nations, like in the aborted attempts in 1947 to establish international administration in both Trieste and Jerusalem. In these cases, sovereignty was deemed to be vested in the U.N.[47] In contrast, the autonomy in the Gaza Strip and Jericho Area is based on an agreement between the two contenders, which eludes the question of sovereignty by artificially maintaining the framework of the Israeli military occupation.

II. International Responsibility for Acts and Omissions of the Palestinian Authority

The question of international responsibility has of course important practical ramifications: who would be responsible for human rights violations if such were to occur in the Gaza Strip and the Jericho Area? Who would be responsible for breaches in agreements with third countries and international institutions concerning capital investment in those areas?

The cautious attitude towards the definition of the status of the PA poses a challenge to international and constitutional lawyers in a legal world still dominated by the Westphalian order of sovereign states. As described above, the parties, due to political and other constraints, deferred the determination of the nature of the future Palestinian entity to the permanent status agreement. I argue, however, that the formal existence of military occupation does not decide the important question of the international responsibility for acts and omissions, including human rights violations, in the areas subject to the jurisdiction of the PA. At the same time, while the PA is no sovereign government, I suggest that to the extent it is actually administering the areas under its

45 See 'Interpretation of the Statute of the Memel Territory (Merits)', (Series A/B, No. 49) 294 (1932), p. 314; Y. Dinstein, *Models of Autonomy*, (1981), p. 299.

46 On this autonomy, see e.g. C. Schreuer, 'Autonomy in South Tirol', in Dinstein, *ibid*, p. 53.

47 On these and other autonomies, see Dinstein, *ibid*; H. Hannum, *Autonomy, Sovereignty and Self-Determination*, (1990); R. Lapidoth, 'Autonomy: Potential and Limitations', 1 *International Journal on Group Rights* 260 (1994).

jurisdiction, it is internationally responsible towards third parties, including individuals.

A. Israel's Responsibility

The Cairo Agreement explicitly absolves Israel from responsibility with respect to international agreements with third parties in economic and some other matters, by recognising the PLO's role as the representative of the PA, empowered to negotiate and sign such agreements on behalf of the PA.[48] With the transfer of powers to the PA, Israel also transfers the responsibility over outstanding and future claims related to the exercise of these powers (Article XXII). Israel does not retain in the agreement international responsibility towards non-Israelis present in the Gaza Strip and the Jericho Area.[49] The question of responsibility for human rights violations is left unanswered in the Accords, despite statements by which the parties commit themselves to respect these rights.[50]

The Cairo Agreement contains a legal paradox: Israel is depicted as an occupant without effective control, and without responsibility for the acts and omissions of the authorities in the area under occupation.[51] The lack of responsibility underscores the conclusion elaborated above, namely that Israel has but a formal status in the areas under the PA's jurisdiction, a status whose significance extends only to the bilateral

---

48 Article VI.b: "[T]he PLO may conduct negotiations and sign agreements with states or international organizations for the benefit of the Palestinian Authority in the following cases only: ..."

49 According to Article V.3, Israel retains authority (and responsibility) over settlements, military locations, Israelis, and external security, and other agreed powers and responsibilities specified in the agreement. The only specified authority with respect to foreigners is the provision of Article I.6 of Annex III, which specifies that tourists in transit to or from Israel on certain roads may be arrested and questioned only by Israeli authorities.

50 Article XIV, entitled "Human rights and the rule of law" provides: "Israel and the Palestinian Authority shall exercise their powers and responsibilities pursuant to this Agreement with due regard to internationally-accepted norms and principles of human rights and the rule of law". Article II.7.h(1) of Annex III (Protocol concerning Legal Matters) provides that the treatment of individuals suspected of committing offences transferred from Israeli to PA custody and vice versa shall comply "with internationally-accepted norms of human rights regarding criminal investigation".

51 Compare Article 6, paragraph 3, of the Fourth Geneva Convention which states that the Convention shall cease to apply one year after the general close of military operations, yet the occupying power shall continue to be bound by a number of provisions "to the extent that such Power exercises the functions of government in such territory". This provision, which relieves the occupant of its duties, envisages an assumption of powers by a local government while the area is still under the occupant's control, as was the case in some European countries following World-War II (see J. Pictet ed., *Commentary: The Fourth Geneva Convention*, (1958), pp. 62-63). As explained above, Israel cannot make use of such an argument, since it does not occupy the Gaza Strip and the Jericho Area.

relations between Israel and the PLO. From the point of view of third parties, Israel should not be regarded as occupant in the Gaza Strip and the Jericho Area. Without exercising effective control, Israel is not responsible for the conduct of the PA under the laws of occupation including the Fourth Geneva Convention. The lack of effective control also suggests that Israel is not responsible for implementing international human rights instruments, such as the 1966 International Covenant on Civil and Political Rights or the 1984 Convention Against Torture.[52] These instruments require the parties to respect the rights enumerated therein "within their jurisdiction," a phrase generally understood to cover all areas and individuals subject to its effective control.[53]

This conclusion seems to be in line with the prevailing expectations. Any Israeli attempt to assume responsibility and intervene in the name of protecting Palestinians' human rights *vis-à-vis* the PA or other Palestinians would not be accepted at face value, would be strongly resisted by Palestinian officials and the goal of protecting human rights would not be attained.

B. The PA's Responsibility

As mentioned earlier, the denial of the PA's international responsibilities, in Article VI.2.a,[54] stems from Israel's interest in denying the PA the conventional attributes of statehood. On the other hand, the realities of Israel's lack of effective control, its displayed disinterest in the fate of the population in the Gaza Strip and the Jericho Area, together with the actual autonomy of the PA in maintaining public order and civil life, all raise the question of the possible international responsibility of the PA in those spheres. The question remains, however, as to how we can recognize the PA's international responsibility without admitting the existence of a Palestinian state.

It is my claim that state sovereignty is not a prerequisite for international responsibility. Therefore, the fact that the PA does not

---

52 On the ratification of these and other human rights convention by Israel, see B. Cohen, 'The Practice of Israel in Matters Related to International Law', 26 *Israel Law Review* 572-573 (1992).

53 T. Buergenthal, 'To Respect and Ensure: State Obligations and Permissible Derogations' in L. Henkin (ed.), *The International Bill of Rights*, (1981), pp. 72, 74; M. Nowak, *CCPR Commentary*, 1993, pp. 41-42. The European Commission of Human Rights determined in a number of cases that "within their jurisdiction" was no more and no less than *under the state party's effective control* (see Applications No. 6780/74 and No. 6950/75, *Cyprus v. Turkey*, 18 Yearbook of the E.C.H.R. 82 (1975), p. 118; Application 8007/77, *Cyprus v. Turkey*, 21 Yearbook of the E.C.H.R 100 (1978), p. 234).

54 "In accordance with the Declaration of Principles, the Palestinian Authority will not have powers and responsibilities in the sphere of foreign relations ..." See also note 37 *supra*.

purport to represent a state does not necessarily prevent its international responsibility. Indeed, in the past it was asserted that "responsabilité et souveraineté territoriales se conditionnent réciproquement".[55] Later, however, it became clear that the important factor in determining responsibility is effective control, rather than sovereignty.[56] If sovereignty is not a prerequisite, international responsibility may then also be attributed to non-state actors.

Indeed, it is beyond doubt today that international organisations, such as the United Nations and the European Union, are internationally responsible for their acts and omissions.[57] The distinction between sovereignty and international responsibility enables the similar recognition of the responsibility of sub-state entities, including autonomies. Contemporary literature advocates such a development.[58]

This development is based on the changing concept of the sovereign state which is challenged both by the movement towards states' integration, and by the increasing legitimacy for external intervention to protect human rights.[59] The growing participation of sub-state entities in international relations also supports this trend.[60] Indeed, if individuals are the subject not only of rights, but also of duties under

---

55 Judge Huber as sole arbitrator in the case of *British Property in Spanish Morocco*, 2 Recueil Int'l Arbit. Awards 615 (1925), p. 636.

56 See I. Brownlie, *State Responsibility*, (1983), pp. 181-183.

57 On the responsibility of these organs for their violations of individual rights see with respect to the U.N.: Exchange of letters Constituting an Agreement between the United Nations and Belgium relating to the Settlement of Claims Filed against the United Nations in the Congo by Belgian Nationals, 20 February 1965, U.N. Jurid. Yearbook 39 (1965); with respect to the European Communities: Case 4/73, *Nold v. Commission* [1974] E.C.R. 491, p. 507; Case 36/75, *Rutili v. Minister of the Interior* [1975] E.C.R. 1219, p. 1232. On this issue, see C. Schreuer, 'The Waning of the Sovereign State: Towards a New Paradigm for International Law?', 4 *E.J.I.L.* 447 (1993), pp. 465-66. On the general question of international responsibility of international organizations, see M. Hirsch, *The Responsibility under International Law of International Organizations Toward Third Parties: Some Basic Principles*, (Ph.D. Thesis, The Hebrew University, Jerusalem, 1994).

58 Schreuer, *The Waning of the Sovereign State*, p. 453: "Rather than grope for the seat of sovereignty, we should adjust our intellectual framework to a multi-layered reality consisting of a variety of authoritative structures. Under this functionalist approach what matters is not the formal status of a participant (province, state, international organisation) but its actual or preferable exercise of functions".

59 On these developments, see e.g. M. Janis, 'International Law?', 32 *Harv. Int'l L. J.* 363 (1992); M. Koskenniemi, 'The Future of Statehood', 32 *Harv. Int'l L. J.* 397 (1992); R. Lapidoth, 'Sovereignty in Transition', 45(2) *J. Int'l Affairs* 325 (1992); H. Steinberger, 'Sovereignty' in R. Bernhart (ed.), *Encyclopedia of Public International Law*, (instalment 10, 1987), pp. 397-418.

60 On international agreements between provinces, cantons, regions and states in federal unions, see Schreuer, *The Waning of the Sovereign State*, p. 450; B. Broms 'Autonomous Territories' in Bernhardt, *ibid*, pp. 7, 8. On the international status of national liberation movements, see J. Barberis, 'Nouvelles Questions Concernant la Personnalité Juridique Internationale', 179 *Recueil Des Cours* 145 (1983–I), pp. 239-268 ; A. Cassese, *International Law in a Divided World*, (1986), pp. 90-99; Benvenisti, *The Israeli-Palestine Declaration*, pp. 544-45.

international law,[61] the recognition of the responsibility of sub-state entities, especially if they control disputed areas, seems a logically trivial, but otherwise imperative, step towards greater efficacy of international norms, particularly in the sphere of human rights. In the same vein, it is suggested that the international responsibility of the PA be recognized. Such a recognition would correspond to the political and social circumstances in the areas under the rule of the PA. Any Israeli interference with the conduct of the PA, in the name of human rights, cannot be expected to bear fruit other than suspicion and disagreement.

A question remains as to the applicability of human rights conventions such as the 1966 Covenant on Civil and Political Rights to the PA's conduct. Two questions are raised here. The first one asks whether these instruments impose responsibility only on states, or does this responsibility extend to non-state actors, including individuals and groups. The prevailing answer to this question is that the duties are owed not only by states, but also by individuals and groups. Human rights instruments focus on the protected right owners rather than on the possible offenders.[62] The second question asks which of the human rights instruments apply to the Palestinian authorities in the West Bank and Gaza. To the extent that the rights contained in these instruments have gained the status of customary international law, they of course apply to the conduct of the PA. As to rights that are still not part of customary law, a number of ways to recognize their applicability to the PA's conduct exist. One way would be to regard the transfer of authority from Israel to the PA as subject to the requirement to abide by those rights under the same international instruments that bind Israel. Another way would consider the existing law prevailing in the areas under the PA's jurisdiction, which is to remain in force, as including those human rights instruments which the Israeli government ratified during the occupation period, and which constrained Israel's conduct in the occupied territories.[63] Finally, a unilateral PA undertaking to respect certain human rights instruments could solve this question. Such

---

61 P. Sieghart, *The International Law Of Human Rights*, (1983), pp. 43-44; J. Paust, 'The Other Side of Right: Private Duties under Human Rights Law', 5 *Harv. Hum. Rt. J.* 51 (1992); A. Kiss, 'La Définition des Devoirs des Individus par les Instruments Internationaux Protégeant les Droits de l'Homme' in J. Jekewitz *et al.*, (eds.), *Das Menschen Recht Zwischen Freiheit Und Verantwortung*, (1989), p. 17.

62 See Paust, *The Other Side of Right*, and see the references cited in his note 5.

63 These instruments were not introduced into the internal legal system of the territories by a military *fiat*, and hence they were not part of the military orders. However, they did change the legal landscape in these territories during the occupation period, since, as part of the relevant international norms, they constrained the conduct of the occupant, whose source of authority is international law. The ratified conventions may thus be treated, in the words of Article VII.9 as "laws ... in effect in the Gaza Strip and the Jericho Area prior to the signing of this Agreement". On this Article, see note 17 *supra*.

an undertaking is being contemplated, as attested by the Palestinian draft Basic Law for the PA in the transitional period.[64]

Conclusion

The DOP and the letters of mutual recognition emitted a clear message that the nature of the Israeli-Palestinian conflict has been transformed. A legal and ideological confrontation based on mutual denial was transformed into a pragmatic conflict contoured mainly by security considerations. Yet this clear message was incompatible with the logic of the transitional period, according to which the final outcome of the process was to be negotiated later. In order to leave all possible bargaining positions open during these later negotiations, the nature of the Palestinian administration in Gaza and Jericho had to be obscured in the Cairo Agreement which implemented the first stage of the transitional period. The concern is, however, that different policies and goals may lead to opposing views as to the powers of the PA, and to different expectations as to its role. And indeed, the attempt in this paper to clarify the nature of the Palestinian rule in Gaza and Jericho has exposed such conflicting attitudes and expectations.

---

64 See Article 8 of the draft, note 18 *supra*, p. 137 (recognition and acceptance of fundamental human rights enshrined in international instruments); Articles 9-33 (enumerating the various rights); and Article 35 (the establishment of an Independent Commission for Human Rights).

4. Some Legal Aspects of the Declaration of Principles: A Palestinian View

Eugene Cotran[1]

Introduction

When the Declaration of Principles (the "DOP") was signed in Washington on 13th September 1993, there was naturally great euphoria. For my part I was full of hope – I wrote an article[2] in which I tried to demonstrate that given the right spirit from *both* sides, and from a *legal* point of view, the Declaration of Principles was a "good Agreement which covers the demands of the Palestinian people, as represented by the PLO, and is consistent with U.N. Resolutions and international law and legality". I was accused of being an optimist and a dreamer. I must confess that my enthusiasm has waned considerably, but not I believe because I misinterpreted the Agreement legally. I still adhere to the view that the DOP constitutes a major advance on previous Israeli positions; if interpreted liberally and in the right spirit and adhered to in broad terms and effect, it does provide a framework for a just and lasting solution to the problem.

First I deal with why I was hopeful.

I. Recognition of Palestinians as a "People"

Prior to the exchange of letters between Chairman Yassir Arafat and Prime Minister Rabin on 9th September 1993, Israel's position was that there was no such thing as a "Palestinian people". Politically, there was the famous (or rather infamous) remark of Golda Meir asserting that Palestinians did not exist. In official Israeli documents the Palestinians were described as a "community of individuals" consisting of "Arab residents of Judea, Samaria and Gaza".

This was swept away by the exchange of letters and the DOP itself which recognised the PLO as the representative of the Palestinian "people".

---

[1] Paper delivered at the Conference in December 1994, but updated to June 1995; see however, postscript at p. 77, below.

[2] Published in the London daily Arabic Newspaper, *Al-Sharq Al-Awsat*, No. 5417 of 27 September 1993 and in *Middle East International*, No. 461, 24 October 1993, pp. 16-17.

The legal importance of this cannot be but over-emphasised for two reasons:

(a) Since the right to "self determination" is said to apply only to a "people", it is a recognition by Israel that the "people" of Palestine have the right to self-determination as outlined in the 1966 Covenant on Civil and Political Rights and the 1966 Covenant on Economic, Social and Cultural Rights, both ratified by Israel on 18th August 1991. On 22nd November 1974 the U.N. General Assembly by Resolution 3236 (XXIX) reaffirmed "the inalienable rights of the Palestinian people to self-determination, national independence and sovereignty".

(b) If Palestinians are a "people" – as now recognised by Israel, there is an implied recognition by Israel that they have *sovereignty* over their land, occupied since 1967. It is a well established rule of international law that in a belligerent occupation situation, sovereignty remains residual in the people who fall under occupation.[3]

II. Recognition of the PLO

The recognition by Israel of the PLO as the representative of the Palestinian people has, it is submitted, two further consequences of prime legal significance, viz. that there is a "*State*" of Palestine and a "*Government*" of the State which is in fact the PLO.

By its Charter, the PLO consists of:

(a) An Executive Committee with a Chairman – "the Executive" branch;

(b) The Palestine National Council (the "PNC"), with a Central Council consisting of one third of the Membership of the PNC, "the legislature or Parliament";

(c) Ten Committees of the PNC which deal with various matters viz. Political, Educational, Economic, Legal, etc.

On 15th November 1988 at Algiers the PNC proclaimed a State of Palestine and resolved that until a Government of Palestine is formed, the Executive Committee of the PLO "shall exercise the powers and duties of the Provisional Government until such time as the formation of the Government is declared". Subsequently, Chairman Arafat was appointed President and some one hundred Governments and States

---

[3] See Lauterpacht, who says that "the occupant is not the sovereign of the occupied territory"; and Pictet, commenting on the Fourth Geneva Convention, who says that occupation is "essentially a temporary, *de facto* situation, which deprives the occupied power of neither its statehood nor its sovereignty".

recognised the State of Palestine. On 2nd December 1988, the UN General Assembly adopted a Resolution acknowledging the Proclamation of the State of Palestine with the designation of "Palestine" instead of "PLO" in the UN system.

From the point of view of international law therefore the position as at the end of 1988 was that:

(a) The PLO was the legitimate representative of the Palestinian people;
(b) A *State* of Palestine was recognised by the international c ommunity; and
(c) The "Government" of the State was the PLO with Chairman Arafat as Head of State or President.

By their recognition, it is submitted that Israel too has now adopted this position. Indeed, they have done more for this reason. There are those international law writers and commentators who say that one of the attributes of Statehood is control of some territory (even if it be very small). By the DOP, control of territory is conceded by Israel to the Palestinians at first in Gaza and Jericho and after elections in the whole of the West Bank, recognising also that the territory will be administered and self-governing as a "single territorial unit".

III. The Declaration of Principles and Independence

Opposers of the DOP have rightly pointed out that there is nothing in the DOP which expressly says that Palestine shall be an independent nation at the end of the 5-year transitional period. It seems to me, however, that having regard to the express and implied recognitions to which I have referred, the fact that full independence must clearly follow full self-government is clear and need not be explicitly expressed. The final goal, as it seems to me, is expressed in the opening words of the DOP and in Articles I, III and IV:

> The Government of the State of Israel and the Palestine Liberation Organization team (in the Jordanian-Palestinian delegation to the Middle East Peace Conference) (the "Palestinian Delegation"), representing the Palestinian people, agree that it is time to put an end to decades of confrontation and conflict, recognize their mutual legitimate and political rights, and strive to live in peaceful coexistence and mutual dignity and security and achieve a just, lasting and comprehensive peace settlement and historic reconciliation through the agreed political process.

Accordingly, the two sides agree to the following principles:

Article I. Aim of the Negotiations
The aim of the Israeli-Palestinian negotiations within the current Middle East peace process is, among other things, to establish a Palestinian Interim Self-Government Authority, the elected Council, (the "Council") for the Palestinian people in the West Bank and the Gaza Strip, for a transitional period not exceeding five years, leading to a permanent settlement based on Security Council Resolutions 242 and 338.
It is understood that the interim arrangements are an integral part of the whole peace process and that the negotiations on the permanent status will lead to the implementation of Security Council Resolutions 242 and 338.

Article III. Elections
1. In order that the Palestinian people in the West Bank and Gaza Strip may govern themselves according to democratic principles, direct free and general political elections will be held for the Council under agreed supervision and international observation, while the Palestinian police will ensure public order.
2. An agreement will be concluded on the exact mode and conditions of the elections in accordance with the protocol attached as Annex I, with the goal of holding the elections not later than nine months after the entry into force of this Declaration of Principles.
3. These elections will constitute a significant interim preparatory step toward the realization of the legitimate rights of the Palestinian people and their just requirements.

Article IV. Jurisdiction
Jurisdiction of the Council will cover West Bank and Gaza Strip territory, except for issues that will be negotiated in the permanent status negotiations. The two sides view the West Bank and the Gaza Strip as a single territorial unit, whose integrity will be preserved during the interim period.

IV. The Three Stages

A more valid criticism of the DOP is the fact that the really thorny issues of "Jerusalem", "Refugees" and "Settlements" (the so-called "permanent status issues") are not agreed upon but are to be negotiated "not later than the beginning of the third year of the interim period" (see DOP, Article V). I shall revert to these matters below, but leaving those aside for the moment, my original hope and optimism was based on a legal interpretation of the DOP that would have three stages:

A. Stage 1

Stage 1 would commence with "Gaza and Jericho", i.e. withdrawal of Israeli military forces and its Civil Administration from Gaza and Jericho; and its replacement by the Palestinian National Authority (the PNA), its government and administration (DOP, Article XIV and Annex II).

This has happened with the Cairo Agreement of 4th May 1994 and the arrival of the Palestinian National Authority to Gaza and Jericho in the same month. The five year interim period commenced on that date (Cairo Agreement, Article XXIII(3)).

B. Stage 2

Interim Agreement: The DOP (Article VII) provides for the negotiation of this Agreement with the goal of holding elections for the Council not later than nine months from the entry into force of the DOP (ie 13 October 1993) (see Article III(2) above), which Agreement "shall specify, among other things, the structure of the Council, the number of its members and the transfer of powers and responsibilities from the Israeli military government and its Civil Administration to the Council. The Interim Agreement shall also specify the Council's executive authority, legislative authority in accordance with Article IX below, and the independent Palestinian judicial organs."

The nine months have long passed, the negotiations go on but are stalled.[4]

The critics say – rightly – if we can't get to Stage 2, when, if ever, are we going to get to the next stage.

C. Stage 3

The third stage is negotiating the thorny "remaining issues", especially those of "Jerusalem", "Settlements" and the "Refugees". This brings me to why my original hopes and optimism have shrunk.

V. The Views of Joel Singer

The starting point is an Article by Mr Joel Singer entitled, "The Declaration of Principles on Interim Self-Government Arrangements: Some Legal Aspects".[5] If Mr Singer was an Israeli independent legal commentator, one would not have been worried, but clearly he is not. The caption under his name in the Article says, "he is the Legal Adviser of the Israel Ministry of Foreign Affairs. He was closely involved in the Oslo negotiations leading up to the signing of the Declaration of Principles with the PLO and is a member of the Israeli negotiating team in the autonomy talks". The caption goes on to state that "the views expressed in this article are his own, and do not necessarily reflect those

4 See postscript, at p. 77, below.

5 1 *Justice*, No. 4, February 1994, published by the International Association of Jewish Lawyers and Jurists.

of the Israeli Government",[6] but since he is the Israeli Government Legal Adviser and reputed to be the draftsman of the DOP and of the Cairo Agreement, it is difficult to see how his views could not but reflect those of the Israeli Government.

I need not deal with Mr Singer's views regarding the Gaza-Jericho Arrangements (pp. 11 to 13 of Article), save to say that what he says is reflected in the Cairo Agreement. More important is what he says regarding the second stage, i.e. the five year Interim Period which commenced on the date of the signing of the Cairo Agreement, i.e. 4th May 1994. Four matters are worthy of special mention:

A. Elections (pp. 5 and 6 of the Article)

At the heart of the DOP is the holding of elections to the new self-governing Council "not later than 9 months" after the entry into force of the DOP, i.e. in June 1994. As pointed out, a year has now passed – the date last mentioned was 1st July 1995 – but it has not happened.[7] Although Annex 1 gives the Palestinians of Jerusalem the *right* to participate in the elections, Mr Singer says that "Israel will continue to oppose any participation of Palestinians of East Jerusalem as candidates in the elections ... participation ... does not require that Palestinians will be able to cast their vote in Jerusalem itself; their votes may be cast at polling stations situated within the territories".

This is a novel and odd way of "participation" to say the least! By its very nature elections are about voting for representatives to represent the electors in the Council – how can it be "democratic" (the word used in Article III) for a Jerusalemite to vote outside Jerusalem for a candidate from Nablus or Hebron, for example!

B. Source of Authority (p. 6 of the Article)

Again at the heart of the DOP is the withdrawal of the military Government and the dissolution of the Israeli Civil Administration once the Council is elected so that the Council replaces them. Article VII (5) says so in clear terms. However, Mr Singer has other ideas. He says:

> On the establishment of the Council, in accordance with Article VII (5), the Israeli Civil Administration will be dissolved; the Israeli military government, on the other hand, will not be dissolved, but will simply withdraw from the West Bank and Gaza Strip to Israel.

---

6 There is a photograph of the signing ceremony on the White House Lawn, Washington, showing Mr Singer presenting the DOP for signature by Mr Shimon Peres for the Government of Israel.

7 See, however, postscript at p. 77, below.

> In this context, the fact that the military government in the West Bank and Gaza Strip will continue to exist is very significant. It emphasizes that, notwithstanding the transfer of a larger portion of the powers and responsibilities currently exercised by Israel to Palestinian hands, the status of the West Bank will not be changed during the interim period. These areas will continue to be subject to military government. Similarly, this fact suggests that the Palestinian Council will not be independent or sovereign in nature, but will be legally subordinate to the authority of the military government. In other words, operating within Israel, the military government will continue to be the source of authority for the Palestinian Council and the powers and responsibilities exercised by it in the West Bank and Gaza Strip.
>
> ...
>
> The provisions of the DOP ensure that Israel, through its military government, shall continue to be the source of authority and, as discussed below, to retain any powers and responsibilities not specifically transferred to the Council.

With respect, this is an extraordinary argument. How can an elected Council be "legally subordinate to the authority of the military government", and how can a "military government" – itself an illegal entity because it is in occupation – be the "source of authority".

As argued earlier,[8] it is well established in international law that sovereignty remains residual in the people who fall under occupation, i.e. the Palestinians through the PLO, and once the Council is elected, through its Council. Sovereignty never resided with the Israeli military government or indeed the Israeli Government and cannot and does not do so by virtue of the DOP. Indeed, if Mr Singer's view were correct, it would amount to legalising the occupation.

C. Jurisdiction of the Council (pp. 6 and 7 of the Article)

It is clear from Article IV of the DOP and the Agreed Minute to Article IV that the jurisdiction of the Council does not cover issues that will be negotiated in the permanent status negotiations viz. Jerusalem, settlements, military locations and Israelis.

But Mr Singer is not content with this functional and personal limitation. He argues that there is a further territorial limitation because of the omission from Article IV and the Agreed Minute of the word "the" or "all" before "West Bank and Gaza". He says:—

> Article IV provides that "the jurisdiction of the Council will cover West Bank and Gaza Strip territory". Significantly, by declining to adopt Palestinian proposals to include the word "all" or "the" before the phrase "West Bank and Gaza Strip", the parties made it clear that they intended that the territorial jurisdiction of the Council will not necessarily cover the entire West Bank and Gaza Strip. The language of Article IV thus follows the wording of U.N. Security Council Resolution 242 which deliberately omitted the word "the" or "all" before the word "territories" in the phrase, "withdrawal of Israeli armed forces from territories occupied in the recent conflict". In both cases, the

---

[8] See p. 68 above and note 3 above.

> omission of the word "the" or "all" was deliberate and meant to leave for negotiation between the parties the extent to which the withdrawal (in the case of Resolution 242) or the Council's jurisdiction (in the case of the DOP) would apply to the West Bank and Gaza Strip. On the basis of this provision, during the Interim Agreement negotiations Israel may seek to exclude from the Council's territorial jurisdiction such areas as state lands or land privately owned by Jews which are located outside the Israeli settlements.
>
> In addition, it is clear that the jurisdiction of the Council will not cover Israeli settlements and military locations which, as noted above, are defined by the Agreed Minute to Article IV as permanent status issues. This list of exceptions is not necessarily exhaustive; indeed, the text of the Agreed Minute to Article IV suggests that they come in addition to the requirement that the extent of West Bank and Gaza Strip territory over which the Council has jurisdiction be defined through negotiations.

It is odd that this view can be an "independent" view since Mr Singer admits that the omission of the "the" is deliberate. He advances the same argument in relation to Article XIV (See p. 11 of his Article), but he seems to have kept the word "the" in that Article viz. "Israel will withdraw from *the* Gaza Strip and Jericho area" (See also Annex II). Again he seems to have forgotten to omit the word "the" in Article I, "... for the Palestinian people in *the* West Bank and the Gaza Strip"; in the second sentence of Article IV, "the two sides view *the* West Bank and Gaza as a single territorial unit"; in Article V(1), "The five-years transitional period will begin upon the withdrawal from *the* Gaza Strip and Jericho area"; in Article VI(1), "and the withdrawal from *the* Gaza Strip and Jericho area"; in Article VIII, "for the Palestinians of *the* West Bank and the Gaza Strip"; and finally in Article XIII, "... a redeployment in *the* West Bank and Gaza Strip".

One hopes that in any event, as has been said in relation to the omission of the word "the" in Resolution 242, that the future of Palestine and Palestinians is not going to depend on the addition or omission of the word "the" or "all" from one Article of the DOP.[9]

D. Displaced Persons or Refugees (p. 10 of the Article)

Mr Singer refers to the 1967 displaced persons or refugees and refers to Article XII dealing with arrangements between the Palestinian Council, Israel, Jordan and Egypt for the modalities of their return.

He states that the question of the 1948 refugees is, under Article V, one of the "remaining issues" to be discussed in the permanent status negotiations. However, he also states that the term "refugees" is not limited to Arab refugees and that the negotiations may specially focus

---

9 It is also surprising that the only official texts of the DOP and of the Cairo Agreement are in English, the language of neither party. The Arabic texts are not official and are translations.

on the large number of Jews who were forced to flee to Israel from neighbouring Arab States. It is difficult to see how the Palestinians or its Council can be blamed or can solve their problem!

My gloom of course does not derive solely from Mr Singer's Article. The real question is whether he is negotiating and drafting in the spirit and sometimes within the clear wording and objectives of the DOP.

VI. The Settlements and Jerusalem

More important than Mr Singer are the instructions he is getting from his superiors. Is the DOP to be taken seriously as the first step towards peace and a *just* solution, to be completed in 5 years, or is it a device for the creation of more facts on the ground by establishing more settlements and extension of settlements, more confiscation of land in Jerusalem and the West Bank, so that the "remaining issues" in the permanent status negotiations become incapable of settlement? More importantly, is the end result an independent State of Palestine with some *22%* of the original area of 1948 Palestine (the whole of the West Bank and Gaza) or some *14%* if the Israeli settlements around Jerusalem and in the West Bank are excluded?

And what about East Jerusalem and the recent land seizure of 133 acres of Arab land in Beit Hanina and Beit Safafa. Mr Singer and the Israeli Government would say that there is nothing in the DOP which says that this and other seizures and extension of settlements cannot be made. The answer is really provided in a *Times* editorial of 13 May 1995, viz.:

> As negotiations between Yitzhak Rabin's Government and Yassir Arafat's Palestinian National Authority continue to lurch in every direction but forward, the Israeli administration has ordered the seizure for Jewish housing of 131 acres of Palestinian land in east Jerusalem. The Israeli public responded with ebullient approval: the Palestinian reaction was marked by resentful indignation. Clearly, by this measure, the seizure does not advance the cause of the now-tattered Declaration of Principles. But Jerusalem was never going to be easy: in fact, it was always going to be this difficult.
>
> ...
>
> The latest seizure of Palestinian land provokes important questions: *Can* the Israeli Government take such action? And *should* it have taken such action? These very questions were stirred earlier this year by the dust of Israeli bulldozers at the Palestinian village of al-Khader, in the occupied West Bank. Mr Arafat described the construction of those new settlements as a "flagrant violation" of the Declaration of Principles, words which he and his political associates were to repeat after the recent seizures in East Jerusalem.
>
> In purely textual terms, the accord does not disallow the kind of action which Israel has just taken. But peace between Israel and the Palestinians is not a matter of text alone: more important even than the letter of the accord is the spirit in which it is interpreted. The seizure of Palestinian land in East Jerusalem runs

> strictly counter to the essence of the Declaration of Principles – just as the continued building of settlements in the West Bank does.

The *Times* is right. The seizure of the land is not only contrary to the spirit of the DOP, but it is also contrary to its intent and letter, since any such seizure will inevitably prejudice the last stage of the DOP which will deal with Jerusalem and settlements. Furthermore the seizure and confiscation is clearly contrary to international law and the Geneva Conventions. So said the whole world in one voice in the Security Council a few days ago in debating a Resolution condemning Israel for the confiscation of the land as illegal and requesting it to withdraw the proposed measure. The USA, however, vetoed the Resolution on the basis that it is for the "parties to solve the matter by negotiations".

The Israeli Cabinet subsequently announced that the proposed measure would be "frozen" – ironically though not because of any pressure from the world or the Arab League (which was proposing to hold an Arab summit to consider the matter), but because there was a motion of no confidence by the few Arab Knesset Members of the Israeli Parliament, supported by the Likud opposition, which would inevitably have led to the fall of the Rabin Government.

Conclusion

It is clear that in future, disputes regarding the implementation of the DOP will have to be resolved politically, rather than legally, though it must not be forgotten that there is a mechanism in the DOP for Resolution of Disputes (Article XIV), first by the Joint Liaison Committee established by Article X, secondly by a "mechanism of conciliation to be agreed upon by the parties" and thirdly by arbitration through an Arbitration Committee.[10]

It is also submitted that the DOP does not in any way relieve the U.N. from its special responsibility to the Palestinian people, especially that the aim of the negotiations is to lead to a permanent settlement based on Security Council Resolutions 242 and 338. The problem, as it seems to me, remains *international* despite the US view that "the parties must solve their own problems". If, therefore, at the end of the day, the second stage (the Interim Agreement leading to elections and redeployment and withdrawal of Israeli forces) is not reached, or if reached, the "remaining issues" cannot be resolved by the end of the five year interim period, the UN itself, as it did in 1947/48 through the partition plan and the internationalisation of Jerusalem, must get

[10] A similar provision is to be found in Article XVII of the Cairo Agreement.

involved in finding a solution to the "permanent status issues", principally Jerusalem, settlements and the 1948 refugees.

Postscript

After months of negotiations the Israeli-Palestinian Interim Agreement on the West Bank and Gaza Strip was signed at Washington on 28th September 1995.[11] Space prevents dealing with it at this late stage of correction of proofs.[12] Suffice it to say that some of Mr Singer's views dealt with earlier,[13] are reflected in the Interim Agreement, especially on the issues of "Source of Authority" after the establishment of the Council (see Article I.5) and the omission of the word "the" from Article XVII.1, 2 and 8 which again deals with the Council's jurisdiction – territorial, functional and personal – in "West Bank and Gaza" omitting "the". The elections to the Council is dealt with in Article II.1 to 4 and in Annex II. Mr Singer does not get his way on the elections in Jerusalem (see Pt. V., A., at p. 76 above). since Annex II (Art VI) provides for Jerusalem residents to vote at five post offices in East Jerusalem. Any candidate must have an "address" in the area under the jurisdiction of the Council (Annex II, Art III).

---

11 For full text, see Appendix, p. 271.
12 October 1995.
13 See Pt. V., pp. 71-75 above.

III. The Structure of Domestic Developments

5. Domestic Politics, Law and the Peace Process: A View from Israel

David Kretzmer

Introduction

Peace-making is a political process, not an academic exercise. Strategic aims, historical claims, international law, international relations, international pressure, economic considerations and a host of other factors play an important role in determining the parties' positions. It is my contention, however, that domestic political constraints are often stronger than any other. Understanding these constraints is therefore essential to any assessment of the prospects of the process itself.

The Oslo Accords and Cairo Agreement reflect a radical change in Israeli perceptions and policies. This change was not welcomed by all Israelis. Nor was the deal between Israel and the PLO acceptable to all Palestinians. Some of the militant Israeli and Palestinian opponents of the deal have resorted to violence and terror, mainly in the hope that by doing so they can create a domestic backlash of Israelis and Palestinians that will thwart the process itself.

The lack of consensus surrounding the Accords and the Agreement, and the terrorist acts that have been planned and carried out by militants, have created serious domestic political constraints both in Israel and in the Palestinian Authority. These constraints often place conflicting demands on the two sides. Thus, for example, the need of the government in Israel to prove to the Israeli public that the Palestinian Authority is taking a tough line against the militant Islamic groups that have taken responsibility for terrorist acts against Israeli citizens may result in Israeli demands for action that could weaken the legitimacy of the Palestinian Authority in the eyes of the Palestinians.

During the process of "getting to peace", domestic political constraints may create tension between the final aim – achieving peace – and the actions taken to overcome such constraints. It seems to me that the Israeli demand at the interim stage that all settlements in the Occupied Territories remain in place is an example of such tension. The closure of the Occupied Territories after terrorist acts in Israel, and the resulting economic hardship for many Palestinian families who are reliant on work in Israel, is another.

It is not with the general question of domestic political constraints that this paper is concerned, however. I am certainly not qualified to discuss the domestic political constraints on the Palestinian side and will confine my discussion to the tension between domestic political constraints in

Israel and legal values. Thus it is with the part the law and legal values have played in dealing with domestic political problems, rather than with the analysis of legal problems, that the paper is concerned.

By ending the regime of occupation, enabling both the Israeli and Palestinian peoples to exercise their right to self-determination and creating conditions of peace, a successful political settlement of the conflict between Israel and the Palestinians will further human rights in the region. However, during the process of getting to peace, domestic political factors may create constraints that have to be overcome if that process is to continue. The problems that I will discuss relate to three human rights issues that are a function of such domestic political constraints. These issues are:

1. The tension between protection of domestic constitutional values and the need to create a political alliance that will support the peace process;
2. The use against "insiders" of security measures that were perceived as being reserved for "outsiders";
3. The measures taken to combat terror, domestic political constraints and the law.

I. Coalition Politics and Constitutional Values

A. The Domestic Political Scene

For two main reasons – the proportional representation system of elections and the existence of three blocs of political forces, centre-left, centre-right and religious parties – no political party in Israel has ever enjoyed the parliamentary majority required to rule in a parliamentary democracy. All Israel's governments have been coalition governments, the backbone of which have usually been one of the two large parties (Labour or Likud) and one or more of the smaller religious parties.

After the last elections the Labour party had what became known as a "preventive bloc" in the Knesset, Israel's parliament. Sixty-one of the 120 Knesset members were either members of the Labour Party or parties to the left of it which would in no circumstances join a coalition led by the Likud. The Likud therefore had no chance of forming a coalition government together with the religious parties and Mr. Rabin, as leader of the Labour Party, was asked to form a government.

Mr. Rabin's government was initially based on a formal coalition agreement between three parties which together had 62 Knesset members: the Labour Party, Meretz and the Shas party, a religious party that represents Jews of Sephardic background. While the negotiations in Oslo were going on, the Shas party left the coalition after its political leader was indicted on charges of corruption. After Shas left the coalition, Mr. Rabin's government was based on a formal coalition between the Labour Party and Meretz, which together have 56 seats. The government also enjoyed the parliamentary support of the Communist Party (the Democratic Peace Front), which has three Knesset members, and the Arab Democratic Party, which has two members.

Mr. Rabin has always been eager to extend the coalition base of his government so as to make it both more representative and somewhat more stable. However, until the negotiations with Syria began to get serious he saw no urgency to the matter as there was little threat to the parliamentary stability of the government. Once the negotiations with Syria got under way, and it became clear that Mr. Rabin was prepared to agree to Israeli withdrawal from most of the Golan Heights, the picture changed. Opposition to withdrawal from the Golan Heights is not limited to the right-wing opposition parties, and Mr. Rabin feared that members of his own Labour Party could threaten the stability of his government if he were to negotiate an agreement with Syria that provided for Israeli withdrawal from the Golan. He therefore regarded extending his coalition base as a political necessity.

The main chance of extending the coalition without changing the peace policy was that Shas could be persuaded to rejoin the government. Shas was indeed prepared to join the coalition and to allow Mr. Rabin to pursue the negotiations with Syria, provided that a referendum would be held on any agreement that involved substantial withdrawal from the Golan. However, it had certain constitutional demands. In order to appreciate the significance of these demands, a short review of recent constitutional developments in Israel is essential.

B. Constitutional Developments in Israel

Until recently Israel was one of the few democratic countries that, like Britain, had no formal constitution. There was no judicial review of legislation, except on very narrow grounds.[1] Thus, even though on most domestic matters (especially those that are not connected with security) the Supreme Court has been fairly rights-minded, it has not been prepared to overrule Knesset legislation that violates basic rights, such as freedom of religion.

Lack of a formal constitution or bill of rights was not for want of trying. Attempts were made over the years to enact a basic law on human rights that would allow judicial review of parliamentary legislation. In recent years the main opposition to such a basic law came

---

[1] I have discussed this whole issue elsewhere. See D. Kretzmer, 'Judicial Review of Knesset Decisions', 8 *Tel Aviv Studies in Law* 95 (1988).

from the religious parties which fear that judicial review of Knesset legislation would endanger arrangements relating to "the status quo in matters of state and religion". These arrangements include lack of civil marriage and divorce, restrictions on public transport and opening of businesses on the sabbath and limitations on the raising of pigs and sale of pork.

Realizing that it was impossible, for political reasons, to enact a general bill of rights, leading proponents of such a bill changed their tactics: they proposed partial bills that deal with those rights that, it was assumed, are less problematical from the point of view of the religious parties. This tactic was successful and in 1992 two basic laws were enacted: the Basic Law: Freedom of Occupation and the Basic Law: Freedom Human Dignity and Freedom.[2] These basic laws do not mention two of the rights that are most problematical for the religious parties: freedom of religion and equality.[3] The Basic Law: Human Dignity and Freedom does, however, mention the notion of human dignity, and the leading justice on the Supreme Court, Justice Aharon Barak, has made it quite clear in his extra-judicial writings that this notion includes a whole gambit of basic rights not specifically mentioned in the law itself, including equality and freedom of religion and conscience.[4] Furthermore, in a recent decision the Supreme Court held that import restrictions on meat that are based on religious grounds are inconsistent with the right of a meat-importer to freedom of occupation.[5]

The enactment of the two basic laws on human rights mentioned above is regarded by many as no less than a constitutional revolution, opening as it does the way to judicial review of parliamentary legislation on the grounds that the legislation is inconsistent with basic human rights or liberties. The staunchest supporters of this revolution have been leading members of the Meretz faction, at the time of writing the Labour Party's only formal coalition partner.[6]

---

2 For a discussion in English of these basic laws see D. Kretzmer, 'The New Basic Laws on Human Rights: A Mini-Revolution in Israeli Constitutional Law?', 26 *Israel Law Review* 238 (1992).

3 The right to equality is problematical because of the application of religious laws in matters of marriage and divorce and the jurisdiction of religious courts in these matters, since both the Jewish and Moslem laws on marriage and divorce may be regarded as discriminatory towards women.

4 See A. Barak, 'Dignity of Man as a Constitutional Right', 41 *Hapraklit* 271 (1994). This view is supported by J. Karp, 'Basic Law: Human Dignity and Freedom – A Biography of Power Struggles', 1 *Law and Government* 323 (1993) and H. Cohn, 'The Values of a Jewish and Democratic State: Reflections on the Basic Law: Human Dignity and Freedom', *Hapraklit*, Jubilee Volume 9 (1993).

5 See *Meatrael* v. *Prime Minister* (decision in H.C.3872/93, unreported).

6 Two of the three political parties that united before the last election to form the united electoral front of Meretz had for years campaigned for a bill of rights and had placed protection of human rights as their major political commitment. The basic laws were

The same constitutional revolution welcomed by the centre-left secular political parties is anathema to the religious parties. They are convinced that they made a serious mistake in allowing the basic laws to be enacted and are looking for a way to undo part of what was done, especially that part that affects the delicate balance between state and religion. Thus it was that the main condition of the Shas party for re-entry into the coalition was that the Labour Party support a minor constitutional counter-revolution. This counter-revolution would consist of three measures:

(1) amendment of the Basic Law: Human Dignity and Freedom so as to provide not only that that basic law will not affect the validity of any laws relating to religious matters, but that laws relating to such matters will become entrenched so that they may be changed only by legislation passed by an absolute majority of the Knesset;

(2) an undertaking of the coalition partners that if the status quo in religious matters is broken, the breach will be remedied by appropriate legislation (a euphemistic way of saying that if the Supreme Court rules that laws relating to religious matters violate basic rights, those laws will be re-enacted so as to guarantee their immunity from judicial review);

(3) enactment of legislation to be proposed by a special committee that will entrench the status quo in matters of state and religion.

C. Progress to Peace and Constitutional Values

The above demands are regarded by constitutional lawyers and political supporters of a bill of rights as totally unacceptable. By seeking to entrench arrangements that place serious restrictions on civil liberties, they pervert the whole rationale of entrenchment, which is to protect democratic institutions and minority rights and not to eternalize political arrangements that restrict basic rights. By guaranteeing in advance that any constitutional decision of a court that advances protection of freedom of religion will automatically be revoked by appropriate legislation, the status of the Supreme Court in judicial review of legislation is seriously undermined.

The signing of a coalition agreement between Shas and the Labour Party in which the Labour Party agreed to meet all the above demands placed the peace-camp, and especially the Meretz faction, in an unenviable position. Widening the coalition was highly desirable if negotiations with Syria, and with the Palestinians, were to progress. The only significant faction which would join the coalition without making

---

submitted as private members' bills by a member of the Meretz faction, then a member of the opposition and now a cabinet minister.

After writing this paper Mr. Rabin successfully negotiated with a three-person break-away faction from one of the right-wing parties to join his coalition.

political demands that could undermine the peace process was Shas. The domestic constitutional price being demanded, however, was one that Meretz could not accept, both on grounds of principle as well as on grounds of political expedience.

This then was the essential dilemma: assuming that because of domestic political constraints the peace process could only be advanced if a wide coalition of forces supported the government, and that the only real potential partner in a wider coalition made demands that undermine domestic constitutional values, should one waive those values for the sake of peace? And if one did, on the basis of the theory that the peace-process must take precedence, was there not some limit to the nature of changes in Israel's constitutional system that one could accept as a price for political support for the process?

At the time of submission of this paper the above questions were placed in abeyance while a case was pending before the Supreme Court which challenged the legality of the coalition agreement between Labour and Shas. The Court subsequently refused to interfere in that agreement, but the delay in the judicial proceedings had given the parties time for reconsideration and the Shas party decided not to join the coalition, ostensibly because of the serious security situation. Be this as it may, the dilemma raised for the peace-camp by the Labour-Shas agreement is a function of the domestic political scene in Israel and not of any particular agreement. It is therefore a dilemma that the peace-camp will most likely have to face in the future as the need continues to build coalitions that will provide political support for the peace process.

II. Dealing with Militant Israeli Opposition

A. Political Background

Israeli government policies after 1967, especially during the 1977–1992 period of Likud government, were aimed at creating facts that would make disengagement from the Occupied Territories politically impossible. During the nineteen-eighties even many opponents of the government's settlement policy were resigned to the view advanced by Meron Benvenisti that this policy had indeed achieved its aim and that repartition of the Land of Israel/Palestine was no longer a feasible option.

The settlement and annexationist policies followed until 1992 were not only a function of the dreams and aspirations of sections of the Jewish public in Israel: they fuelled those aspirations and created expectations both among the Jewish settlers in the Occupied Territories, and among some sections of the Israeli public, that Israel would retain sole control of the Greater Land of Israel permanently. The direction of the present peace-process between Israel and the Palestinians has shaken the very foundations of these aspirations and expectations.[7] Pro-annexationist forces in Israeli see their dreams being shattered; Jewish settlers on the West Bank and in Gaza sense that they will be forced at a later stage of the process to leave homes that were generally built with the whole-hearted support and encouragement of the government.

Domestic opposition in Israel to the Oslo Accords and Cairo Agreements may be divided into a number of camps:

1. Parliamentary Opposition by the Right

This opposition was initially unable to stir up public opinion against the peace agreements with the Palestinians. However, the prospect of an agreement with Syria, under which Israel would relinquish control of the Golan Heights, and a number of terrorist attacks against Israeli targets, have increased its chances of creating a parliamentary coalition that could threaten the stability of Mr. Rabin's government. The threat of such a parliamentary coalition is the direct cause of the constitutional manoeuvres that were discussed above.

2. Extra-parliamentary Opposition

Led by Jewish settlers from the West Bank and Gaza, this camp, which has followed traditional forms of protest, such as demonstrations and sit-ins, has mounted a campaign to delegitimize the Rabin government. This campaign rests on three main claims:

(a) No Israeli government has the right to give up part of the traditional homeland;

(b) The Labour Party and its leader, Mr. Rabin, have broken their pre-election pledge not to negotiate with the PLO;

(c) Mr. Rabin's government does not enjoy a "real" parliamentary majority, since it is dependent on the support of the Arab parties in the Knesset.[8]

The premise of this final claim is that the Arab citizens of Israel are less than full citizens in a state that defines itself as the state of the Jewish people. They are not legitimate partners in decisions relating to

---

7 I stress that the aspirations are inconsistent with the direction of the peace process and not with the agreements that have so far been concluded, since those agreements provide for the continued presence of the Israeli settlers on the West Bank and in Gaza.

8 Mr. Rabin's government rests on a formal coalition between the Labour Party and Meretz, which together have 56 of the 120 members of the Knesset, and the support of the five members of the Communist Democratic Peace Front and the Arab Democratic Party. Two of the three Front members are Arab, as are the overwhelming majority of its voters. As its name suggest, the Arab Democratic Party is an entirely Arab party.

the security of the state or its ideological direction.[9] More recently the delegitimization campaign has also rested on the claim that the Rabin government is resorting to non-democratic means to crush its political opponents.

3. Extra-legal Opposition

This has comprised individuals and groups that have resorted to violence and terror, the most horrific instance of which was the murder of 29 Muslim worshippers in the Cave of the Patriarchs in February 1994. It is the way these groups and individuals have been dealt with that will concern me in the present section.

B. Security Powers and Interrogation Methods

Israel's legal system includes a corpus of security legislation that places in the hands of the executive branch of government wide powers to impose severe restrictions on the fundamental liberties of the individual. Much of this legislation was passed during the period of the British Mandate over Palestine but was not revoked after Israel became independent. Other legislation was enacted by the Knesset.

Among the powers included in this legislation are the following:

(a) Administrative detention;

(b) Town arrest;

(c) Declaration of an organization as an unlawful organization;

(d) Denial of right of an interrogatee to meet with counsel for a period of fifteen days.

Alongside the formal security powers, the security authorities have been given license to use "special means" in interrogation of suspects. The background to this license is revealing.

Over the years allegations have been made time and again by interrogatees and Israeli, Palestinian and foreign human rights organizations that torture and cruel and degrading forms of treatment have been used by the authorities in interrogation of Palestinian detainees. A Commission of Inquiry, set up by the government in 1987 and headed by a former president of the Supreme Court of Israel, Justice Moshe Landau, confirmed that force had indeed been used in many interrogations.[10] In dealing with the methods of interrogation that

---

9 This argument was advanced quite explicitly in an article published in the daily *Ha'aretz* by a former Knesset Member of the one of the smaller right-wing parties. See Y. Tzidon, 'The Kohalani Law and Democracy', *Ha'aretz*, 2 October 1994, p. B4.

10 See Report of the Commission of Inquiry into the Methods of Investigation of the General Security Service (G.S.S.) Regarding Hostile Terrorist Activity (Jerusalem, October, 1987). The Commission was established after it was revealed that a Circassian officer in the IDF who had been convicted of serious security offences had made statements under severe duress by the security services.

would be acceptable in the future, the Commission categorically stated that use of torture was unacceptable. However, it held that in cases in which it is essential to obtain information needed to protect the security of the state and its citizens, the interrogators could use forms of non-violent psychological pressure, and that if these were not effective, a moderate degree of physical pressure could be used.[11]

Two reports published by B'Tselem, The Israeli Information Center for Human Rights in the Occupied Territories, after the report of the Landau Commission was published, charged that force was still being used in interrogations, even when the detainees were not suspected of actual terrorist activity.[12]

C. Uses of Legal Framework and Interrogation Methods

The background and political justification offered for both the continued existence of the special security legislation mentioned above, and the extraordinary leeway granted to the security services in interrogations are, of course, the security situation of Israel in the context of the Arab-Israel conflict, and more specifically the nature of the conflict with the Palestinian people. This is made most clear in the Report of the Landau Commission. That report devotes two sections to an analysis of "Terrorist Organizations and the Armed Struggle" and to a description of the difficulties that the security services encounter in acquiring information during interrogations. The premise of the Commission was that if the security services were confined to the methods of interrogation used in ordinary criminal investigations they

---

11 Id., Para. 4.7.

12 See B'Tselem, The Israeli Information Center for Human Rights in the Occupied Territories, *The Interrogation of Palestinians During the Intifada: Ill-treatment, "Moderate Physical Pressure" or Torture?*, (March 1991); *The Interrogation of Palestinians During the Intifada*, (Follow-up Report, March 1992).

After this paper was written, following the terrorist attack on a bus in Tel Aviv which resulted in the death of twenty-two people, a special ministerial committee which overlooks the secret security services, gave those services permission to employ the 'special means' in interrogation of all detainees suspected of being members of militant Muslim groups involved in the campaign of terrorist acts. In April 1995, a Palestinian detainee died from injuries caused during interrogation, apparently due to 'shaking'. After an investigation carried out by the special Ministry of Justice unit for investigation of police and security agents, it was announced that one of the interrogators would be charged before the special disciplinary court headed by a judge that deals with disciplinary charges against members of GSS. The decision not to press criminal charges was severely criticized. It seems fairly obvious that the reason that criminal charges were not pressed is that 'shaking' is allowed under the guide-lines. The interrogator will probably be charged only with 'shaking' more than allowed, and not with causing the death of the detainee, which may very well have resulted from the 'shaking' permitted under the guide-lines. At the time of writing a case is pending before the Supreme Court challenging the legality of the guide-lines set down by the Landau Commission and the ministerial committee.

would not be able to obtain the information needed to thwart hostile terrorist activity. The conclusion was that moderate force could be used when necessary in cases of "hostile terrorist activity or political subversion that is illegal under the laws in Israel or in the territories."

Use of the special security legislation and of the special interrogation methods as one of the means of managing the conflict with the Palestinians has had a number of implications. One of them has been that all opposition to the wide-scale use of this legislation and to the interrogation methods of the security services has been perceived as politically motivated criticism that is necessarily connected to one's attitude on the wide political issues. Arguments based on universalistic concepts of human rights have been seen as expressions of identification with the political or national aspirations of the Palestinians whose rights were being violated, or even as expressions of support for terrorist acts carried out by Palestinians. The best example of this phenomenon was the public reaction to the petition of the Association for Civil Rights in Israel (ACRI) against the deportation of 400 Hamas activists in December 1992. The prime minister himself, Mr. Rabin, referred to ACRI as the "Association for the rights of the Hamas". A more recent example was the public incredulity when ACRI petitioned the Supreme Court to prevent demolition of the home of the terrorist who blew up the bus in Tel Aviv in October 1994, thereby killing twenty-two persons and wounding many others.

The activities of Israeli human rights organizations against use of security powers and use of force in interrogations have sometimes received parliamentary and public support by Knesset members of the left. Politicians on the right, however, have usually expressed unqualified support for the use of special security powers and for the interrogation methods of the security forces. They have also been highly critical of these human rights organizations. This was most apparent when the first B'Tselem report on the interrogation of Palestinian detainees was published. Leading right-wing politicians and figures expressed anger at B'Tselem for publishing the report, claiming either that the report was unreliable as it relied on the testimony of Palestinian detainees, or that even if the allegations were well-founded in fact, the security forces could not be faulted for using the interrogation methods described in the report.[13]

D. The Right Discovers Human Rights

As long as those on the receiving side of special security powers, such as administrative detention and interrogation methods, were Palestinians,

---

[13] For a description of these reactions to the report see B'Tselem, *Interrogation of Palestinians during the Intifada*, Follow-up Report, pp. 10-13.

the right-wing in Israel was wholly supportive of the security services and highly critical of human rights organizations that dared to challenge them. Their assumption that these powers and interrogation methods could be used on "the other guys" and never on themselves was rudely shattered when the decision was taken to use some of the powers against radical right-wing forces opposed to the peace process who had planned or supported terrorist acts against Palestinians.

The first case of major resort to security powers against Israeli citizens came in the wake of the Hebron massacre in February 1994. While it was assumed, and later confirmed by a formal judicial commission of inquiry, that the perpetrator of the massacre had acted on his own, the government decided to act against the most extreme Jewish political organization that was active both in the Occupied Territories and in Israel itself, the 'Kach' movement founded by Meir Kahane. The movement was declared a "terrorist organization" under the Prevention of Terror Ordinance and a few of the movement's leaders were placed in administrative detention.

Use of administrative detention should have shocked no one, for during the *intifada* thousands of Palestinians were held under administrative detention for long periods of time. However, so deeply had parts of the right internalized the division between "them" and "us" that they expressed outrage at the "governmental terror". Their outrage was aimed both at the very use of the measure of administrative detention against Jews, as well as the fact that in some cases the law of administrative detention that was employed was the military law that applies on the West Bank, rather than the more liberal domestic law in Israel that subjects all cases of administrative detention to stringent judicial review by the ordinary courts. These sections of the right had accepted as self-evident the legitimacy of the practice that been established over the years under which the Jewish settlers in the Occupied Territories were in fact not regarded as subject to the military regime that was in effect in those territories. Their division was clear: one set of laws for the Palestinians; another for the Israelis living in the same territory.

Security powers were employed again when a number of people were arrested on suspicion of stealing arms from the IDF in order to hand them over to right-wing militants who were planning terrorist attacks on Arabs. The security forces invoked the security provisions, used frequently when Palestinians are under interrogation, according to which access to counsel was denied on security grounds for a period of fifteen days. When one of the first detainees was brought for remand before a judge he alleged that he had been subjected to harsh treatment by the interrogators. A public outcry ensued in which politicians of the right, up until then the stalwart supporters of the security services, attacked those same services. The very people who had always denied the credibility of Palestinian reports about the interrogation methods of the security services now accepted as totally credible the allegations made by the Israeli detainees, even though, given their attempt to delegitimize the Rabin government, they had every reason to exaggerate in describing the methods of the security service.

The right wing opposition parties demanded a special session of the Knesset to deal with the interrogation methods and use of security powers by the government. Right wing politicians, never known for their sensitivity on questions of human rights, declared that they would propose legislation to prevent denial of access to counsel, to limit the use of administrative detention and to increase control over the practices of the security services.

E. Universalization of Human Rights Values

I have mentioned above that given the use of security powers and special interrogation methods as part of a strategy of conflict-management, it is very difficult in Israel to convince the public that universalistic concepts of human rights are relevant when the people whose rights are being violated are "the enemy". It does not seem to me that this situation is peculiar to Israel. Human rights organizations in Israel have for years made little progress in convincing the public (or the courts) that the wide use made of security powers and special interrogations methods involve unacceptable violations of human rights, even in a situation of conflict and violence. The interesting question was whether there would be greater willingness to universalize human rights values now that the victims of alleged human rights violations were not members of the outsider enemy group. Would it perhaps be possible at least to convince people that one of the dangers of arming the authorities with wide security powers is that one can never be sure against whom they will be employed?

Various strategies were adopted in order to exploit the climate that had been created with the use of the security powers against members of the militant right. ACRI lawyers agreed to represent members of extreme right-wing organizations who had been placed under administrative detention or town arrest. They did so because of the principled stand the organization had always taken on the question of administrative detention, but they obviously also hoped that this would help persuade the public that the opposition to such detention must be based on universalistic grounds. The Public Committee Against Torture in Israel, which for a long time had attacked the license given by the Landau Commission to use of moderate force in interrogations, submitted a petition to the Supreme Court in which it asked the Court to annul the recommendations of the Landau Commission and to subject the security services to the law. Articles were written in the press calling for changes in the law.[14]

It is too early to judge whether the attempts to exploit the use of security measures and special interrogation methods against right-wing militants in order to bolster the universalistic nature of human rights will be successful. The present writer is not overly optimistic. It seems that the message being pervaded by the right was not that "you can't do that sort of thing", but that "you can't do that sort of thing to us".

Situations of national and ethnic conflict are not conducive to human rights discourse. While those committed to human rights values must continue to demand that recognized standards be maintained even in such situations, the real chance for enhancing respect for human rights lies in reducing the conflict. One would hope that the new political order that is being created between Israel, the Palestinians and the Arab World will create an atmosphere conducive to protection of human rights. This new order should ideally include a regional human rights treaty that may contribute to acceptance of universalist concepts of human rights.

III. The Peace Process, Terror and Domestic Politics

A. The Dangers of Terror

Opinion polls in Israel show quite clearly that support for the government's peace policy drops after acts of terror against Israeli civilians. The opposition is quite aware of this. Some opposition politicians never miss the opportunity of telling the public that the acts of terror are a direct result of the government's policies and the weakness it has displayed. After the bombing of the bus in the centre of Tel Aviv, the public were told that the government had abandoned their security.

In the current situation one of the dangers of terrorism that must be taken into account is the real possibility that the terrorist acts of fanatical fundamentalist Muslims and Jews will achieve their immediate goal: to kill the chances of a compromise between Israelis and Palestinians.[15] That goal will be achieved if terror causes people to lose

[14] See, for example, the article by Professor Uriel Procaccia, a professor of law at the Hebrew University and a former chairperson of B'Tselem, calling for revocation of the Landau Commission's recommendations, *Ha'aretz*, 14 September 1994, p. B1.

[15] In dealing with the aims of terror one might have to distinguish between short-term and long-term aims. Destroying the present peace process may be regarded as the short-term aim that leads towards achieving the long-term. This may be the establishment of a fundamentalist state.

faith in the peace process. It is therefore obviously in the interests of both Israelis and Palestinians committed to peace that effective measures be taken to stop the terror.

What kind of measures can be taken to counter terror? Regrettably, lawyers do not have a ready answer to this question. What they must do, however, is to stress that one of the main dangers of terrorism, besides the obvious danger of innocent people losing their lives or being wounded, is that the state will respond with repressive measures that in some cases may be as bad, if not worse, than the terrorist acts themselves.

Repressive measures in response to terrorism face at least two types of criticism. First, such measures are not necessarily effective in combatting terrorism. In fact, they may very well be counter-productive, both in the short and long run. In the present situation, resentment caused by repressive measures against Palestinians may increase both the number of Palestinians who are prepared to resort to terror as well as the number of those who despair of the peace process. Second, measures that are inconsistent with legal values and with human rights standards must be ruled out on grounds of principle.

The vast contemporary literature on terrorism in the democratic state mentions one other type of criticism against repressive measures: that they are likely to undermine the government's legitimacy in the eyes of its own population.[16] It is, of course, doubtful how helpful all this literature is in the situation that concerns us. For while Israel itself is a democratic state, democratic values have had little influence over the way it has ruled the West Bank and Gaza for twenty-seven years as an occupying power. But even if that literature has some bearing on the present situation, the above point of criticism does not hold. As I stressed in the discussion of the measures taken against Israeli terrorists or suspected terrorists, in a situation, such as the present, of ethnic or national conflict, people distinguish between measures taken against the other group and measures taken against themselves. In such a situation, repressive measures against the other side may actually enhance the government's legitimacy in the eyes of its own constituency.

The political leadership in Israel finds itself in a bind. It does not have an operational answer to sporadic acts of terror and can only hope that by pursuing the road to peace the incentive to carry out such acts will eventually be reduced. However, those acts of terror are undermining its authority to do just that. The temptation in such a case is to carry out demonstrative acts that may not deal with the terror itself, but will

16 See P. Wilkinson, *Terror and the Liberal State*, (1977), p. 124; G. Wardlaw, *Political Terrorism, Theory, Tactics and Counter-Measures*, (2nd edn, 1989), p. 70. Other works dealing with the topic include: A. Cassese, *Terrorism, Politics and Law*, (1989); L.B. Weinberg and P.B. Davis, *Introduction to Political Terrorism*, (1989); D.J. Hanle, *Terrorism, The Newest Face of Warfare*, (1989); R.G. Frey and C.W. Morris (eds.), *Violence, Terrorism, and Justice*, (1991).

enhance the government's political authority to continue the peace process. Arguing that such acts are ineffective in combatting the terror, and that they may even aggravate the situation, becomes besides the point. For even if the terror is not contained, the hope is that these measures will at least prevent terror from achieving its political goal.

In such a situation, the only arguments that can be made against repressive measures are those that rely on principle. What are the prospects of such arguments having some influence?

B. The Supreme Court, Legal Values and Domestic Constraints

The reluctance of domestic courts to interfere in security decisions in times of crisis or emergency has been well researched.[17] It is not difficult to find explanations for this reluctance. Courts are not eager to place themselves in a position in which they may be charged with responsibility for harm to security of the state or of the public. In the short-term the decision not to interfere in the decision of another decision-making body is safer than the decision to interfere.[18]

Since soon after the occupation of the West Bank and Gaza began in 1967, the Supreme Court has reviewed the legality of acts carried out there by the authorities. Perceptions of the role this review by the Court has played differ widely. Members of Israel's legal and political establishment generally share the view that the Court has ensured the rule of law in the Occupied Territories.[19] This perception is not shared by many Israeli academics, nor by Palestinian and foreign observers. They take the view that the main function of the Court has been to provide legitimization for the actions of the authorities.[20] A third

17 See Alexander, 'The Illusory Protection of Human Rights by National Courts During Periods of Emergency', 5 *Human Rights Law Journal* 1 (1984); Brennan, Jr., 'The Quest to Develop a Jurisprudence of Civil Liberties in Times of Security Crises', 18 *Israel Yearbook on Human Rights* 11 (1988).

18 This phenomenon is consistent with the tendency of decision-makers who deal with decisions that involve risks to prefer omissions to commissions. See Ritov and Baron, 'Status Quo and Omission Biases', 5 *Journal of Risk and Uncertainty* 49 (1992); Ritov and Baron, 'Reluctance to Vaccinate – Omission Bias and Ambiguity', 3 *Journal of Decision Making* 263 (1990).

19 This perception of judicial review by the Supreme Court rests, first and foremost, on the enormous prestige that the Court enjoys both in Israel itself, and among members of the legal and judicial professions in other countries. It is bolstered by the lack of a precedent for review by courts of an occupying power over acts of the military authorities in occupied territory. Cases in which the Court has actually interfered in decisions of the authorities are also cited as evidence of the legal constraints placed on the authorities through the mechanism of judicial review.

20 Besides general theories about the legitimizing role of law and legal institutions, this perception relies largely on statistical evidence: almost all of the hundreds of judgments relating to the Occupied Territories have been decided in favour of the authorities, sometimes on the basis of highly dubious legal arguments. It is true, indeed, that in a few cases the Court has decided against the authorities. However, these "landmark

perception, shared by members of the defence establishment and some politicians on the right, is that the Court has hampered the freedom of action of the security authorities, thereby impairing the effectiveness of the measures they take to control violence and terror.[21]

Whichever perspective one adopts towards the general function of the Supreme Court of Israel in cases connected with the Occupied Territories, it would be difficult, if not impossible, to substantiate the claim that the Court has in any significant way hampered the discretion of the authorities in employing a wide range of security powers. While the Court has imposed some procedural requirements on the authorities,[22] it has almost without exception bowed to the discretion of the authorities in the use of their wide security powers. The jurisprudence of the Court would therefore seem consistent with the general trend of domestic courts mentioned above.[23]

While the trend of domestic courts is all too clear, another factor enters play. Crises and emergencies end, and when they do it often transpires, even to the judges themselves, that the stand taken by the courts was demanded neither by the law nor by the exigencies of the security situation.[24] As the end of the occupation comes into sight, there was some chance that this would begin to filter through and that there would be a change in direction by the Court. Furthermore, the enactment of the Basic Law: Human Dignity and Freedom in March, 1992, has had an inordinate influence on judicial and legal discourse and there was the possibility that this would have some impact on the Court's approach in cases dealing with the Occupied Territories.

---

cases" only serve to enhance the legitimising function of the Court by reinforcing the "image of the court as an impartial body which boldly challenge[s] the government in pursuit of justice". See R. Shamir, '"Landmark Cases" and the Reproduction of Legitimacy: The Case of Israel's High Court of Justice', 24 *Law and Society Review* 781 (1990), p. 795.

21 As the cases in which the Court has actually interfered in decisions of the military are few and far between, it would be difficult to claim that it has actually prevented the military authorities from using measures that they consider necessary. The negative attitude of Mr. Rabin and like-minded members of the security establishment rests on the notion that the mere accountability of the military before an outside body undermines its authority and that the delays caused by judicial review reduce the deterrent effect of some measures, such as deportations and house demolitions.

22 The most significant requirement is the demand to provide a hearing, and a chance to petition the Court, before demolition of a house under regulation 119 of the Defence Regulations (Emergency), 1945. See *Association for Civil Rights in Israel* v. *Commander of Central Command* 43 (2) P.D. 529 (1989).

23 Defenders of the Court's record always point to a factor that cannot be ignored. While the cases in which the Court has interfered are few and far between, in many cases the authorities have stepped down before a decision was rendered. On some occasions they have done so after a petition was submitted to the Court, because they are reluctant to defend their decisions. In other cases, they have stepped down during the proceedings themselves after the judges have expressed criticism of their position.

24 See Brennan, *The Quest to Develop a Jurisprudence*.

There were indeed some initial signs of change. While the Court had consistently refused to interfere in the demolition of houses as a punitive measure,[25] in the last two years a justice recently appointed to the Court has dissented in two house demolition cases.[26] More significantly, in a decision written by a judge who had previously refused to interfere in many similar cases, the Court unanimously intervened in the decision of the military commander to demolish a house on the grounds that the damage caused to innocent people was disproportional.[27]

On the evening of the suicide bombing of the bus in Tel Aviv, Mr. Rabin gave a press conference that was broadcast on national television. In this broadcast he repeated a theme that he has mentioned on many an occasion: if only the law and the lawyers wouldn't get in his way he could find effective ways of fighting terror.[28] While Mr. Rabin stated that he was not aiming his criticism at the Supreme Court, as that court only applied the law, very few people entertained doubts that the target of his criticism was not only the law, but the Court.

As mentioned above, the failure of the Israeli security services to counter all terrorist acts cannot seriously be attributed to a lack of legal powers or to restraints placed on use of those powers by the Court. Nevertheless, the perception that it is because of the law and the Court that the authorities cannot wage a successful battle against terror is hardly one that the Court would want to encourage. The Court was therefore placed in an unenviable position when ACRI lawyers, representing the family of the terrorist who had been killed by the bomb he carried onto the bus in Tel Aviv, petitioned it to restrain demolition of the family's home.

There is no need to rehearse the legal arguments against the demolition here. In previous cases the Court had dismissed all arguments against demolition of houses based on international law and general principles of Israeli law. However, the Court had never upheld demolition of the house of a person who had been killed, and the main

25 I have elsewhere reviewed the record of the Court on this issue: see Kretzmer, 'Judicial Review Over Demolition and Sealing of Houses in the Occupied Territories' in I. Zamir (ed.), *Klinghoffer Book on Public Law*, (1993), p. 305. And also see Simon, 'The Demolition of Homes in the Israeli Occupied Territories' 19 *Yale Journal of International Law* 1 (1994).

26 See the judgments of Justice M. Cheshin in *Khisrahn* v. *Military Commander* (1991) 46 (ii) P.D. 150; *Alamrin* v. *Military Commander* (1992) 46 (iii) P.D. 693.

27 See the decision of Justice Barak in *Tourkman* v. *Minister of Defence* (unreported decision in H.C. 5510/92).

28 The most revealing statement by Mr. Rabin was one of the explanations he originally offered to the Israeli public for his willingness to hand control over Gaza to the PLO:

I hope that we will find a partner that will be responsible in Gaza for the internal Palestinian problems. It will deal with Gaza without the problems of the High Court of Justice, without the problems of B'tselem and without the problems of all kinds of sensitive souls and all kinds of mothers and fathers. See *Yediot Aharanot*, 3 March 1993, p. 4.

argument was that in such a case it was no longer possible to speak of punishing the perpetrator himself. The demolition should therefore be regarded both as a clear case of collective punishment that is outlawed by international law, as well as an action inconsistent with the notion of human dignity, now constitutionalized by the domestic legal system.[29]

In a four-to-one decision handed down on 17 November 1994, the Court dismissed the petition.[30] I do not intend to analyse the decision itself. Its highly formalistic and technical reasoning does not become a court whose jurisprudence is generally anything but formalistic and technical. The most telling part of the judgment is the section in which the Court deals with the recent decisions in which the one justice had dissented against house demolitions, and the latest case in which the Court itself had intervened to prevent a demolition. The Court stated:

> It is binding precedent that in applying the said sanction great care and reasonable proportionality are required …
>
> All the judges on this Court are concerned that these criteria be met. Against the background of this concern with the seriousness of the damage to outsiders, who had no part in the terrorist's acts, and who could not even have known of his involvement in terrorist activity, we have not hesitated, in every suitable case, to express our position during the course of the proceedings; and our remarks have more than once prompted the security authorities to agree (without waiting for a judicial decision) to moderate the damage to living quarters of others which are in the building that is to be demolished.[31]

Whether the Court realised it or not, this dictum is a sad statement of its position in such cases. Its role is to try and influence the authorities to moderate their actions. It cannot, however, take responsibility for actually interfering in decisions, especially when the authorities claim that the measure will deter terrorist attacks.

Mr. Rabin's attempt to blame the law and the Supreme Court for his inability to combat terror now seems even less persuasive than it was before. My conclusions, however, are no more encouraging than they were in discussing the universalization of human rights values. The hope that law and legal institutions will be able to give adequate protection to human rights in times of national conflict, terror and political instability

---

29 In analyzing the notion of "human dignity" in the Basic Law, Justice Aharon Barak has written: "Human dignity sees a person as an end and not as a means to achieve the ends of others." See Barak, *Interpretation in Law*, (Volume III, Constitutional Interpretation, 1994), p. 421.

30 The dissenting judge was Justice Cheshin, who had dissented in the previous cases. In a moving judgment he stated that the situation was indeed one of war. But he was not an expert in law and could only analyze the case according to the legal principles which he had been taught. He reached the conclusion that while the death of the terrorist did not prevent imposition of the sanction, that sanction could only be applied to the room in which the terrorist had lived. As it was impossible to separate this room from the rest of the house that house could not be demolished.

31 See *Naazal* v. *Military Commander* (unreported decision in H.C. 6026/94), p. 9.

is not very bright. This is not a reason to give up the attempt to use them to achieve that goal. It is, however, one more reason for finding every possible avenue to make sure that the road to peace is not abandoned.

6. The Draft Basic Law for the Palestinian NationalAuthority During the Transitional Period

Anis Al-Qasem

Introduction

The decision to have and enact a Basic Law for the emerging Palestinian authority was taken by the Palestine National Council (PNC) immediately after its approval of the Declaration of Independence and the Political Statement on 15 November 1988.

The Declaration of Independence meant the emergence of the Palestinian State, which was later recognised by about one hundred states, and the political statement meant the starting of a political process which, it was hoped, would lead to the effective exercise of sovereign powers in the Occupied Territories. This would have become possible through the implementation of Security Council Resolution 242 and the consequent withdrawal of Israeli troops from the West Bank and the Gaza Strip.

The need would then arise for a Basic Law so that the new entity would start in an organised manner. In anticipation of such an eventuality and because of the logistic and financial difficulties often met in holding sessions of the PNC, I proposed a motion under which the PNC would authorise the Central Council to approve a Basic Law for the new State of Palestine.

The Central Council, which consists of about 100 members (compared with 430 PNC membership) elected by the PNC from amongst its members and which was created by a special resolution of the PNC, could meet and act more quickly and would afford greater opportunity for discussion. Mr Arafat, the PLO Chairman, opposed the motion on the grounds that it was not necessary at that moment in time. However, I refused to withdraw it and insisted on putting it to the vote. The motion was carried by a large majority, despite the dissenting vote of the Chairman.

I. Constitutional History

The operative constitutional history of Palestine in recent times can be divided into the following phases:[1]

A. the Ottoman Caliphate;
B. the British Mandate;
C. the period between 1948 to 1967;
D. Israeli Occupation.

A. The Ottoman Caliphate

Prior to 1917, when British forces occupied Palestine in the course of the First World War, the country formed part of the Ottoman Caliphate. Its inhabitants were Ottoman citizens with the full rights of citizenship accorded by the Constitutions of 1876 and 1908. The two constitutions recognised the right of every Ottoman citizen to elect and be elected to national representation in the Ottoman parliament. Palestinians elected their representatives and participated fully in the political life of the Caliphate in the same manner and to the same extent as other Ottoman citizens. As part of the Caliphate, Palestine, like Turkey itself, did not have sovereign political status or its own independent constitution: its constitution was that of the Caliphate itself.[2]

B. The British Mandate

This phase started with the British military occupation in 1917 and ended with the surrender by Britain of its mandate and its departure on 14 May 1948. The British rule over Palestine was marked by the deprivation of the Palestinians of the political rights they enjoyed and exercised while citizens of the Ottoman Caliphate. This is a tragic reflection on the first contact between Palestine and a Western democracy in modern times. In 1922, Britain, as the mandatory power in pursuance of a mandate given to it by the Council of the League of Nations on 24 July 1922, enacted a constitution for Palestine in the form of an Order-in-Council entitled "The Palestine Order-in-Council, 1922". Under that Order-in-Council, the Government of Palestine was entrusted to a High Commissioner to be appointed by the King of the United Kingdom, assisted by an Executive Council appointed by the British Government.

---

[1] For a discussion of the development of the legal system in Palestine, see Anis F. Kassim, 'Legal Systems and Developments in Palestine', 1 *Palestine Yearbook of Int'l Law* 19 (1984).
[2] Henry Cattan, *The Palestine Question*, (1988), pp. 7-8.

Part III of the Order provided for the establishment of a Legislative Council "[f]rom and after a date to be fixed by the High Commissioner". That date was never fixed. The Palestinians protested against the composition of the Council and its powers. The Council was to consist of twenty-two members in addition to the High Commissioner, of whom ten would be "official" members and twelve "unofficial" ones. The ten official members were members of the Executive Council, who were all British heads of departments appointed to implement the Balfour Declaration on the creation in Palestine of a Jewish national home. The twelve unofficial members were to be elected in accordance with such Order-in-Council or Ordinance or other legislative enactment as may from time to time provide for elections to the Council. In pursuance of this provision, the mandatory power have departed from democratic principles and apportioned the twelve seats on a sectarian basis, with the result that when Jewish representation was added to the official members, a clear majority would be obtained in support of the Zionist programme for Palestine: the rights and interests of the vast majority of the population, the Palestinian Arabs, would suffer and their views would not be given any weight. The Palestinians rejected the election formula and no elections were ever held, despite British promises to reconsider.

The powers of the Legislative Council did not cover legislation in general. The Council could legislate "for the peace, order and good government of Palestine". Even with such limited legislative powers, "[n]o Ordinance shall take effect until either the High Commissioner shall have assented thereto and shall have signed the same in token of such assent, or until the assent of His Majesty thereto has been given by Order-in-Council or through a Secretary of State".

All of this represented a retrogressive step for the Palestinian experience of democratic institutions and constitutional government. It is instructive to note that the Order-in-Council did not contain any specific provisions guaranteeing civil or political rights. It was only concerned that no Ordinance passed by the proposed Legislative Council should "restrict complete freedom of conscience and the free exercise of all forms of worship, save in so far as is required for the maintenance of public order and morals; or which shall tend to discriminate in any way between the inhabitants of Palestine on the ground of race, religion or language". The whole term of the British mandate was characterised by the imposition of the most oppressive emergency regulations which strangled the civil and political rights of the Palestinian population and which were utilised by the Israelis during their occupation of the West Bank and the Gaza Strip to violate the human rights of the Palestinians. Thus the British mandate ended with the destruction of the civil and political rights enjoyed by and guaranteed to the Palestinians under the Ottoman constitution, coupled with the danger to their very national and physical existence.

C. The Period between 1948 to 1967

The British Government referred the question as to the future of Palestine to the United Nations and on 29 November 1947 the General Assembly, by resolution 181(II), recommended a Plan of Partition dividing the country into two states: one Arab and one Jewish with an economic union. The British Government declared its intention to withdraw from Palestine by 14 May 1948, and on 15 May Israel was created. The 1948 war ended with Israel occupying more land than that allotted to it under the Partition Plan. The remainder of Palestine, the areas which have become known as the Gaza Strip and the West Bank, fell under Egyptian and Jordanian occupation respectively. A new chapter in the constitutional history of Palestine was opened.

1. The Gaza Strip

Egyptian administration of the Gaza Strip started on 26 May 1948. At first, the Order-in-Council of 1922 was legislatively retained with the authority of government vested in an Egyptian administrative governor. The complete break with the constitutional past came on 29 March 1962 when a constitutional Basic Law, promulgated by the Egyptian President, Gamal Abdul Nasser, came into force and replaced the British Order-in-Council of 1922.

The 1962 Basic Law provided for a Governor General, an Executive Council, a Legislative Assembly and an independent judiciary. The Governor General was to be appointed by the Egyptian President and was always an Egyptian high ranking officer. He was to promulgate laws passed by the Legislative Assembly, with a right of veto over such legislation. However, a law vetoed by him would become law if, after its return to the Legislative Assembly, it was passed by three quarters of the Assembly's members. A provision of this kind is not unusual even in permanent constitutions of independent states.

The Executive Council was to consist of the Governor General, his deputy, and nine heads of department. The Deputy Governor General and the heads of department were to be appointed by the Egyptian Minister of War. Throughout Egyptian administration of the Strip, no Palestinian was appointed as head of department. Palestinians were thus not given the opportunity to exercise and gain experience at ministerial level. There was nothing in the 1962 Basic Law which would have prevented such an appointment, but it was not made.

The Legislative Assembly comprised (1) the Governor General, as Chairman, (2) members of the Executive Council, (3) twenty-two members elected by the local committees of a newly created single party called the Palestinian Arab National Union in Gaza (PANU) and ten more members of recognised ability chosen by the Governor General who qualified for nomination to local committees of PANU. These thirty-two members were Palestinians and thus a Palestinian majority was numerically guaranteed: the passage of legislation, despite the veto, was also guaranteed. Under this 1962 Basic Law, all Palestinians were ipso facto members of PANU, and, theoretically, all would have participated in the election of the local committees which would choose the 22 members of the Assembly, and the other ten would have had the qualifications for nomination to the local committees. It was a complicated system of indirect representation in line with a single party system, which was the same system applicable at the time in Egypt itself.

No laws would be enacted which were not passed by the Legislative Assembly and endorsed by the Governor General. The Assembly was thus a proper legislative body. However, no constitutional powers were given to the Assembly in respect of the Executive Council or the Governor General. Neither would require the approval of or could be removed by the Assembly. The presence of the Governor General as Chairman of the Assembly would not encourage, constitutionally, independence of the legislature. However, Egyptian benign rule which was characterised by the consensus of the population made these legal niceties inconsequential.

Basic human rights were, to a good measure, provided for. The protection of human rights was further guaranteed by a tradition of an independent judiciary and a public prosecution service staffed by Egyptian judges and public prosecutors and the High Court retained its jurisdiction over the review of administrative acts. In fact, Palestinian Gazans under Egyptian administration enjoyed a larger measure of human rights than their Egyptian counterparts in Egypt itself, and were able to gain some measure of constitutional experience denied to them under British rule.

2. The West Bank

As with Egypt in the Gaza Strip, Jordan did not start its administration of the West Bank as a belligerent occupier. It enacted various pieces of legislation which gave the King the powers entrusted to the King of the United Kingdom and the High Commissioner for Palestine under the Palestine Order-in-Council. A military governor was appointed to administer the territory, assisted by Palestinian deputies. Some Palestinian notables held a conference in Jericho on 1 December 1948 and resolved to petition the King of Jordan to unify both banks of the River Jordan in one state. On 24 April 1950, both houses of the Jordanian parliament adopted a resolution formally responding to the petition, and from that date the West Bank was incorporated into the Hashemite Kingdom of Jordan, and Palestinian residents of the West Bank became Jordanian citizens.

As citizens of the Kingdom, Palestinians became subject to the Jordanian constitution and enjoyed in law all the rights of Jordanian citizenship. Membership of both houses of Parliament was equally divided between the two banks and Palestinians were appointed to the Council of Ministers mainly on the basis of equality in numbers, though the office of Prime Minister was rarely occupied by a Palestinian. General and municipal elections were held in both banks and political parties were active. At that time, Jordan had not adopted a one party system, and in fact never did. Palestinians were active in all political parties.

Palestinians in the Hashemite Kingdom of Jordan gained experience and sophistication in constitutional and political activities, though they were resentful of the concentration of power in the hands of the Monarchy. Nevertheless, their experience in government, at all levels, exceeded that of the Palestinian Gazans who never occupied ministerial positions or conducted foreign affairs. Certainly, they enjoyed more rights than under the British mandate.

D. Israeli Occupation

Palestinian constitutional development was severely arrested under the Israeli occupation of both the Gaza Strip and the West Bank in 1967. Israel came as a belligerent occupier with a political agenda which was diametrically opposed to the rights and interests of the Palestinians in the remainder of Palestine. Israeli military governors were entrusted with legislative, executive and judicial powers. Israel showed no respect for the Fourth Geneva Convention and was frequently condemned by the Security Council, the General Assembly and other organs of the United Nations for its violations of the Convention and the human rights of the Palestinians. The rule of law suffered considerably and Israeli courts failed to provide protection. The emergency regulations of the British mandate were revived and vigorously applied. Although occupation is still there and has lasted for 27 years, no Israeli attempts were made at the revival of constitutional institutions which previously existed or at the building of alternative genuine institutions. Israel even suspended the only form of election which it first allowed: municipal elections. The creation of a Palestinian National Authority, in pursuance of the Oslo Declaration of Principles of 1993, is a first tentative step in the right direction. However, there is no certainty as to the future, and Israel has yet to recognise the right of self-determination for the Palestinian people which would permit them to build with confidence their institutions in the West Bank and Gaza.

II. Palestinian Independent Constitutional Attempts

Neither under the British mandate nor in the Gaza Strip under the Egyptians or in the West Bank under the Jordanians did Palestinians have a role in the creation of the constitutional system which governed them. However, in 1948 and 1964 they attempted to do that: first through the ill-fated All Palestine Government and second through the Palestine Liberation Organisation (PLO). The third is, of course, through the Draft Basic Law, which is the main subject of this paper.

A. The All Palestine Government

The failure to prevent the creation of Israel and the Palestinians' need to express themselves as a government of the whole Palestinian territory prompted the Arab High Committee, which at that time represented the Palestinian people, to convene a national conference in Gaza on the 2nd and 3rd of October 1948. Attendants were representatives of various Palestinian organisations, activists in the political field, notables and professionals. The conference resolved to establish an All Palestine Government and adopted a Provisional Law for that Government.

The Provisional Law consists of eighteen Articles in all. It declared that it was "provisional" and would apply until a constituent assembly was elected to enact a constitution for the country and to choose the form of government. Under the Provisional Law, the All Palestine Government was to be composed of: (1) a national assembly, (2) a council of ministers and (3) a supreme council.

Pending the elections, the national assembly was to consist of members representing the various bodies and individuals invited to attend the conference. No definition is given as to the powers of the assembly, but, probably, it was intended to be a parliament. Since the assembly did not conduct any activity other than the approval of the Provisional Law, one cannot evaluate its role with any certainty.

The supreme council was to consist of three members: the chairman of the national assembly, the prime minister and the president of the supreme court. The council was envisaged as a collegiate head of state, with similar powers.

Under the Provisional Law, the All Palestine Government was to exercise power over all mandated Palestine, which would include that part declared as Israel. The creation of the All Palestine Government implied an expression of refusal to recognise the state of Israel.

A judiciary, independent from both the legislative and executive organs of government, is provided for. There is no reference to basic rights and fundamental freedoms. These were not the main pre-occupation of the attendants who were more concerned about the national rights and very existence of their people.

The Government exercised no authority over the Palestinian territory, the Gaza Strip and the West Bank, which was in Arab hands. Differences among Arab states had precluded such assumption of authority. Its main visible achievement was the issue of passports to

Palestinians who needed them. Such passports were, at the time, recognised by some Arab states. The unification of the West Bank with Jordan in 1950, eroded further its theoretical authority. The 1962 Egyptian constitution for Gaza gave no role to that government in the administration of the Strip, although Egypt treated it as Palestinian territory and its inhabitants as Palestinian citizens. Even the seat of government was in Cairo and not on Palestinian territory. Its representatives attended meetings of the League of Arab States of which Palestine was a full member. However, it failed to influence the course of events and contributed little to Palestinian constitutional developments or experience, and passed away with the death of its first and last head of government, Ahmad Hilmi, in 1963.

B. The Palestine Liberation Organisation (PLO)

The demise of the All Palestine Government left the Palestinians without a recognised body to represent them and to pursue their rights. The first summit of Arab Heads of State, which was held on 13-16 January 1964, resolved "to establish a Palestinian entity which would express the will of the Palestinian people and create a body which would pursue its rights". The summit charged a well-known Palestinian lawyer, Ahmad Shuqairi, who had distinguished himself as representative of Syria at the United Nations and who had been appointed to represent Palestine within the League of Arab States, with the duty of contacting Palestinians in their places of concentration in order to establish a body which would speak for them and work for the liberation of their country. Shuqairi's efforts and visits led to the convening of a conference in Jerusalem (which at that time was still in Arab hands) on 28 May 1964. The conference was attended by 397 invitee-participants amongst whom were notables, ministers, parliamentarians, mayors, members of village councils, members of the legislative assembly of Gaza, heads of chambers of commerce and representatives of various professional organisations, trade unions, diaspora Palestinians and refugee camps. The conference adopted a declaration announcing the creation of the PLO,[3] the Palestine National Covenant and the PLO Basic Law. It elected Ahmad Shuqairi as Chairman of the Executive Committee of the PLO provided for in the Basic Law and authorised him to select the 14 members of the Committee. The conference further decided that it would be the Palestine National Council provided for in the PLO Basic Law until elections were held for the membership of the Council.

---

[3] The declaration was drafted by Raji Sahyun, Dr. Muhammed Khalil and the writer and was adopted by acclamation.

The National Covenant expressed the commitment of the Palestinian people to the liberation of their country, the methods to achieve that objective and other matters of national, Arab and international importance in connection with the Palestine question. The Covenant, as approved, consisted of 29 Articles and was intended as the most binding document in modern Palestinian history.

The PLO Basic Law forms an annex to the Covenant as part thereof. Under its provisions, all Palestinians are deemed members of the PLO. The PLO is their home and representative. Under its provisions, the institutions of the PLO are: the Palestine National Council (PNC), the Executive Committee and the Palestine National Fund.

The PNC stands as the highest organ of the PLO constitutional institutions. It is the Palestinian Parliament in Exile. Its members were to be elected in accordance with an electoral regulation to be made by the Executive Committee. After the formation of the PLO, Shuqairi sought the agreement of the various Arab governments where Palestinians resided to arrange for the holding of elections. None gave its consent, and in consequence thereof, a formula was agreed between the PNC Bureau, the Executive Committee and the constituent organisations as to membership. All liberation organisations, professional organisations, trade unions, refugee camps, in addition to independents and diaspora Palestinians are represented within it.

As the highest organ, the PNC lays down the general PLO policy; it elects the Chairman and members of the Executive Committee and Chairman of the Palestine National Fund who, on election, becomes a member of the Executive Committee. During its sessions which, under the PLO Basic Law are to be held annually, the PNC can establish such committees as it deems necessary. By resolution, the PNC, in its seventeenth session of November 1984, created ten permanent committees to which matters can be referred by the Executive Committee, through the President of the PNC. The most active of these committees has been the Legal Committee.

The logistical and financial problems faced in holding regular annual meetings of the PNC, prompted it, in the same 17th session, to create a Central Council to which the Executive Committee reports and which takes binding decisions in all matters referred to it. However, this Council cannot appoint or dismiss members of the Executive Committee, amend the Covenant or deal with the budget. It has about 100 members elected by the PNC from its membership, this number to include members of the Executive Committee and the Chairmen of the ten permanent committees.

The PNC is autonomous and independent from the various organisations which are members. It does not lay down their policies and is not involved in any manner in their activities nor is it responsible for these activities. It is not bound by any agreements concluded by or between them, and the Legal Committee has refused to sanction or recommend to the PNC the implementation of agreements concluded between major organisations which were found in contravention of the PLO Basic Law or the Internal Regulations of the PNC.

The establishment of the PNC saw the growth of parliamentary experience and traditions, and the appearance of political pluralism and parliamentary opposition. The Chairman of the PNC and his deputies, who are elected by the members, have consistently guaranteed freedom of speech to all members, and criticism of the PLO Chairman has often been voiced in strong terms. Through strict observance of the Basic Law and the Internal Rules of the PNC, sometimes in extremely difficult conditions, as was the case regarding quorum and issues raised during the Amman session in 1984, the beginnings of attention to and observance of the rule of law was witnessed in the workings of the PNC.[4] It should be recalled that the PLO is perhaps the only liberation movement which, from its inception, has bound itself by public institutions and publicly known rules. Sessions of the PNC have always been public, something unknown for liberation organisations. Palestinians have gained much parliamentary experience through membership of the PNC, have accepted the existence of opposition as a valid exercise of the right to freedom of speech and pluralism in the exercise of the right to free association and free speech.

The Executive Committee is the PLO's council of ministers. Its members are elected and dismissed by the PNC before whom it is jointly and severally responsible. Each member heads a department and carries out the responsibilities of his department.

Amendment of the National Covenant and the PLO Basic Law are intentionally made difficult in order to insure that such amendment has the support of a substantive majority. Approval of two thirds of the total PNC membership is required. Moreover, in order to prevent any group and its supporters from dominating the PNC, the quorum is also placed as high as two thirds.

The PLO has had its ups and downs, but it has succeeded, through its institutions, in preserving Palestinian identity, in struggling for Palestinian rights and in shifting the Palestine cause from being a refugee cause to being a struggle for nationhood and national independence. It achieved international recognition and status and was the first ever liberation movement to be given Observer status at the

---

4 In that session, which was boycotted by opposition organisations, a petition, in accordance with PNC rules, was presented for the termination of the membership of those involved in armed conflict with PLO forces in the Lebanon in 1982, 1983. The Legal Committee insisted on full observance of the rules on termination which required notice to challenged members of the change and an opportunity to defend themselves, and that a two thirds majority of total PNC members must approve the termination. The debate on the report of the Committee was the longest in the history of the PNC and was finally adopted by a large majority. Membership of the PNC was thus safeguarded to afford complete freedom of opinion.

United Nations and to participate in Security Council debates. Ultimately, the PLO was recognised by Israel as being the party with the representative authority to deal with in solving the Palestine problem, something which was previously anathema to the Israeli establishment.

III. The Draft Basic Law for the National Authority

A. The Need for a Basic Law

As mentioned previously, the PNC resolved on 15 November 1988 to authorise the Central Council to enact a Basic Law. The need for a Basic Law at this stage has been questioned by some Palestinians whose views deserve high respect. In an interview given to the Arabic magazine *al-*Watan al-Arabi of 4 March 1994, Dr Anis F. Kassim raised the question in the on-going debate about the Draft within the Palestinian community. The need has arisen not simply because a new state is being born, but also because of the legal heritage the new entity will succeed to. During the periods of the Ottoman Caliphate and under British mandate, the two territories destined to form the territory of the new Palestinian state, the Gaza Strip and the West Bank, formed part of one political entity with the same constitution and laws. However, from 1948, they separated: the Gaza Strip fell under Egyptian administration while the West Bank became, as of 1950, part of the Hashemite Kingdom of Jordan. The constitutional position had changed: the West Bank became subject to the Jordanian constitution and the Gaza Strip, as of 1962, became subject to its own constitution which was enacted by the Egyptian President and which entrusted powers to him, to the Egyptian Minister of War, to a General Governor, to an Executive Council respectively appointed by them and to a Legislative Assembly which was to be elected in a particular manner. During this period of separation, laws were enacted by the respective legislative authorities. The constitutional and legal situations were no longer the same. Then came Israeli occupation which, in both administration and legislation, maintained the separateness of the two entities.

When a new Palestine is to be created, that complex situation has to be attended to. The various authorities of the state have to be redefined on a unitary basis. A transition law which, for example, may attempt to apply to the new entity the 1962 Gaza constitution would in effect amount to a new Basic Law. There would be the need to transfer powers from the Egyptian President and Egyptian Minister of War to new Palestinian counterparts, the office of the Governor General would have to be thought out and would cease to exist, and the Legislative Assembly would have to be reconsidered and re-defined both as to membership and constitution. For example, the Governor General, who was under the 1962 constitution the head of the Executive, is also the Chairman of the Legislative Assembly. Within the PLO constitutional structure a successful struggle was waged, as early as the second session in 1965, to separate the office of the Chairman of the PNC from that of the Chairman of the Executive Committee, and it would be a retrogressive step to combine the two offices in one person. Rules for the governing of an independent state, which were not attended to under Egyptian administration, would have to be introduced. By its terms, the 1962 Gazan constitution was naturally limited to Gaza. Territorial extension of application would thus become necessary. A similar exercise would have to be undertaken if the constitutional situation prevailing in the West Bank were to be amended and territorially extended.

In 1948, it was a relatively simple legal exercise for the Egyptian and Jordanian governments to legislate the transfer of the exercise of powers from the King of the United Kingdom and the High Commissioner for Palestine under the Palestine Order-in-Council of 1922 to appropriate Egyptian and Jordanian authorities. It was also equally simple for the Israelis to transfer power from the Egyptians and Jordanians. However, like everything else, it will not be that simple for the Palestinians. First, there is the need to reunify the two areas into one single constitutional entity. Secondly, there are in existence Palestinian constitutional institutions which encompass and represent the whole Palestinian people through the institutions of the PLO, and the transfer of powers would not fit neatly within these institutions. Thirdly, neither previous constitutional arrangement would be suitable for the new situation. For example, there would be no place for a governor general as provided under the 1962 Gazan constitution, and therefore, the whole chapter on that office as well as any references to it would have to go. That would leave the head of the executive and of the legislature unprovided for, although the former office is held by the President and the second is separate from it under the PLO constitution and PLO resolutions. Under PLO constitutional arrangements, the national authority which is to exercise executive power within the unified Palestinian areas is to be appointed by the PLO Executive Committee, while the Executive Council under the 1962 Gazan constitution was appointable by the Egyptian Minister of War, and that competence has to be transferred. The Legislative Assembly would have to be entirely re-organised, and, for the time being, its powers transferred to another organ within Palestinian constitutionality. And so on. The cleanest and most direct solution which could also remedy some shortcomings and fill in constitutional gaps would be to act within Palestinian constitutionality and enact a new Basic Law which would tie-up with Palestinian constitutionality, reflect the new realities, Palestinian experiences, developed political thinking and the world revolution regarding human rights and their protection. A law, and there must be a law, of transfer of powers and constitutionality would not be the simple or good answer.

B. Preparation

The Draft Basic Law for the National Authority during the Transitional Period (the Draft) has not been the first attempt at drafting a Palestinian constitutional document. In 1974, when the PNC offered, as a demo cratic solution to the Palestine problem, the establishment in the whole of mandate Palestine of a democratic secular non-sectarian state in which Palestinians and Israelis would enjoy equal rights, I was asked by the PLO leadership to prepare a draft constitution expressive of that offer. The draft was prepared, but shelved because of Israeli rejection of even considering the solution. I still think that that would have been the best solution. Both peoples would have satisfied their ideology of treating Palestine as their country, they would live together in peace without one claiming the destruction of the other party and their special requirements could have been met within a loose constitutional form.

After the Declaration of Independence and the adoption of a resolution authorising the enactment of a Basic Law and charging the PLO Executive Committee with the powers of government pending the appointment of such government by the Central Council and the election of Mr Arafat as President, members of the Central Council, and particularly the opposition, frequently raised the question of a government law. A number of drafts were prepared setting out a government organisation.[5] Those drafts were communicated to the Executive Committee member in charge of legal matters, Jamal Sourani, for the consideration of the leadership and the Committee. However, those attempts failed to produce any tangible result and were never presented to the Central Council.

The Madrid Conference and Palestinian-Israeli negotiations created the possibility of a two state solution, of which Palestine would be one. Work was started on the basis of a fully fledged Palestine state. However, that was also shelved because of the agreement resulting in the Declaration of Principles (DoP) between the PLO and the Israeli government signed in Washington on 13 September 1993. The DoP provided for a transitional period, the appointment of a Palestinian National Authority to which powers would be transferred and for

---

5 His Honour Eugene Cotran, a colleague and compatriot, English barrister and presently Circuit Judge, volunteered his assistance and has generously given time and effort to help in the preparation of these drafts. After the preparation of the first draft of the Basic Law, he continued his contribution with devotion, responsibility and learning. While any shortcomings can only be mine, the credit must be shared by him.

elections to a Council which would have legislative and executive powers.

Following the signing of the DoP and at a number of meetings of the Executive Committee with the original negotiating team, the question of government organisation was raised. At meetings which I attended as Chairman of the PNC Legal Committee, I advanced the view that a Basic Law should be passed in pursuance of the resolution of the PNC which had anticipated such possible developments. The suggestion was approved at an Executive Committee meeting in November 1993 and I was asked to start the process.

A first draft was prepared and presented to the Executive Committee at its meeting on 5 December 1993. The Draft received a first reading, and Chairman Arafat proposed its circulation to all organisations for study and comment in preparation for a second reading. Before the meeting, accompanied by Mr Sourani, I had a private meeting with Chairman Arafat to brief him on some aspects of the Draft, particularly those dealing with the office of President. For some time, the question of the term of the President has been raised at meetings of the Central Council, with no conclusive results. The Draft offered an opportunity to tackle the problem. It provided that the term would be five years and that no person may hold the office for more than two successive terms. I expected opposition because such provision represented a fundamental departure from the prevailing constitutional situation in the Arab states, and the PLO Basic Law did not attend to the matter. Mr Sourani, who supported the proposed provision, also supported my presentation. We told Mr Arafat, who showed some initial reluctance, that a true leader would think of the future of his people and would leave them institutions which would protect them from the rise of dictatorship through the manipulation of constitutional provisions, such as the absence of a provision which does not limit the chances of re-election. A responsible leader would not fashion a constitution to his measurement because there is no certainty that those who would follow would be as significant, and constitutions which were formulated on personal considerations had failed in the protection of the people from disguised or open dictatorship. Mr Arafat indicated his agreement. At that same meeting of the Executive Committee, Mr Arafat also suggested that I hold a meeting of the PNC Legal Committee to consider the Draft. The difficulty of holding meetings of PNC committees has been financial because members have to come from a number of countries. However, a meeting of the Legal Committee in the circumstances was justified.

On 10 December 1993, the meeting of the Legal Committee was held in Amman. Some prominent Palestinian lawyers in Amman were also invited to attend. The meeting considered the Draft, suggested some amendments and left the door open for further amendments in the light of comments received as a result of the circulation of the Draft. The Draft was published in December 1993 in a Jerusalem newspaper. The publication created the anticipated general public interest since it was the first time in the history of Arab legislation that a constitutional document was published for public comment before enactment. The policy of publication for comment was intended to provide a radical departure from the tradition of secret legislation practised not only by overnight legislation in some Arab countries but also from the persistent Israeli practice of enacting military orders only to be seen on sudden application before an Israeli military tribunal trying a Palestinian for an offence created by a secret Israeli military order.

As a result of the publication and circulation of the Draft, I started receiving comments, verbal and written. Palestinian women's organisations sent a long memorandum regarding women's rights. In particular, they raised a question as to the non-reference in the Draft to equality of rights between men and women. The Draft was developing rapidly into a second draft.

I received an invitation from the Jerusalem Media and Communication Centre (JMCC), a Palestinian NGO based in Jerusalem, to participate in a conference they organised on 4 February 1994 regarding the challenges of the transitional period to Palestinian society. I was to address the conference on the Draft. It had been thirty years since I had been to Jerusalem. The last time I had been there was in 1964 when I attended the meeting which created the PLO and chaired the committee which prepared the National Covenant and the PLO Basic Law. I hesitated, but accepted because it was necessary to hear the views of our people in the Occupied Territories directly and to explain to them the document which had already been published in Jerusalem, translated into English and circulated by the JMCC.

I attended the conference, presented the Draft and listened to comments most of which concerned the powers of the President, as will be explained below. Palestinian dailies, *al-Quds* and *al-Nahar*, of 5 February 1994, gave full reports of the proceedings and my intervention and *al-Nahar* published on the same day the full text of the second Draft. On 6 February, I gave a lecture on the Draft to the students and faculty of the Jerusalem Law College and again that was fully covered the next day by the above-mentioned two dailies. On the same day I held two independent meetings with a number of judges and members of the legal profession in the West Bank and Gaza. On 8th February, I had a long meeting with representatives of Palestinian women's organisations and discussed their concerns. On 11th February, *The Jerusalem Post* published a long interview in its supplement "News In Focus", and, on the same day *The Jerusalem Times* published its own interview. Interviews were given to Israeli TV, to the Arabic radio service, whose report was quoted in the London-based Arabic daily *al-Quds-al-Arabi* on 5, 6 and 9 February 1994, as well as to outside TV services and foreign correspondents. Western consular missions in Jerusalem showed clear interest in the matter and I was invited to meet the Consul Generals of the United Kingdom, the United States and France. The German Embassy in Tel Aviv sent two of its members to meet me in Jerusalem. Intentionally, I did not try to meet any Israeli official, and none contacted me. For me, the subject was entirely a Palestinian affair which did not call for any Israeli input or approval. I left Jerusalem on 12 February back to my base in London to digest the fruits of my mission.

The Chairman of the Judicial Committee, an ad hoc committee formed by Mr Arafat to consider the future of the judiciary, sent the comments of the committee on the section dealing with the judiciary. I travelled to Tunis on 3 April 1994 to meet him and discuss. We agreed on the amendments. We met Mr Arafat with the Acting Chairman of the PNC and told them that the Draft was almost ready. By 1 May 1994 consultations were concluded and the third Draft was ready. Mr Cotran and I translated it into English, and I sent both the Arabic and English translation to the Jerusalem Media and Communication Centre in Jerusalem for publication in Jerusalem. They published the Draft in their occasional document series as No 1, June 1994.[6]

It was the agreed plan that once the stage of consultation was completed, a meeting of the Central Council would be held to consider it. That meeting has not been held to date, and the Draft remains a draft. However, it has started affecting Palestinian life. It has been relied upon to protest against violations of human rights, and the oath taken by President Arafat was the oath set out in the Draft. A conference has been organised for 8 December 1994, this time in Nablus, the largest Palestinian town in the West Bank, by another Palestinian NGO, the Center for Palestine Research and Studies (CPRS), solely to consider the Draft and the proposed elections plans, and I was invited to speak about the Draft.[7]

C. Main Features of the Draft

1. The Draft and the Elected Council

The Draft is intended for the transitional period, and not as a permanent constitution, although it has some features of such a constitution. The transitional period draws a line at the proposed general elections. The Draft took note of that line. It recognised that when elections take place, the elected body would be the appropriate body to determine a number of important issues and should not be bound by some predetermined positions taken before the elections. Since the British mandate, the Palestinians have been denied the right to elect their national

---

[6] See Annex to this Chapter, p. 137, post.

[7] A Committee consisting of the writer, Judge Eugene Cotran and prominent lawyers from the West Bank and Gaza are now considering a Fourth Draft especially in the light of the Interim Agreement set out in the Appendix, p. 271, post.

representatives, and it would not be an encouraging beginning for the first elected body to find itself bound by a form of government not having been approved by it. The Draft concentrated therefore on matters necessary for the first part of the transitional period before the emergence of the elected body and on such matters as have been of concern to Palestinians or those which are the subject of consensus. Nevertheless, even these provisions can be amended by the elected body, in accordance with Article 7(2) of the Draft, which provides:

> Subject to Articles 48 and 106, this Basic Law may not be amended except by a two thirds majority of the elected legislature.

Article 48, which will be discussed shortly, provides:

> The Legislature shall lay down its rules of procedure and shall prescribe the rules relating to the enactment of laws and its relationship with the Executive Authority and the formation of the Government and such laws shall be treated as a sequel to this Basic Law.

And Article 106 provides:

> None of the fundamental rights and freedoms enshrined in this Basic Law may be suspended, and such rights and freedoms shall remain governed by the provisions of this Basic Law and the laws enacted in pursuance thereof.

The elected Council is conceived under the Draft as marking an important juncture in constitutional development and exercise of powers, and that is reflected in important provisions. Under Article 47, the Council of National Authority (CNA) is to exercise legislative power until the election of the Legislature, in which event legislative authority would be exercised by the Legislature. Under Article 58(2) the CNA is to continue in office until the first elections and thereafter in a caretaker capacity until a government is formed in accordance with the law, rules and regulations to be established in that regard by the Legislature in accordance with Article 48. The elected Council is therefore called upon, as one of its first tasks, to consider the Draft, amend where amendment is necessary with the majority required and set out the rules of government. The anticipation is that the elections would be free and open to all the political forces within the Palestinian community. In that event, it is only proper that such a Council should be given the power to organise the system of government for the remainder of the transitional period.

2. General Provisions

The General Provisions of the Draft in Chapter One deal with matters about which there is general consensus amongst Palestinians. It was necessary to assert that the Palestinian people are the source of all authority which, during the transitional period, is to be exercised by the authorities and in the manner provided for in the Draft (Article 1). In view of Israeli allegations and past constitutional history, this provision removes any ambiguity as to sovereignty, the source of authority and the authorities in the transitional period in whom the authority to govern is vested.

Article 2 reiterates the form of government to which the Palestinians have committed themselves in the Declaration of Independence of 1988. It provides for parliamentary democracy and pluralism "with consideration by the majority for the rights and interests of the minority and respect by the minority of the decisions of the majority". I believe this is the first time that consideration for the rights and interests of the minority is constitutionally provided for in this manner. A democracy is not a democracy if simply based on numerical majorities and such majority can disregard the rights and interests of the minority. Article 3 makes it clear that, for the Palestinians, Arabic, which is their language, is the official language of Palestine. There is nothing in the Draft which would infringe on the right of people to use the language of their choice in their private relations, in schools, in publications or otherwise. Article 4 describes the traditional Palestinian flag.

Article 5 declares Jerusalem as the capital of Palestine. In the first draft, no such reference to a capital was made, and the question was raised and settled during my visit to Jerusalem. Jerusalem, under the DoP, was made subject to negotiations during the transitional period. In spite of that provision, the Israeli government kept insisting on a position which took no note of the DoP stipulation. In the circumstances, it was felt necessary to assert the Palestinian position which has never been challenged except by Israel, while Israeli claim to Jerusalem has been rejected by the Security Council and General Assembly resolutions which treated Jerusalem as occupied territory, even after the signing of the DoP. This provision was highlighted by the media and particularly by a report from Jerusalem by the Associated Press correspondent in Jerusalem, Mr Ghazali, who, on 27 May 1994, conducted a telephone interview with me and sent out his dispatch. The subject was taken up by the media and I was interviewed as if it was the first time that the Palestinians have declared their position on Jerusalem.

Article 6 deals with sovereignty over natural resources. It has followed the lines of the UN Declaration on the subject adopted on 14th December 1962 by the General Assembly. Because of unlawful Israeli exploitation of Palestinian waters and their claim to share in such waters, it has become necessary to re-assert Palestinian sovereignty over their natural resources.

Article 7 is important for judicial review. It declares null and void legislation which is inconsistent with the provisions of the Basic Law. As will be seen in Chapter Six on the Judicial Authority, the Draft provides for the creation of a constitutional court which would be empowered to determine the constitutionality of legislation. Paragraph 2 of the same Article, provides for the manner of and restrictions on amendments to the Basic Law. The Draft has attempted to safeguard basic rights and freedoms provided for therein from being subject to amendment. These provisions are the Bill of Rights for the Palestinian people.

Intentionally, the Draft avoids the inclusion of issues that may be divisive at this stage within the Palestinian community, such as the religion of the state, the sources of legislation and boundaries. It has been the regular practice in Arab States to provide that Islam is the religion of the state and *shari'a* (Muslim jurisprudence) as the source, the main source or a source of its legislation. Within the Palestinian community there are various trends on the subject: the secular, the modernist and the fundamentalist. It was thought that such an issue should be decided in an atmosphere of freedom when the time comes for the preparation of a permanent constitution, and when the question was raised, that was the answer that was given.

3a. Fundamental Rights and Freedoms

This Chapter attempts to remedy the situation which has prevailed for most of this century. Under the British mandate, Palestinians were denied the exercise of political rights and lived for most of the mandate under emergency regulations which effectively suspended all civil rights. Israeli occupation was even more destructive and violative of all political, civil, cultural, economic and social rights. Under the new Palestinian entity, it is imperative that, even during the transitional period, such rights should be guaranteed and protected by a constitutional document from the very beginning. It was for that reason that a general provision of the character of Article 8[8] was included in order to bring into respect the international achievement in the protection of human rights. It is recognised that a Basic Law is not the proper place for the declaration of, recognition of, and respect for international covenants, conventions, agreements or declarations. However, although such a declaration would not amount, in law, to adherence, internally such instruments on human rights could be deemed to form part of the law by virtue of a provision such as that in Article 8. Deliberately, the instruments named are those of general application rather than those specific to a particular right, such as the

---

8 While preparing the draft permanent constitution, the British Foreign Office, at my request, offered to assist through Mr Henry Steel, a constitutional consultant and member of the British delegation to the UN Commission on Human Rights. As stated above, the project was abandoned. However, in a meeting with Mr Steel on 29th March 1993, he gave valuable advice particularly on the chapter dealing with basic rights and fundamental freedoms. Article 8 was suggested by him, and was retained for the Basic Law.

right not to be tortured, or to a section of the community, such as women, children or workers. It would have been too long a provision to set out all human rights instruments and the omission of one could raise questions as to its applicability. The Universal Declaration and the two Covenants are detailed and wide enough in their application and the rights they provide for to make it unnecessary in a Basic Law to have specific reference to special conventions. The reference to the Convention on the Elimination of All Forms of Racial Discrimination is justified by the racial discrimination from which the Palestinians have suffered under Israeli occupation and still suffer from in Israel itself. This Article 8 binds the Palestinian authorities to adhere to the international conventions on human rights as soon as such adhesion becomes possible.

The Draft was not satisfied with the generality of Article 8. Few would have read or been acquainted with the detailed provisions of international conventions or even with the Universal Declaration on Human Rights. The remainder of this Chapter sets out human rights and fundamental freedoms based mainly on the Universal Declaration and the two Covenants.

The first right provided for in Article 9 is the right of every person to life. This right has rarely been recognised for the Palestinians. Palestinian lives are terminated daily by an Israeli shoot to kill policy, which seems to have been sanctioned at the highest Israeli level through the pardon given by the Israeli President to the four Israeli members of the secret service who killed a Palestinian prisoner arrested alive in full view of foreign journalists. Palestinian factions have fought battles at which only Palestinian blood was spilt. Refugee camps have been the target of Israeli air attacks with the indiscriminate killing that resulted, and such camps have been besieged and bombarded by militias. The massacres at Sabra and Shatila refugee camps in 1982 were only two amongst the many massacres committed by Israel against the Palestinians. It is therefore essential to state this right to life as the first in the list of rights.

Article 10 declares that "women and men shall have equal fundamental rights and freedoms without discrimination". This Article did not appear in the first draft on the assumption that proper legal construction of the rights and freedoms as set out in the Draft would make such a provision superfluous. However, Palestinian women's organisations feared that the Draft Basic Law is depriving them of a position enunciated in the Declaration of Independence. They raised the point in memoranda and in my meeting with them in Jerusalem. The lawyers among them accepted the explanation. However, because women's rights is an issue in the Arab world and to allay their fears, it was decided to forego the legal niceties of drafting and to introduce a specific provision and highlight it as the second provision after the right to life. Women's organisations raised other issues which mainly pertained to personal status. It was explained and accepted that a Basic Law was not the place for such subjects and that has to be attended to in special legislation. With their full participation in public life guaranteed to them by the Draft, they could make their own opinions influential.

It is not intended to go through all the fundamental rights and freedoms provided for in the Draft. They mainly follow the provisions of the two Covenants and the Universal Declaration. All of these rights and freedoms are of particular importance to the Palestinian people: the right to participate in public life (Article 12); the right to liberty and security of person (Article 13); the right to freedom of thought, conscience and expression and publication of opinion (Article 14); freedom of formation of political parties (Article 15); freedom of the press, printing and the media (Article 16); freedom from arbitrary or unlawful interference with privacy, family, home or correspondence and from unlawful attacks on honour or reputation (Article 17); security of the home is guaranteed (Article 18); the right to own private property without interference except in accordance with the law and for public interest (Article 19); freedom of economic activity is guaranteed (Article 20); the families of martyrs, the injured and the handicapped (and there are so many) have the right to care and rehabilitation (Article 21); mothers, children, the family, the young and the youth have the right to protection and to the availability of proper opportunities for the development of their talents (Article 22); work is a right, duty and honour and the Palestinian authorities should endeavour to provide equal opportunities to citizens to enable them to exercise this right under laws which provide for social justice, and forced labour is prohibited (Article 24); the right to education, public and private is guaranteed (Article 25); the right to peaceful assembly and freedom of association is recognised (Articles 26 and 27); the surrender of persons granted political asylum in accordance with international law is prohibited (Article 29); the right of every person to address the public authorities on personal matters of concern to him or on public matters is guaranteed (Article 30); freedom of belief and worship and exercise of religious functions are guaranteed (Article 32).

Special reference must be made to Articles 28, 31 and 33. Article 28 provides:

> No Palestinian may be deported, deprived of his nationality, prevented or prohibited from returning to or leaving Palestine or surrendered to any foreign authority except in accordance with extradition agreements.

Palestinians have suffered considerably from Israeli policies of deportation in violation of the Fourth Geneva Convention and they must be reassured. They must also be assured that under no circumstances will they be deprived of their Palestinian nationality. This point is of special importance because of the practice of some Arab states in depriving those citizens who criticise or oppose the regime of their nationality. Palestinians must also be free to leave and return without hindrance or the requirement of an exit visa as is the practice of some Arab countries. A Palestinian should also feel assured, after bitter experiences of extradition cases, that he will not be extradited except in accordance with extradition agreements.

Article 31 provides:

> Jerusalem is a city holy to the three divine religions. In compliance by Palestine with its spiritual heritage, Palestinian authorities shall provide conditions for tolerant co-existence between religions in Jerusalem and the rest of Palestine.

Article 31 is taken from the Declaration of Independence adopted by the PNC on 15th November 1988. It expresses the fundamental tolerance of the Palestinian community throughout the history of Palestine under Arab rule. Historically, the destruction of the Jewish temple was at the hands of occupiers and not indigenous Palestinians. Similarly, the exile of the Jews from Jerusalem was not the act of the Palestinian Arabs and it was when Palestine fell under Muslim rule that the Jews were allowed to return to Jerusalem. Under Arab Muslim rule, there have been more churches in Jerusalem than mosques, and, from the twelfth century, the keys to the Church of the Holy Sepulchre in Jerusalem have been entrusted by the Christian communities to a Muslim family. Article 31 attempts to restate this tradition and make it binding on Palestinian authorities as a legal obligation.

Article 33 provides:

> Freedom of access and visit to holy places and religious buildings and sites are guaranteed for all, citizens and non-citizens, without discrimination. Freedom of worship for the followers of such places is also guaranteed. The exercise of the foregoing freedoms shall be subject to the requirements of public security, order and morality.

Article 33 is based on the United Nations Partition Resolution which required both the Arab and Jewish states to incorporate in their constitutions certain guarantees, including the right provided for in this Article. Israel has failed to meet this condition and has drastically interfered with Muslim places of worship, such as the Hebron Mosque where the massacre took place. However, for the Palestinians, it has been their tradition all along not to interfere with places of worship of other religions and to provide protection to such places.

3b. Protection of Fundamental Rights and Freedoms

Unlike a number of constitutions, including the Arab constitutions, the Draft Basic Law does not make fundamental rights and freedoms "subject to or in accordance with the law". In many cases legislation has compromised the constitutional right and deprived it of its significance. For that reason, the Draft Basic Law does not subject such rights and freedoms to legislation without, where some legislation may become necessary, setting down the criteria by which the constitutionality of such legislation can be tested. The reasons which may justify the imposition of some restrictions where required are clearly set out and such reasons have to be satisfied for the restrictions to be valid and legal. This is the first protection envisaged under the Draft Basic Law.

The second protection is provided for in Article 34 which states:

> Every person whose fundamental rights or freedoms, as provided in this Chapter and Chapter Three, have been violated shall have the right to challenge the violation before courts of law and to demand compensation, where appropriate.

By virtue of this provision a personal right is created for any person whose fundamental right or freedom has been violated to apply to the courts of law for the removal of the violation and for compensation where appropriate. Laws normally provide for such protection. However, it was thought that a constitutional right would provide an all-embracing remedy, particularly in the present complex legal situation in Palestine resulting from its mixed and unfavourable heritage.

The third protection is afforded by the creation in Article 99 of a Constitutional Court and a High Court before which the constitutionality and legality of legislation and administrative acts can be challenged.

The fourth protection is provided in the Chapter dealing with the Rule of Law in Article 46 under which it is made a criminal offence subject to prosecution and punishment for any public official required by law to execute decisions of the courts to refuse or suspend such execution. The right given under this Article is a direct right to bring criminal action before the competent court and has been provided for to ensure judgement enforcement by creating immediate responsibility of the official directly involved.[9]

The fifth protection is provided for in the last paragraph of Article 99 which provides that "no law, administrative order or action may be excluded from review by the judiciary".

The sixth protection is afforded through the creation of an independent commission for human rights with its own juridical personality to monitor and ensure the observance of human rights and freedoms in Palestine. Such Commission already exists under Dr Hanan Ashrawi, and Article 35 of the Draft Basic Law gives it constitutional recognition.

---

[9] On 31st July 1951, the Israeli Supreme Court delivered a judgement in favour of the Israeli-Palestinian inhabitants of the village of Ikrit declaring their right to return to their village. Instead of complying with that judgement, the Israeli Air Force razed the village to the ground. The same fate befell the other village Kfar Berem. See Sabri Jiryis, *The Arabs in Israel*, (1976), pp. 90-94.

4. The Rule of Law

This Chapter Three on the Rule of Law is based mainly on Chapter Four, Articles 64–72, of the Egyptian Constitution of 1971, and establishes that the rule of law is the basis of government in Palestine (Article 36), that all Palestinian authorities and organs as well as individuals and persons in Palestine shall be subject to the law and shall be accountable for its violation (Article 37). The Draft Basic Law added accountability which is not to be found in the Egyptian text of Article 65. The same Article 37 continues to provide that the independence of the judiciary, its immunity, respect for and execution of its decisions are basic guarantees for the protection of rights and freedoms and the establishment of the rule of law. The Draft adds to a similar Egyptian text the words "and for the establishment of the rule of law", because the rule of law would lose its effectiveness if decisions of the courts can be disregarded.

Article 38 is more comprehensive than its counterpart in the Egyptian Constitution (Article 68) and provides:

> All persons shall be equal before the courts and the law, and are entitled to the equal protection of the law without discrimination on any ground such as race, colour, sex, language, religion, political or other opinion, national or social origin, birth or other status.

The abuse of the rule of law by Israel in respect of the Palestinians has been mainly responsible for the comprehensiveness of this provision, which is not limited to citizens but applies to all, since any person who happens to be in Palestine must enjoy equal protection of the courts and the law. "The right to recourse to the courts", provides Article 39, "is guaranteed for everyone and no administrative act may exclude its review by the courts".

Article 40 provides for the presumption of innocence in criminal matters and for the right of defence, and Article 41 provides for punishment as being personal to the offender (and would not include his family or their house, as has been and still is Israeli practice recently supported by a decision of Israeli courts which permitted the blowing up of the house of a suicide bomber), prevents retroactivity of criminal legislation unless more beneficial to an offender, and prohibits collective punishment. The breadth of this provision is not to be found in the Egyptian Constitution.

Article 44 provides as follows:

> All persons deprived of their liberty shall be treated with humanity and with respect for the inherent dignity of the human person.

This Article is taken from Article 10(1) of the International Covenant on Civil and Political Rights. This provision would apply to all those deprived of their liberty, whether in prisons, mental or psychiatric institutions or wherever, and should be read in conjunction with Article 11 which provides:

> All persons are equal in human dignity. No person shall be subjected to torture or to cruel, inhuman or degrading treatment or punishment. In particular, no person shall be subjected without his free consent to medical or scientific experimentation. No effect shall be given to any statement obtained as a result of or the threat of torture, cruel, inhuman or degrading treatment.

It would be sufficient to recall the treatment of Palestinian detainees and prisoners at the hands of the Israeli occupying authorities to see the justification, if justification is needed, for the inclusion of these two provisions in the Draft Basic Law. The Israeli Landau Commission investigating torture of Palestinians found it acceptable to use "reasonable" force to obtain confessions, and Landau was a judge of the Israeli Supreme Court.

Detention without charge for indefinite periods and without trial marked Israeli "respect" for the rule of law as far as the Palestinians were concerned. For that reason, Article 45 has provided for prompt information of the cause of detention and the nature and cause of the charge and for a trial without undue delay in the presence of the accused in a manner which guarantees defence through a lawyer of the accused's choice.

5. Legislative Authority

The provision on legislative authority in Chapter Four, Articles 47–49, takes account of the division of the transitional period into two: before and after elections. Article 47 provides that the Council of National Authority created by the Basic Law would exercise legislative authority during the transitional period until the election of a legislature which would thereupon exercise legislative authority. There is a necessity to legislate prior to the elections in order to meet the new situation, and the only authority which could be given that power is the Council of National Authority. Reference has already been made to Article 48 which authorises the elected body to legislate a sequel to the Basic Law setting out the details of the form of government.

Although the elected Council is to lay down the form of government which would cover the rules pertaining to the Council itself, it was felt necessary to provide a protection to the Council from suspension while it is deliberating on the issues in hand. Article 49 therefore provides:

> The legislative authority may not be suspended nor the immunity of its members be affected.

6. The Executive Authority

Chapter Five deals with the Executive Authority under the following subjects:

(a) the President;
(b) the Council of National Authority;
(c) Security Forces and the Police;
(d) Public Councils and Institutions;
(e) Local Government;
(f) General Provisions.
(g) Finance.

(a) The President

Following the Declaration of Independence, a President for the State of Palestine has been elected, has been recognised by those who recognised the state of Palestine and has been treated as head of state. Consequently, his office must have its constitutional place in the Basic Law. The elected President is the Chairman of the Executive Committee of the PLO and exercises the powers granted to him in that capacity under the PLO Basic Law or in pursuance of resolutions of the PNC, the Central Council or the Executive Committee. Article 50 preserves for him those powers which he exercises independently of the National Authority and within the framework of the PLO constitutional institutions. However, Article 50 also makes him "the head" of the National Authority in order to create a constitutional connection through him between the National Authority and the PLO constitutional bodies.

Two issues have frequently been raised in the course of PLO meetings at various levels, and particularly in the Central Council: (a) the term of presidency, and (b) the appointment of a vice president. Within the framework of the PLO, as a liberation movement, there is no provision in the PLO Basic Law as to either, and neither point was raised while the PLO Basic Law was being considered. However, since the leader's election was left to the PNC, change was possible in changing circumstances, and change indeed took place. Mr Shuqairi, the first PLO Chairman, was replaced by Mr Arafat in 1968 when the Palestinian liberation movements came to the forefront of the Palestinian struggle and the whole of Palestine fell under Israeli occupation. However, the office of a president is different from that of a leader of a liberation movement.

The drafting of the present Basic Law was thought to be the opportunity to remedy the two situations. As to term, Article 52 provides:

> The term of the Presidency shall be five (5) years and no person may be President for more than two consecutive terms. The first term of the first President and any successor in the transitional period shall expire with the expiry of the transitional period.

This provision has remained unchanged (except for the addition of the words "and any successor") throughout the preparation of the Draft.

Apart from the Lebanese constitution, no limitation is provided in any of the Arab republican constitutions as to the number of terms a person can be president, with the result that, once in power, only death has succeeded in removing an incumbent. The Draft Basic Law has refused to follow such a precedent, and treats the present term of Mr Arafat as his first, with the right to present himself for election as President only once more. The transitional period, under the DoP, is deemed to last five years, and that would be in line with the provision as to term. However, it is likely that the transitional period may last longer, in which case the first president and any successor would remain in office until the end of the transitional period in order to conclude the negotiations.

The second problem as to a vice president is finally solved as provided in Article 53:

> If the office of the President becomes vacant or if the President becomes permanently incapacitated, the Chairman of the Palestine National Council shall assume his powers and duties in a caretaker capacity until a new President takes office, which shall be no more than 60 days from the date of occurrence of the vacancy or the proof of permanent incapacity.

The Basic Law does not give the President any special powers. He would be, in accordance with Article 54, the Commander-in-Chief of the Palestinian forces, presently represented by the Palestine Liberation Army which has not been disbanded. Under Article 55:

> The President shall sign and promulgate laws within 30 days after their approval by the Legislative Authority, and if not signed within the said period, such laws shall be deemed promulgated.

The President is not given a veto power on legislation. He is required to sign and publish within thirty days, failing which the draft law becomes law on the expiry of that period without his signature.

In line with other constitutions, Article 56 authorises the President to grant special pardons and to commute sentences. General pardon would require a law.

Under Article 60(3), the President is to perform the powers and duties of the Chief Minister until elections are held and a government is formed in accordance with the applicable provisions of the Basic Law. The other power given by the Basic Law to the President is the appointment of the first Chief Justice (Article 96). This matter will be discussed later.

(b) The Council of National Authority

This Council is regulated by Articles 58–78. Most of these Articles are regulatory in nature and would normally appear in a government law regulating the workings of the government. Consequently, it is not intended here to deal with them in any detail.

The constitutional position of the Council of National Authority (CNA) within Palestinian constitutionality is perceived in Article 58. The Central Council has authorised the Executive Committee to appoint members of the CNA, with the Executive Committee as the Council's reference authority in the matters falling within the Council's competence. This constitutional link is further explained in Article 63 which provides:

> The Chief Minister and Ministers of the Council are jointly responsible to the Executive Committee of the PLO for the general policy of the country as is within the competence of the Council and each Minister is responsible to the Executive Committee for the actions of his Department.

Under the Draft, there will be a Chief Minister and ministers. The first draft anticipated a severance between the office of President and that of the Chief Minister. It was thought it would not be proper to combine the two into one for accountability purposes because the President would be the head of both the CNA and the Executive Committee before whom the CNA is responsible. It was clear, however, that Mr Arafat was not in favour of creating a new head. A compromise solution was arrived at which is expressed in Article 60(3) under which the President would exercise the powers and duties of the Chief Minister until a new government is formed in accordance with the rules to be established by the elected assembly.

The powers of the CNA are generally set out in Article 59. The CNA would be generally responsible for the government and administration of the affairs of the country. Obviously, the CNA would be in no position to govern except to the extent competencies are transferred to it under the DoP. However, the CNA cannot exercise the powers of the higher constitutional institutions of the PLO, i.e. the Executive Committee, the Central Council and the PNC. In particular, the CNA cannot conclude international agreements or deal with foreign governments: such powers are reserved to the PLO as such which is the body recognised on the international level as representing the Palestinian people.

Reference should be made to two Articles in this section which are innovative and intended to handle shortcomings in administration and public participation in the decision making process. Article 76 provides:

> In the provision of administrative services and attending to the rights of individuals, simplification of procedures, expeditiousness and propriety in performance shall be observed within the limits of the law and public interest.

Administrative routine and the difficulty of obtaining one's rights in dealing with Arab administrations has been a vexing problem. This provision may help to alleviate the problem.

The second Article to which reference should be made is Article 77 which provides:

> The executive authority shall avail the widest opportunity for the participation of citizens, political parties, trade unions and other organisations in the discussion of policies, through announcing such policies and consultation with the said bodies.

This provision represents democratic practice, which was followed in the drafting of the Basic Law, and it was thought that it would be proper to provide for it to ensure public participation in the decision making process. In fact, this provision has already been put into effect not only through the consultations on the Basic Law, but also by the CNA itself when it published a proposed investment law for public comment on 18 October 1994 in a Jerusalem daily.

(c) Security Forces and the Police

Article 79 deals with this subject by providing:

> (1) Security forces and the police are a regular force created for the service of the people, protection of society and to maintain security and public order. It shall perform its duties within the limits provided by law with full respect of rights and freedoms without prejudice or discrimination. All persons must cooperate with and assist the police in the performance of their duties.
>
> (2) Security forces and the police shall be regulated by law.

Most Arab constitutions have a similar provision. However, the proviso that the performance of duties must be "with full respect of rights and freedoms without prejudice or discrimination" is added. The addition was inspired by the literature on the origins of the British police system, and is intended as a limitation on police power in the exercise of their duties even within the law. Only those who violate the law in a demonstration, for example, are to be denied the right to participate, while the other participants should be allowed to continue exercising their right to demonstrate peacefully.

(d) and (e) Public Councils and Institutions and Local Government

Article 80 on Public Councils and Institutions follows the traditional line of providing authority for their creation and the establishment of councils and institutions with juridical personality.

Article 81 deals with local government. In addition to the normal provisions, this Article draws attention to the role of local governments "in the preparation and implementation of the development plans and the supervision of the various fields of activity", and requires the law on local government to provide for such a role.

(f) General Provisions

The four Articles of this section are concerned with the conduct of administration in the manner provided by law. Article 82 prohibits the signing or undertaking of financial obligations except within the allocations provided for in the law, and deprives any disposition in contravention of the provisions of this Article of any legal effect. Article 83 prohibits administrative units and officials from taking decisions or giving instructions in contravention of laws in force. Article 84 provides that administrative units are entitled to exercise the powers, carry out the duties and issue resolutions, instructions and regulations for that purpose within the mandate prescribed to each unit by law. All these provisions are introduced to ensure observance of the law in administration, and to remedy shortcomings in PLO procedures.

(g) Finance

The section on finance, Articles 86–93, follows traditional lines regarding the imposition of taxes, preparation of budget, collection of public funds and the procedure for spending therefrom, the determination of the financial year, a provision to cover delay in approval of the budget by law, payment of all receipts in taxes and other revenue to the public treasury, the creation of an independent Audit Office, public loans and banking legislation.

7. The Judicial Authority

During the British mandate, there was one judicial system for the whole of Palestine comprising civil and religious courts. The creation of Israel in 1948 and the legal separation of the Gaza Strip and the West Bank which fell, respectively, under Egyptian and Jordanian administration, led to the separate development of the laws and the judicial system in the two areas. Then came Israeli occupation which affected the judicial system in a material manner in both areas, but the separateness was maintained. A brief discussion would show the significance of the provisions of the Draft Basic Law on the judiciary.[10]

---

[10] For a general discussion, see the report of the International Commission of Jurists, *The Civilian Judicial System in the West Bank and Gaza: Present and Future*, (June 1994), and a report prepared by Ali Safarini, Shukri Nashashibi, Fuad Shehada, Raja Shehadeh, Salwa al-Sayegh and Tawfiq Abu Ghazala, *Towards the Reconstruction of a Unified Independent Palestinian Judicial Authority in the West Bank and the [Gaza] Strip*, (Jerusalem, June 1994).

(a) The West Bank
(i) Jordanian Administration
The Jordanian Constitution of 1st January 1952, which was the constitution that became operative in the West Bank on union with Jordan in 1950, provided for three types of courts:

(i) Regular courts with jurisdiction over all persons in civil and criminal matters, including actions brought by or against the government, but with the exception of matters which fell within the jurisdiction of religious or special courts;

(ii) Religious courts which had jurisdiction in personal matters over Muslims and non-Muslims;

(iii) Special courts established by special legislation.

The regular courts comprised magistrate courts, courts of first instance, appeal courts and a court of cassation. As a High Court, the Court of Cassation was an administrative court with power to annul administrative decisions and any action which was contrary to the constitution or the law. The High Court also had jurisdiction to consider applications by persons who were unlawfully detained (habeas corpus jurisdiction). However, the Court had no jurisdiction to consider constitutionality of legislation or to annul regulations which were in contravention of the law. Its jurisdiction in that regard was limited to annulment of acts taken in pursuance of an unlawful regulation.

(ii) Israeli Rule
By Military Orders 1 and 2 of 1967, all legislative, executive and judicial powers were assumed by the Israeli military administration. The military administration repealed legislation which permitted appeal to the Court of Cassation, thus repealing a vital step in litigation. The jurisdiction of the Court of Cassation as a High Court was transferred to the Court of Appeal. However, the courts were prohibited from considering any civil or criminal action or taking any preliminary ruling against the State of Israel, the authorities and officials thereof, the Israeli Army and soldiers, bodies designated by the military authorities, employees of such bodies or any person employed by the Israeli Army (Military Order 164). By Order 841, the Israeli Area Commander, the Military Prosecutor General, the Legal Adviser or any person authorised by him was empowered with the authority to close a criminal investigation or order suspension of criminal proceedings in progress before a court if in his opinion, there was no interest served by the investigation or trial or because of lack of sufficient evidence. This order undermined the independence of criminal investigation or trial, and there were cases in which prosecution was withdrawn from local courts.

Objection Committees were established by Military Order 172, which greatly reduced the role and jurisdiction of local courts as provided in laws in force before the occupation. These committees were not bound to follow any prescribed procedure, the person in charge could lay down the procedure he deemed appropriate without the need to publish such procedure, the committees could meet in camera and their decisions were mere recommendations to the Israeli Area Commander who could reject them. Each committee was composed of three Israeli members. The establishment of these committees with wide jurisdiction constituted the most serious challenge to the independence of the judiciary and the rule of law. The jurisdiction of these committees included, for example: matters pertaining to land and government property, abandoned property, expropriation, registration of land not previously registered, customs and income taxes, transport of goods, patents, regulation and exploitation of natural resources, companies and banks, supervision over public bodies and over the appointment, dismissal and pensions etc. of public officials.

At the beginning of the occupation, and by virtue of Military Order 3, the Area Commander was authorised to establish military courts to consider matters affecting security and public order. By that Order, the military courts were bound to apply the Fourth Geneva Convention. However, that provision was repealed by Order 374. Then came Order 30 which gave the military courts jurisdiction in criminal matters which had fallen within the jurisdiction of local courts. This position was confirmed by Orders 378 and 842. Judges were Israeli military officers, some of whom were without legal qualifications.[11]

(b) The Gaza Strip

(i) Egyptian Administration

The Constitutional Order of 1962 provided that the formation of courts and the determination of their jurisdiction should be provided for in the law. No law was promulgated affecting the judicial system which remained as it was under the British mandate. Prior to that, by Order 6 made on 1 June 1948, the Egyptian Administrative Governor ordered the continued existence of the courts in the performance of their functions in accordance with the laws in force at the end of the British mandate. The Court of Appeal, acting as High Court, had jurisdiction to annul administrative orders and to order the release of persons unlawfully detained. The Egyptian administration did not disturb the judicial system or the laws in any adverse direction.

(ii) Israeli Occupation

What was done in the West Bank was also done in the Gaza Strip.

---

[11] For a discussion, see the report prepared jointly by Al-Haq – Law in the Service of Man – and the Gaza Centre for Rights and Law, *Justice? The Military Court System in the Israeli Occupied Territories*, (February 1987).

(c) The Draft Basic Law

The need to restore a proper unified judicial system and the rule of law are imperative for the new Palestinian entity. It is necessary to re-establish the independence of the judiciary, to re-create a court of cassation, to restore jurisdiction in respect of acts of the administration and to remedy the shortcomings of the past by creating a constitutional court.

Article 94 provides that the judicial authority will be an independent authority and that the powers exercised by the Supreme Court and the other Courts will be in accordance with the Basic Law and any other law. A head of the Judicial Authority, the Chief Justice of Palestine, is provided for in Article 96 so that, like the other two authorities, the Judicial Authority will have its Head and spokesman. In creating this post, the Palestinian tradition under the British mandate has been kept. The Chief Justice must be a judge of the Supreme Court and is to be appointed by Presidential Decree with the approval of the High Judiciary Council. Since this Council will come into being only after the enactment of the relevant legislation, and its approval would not therefore be possible, the first Chief Justice and only the first will be appointed by Presidential Decree without the involvement of a non-existing Council (Article 96).

Article 97 provides for the establishment of a High Judiciary Council with the Chief Justice as its Chairman. This Council would be responsible for the appointment, promotion, transfer and discipline of judges, in accordance with special legislation to be issued in that regard. As a further safeguard, the Article provides that "the opinion of the Council shall be taken in respect of draft legislation pertaining to the organisation of the judicial authority, including the public prosecution".

Article 95 provides:

> Judges shall be independent and, in their judicial function, shall be subject only to the law. No other authority may interfere in individual cases or in the administration of justice.

Article 99 provides for a Supreme Court comprising:

(a) a High Constitutional Court;
(b) a Court of Cassation;
(c) a High Court of Justice.

Thus, the Court of Cassation would be restored so that appeal on points of law in civil, criminal and commercial matters can be decided. The High Court would also be restored with jurisdiction over administrative and other disputes in the manner provided for in law. A

Constitutional Court would be created with exclusive jurisdiction over judicial review of the constitutionality of laws and regulations and with the power to construe laws. The restoration of the High Court and the creation of a Constitutional Court would provide protection against administrative arbitrariness, unlawful acts or decisions and unconstitutionality of laws and regulations. For pre-Israeli legislation in the West Bank and Gaza, constitutionality could not be challenged: only the effect could be remedied. As has been stated above, Israeli Military Orders deprived local courts of the jurisdiction they had in this regard.

To make judicial review of legality and constitutionality effective, the last paragraph of Article 99 provides:

> No law, administrative order or action may be excluded from review by the judiciary.

By Article 101, public and Government cases, in line with pre-Israeli occupation legislation, are to be conducted by the Attorney General. In the second draft, it was conceived that the Attorney General would occupy a ministerial position to make him accountable, politically, for failures in the observance of the rule of law by the government. However, that would have been a great departure from existing practice in the whole Arab world, and might infringe on the independence of the Attorney General as the person responsible for criminal prosecution and conduct of government cases.

8. Concluding and Transitory Provisions

Article 103 determines that this Basic Law is to apply during the transitional period, but it shall not affect the powers and duties of the PLO and its organs, including its powers to represent the Palestinian people in foreign and international relations and relations with foreign governments and international organisations.

Article 104 provides for the promulgation and publication of laws to put an end to Israeli practices of failing to publish military orders, and Article 105 provides for the non-retroactivity of legislation. Article 106, which has already been discussed, protects fundamental rights and freedoms from suspension for any cause. Article 107 provides for the continuity of laws, regulations and decisions in force in the Gaza Strip and the West Bank to the extent that they do not conflict with the provisions of the Basic Law. Military Orders which are contrary to the provisions of this Basic Law would thus become ineffective.

It must be emphasised that this Basic Law is still a draft, and comments are still welcome to put it into its fourth draft.[12] Nevertheless, it has aroused considerable interest amongst Palestinians who are now relying on it in defence of their rights and fundamental freedoms from violation by Palestinian authorities.

---

12 See footnote 7 at p. 116 above.

Annex
Basic Law for the National Authority in the Transitional Period*

Third Draft

CHAPTER ONE
GENERAL PROVISIONS

ARTICLE 1
The Palestinian people are the source of all authority which shall be exercised, during the transitional period, through the legislative, executive and judicial authorities in the manner provided for in this Basic Law.

ARTICLE 2
The government of Palestine shall be based on parliamentary democracy and pluralism, with consideration by the majority for the rights and interests of the minority and respect by the minority of the decisions of the majority.

ARTICLE 3
The Arabic language shall be the official language of Palestine.

ARTICLE 4
The flag of Palestine shall be of the following colours and dimensions: Its length twice its width, divided horizontally into three equal parallel parts, the upper black, the middle white, and the lower green, thereon placed from the base a red triangle whose base and height equal the breadth and half the length of the flag, respectively.

ARTICLE 5
Jerusalem shall be the capital of Palestine. During the transitional period the Palestinian Authorities may set up the Government Headquarters in any other place in Palestine.

---

*This is the third draft which is still under discussion in the Palestinian circles. Its has not yet been presented to the Central Council for consideration and approval. A fourth draft is in the course of preparation (see footnote 7 at p. 116 above).

ARTICLE 6

Sovereignty over the national resources in Palestine is vested in the Palestinian people, and shall be exploited and disposed of in the interests of the Palestinian people according to law.

ARTICLE 7

(1) This Basic Law shall be the Supreme Law of Palestine in the Transitional Period and any other law which is inconsistent with any of its provisions shall be null and void;
(2) Subject to Articles 48 and 106, this Basic Law may not be amended except by a two thirds majority of the elected legislature.

CHAPTER TWO
I. FUNDAMENTAL RIGHTS AND FREEDOMS

ARTICLE 8

Palestine recognises and respects the fundamental human rights and freedoms prescribed in the Universal Declaration of Human Rights, the International Covenant on Civil and Political Rights, the International Convention on the Elimination of All Forms of Racial Discrimination and other Conventions and Covenants which secure such rights and freedoms. Palestinian authorities shall adhere to the said international agreements.

ARTICLE 9

Every person has the right to life.

ARTICLE 10

Women and men shall have equal fundamental rights and freedoms without any discrimination.

ARTICLE 11

All persons are equal in human dignity. No person shall be subjected to torture or cruel, inhuman, or degrading treatment or punishment. In particular, no person shall be subjected without his free consent to medical or scientific experimentation. No effect shall be given to any statement obtained as a result or under the threat of torture, cruel, inhuman or degrading treatment.

ARTICLE 12

Every person shall have the right to participate in public life and to nominate himself to public office in accordance with the law.

ARTICLE 13

Every person has the right to liberty and security of person. No person shall be subjected to arbitrary arrest or detention. No person shall be deprived of his liberty except on such grounds and in accordance with such procedures as are established by law.

ARTICLE 14
Every person shall have the right to freedom of thought, conscience and expression and publication of his opinion either orally, in writing, or in the form of art or through any other form of expression, subject to observance of restrictions imposed by law for the respect of the rights or reputations of others, the protection of national security or of public order or of public health or morals.

ARTICLE 15
The freedom of formation of political parties is guaranteed provided that their aims and activities do not conflict with the basic principles prescribed in this Basic Law and that they conduct their activities in a peaceful manner. The law shall set out the rules governing the formation of political parties.

ARTICLE 16
Subject to the provisions of Article 14 of this Basic Law, the freedom of the press, printing, publication and media is guaranteed. Censorship of the press is prohibited, and no newspaper shall be subject to warning, suspension, or termination, through governmental or administrative action.

ARTICLE 17
No person shall be subject to arbitrary or unlawful interference with his privacy, family, home or correspondence, or to unlawful attacks on his honour or reputation. The law shall provide protection against such interference or attacks.

ARTICLE 18
Security of the home is guaranteed; it may not be entered or inspected except in pursuance of a reasoned judicial order and in accordance with the law.

ARTICLE 19
Every person is entitled to his own private property, interference in which shall be prohibited except in accordance with the law and for the public interest. Private property may not be expropriated except for public interest in consideration of fair compensation and in accordance with the procedure laid down in the law.

ARTICLE 20

Freedom of economic activity is guaranteed. The law shall set out the rules and extent of supervision in pursuance of the requirements of public interests.

ARTICLE 21

The families of martyrs, the injured and the handicapped have the right to care and rehabilitation, which shall be provided by the Palestinian authorities.

ARTICLE 22

Motherhood, childhood, the family, the young and the youth have the right to protection and the availability of proper opportunities for the development of their talents. Such protection is a duty on society to be discharged by the Palestinian authorities within the limits stipulated by law.

ARTICLE 23

The law shall set out the rules pertaining to social security.

ARTICLE 24

Work is a right, duty and honour. The Palestinian authorities shall endeavour to provide equal opportunities to citizens to enable them to exercise this right under laws which provide for social justice. No one shall be required to perform forced or compulsory labour except in the following circumstances:

(1) Any service of military character or any national service required by law, save for conscientious objectors;

(2) Any service exacted in causes of emergency or calamity threatening the life or well-being of the community;

(3) Any work or service which forms part of normal civil obligations.

ARTICLE 25

(1) Every person has the right to education which shall be free and compulsory until the secondary stage in public institutions. The Palestinian authorities shall endeavour to provide education at all stages;

(2) Minorities, religious or otherwise, and others who meet the conditions prescribed by law shall have the right to establish private schools and educational institutions, provided they observe the general conditions laid down in the law;

(3) The education authorities shall supervise all education. Universities and centres of scientific research shall enjoy respect and autonomy in the manner provided in the law.

ARTICLE 26

The right to peaceful assembly is recognised. No restrictions may be placed on the exercise of this right other than those which are prescribed by law and which are necessary in a democratic society in the interests of national security or public safety, public order, the protection of public health or morals or the protection of the rights and freedoms of others.

ARTICLE 27

(1) The right to freedom of association with others is recognised to all persons, including the right to form and join trade unions for the protection of their rights;

(2) No restrictions may be placed on the exercise of this right other than those which are prescribed by law and which are necessary in a democratic society in the interests of national security or public safety, public order, the protection of public health or morals or the protection of the rights and freedoms of others. This Article shall not prevent the imposition of lawful restrictions on members of the security forces and the police in their exercise of this right.

ARTICLE 28

No Palestinian may be deported, deprived of his nationality, prevented or prohibited from returning to or leaving Palestine or surrendered to any foreign authority except in accordance with extradition agreements.

ARTICLE 29

The surrender of persons granted political asylum by the Palestinian authorities in accordance with international law is prohibited.

ARTICLE 30

Every person has the right to address the public authorities on personal matters of concern to him or on public matters.

ARTICLE 31

Jerusalem is a city holy to the three divine religions. In compliance by Palestine with its spiritual heritage, Palestinian authorities shall provide conditions for tolerant co-existence between religions in Jerusalem and the rest of Palestine.

ARTICLE 32

Freedom of belief and worship and exercise of religious functions are guaranteed, subject to non-violation of public order or morality.

ARTICLE 33

Freedom of access and visit to holy places and religious buildings and sites are guaranteed for all, citizens and non-citizens, without discrimination. Freedom of worship for the followers of such places is also guaranteed. The exercise of the foregoing freedoms shall be subject to the requirements of public security, order and morality.

II. PROTECTION OF FUNDAMENTAL RIGHTS AND FREEDOMS

ARTICLE 34

Every person whose fundamental rights or freedoms, as provided in this Chapter and Chapter Three, have been violated shall have the right to challenge the violation before the courts of law and to demand compensation, where appropriate.

ARTICLE 35

An independent Commission for Human Rights with judicial personality shall be established by law to monitor and ensure the observance of human rights and freedoms in Palestine. Its formation, functions, and powers shall be defined by law and shall be without prejudice to any powers given to individuals, to the Attorney General, to the Audit Office and to the Courts under this Basic Law or any other law.

CHAPTER THREE
THE RULE OF LAW

ARTICLE 36

The rule of law is the basis of government in Palestine.

ARTICLE 37

All Palestinian authorities and organs as well as all individuals and persons in Palestine shall be subject to the law and shall be accountable for its violation. The independence of the judiciary, its immunity, respect for and execution of its decisions are basic guarantees for the protection of rights and freedoms and the establishment of the rule of law.

ARTICLE 38

All persons shall be equal before the courts and the law, and are entitled to the equal protection of the law without discrimination on any ground such as race, colour, sex, language, religion, political or other opinion, national or social origin, birth or other status.

ARTICLE 39

The right of recourse to the courts is guaranteed for everyone and no administrative act or decision may exclude its review by the courts.

ARTICLE 40
Everyone charged with a criminal offence shall be presumed innocent until proved guilty in a lawful trial in which he has been afforded guarantees to defend himself. Every person charged with a serious criminal offence shall have a lawyer to defend him.

ARTICLE 41
(1) Punishment is personal, and no one shall be held guilty of any criminal offence on account of any act or omission which did not constitute a criminal offence, under national or international law, at the time when it was committed. Nor shall a heavier penalty be imposed than the one that was applicable at the time when the criminal offence was committed. If, subsequent to the commission of the offence, provision is made by law for the imposition of the lighter penalty, the offender shall benefit thereby. No one shall be liable to be tried or punished again for an offence for which he has already been finally convicted or acquitted in accordance with the applicable law and penal procedure;
(2) Collective punishment is prohibited.

ARTICLE 42
Except in cases of flagrante delicto, no person may be arrested, searched, detained or have his liberty restricted in any manner or prevented from free movement, except by order given by a component court or the prosecution service in accordance with the law and only where such is required for the needs of the investigations and security of society. The law shall determine the period of detention on remand. No detention or imprisonment is permitted except in places which are subject to laws regulating prisons.

ARTICLE 43
Except where otherwise is provided by law, criminal actions shall only be instituted by order of a judicial body.

ARTICLE 44
All persons deprived of their liberty shall be treated with humanity and with respect for the inherent dignity of the human person.

ARTICLE 45
Every person who has been arrested or detained shall be informed promptly on his arrest of the cause thereof, and shall, without delay, be informed in detail and in a language which he understands of the nature and cause of the charge against him. He shall be given adequate time and facilities for the preparation of his defence and to communicate with a lawyer of his own choosing. He shall be tried without undue delay in his presence in a manner which guarantees defence through a lawyer of his own choosing.

ARTICLE 46
Judgements shall be given and executed in the name of the people. It shall be a criminal offence subject to prosecution and punishment in the manner provided in the law for any public official required by law to execute decisions of the courts to refuse or suspend such execution. In this event, the person in whose favour judgement has been given shall have the direct right to bring a criminal action before the competent court.

CHAPTER FOUR
LEGISLATIVE AUTHORITY

ARTICLE 47
The Council of National Authority by this Basic Law shall exercise legislative authority during the transitional period until the election of a Legislature which thereupon shall exercise the legislative authority.

ARTICLE 48
The Legislature shall lay down its rules of procedure and shall prescribe the rules relating to the enactment of laws and its relationship with the Executive Authority and the formation of the Government and such law shall be treated as a sequel to this Basic Law.

ARTICLE 49
The legislative authority may not be suspended nor may the immunity of its members be affected.

CHAPTER FIVE
EXECUTIVE AUTHORITY

I. THE PRESIDENT

ARTICLE 50
The Chairman of the Executive Committee of the Palestinian Liberation Organisation (hereinafter referred to as the "PLO") shall be president and the head of the National Authority and shall exercise the powers prescribed for him in the Basic Laws of the PLO, the resolutions of the Palestine National Council, the Central Council of the PLO and the Executive Committee of the PLO as well as the powers prescribed in this Basic Law.

ARTICLE 51
Before assuming office, the President shall take the following oath in the presence of the Bureau of the Presidency of the Palestine National Council: "I swear by Almighty God to be faithful to the Nation of Palestine and to its national heritage and to preserve this Basic Law and the law, serve the Palestinian People and faithfully carry out the duties entrusted to me according to the law."

ARTICLE 52
The term of the Presidency shall be five (5) years and no person may be President for more than two consecutive terms. The first term of the first President and any successor in the transitional period shall expire with the expiry of the transitional period.

ARTICLE 53
If the office of the President becomes vacant or if the President becomes permanently incapacitated, the Chairman of the Palestine National Council shall assume his powers and duties in a caretaker capacity until a new President takes office, which shall be no more than 60 days from the date of occurrence of the vacancy or the proof of permanent incapacity.

ARTICLE 54
The President is the Commander-in-Chief of the Palestinian forces.

ARTICLE 55
The President shall sign and promulgate the laws within 30 days after their approval by the Legislative Authority, and if not signed within the said period, such laws shall be deemed promulgated.

ARTICLE 56
The President may grant a special pardon and commute sentences. General pardon shall be prescribed by law.

ARTICLE 57
The President shall exercise his powers through Resolutions and Decrees in the manner prescribed by law.

II. THE COUNCIL OF NATIONAL AUTHORITY

ARTICLE 58
(1) A council to be known as the Council of National Authority (hereinafter referred to as the "Council") is hereby established. It shall be appointed by the Executive Committee of the PLO, which shall be the Council's reference authority in the matters falling within the Council's competence;

(2) The Council shall continue in office until the first elections and thereafter in a caretaker capacity until a government is formed in accordance with the law, rules and regulations to be established in that regard by the Legislature in accordance with Article 48.

ARTICLE 59

The Council shall generally be responsible for the government and administration of the affairs of the country.

ARTICLE 60

(1) The Council shall be composed of a Chief Minister and such other Ministers as the public interest may require. The resolution of appointment shall designate a Department for which the Minister shall be responsible;
(2) A Minister may hold more than one portfolio, as may be determined in the resolution of appointment;
(3) The President shall perform the powers and duties of the Chief Minister until elections are held and a government is formed in accordance with Articles 48 and 58(2).

ARTICLE 61

The Chief Minister and Ministers of the Council shall, before assuming office, take the oath provided for in Article 51 of this Basic Law in the presence of the President.

ARTICLE 62

Neither the Chief Minister nor any Ministers of the Council may purchase or lease any government property, not even through public auction, nor may any one of them have a financial interest in any contract concluded with government bodies, nor may he, while being a member of the Council, be a member of the board of directors of any company or carry on a trade or practice a profession or receive a salary or any other remuneration from any company or any other source.

ARTICLE 63

The Chief Minister and Ministers of the Council are jointly responsible to the Executive Committee of the PLO for the general policy of the country as is within the competence of the Council and each Minister is responsible to the Executive Committee for the actions of his department.

ARTICLE 64

The Chief Minister of the Council in additional to such powers as may be granted to him by law, shall direct the work of the Council, supervise the implementation of its resolutions and the activities of the various Departments and their exercise of the powers allocated to them and the implementation of the policy determined by the Council.

ARTICLE 65
The powers of the various Department shall be determined by regulations made by the Council and endorsed by the President.

ARTICLE 66
(1) Every Minister shall be the head of his Department and shall be responsible for all matters pertaining to his Department;
(2) The Chief Minister of the Council shall deal with matters falling within his competence and powers and shall refer all other matters for decisions by the Council.

ARTICLE 67
Without prejudice to the generality of Article 59 of this Basic Law, the Council shall have the following powers:
(1) To lay down the general policy within the powers entrusted to the Council in the light of submissions by Ministers;
(2) Implementation of the general policies laid down by the appropriate Palestinian authorities;
(3) Preparation and approval of the general budget;
(4) Supervision of the administrative organs;
(5) Follow up on the implementation of laws and ensuring observance thereof;
(6) Follow up performance of their duties and powers by the various Departments and all other units of the administrative organ;
(7) Consideration of the proposals and policies of the various Departments in respect of the performance of their powers;
(8) Any other powers entrusted to the Council by this Basic Law or any other law, including the legislative power in the manner set out in Article 47 of this Basic Law.

ARTICLE 68
The Council shall meet regularly at the invitation of the President or the Chief Minister of the Council. A simple majority shall form a legal quorum. Resolutions of the Council shall be signed by the Chairman of the Meeting and the Ministers and shall be implementing by them, each within his competence. The Chairman of the Meeting shall be the President if he attends, or if he does not attend, the Chief Minister.

ARTICLE 69
The Council shall have a Secretary General who shall organise its meetings, prepare the agenda and minutes of the meetings, follow up the implementation of its resolutions and keep the papers and files of the Council. The Secretary General shall be appointed by resolution of the Council and shall carry out his duties in accordance with instructions given by the Council or its Chairman, as the case may be. The Secretary General shall attend meetings of the Council. However, he may not

participate in the deliberations unless so requested and he shall not have the right to vote on resolutions of the Council.

ARTICLE 70

Every Minister shall have the following powers within his Department:

(1) Propose the general policy of the department and supervise its implementation after its approval;

(2) Supervise the conduct of affairs in his Department and give the necessary instructions in that respect;

(3) Implement the budgetary provisions pertaining to his Department;

(4) Propose legislation pertaining to his Department;

(5) Delegate, as need be, some of his powers to the Under-Secretary of the Department, heads of divisions or senior officials in the Department;

(6) Any other powers entrusted to him by laws, regulations and resolutions made in pursuance thereof.

ARTICLE 71

Each Department shall have an Under-Secretary appointed by the Council. The Under-Secretary shall administer the affairs of the Department under the supervision of the Minister concerned and in accordance with his instructions. In particular, he shall supervise the officials and employees of the Department and its divisions and shall follow up the implementation of the policy and plans approved for the department. the Under-Secretary shall also carry out such powers as may be delegated to him by the Ministers concerned in pursuance of Article 70(5) of this Basic Law.

ARTICLE 72

Each Department shall comprise the Minister and his office, the Under-Secretary and divisions as may be determined in the structural organisation of the Department. The divisions shall be directly responsible to the Under-Secretary. Each Department must have central administration for financial and administrative affairs, and, where necessary, for legal affairs. These central units shall serve the whole Department as well as the councils and specialised institutions attached to the Department.

ARTICLE 73

Divisions in each Department shall be established and cancelled by the Minister concerned within the budgetary allocations for his Department. The resolution establishing the division shall determine its competence.

ARTICLE 74

Each Minister shall submit to the council detailed reports on the activities of his Department, its policies, plans and achievements compared with the aims set out for the Department in the general plan and also submit the Department's proposals and recommendations as to its future policy. These reports shall be submitted on a regular basis so that the Council will be fully informed of the activities and policies of each Department.

ARTICLE 75
The appointment of officials and their terms of employment shall be in accordance with the laws in force in that respect.

ARTICLE 76
In the provision of administrative services and attending to the rights of individuals, simplification of procedures, expeditiousness and propriety in performance shall be observed within the limits of the law and public interest.

ARTICLE 77
The executive authority shall avail the widest opportunity for the participation of citizens, political parties, trade unions and other organisations in the discussion of policies before their determination, through announcing such policies and consultation with the said bodies.

ARTICLE 78
The Council, its Chief Minister and Ministers shall exercise the powers and competence provided for their predecessors in legislation in force on the effective date of this Basic Law, until such laws are amended or replaced, as the case may be.

III. SECURITY FORCES AND THE POLICE

ARTICLE 79
(1) Security forces and the police are a regular force created for the service of the people, protection of society and to maintain security and public order. It shall perform its duties within the limits provided by law with full respect of rights and freedoms without prejudice or discrimination. All persons must cooperate with and assist the police in the performance of their duties;
(2) Security forces and the police shall be regulated by law.

IV. PUBLIC SCHOOLS AND INSTITUTIONS

ARTICLE 80
Specialised public schools and councils shall be established by resolution of the Council to assist the Council in formulating policies within the general fields of activity. Such councils and institutions may be autonomous bodies enjoying juridical personality exercising activities

entrusted to them under their respective resolutions; in which case they shall be established by law.

V. LOCAL GOVERNMENT

ARTICLE 81

For purposes of local government the country shall, by law, be divided into administrative units and municipalities enjoying judicial personality. Each unit shall have a popular council directly elected in the manner provided in the law. The law shall determine the competence of such administrative units, their financial resources, relations with central authority, their role in the preparation and implementation of the development plans and supervision of the various fields of activity. Division shall be, as far as possible, on the basis of number of inhabitants and their concentration.

VI. GENERAL PROVISIONS

ARTICLE 82

No administrative unit or any official thereof may sign or undertake a financial obligation except within the allocations provided for in law, and no effect shall be given to any disposition in contravention of this provision.

ARTICLE 83

No administrative unit or any official thereof may take decisions and issue instructions or regulation in contravention of laws in force, and no effect shall be given to decisions, instructions or regulations for the purpose within the mandate prescribed to it by law.

ARTICLE 84

Each administrative unit shall be entitled to exercise the powers, carry the duties and issue resolutions for the purpose within the mandate to it by law.

ARTICLE 85

Appointment to public offices and specialised councils and institutions shall be on the basis of competence, experience and ability to perform in accordance with the nature of the public office and functions and aims of the council or institution.

VII. FINANCE

ARTICLE 86
General taxes and duties may not be imposed, amended or repealed except by law, and no total or partial exemption may apply except in the circumstances provided for in the law.

ARTICLE 87
The law shall set out the rules pertaining to the preparation of the general budget and for the disposition of funds allocated therein.

ARTICLE 88
The law shall set out the rules governing the collection of public funds and the procedure for spending therefrom.

ARTICLE 89
The beginning of the financial year shall be determined by law. If the budget law is not passed before the commencement of the new financial year spending shall continue on the basis of monthly allocations of one twelfth of the previous budget for each month.

ARTICLE 90
All that is received in taxes and other revenue must be paid to the public treasury and included in the budget. No part of the funds of the general budget may be allocated or spent for any purpose whatsoever except in accordance with the law.

ARTICLE 91
An Audit Office shall be established and its autonomy shall be guaranteed by law. The Office shall be attached to the Council, and shall assist the administrative organ in supervising the collection of public revenue and spending therefrom within the limits set by the budget. The Audit Office shall submit to the Council an annual report regarding its activities, observations showing financial violations, if any, and the responsibility arising therefrom. The Audit Office, after the establishment of the Legislative Council, shall become attached to the said Council and shall submit its report to the government.
The law shall provide for the immunity of the head of the Audit Office and shall give him the powers necessary for him to carry out his duties in the possible manner.

ARTICLE 92
Public loans shall be confirmed by law. A public loan may be concluded or guaranteed by a law or within the allocation prescribed for that purpose in the budget law.

ARTICLE 93
Banks shall be regulated by law.

CHAPTER SIX
THE JUDICIAL AUTHORITY

I. THE JUDICIARY

ARTICLE 94
The judicial authority shall be an independent authority to be exercised by the Supreme Court and other Courts in accordance with this Basic Law and any other law.

ARTICLE 95
Judges shall be independent and, in their judicial function, shall be subject only to the law. No other authority may interfere in individual cases or in the administration of justice.

ARTICLE 96
There shall be a Chief Justice of Palestine who, in that capacity, shall be the Head of the Judicial Authority and President of the Supreme Court. The Chief Justice shall be a judge the Supreme Court appointed by the Presidential Decree with the approval of the High Judiciary Court except that the first Chief Justice appointed in pursuance of this article shall not require such approval.

ARTICLE 97
A High Judiciary Council shall be established by law with the Chief Justice as Chairman. The law shall establish the composition and powers of this Council as well as its rules of procedure. The opinion of the Council shall be taken in respect of draft legislation pertaining to the organization of the judicial authority, including the public prosecution.

ARTICLE 98
(1) The law shall provide for the rules governing the appointment, transfer, secondment and promotion of judges and other matters pertaining to the judiciary;
(2) Judges shall be irremovable, and the law shall regulate their disciplinary accountability.

ARTICLE 99
A Supreme Court shall be established by law comprising:
(1) A High Constitutional Court which shall have exclusive jurisdiction of judicial review of constitutionality of laws and regulations and construction of legal provisions in the manner prescribed by law;

(2) A Court of Cassation in criminal, civil, and commercial matters in the manner prescribed by law;
(3) A High Court of Justice which shall have jurisdiction over administrative and other disputes in the manner prescribed by law.
The law shall determine the types of other courts, their organization, jurisdiction and procedure.
No law, administrative order or action may be excluded from review by the judiciary.

ARTICLE 100
Hearings shall be in public, unless the court determines otherwise in the interests of public order or morality, and in all cases judgements shall be pronounced in open court.

II. ATTORNEY-GENERAL AND PUBLIC PROSECUTIONS

ARTICLE 101
Public and Government cases shall be conducted by the Attorney-General in the name of the people.

ARTICLE 102
(1) The appointment, transfer and dismissal of the Attorney-General and public attorneys in his office shall be in the manner and subject to the conditions prescribed by law;
(2) The law shall determine the powers, competence and formation of the service.

CHAPTER SEVEN
CONCLUDING AND TRANSITORY PROVISIONS

ARTICLE 103
This Basic Law shall apply during the transitional period, but shall not affect the powers and duties of the Palestine Liberation Organization and its organs including its powers to represent the Palestinian people in foreign and international relations and relations with foreign governments and international organizations.

ARTICLE 104
Laws shall be promulgated in the name of the Palestinian people, and shall be published in the Official Gazette after signature and promulgation by the President. They shall come into force 30 days from publication unless the law provides otherwise.

ARTICLE 105

The provisions of laws and legislative resolutions shall not apply except to matters occurring as from the date on which they come into force. Where required and in non-criminal matters, laws may provide otherwise.

ARTICLE 106

None of the fundamental rights and freedoms enshrined in this Basic Law may be suspended, and such rights and freedoms shall remain governed by the provisions of this Basic Law and the laws enacted in pursuance thereof.

ARTICLE 107

Laws, regulations and decisions in force in the Gaza Strip and the West Bank before the coming into effect of this Basic Law shall remain in force to the extent that they do not conflict with the provisions of this law, until they are amended, repealed or replaced in pursuance of this or any other law.

ARTICLE 108

This Basic Law shall be published in the Official Gazette and shall come into force on the date of appointment of the Council of National Authority.

IV. Economy and Law

7. Legal Aspects of Israeli-Palestinian Economic Relations

Celia Wasserstein Fassberg

This paper deals with the legal framework of Israeli-Palestinian economic relations. These encompass the economic relations between Israel and the Palestinian Authority, and commercial relations between Israelis and Palestinians. This legal framework is embodied in the various parts of the Cairo Agreement.[1]

The Protocol on Economic Relations ("the Economic Protocol"), attached to the Cairo Agreement, opens with a declaration that, "the parties view the economic domain as one of the cornerstone(s) in their mutual relations with a view to enhance (sic) their interest in the achievement of a just, lasting, and comprehensive peace". The Parties declare that they will cooperate in this field in order "to establish a sound economic base for these relations, which will be governed in various economic spheres by the principles of mutual respect of (sic) each other's economic interests, reciprocity, equity and fairness". This declaration has been reinforced in recent months by the Middle-Eastern Economic Summit Conference in Casablanca, by talk of establishing a Regional Development Bank for the Middle East, by Israel's peace treaty and relatively cordial relations with Jordan, and by the dizzying pace at which economic relations are being established and developed between the Arab countries and Israel.

The discourse of regional integration and cooperation suggests that regulating Israeli-Palestinian economic relations in an agreement is intended to contribute to the establishment of some form of regional economic union.

Economic relations between societies are expressed by two separate types of rules. The first type of rules are those which determine the terms on which foreign economic activity is introduced and performed. These constitute a regulatory framework which tells us such things as whether imports are allowed, whether they are restricted in quantity or quality, whether licences are required, and whether taxes are imposed. The second type of rules are those which determine the terms on which individual

[1] The Cairo Agreement on the Gaza Strip and the Jericho Area, signed on 4th May 1994, seeks to implement the Declaration of Principles on Interim Self Government Arrangements signed in Washington on 13th September 1993, and, in particular, to put into effect its Protocol on Withdrawal of Israeli Forces from Gaza and the Jericho Area. This Agreement was designed as an interim agreement, pending a permanent solution.

transactions are made, performed, and enforced. These constitute a facilitative framework, and tell us how contracts are made, which law governs them, whose courts can adjudicate disputes, and how judicial decisions can be enforced.

Agreements on economic relations usually use legal rules in order to reduce barriers to trade. The greater the union anticipated, the more willing the parties are to reduce and coordinate regulatory barriers, and the more likely they are to cooperate and coordinate on the facilitative level. In view of the declaration in the Economic Protocol and the prevailing rhetoric of economic cooperation, I have tried to examine the regulatory and facilitative arrangements in the Israeli-Palestinian agreements in order to identify the degree of economic union they anticipate.

The operative legal framework is provided in three separate sections of the Cairo Agreement. The first set appears in the Cairo Agreement itself. The second set appears in the Economic Protocol,[2] and the third set appears in the Protocol Concerning Legal Matters.[3]

1. The Cairo Agreement grants the Palestinian Authority legislative, executive, and judicial powers and responsibilities. Among the powers mentioned explicitly are the power to conclude contracts and international agreements and the capacity to sue and be sued.[4] This constitutes international recognition on Israel's part of a Palestinian legal identity.[5] It does not constitute recognition of a Palestinian state or sovereign.[6] But it does acknowledge, from Israel's point of view, an entity separate from Israel and, more significantly, separate from both Jordan and Egypt – the previous controllers of the territory. In other words, it acknowledges the existence of a *new* entity.[7] This bilateral

---

2 This Protocol was signed in Paris, before the Cairo Agreement, on 29th April 1994. It is Annex IV to the Agreement.

3 This Protocol was signed together with the Cairo Agreement and is Annex III.

4 See Articles V and VI of the Agreement.

5 This basis for the governmental powers of the Palestinian Authority is of course very different from the internal constitutional source of such powers from the Palestinian perspective.

6 Since the Palestinian Authority has the capacity to sue and be sued, and since it is not recognised as a state, the doctrine of sovereign immunity should not apply to it. As a result, it is presumably subject to suit in any competent court for any legal act for which it might be held liable (see infra). The relationship between the PLO and the Palestinian Authority is not defined. An interesting question is whether the Palestinian Authority could be held liable for injuries caused by PLO terrorist activities performed prior to the Agreement.

7 Hereafter, the Territory. The existence of a separate *legal* system in the areas administered by Israel since 1967 was recognised and formally maintained by Israel throughout. The law existing in the territories prior to the Israeli administration remained in force subject only to modification by the Military Government. The recognition accorded by this Agreement does not create a new legal system. It merely signals the withdrawal of military control

recognition has no immediate significance or implication as far as other states or international organisations are concerned.[8] It is, however, crucial to the establishment of economic relations between the two parties since it recognises the Palestinian Authority as an autonomous actor in the economic domain. Without a formal legal identity, and without recognition of its policy-making and administrative powers on the part of Israel, the Palestinian Authority could not function as a trading partner.

2. The Economic Protocol establishes the regulatory framework within which economic activity will take place between the two economies. It deals with a very broad range of issues. It establishes movement of agricultural produce[9] and industrial goods[10] between the Parties free of

---

from these two existing, non-Israeli, systems and recognises their new unified political framework. The Agreement provides for similar continuity in substantive law despite the formal change: "Laws and military orders in effect in the Gaza Strip or Jericho Area prior to the signing of this Agreement shall remain in force, unless amended or abrogated in accordance with this Agreement." (Article VII.9). This provision creates two interesting situations. The first – that the Palestinian Authority is committed formally to applying law imposed by the Israeli Military Government. The second – that the legal system to be applied by the Palestinian Authority in the Territory, which is made up of two separate territorial units, the Gaza Strip and the Jericho Area, is founded upon existing law, which is also made up of two separate and different legal units. The law in the Gaza Strip (which, as Mr. Raja Shehadeh pointed out to me, was never annexed by Egypt or subjected to Egyptian law) has as one of its principal foundations, British Mandatory law, whereas the law of the Jericho Area has as one of its principal foundations, Jordanian law. Integrating these into one system is a practical matter of no little difficulty. In the meantime, it is somewhat difficult to conceive of one legal system in the Territory.

8 Even if the agreement is regarded as an international agreement and even if the PLO, or perhaps more appropriately, the Palestinian Authority, is to be regarded as a subject of international law (see E. Benvenisti, 'The Israeli-Palestinian Declaration of Principles: A Framework for Future Settlement', 4 *E.J.I.L.* 542 (1993), pp. 542-545), it is not clear to what extent the legal entity established by the Agreement should be recognised by other states.

9 Article VIII.1. This provision is subject to "exceptions and arrangements". These relate to veterinary and plant-protection supervision, which are coordinated, and include a schedule of quantitative restrictions on the sale of poultry, eggs, melons, potatoes, cucumbers, and tomatoes. These quantitative restrictions are laid down on a scale according to which they will be eliminated completely by 1998, when each party will be free to introduce unlimited amounts into the other's market (Article VIII.10). The implementing law in Israel requires a permit for the transportation of those agricultural goods on which quantitative restrictions have been imposed as a means of supervising the quantities (*Sefer Huqim* 1497 (1994)).

10 Article XI. Industrial goods are not defined. As a result, the provisions on agriculture and industry provide for free trade in almost every conceivable area.
The anticipated freedom from *any* restriction, including customs duties and import taxes, appears to require that non-tariff barriers be removed. For example, it is explicitly provided that indirect tax rebates or benefits and subsidies to sales are not allowed in trade between the two parties (Article IX.2.c). At the same time, however, the entire arrangement is subjected to each side's legislation. Non-tariff barriers that are not explicitly forbidden might then be introduced by means of primary or secondary legislation.

customs duties and import taxes. It coordinates customs policy,[11] taxation,[12] monetary affairs,[13] and the reciprocal licensing of banks and insurance companies.[14] It provides in detail for movement of labour, and for coordination of social insurance, work accident insurance and pension schemes.[15] It coordinates tourism policy,[16] and it harmonises road accident liability laws.[17]

3. The Protocol Concerning Legal Matters establishes the facilitative framework within which individual transactions are conducted and enforced. It coordinates rules of jurisdiction, and guarantees enforcement of judgments.[18] It also provides for extensive cooperation in the course of judicial proceedings.

The broad scope of issues coordinated in these provisions suggests that a very close economic union is anticipated. A good model of economic union against which these arrangements can be measured is the European Union. There, in order to form one market, its members instituted the four freedoms; the freedom of movement of persons, capital, goods, and services. These freedoms were buttressed by abolishing tariff and quantitative restrictions and by establishing a common customs barrier. Policies in certain fields were harmonised or approximated in order to equalise competition, to unify trade conditions, and to eliminate discrimination within the market. Finally, rules of jurisdiction, choice-of-law, and enforcement of judgments were unified in the commercial field.

The relationship between Israel and the Palestinian Authority is structurally similar – many of the same issues are coordinated. But upon examination, it turns out to be very different in substance. Its rules do not seem designed to bring about union.

---

11 Article III.5. Israeli officials will collect the duty on goods imported through Israeli entry points and destined for the Palestinian Authority.

12 Israel will transfer to the Palestinian Authority 75% of the income tax collected from Palestinians from the Territory employed in Israel and 100% of the tax collected from Palestinians employed in the Settlements. Each side is entitled to determine its own tax policy and, among other things, to levy taxes on the economic activity of individuals and corporations carried out in the other's territory (Article V). As far as indirect taxes are concerned, each Party is free to fix its own, but purchase tax will not differentiate local from imported goods. While the rate of VAT in Israel is 17%, it will be 15%-16% in the Territory (Article VI).

13 Article IV.

14 Article IV.8, Article XI.12.

15 Article VII.

16 Article X.

17 Article XI.

18 Article IV.4.

The principle of free movement of industrial and agricultural goods is laid down. But none of the supporting mechanisms for creating one market are introduced. There are no provisions guaranteeing equal competition or dealing with practices which distort the market and disadvantage foreign goods.[19] Similarly, there is at present no mechanism for establishing and implementing common agricultural or industrial policy.[20] The agreements also have no general provision on harmonisation of any of the commercial laws. Harmonisation is limited to road accident liability insurance and tourism policy. But even here, the road accident liability scheme is not a joint one; the Palestinian Authority is required to adapt itself to the scheme already existing in Israel.

The coordination of customs policy is also not typical. On the one hand, the common customs barrier is not complete. Each Party has its own customs barrier. But while the import policy of Israel is not restricted in any way, the freedom of the Palestinian Authority to determine its own import policy is closely defined. The Authority is free to set its own import and customs policy only with respect to certain specified goods, from specified countries,[21] and only up to the limit of local market needs.[22] As a result, the rules of origin appearing in the agreement fulfil an unusual role. Normally they define the goods eligible for free trade between the parties themselves. Here they define and restrict the goods which the Palestinian Authority may import from *other* countries.

Even where the customs barrier is coordinated, no real union is formed: the agreement leaves the Palestinian Authority free to set its own customs rate but requires that this rate not fall below the Israeli rate. There is no institutional mechanism for consultation and for joint action on adapting or changing the rates. The parties agree to adopt a common import policy, but it is again Israel who determines that policy.[23] The only joint action

---

19 It is explicitly provided that the Palestinian side may encourage and develop local industry by grants, loans, research and development assistance, and direct tax benefits as well as by other methods employed in Israel. It is, however, not unusual to find such rules in free trade agreements. The US-Israel Free Trade Agreement, for example, made special temporary provision for "infant industries" in Israel.

20 Annex II of the Cairo Agreement, the Protocol Concerning Civil Affairs, does anticipate that the Parties will take measures to reach compatible standards of disease control in plants and animals (Article II.B.20) and compatible standards in the field of transportation (Article II.B.19). It also provides for cooperation in the field of environmental protection (Article II.B.35).

21 Jordan, Egypt, Arab countries, Muslim countries, and other countries as agreed between the Parties (Article III.2.a.(1) and (2), of the Economic Protocol).

22 The rules restrict the Palestinians' freedom to set their own import policy with respect to these goods by limiting it to local market needs (Article III of the Economic Protocol). The determination of local market needs is to be carried out by both parties jointly.

23 This provision may eventually bring about a uniform customs barrier. If the Palestinian Authority imposes higher tariffs than Israel, the goods imported through the Territory and

anticipated in this context is in determining Palestinian market needs for the purposes of limiting its independent import policy.

In a similar way, the rules on monetary affairs do not bring about free movement of capital. There is free movement in the sense that Israeli currency can be used for any transaction in the Territory.[24] But that currency is not a joint one; it is the currency of only one of the parties – Israel. It is anticipated that the Palestinian Authority will have its own currency,[25] but there is no indication that this will circulate in Israel too, or indeed that there will be any joint currency. The Protocol also includes rules regulating the Palestinian right to convert Israeli shekels into foreign currency.[26] These rules do establish consultative mechanisms, but the purpose is clearly not to establish a common monetary policy, but rather to control the Palestinian use of Israeli currency for the purposes of Israeli monetary policy.

The provisions concerning the movement of persons and of services are also not characteristic of an agreement seeking economic union. With respect to persons, far less than free movement is granted in either the economic or the political sense. The Protocol lays down that both sides will attempt to maintain "normal" movement of labour between them.[27] It provides that the placement and employment of workers from each side will be through the employment service of the employing side[28] and in accordance with its legislation. Although these rules are formulated as even-handed reciprocal rules, it seems to be anticipated that the flow of workers will continue to be from the Palestinian Authority to Israel and that all the workers will be of the type referred to in Europe as Frontier

---

circulated freely in the Territory and in Israel will be at a competitive disadvantage. In the meantime, however, it protects the Israeli economy by not permitting the import and free circulation of goods at a lower cost (or a higher profit margin) than by import through Israel.

An interesting feature of the agreement is that when goods are imported through Israeli entry points, Israeli officials will collect the duties on behalf of the Palestinian Authority.

24 Article IV.10.a.

25 Article IV.10.b.

26 Article IV.16-19. The Palestinian Authority can convert Israeli shekels into foreign currency via the Bank of Israel in an amount equal to the difference between the total value of goods and services purchased in Israel from the Territory minus the total value of goods and services purchased in the Territory from Israel plus any accumulated amounts of foreign currency previously converted by the Palestinian Authority into shekels. Consultation on this issue is provided for.

27 Article VII. The normal movement of labour is subject to each side's right to determine from time to time the extent and conditions of the labour movement into its area. This provision, although formulated as a reciprocal right, serves the Israeli policy of closing the border and stopping the flow of Palestinians into Israel in the wake of terrorist attacks.

28 The Palestinian employment service has the right to regulate the employment of Palestinian labour in Israel (Article VII.1).

Workers, workers who cross the border in the morning to work and in the evening to return home, and who have no right to live in the area in which they work.[29]

Similarly, none of the rights normally associated with free movement of persons and services are granted here. Virtually no mention at all is made of the right of establishment, which is a necessary component of the free movement of labour and professionals.[30] Indeed, the law of the Military Government which is imported into the Agreement in this context specifically denies Palestinians the right of establishment in Israel. No provision is yet made for the mutual recognition of diplomas and qualifications;[31] no provision requires striking out residency or nationality requirements from local standards for professional qualification; there is no guarantee of non-discrimination in government procurement contracts; there is no provision in the various agreements guaranteeing that there will be no discrimination in choosing workers, and in their terms of employment. The Protocol does provide for cooperation with respect to social insurance, work accident insurance, health insurance, and pension schemes. But it is not at all clear whether these arrangements are designed

---

29 No provision is made here for the right to enter, reside in, and exit the territory of the side in which the worker is going to be employed and no provision is made for a worker's family to accompany him. The rules on passage from one area to the other appear in Annex I of the Cairo Agreement which deals with Withdrawal of Israeli Forces and Security Arrangements. Israelis entering the Territory are only required to carry identification, and driving licence and vehicle registration documents recognised in Israel. The Palestinian Authority has no power to prevent their entry into the Territory under the Agreement. By contrast, Israel can prevent or limit entry of Palestinian residents to Israel for safety and security reasons (Article VII, Annex I) and the entry of residents of the Territory to Israel is subject to Israeli rules and procedures (Article VII, Annex I). Passage between the Jericho Area and Israel via the West Bank is governed by the pre-existing rules of the Military Government. Under these rules, workers from the Gaza Strip and Jericho may enter Israel only in order to work, and under the terms of a work permit. They may not sleep in Israel (Article II.B.27.c. of the Protocol Concerning Civil Affairs requires that a Palestinian resident entering Israel from the Gaza Strip or Jericho Area show his identity card and, where necessary, an entry permit).

30 The only mention of the right of establishment is in connection with banks and insurance companies. The existing branches of Israeli banks in the Territory will be licensed by the new Palestinian Monetary Authority (Article IV) and, if Israel treats Palestinian banks as it treats other foreign banks, the Palestinian Authority will treat further Israeli requests for branches in the Territory as it treats other foreign requests. Insurers from both sides may apply for a licence from the other side according to the rules governing foreign insurers, and the parties agree that there shall be no discrimination against such applicants (Article XI.12).

31 The Protocol Concerning Civil Affairs does anticipate that the Parties will establish procedures for mutual recognition of professional certificates and diplomas (Article II.B.8). Article XI.10 further requires joint approval of operators of commercial air services to, from, and between the Gaza Strip and Jericho Area. Only pilots licensed in Israel or in a member state of the IACO maintaining bilateral aviation relations with Israel can be approved.

to protect the rights of the individual worker and promote free movement of labour or rather to release Israeli institutions and employers from liability, without, at the same time, creating any substitute liability in the Palestinian authorities.

As the coordination of customs matters suggests, these rules are not designed to encourage economic unification or integration. Similarly, it is significant that, just as no institutions are anticipated for the harmonisation of laws and coordination of policies, the institutions established for implementing the agreement are relatively modest as compared with the institutions of the EEC; they do not provide for the possibility that disputes may not be amicably resolved by the Parties, and they do not anticipate any institution resembling the European Court of Justice.[32] The entire structure seems designed rather to establish the Palestinian Authority as an economic actor, and to limit its power in order to protect the Israeli economy.

The facilitative arrangements reveal a similar ambivalence. On the one hand, the Protocol Concerning Legal Matters establishes a very close system of cooperation.[33] In civil cases, each side takes upon itself to serve legal documents issued by the judicial organs of the other party within the territory under its control.[34] No conditions and no restrictions are attached to this provision.[35] So too, each Party will take evidence from

---

[32] Article II provides for the establishment of a Joint Economic Committee. This Committee is charged with implementing the Protocol. Each side may request that an issue be reviewed by the Committee. Trade agreements usually have far more sophisticated institutional arrangements, including a hierarchy of institutions for different levels of unresolved disputes. The Cairo Agreement does include a rather more sophisticated dispute resolution mechanism (Article XVII). The relationship between the mechanism established by the Economic Protocol and that established by the Cairo Agreement is not clear.

[33] This Protocol deals with jurisdiction and legal assistance in civil and in criminal matters. It anticipates that further arrangements will be negotiated in the future.

[34] Article IV.1. The provision extends to subpoenas too. This means that Israel will serve all documents in Israel and the Settlements (and also presumably in the rest of the West Bank), and the Palestinian Authority will serve all documents in its territory, irrespective of the identity of the addressee.

[35] The commitment is very important for Israeli law since its jurisdiction in civil matters depends on the service of summonses. This is true for service out of the jurisdiction too which, however, requires leave of the court and is subject to judicial discretion, exercised in a closed list of circumstances (Rule 500, Rules of Civil Procedure 1984). In 1969, Israel made special provision for service in all the administered territories in accordance with Israeli law, as if they were part of Israel, without having to obtain leave from the court (Rules of Civil Procedure (Service of Documents in the Administered Territories) 1969). The rules permit such service on anyone in "the area", and "the area" is defined as "any territory held by the Israel Defence Forces". This willingness to treat the territories as part of Israel for the purpose of serving documents was justified by the fact that, even though a separate legal system exists in the administered areas, no foreign sovereign is involved whose powers would be undermined by Israeli service of documents. The Palestinian Authority is not a state, as we have seen. But Israel does recognise its territorial jurisdiction, created by the transfer of territory from the Israel Defence Forces to the

witnesses[36] and issue interim orders[37] for civil cases conducted in the courts of the other Party. Civil judgments will be reciprocally enforced almost automatically,[38] and judgments will be reciprocally executed as if they were local judgments.[39]

Palestinian Authority. It would then seem reasonable to assume that the territory of the Palestinian Authority is not considered territory held by the Israeli Defence Forces and that, under Israeli law, documents cannot be served there automatically. Leave must then be obtained, as is the case whenever the person to be served is outside Israel. The reciprocal service of documents agreed upon by the Parties simply guarantees that such documents will reach their destination and that Israeli jurisdiction will be established over the person served.

36 This provision is a little surprising in view of the provision on serving subpoenas. Although it seems to correspond with another rule permitting each Party to summon witnesses for proceedings held in the territory of the other Party, that provision is brought in the criminal context, not in the chapter on civil legal assistance.

37 Article IV.2.b. In the civil context, such orders have effect only within the territory under the control of the issuing Party. As a result, judicial organs "under the responsibility of both Parties" are authorised to issue interim orders for the area under their control even when the civil action is being conducted in the courts of the other Party. It is not clear whether this means that the two Parties will establish a joint organ empowered to issue orders valid in both territories for such cases or rather that each Party will be able to issue interim orders for the benefit of proceedings taking place in the courts of the other. Despite the unfortunate use of the word "both" instead of "each", the reference to "courts of the other Party" suggests that the intention was to permit each side to issue orders for the benefit of the other. This would place the Palestinian Authority in a better position in this regard than any foreign national legal system, since Israel does not issue such orders for foreign litigation.

38 Article IV.4. One condition is that the judicial organ issuing the judgment had jurisdiction to render the judgment. The term "jurisdiction" is not defined here. In view of the important distinctions between different types of jurisdiction that can be relevant for the purpose of enforcing foreign judgments (for example, the distinction between jurisdiction under the law of the issuing forum and jurisdiction under the law of the enforcing forum), the absence of a clear explanation of what is required here undermines the apparent simplicity of the enforcement process. Another condition is that enforcement of the judgment is not contrary to public policy. No other defence is permitted. Although no such limitation appears in the Protocol, the Israeli implementing law (*Sefer Huqim* 1497 (1994)) provides for enforcement only of final judgments from the Palestinian Authority in Israel. This is consistent with the fact that interim orders (which, by their nature, are not final) are treated separately. Nonetheless, the finality contemplated here – after all appeals have been exhausted – seems to correspond to the finality required in the Foreign Judgments Enforcement Law 1958 (12 *L.S.I.* 82) – exhaustion of the possibility of appeal (rather than that required in enforcement by action on the judgment – that the judgment be *res judicata*). Since interim orders can be final in the required sense, it is not quite clear why they were treated separately.

39 In the process of executing any judgment against an Israeli, Palestinian execution offices are empowered to issue orders against Israeli property in the Territory. Such orders will be executed by Israeli authorities with the assistance of the Palestinian Authority, but can also be executed by the Palestinian Police alone, if Israel has notified the Palestinian Authority that it has no objection. The only restriction on the power of Palestinian execution offices seems to be that they may not issue orders concerning the personal freedom of Israelis –

Here too, however, the impressive cooperative structure does not bring about unification or integration. Quite the contrary. The rules on jurisdiction in the same Protocol confirm that the discourse of cooperation obscures a very different reality.

First of all, this Protocol does not harmonise substantive law.[40] Similarly, there is no indication of the anticipated scope of Palestinian or Israeli law with respect to activities involving elements from the other Party.[41] The only provision to deal with this issue lays down that Israelis conducting commercial activity in the Territory are subject to the civil law prevailing there relating to such activity.[42] This is a curious provision. Firstly it does not address the fact that the civil law prevailing in the Territory is not uniform: the law governing the Jericho Area is of Jordanian origin, while that governing the Gaza Strip has its origins in British Mandatory law.[43] In an individual transaction, it may be relatively easy to identify which of the two laws applies. But which of them is "the prevailing civil law" when, for example, the Israeli is dealing with the Palestinian Authority itself, for example in commercial activity designed to benefit all the residents of the area? Secondly it is not clear whether the provision restricts or expands the scope of Palestinian law. Does it mean that *all* local commercial law must apply, and that the Parties cannot contract out of it? Or does it imply that Israelis in the Territory are bound *only* by the local *commercial* law, and that no other portions of Palestinian law apply to them? Does it simply clarify that *mandatory* provisions of local commercial law will apply? If so, how does this somewhat self-evident idea coexist with the fact that Israelis are totally exempt from local *criminal* law?[44]

The absence of any kind of coordination or harmonisation on these questions of legislative jurisdiction makes economic activity difficult, because the parties will not be able to anticipate which law applies, and to what extent they are free to choose an applicable law. The rules with respect to judicial jurisdiction are even more troubling. The provisions

only Israeli offices are so empowered. The execution of such orders, like that of orders against Israeli property, is in the hands of Israel, unless this power is renounced.

40 It harmonises only the régime of automobile accident liability.

41 It then assumes the existence and application of choice-of-law rules in local courts and the use of normal choice-of-law rules in foreign courts.

42 Article III.2.

43 Although this area was controlled by Egypt prior to 1967, it was never annexed to Egypt and was not subjected to Egyptian law. As mentioned earlier, *supra*, note 7.

44 The Protocol Concerning Legal Matters deals with criminal matters too, and the rules on criminal jurisdiction make it clear that judicial and legislative jurisdiction go hand in hand in the criminal area. One of the striking features of these rules is that they insulate Israelis from any Palestinian criminal jurisdiction, even within the territory under Palestinian control.

deal only with the jurisdiction of the Palestinian Authority. Israeli jurisdiction is still defined by Israeli law, and it turns out that it is much broader than the jurisdiction accorded the Palestinian courts.

Although the courts of the Authority are empowered to deal with all civil matters, subject to the Agreement,[45] they have no civil jurisdiction over actions against the State of Israel or her organs.[46] Similarly, they have no civil jurisdiction over actions to which Israelis[47] are a party, except in specified cases, where the Authority has an overwhelming interest in the case, or where the Israeli concerned can clearly be taken to have subjected himself to Palestinian jurisdiction.[48] It is interesting that the Protocol does not establish that Israel has exclusive jurisdiction in all the cases in which the Authority is denied jurisdiction. It simply removes them from the jurisdiction of the Palestinian courts. This means that while any court in the world may adjudicate such cases, if it has jurisdiction under its internal rules, only the courts of the Palestinian authority may not.

---

45 Article III.1. Here again, interesting questions arise in international law. The document is a purely bilateral agreement (the United States, the Russian Federation, and Egypt are involved only as witnesses). Even the internal constitutional documents which will establish legislative, judicial, and executive functions within the Palestinian Authority have no external force, as such. In view of the fact that the Authority is not a state, it is not at all clear how other states should treat its law, its acts, and its decisions in the realm of private law. Its law would probably be applied in a conflict-of-laws case simply as the law in force in the territory, as a fact. The enforcement of its judgments might prove more difficult, since many systems enforce only judgments given by the courts of foreign *states*.

46 Article III.4.

47 Although the term "Israelis" is said to include "also" Israeli statutory agencies and corporations registered in Israel (Article I.d), neither the Cairo Agreement nor the Protocol Concerning Legal Matters specifies the fundamental meaning of the term. The Israeli implementing law defines the term, for the purposes of Israeli Emergency Regulations governing some of these arrangements, as persons registered in the Population Registry and corporations registered or established in Israel. This definition does not include non-Israeli Jews, who are not registered in the Population Registry, but who are eligible for citizenship under the Law of Return. Such people are considered Israeli for many of the purposes of Israeli law in the West Bank territories which continue to be administered by Israel.

48 Where the subject matter of the action is an ongoing Israeli business situated in the Territory (the Israeli implementing law denies Israeli courts jurisdiction over these cases); where the subject matter of the action is real property situated in the Territory (the Israeli implementing law denies Israeli courts jurisdiction over these cases too); where the defendant consented in writing to the jurisdiction of the Palestinian courts; where the plaintiff is Israeli. It is also anticipated that other cases will be agreed upon by the Parties (which will presumably override any absence of consent on the part of the litigating parties). Some initial questions raised by these provisions are: when is the subject matter of the action an ongoing Israeli business situated in the Territory? Does the business concern itself have to be the subject matter – its existence, its solvency etc. – or can the relevant subject matter be a question concerning its activities? When the subject matter of the action is real property in the Territory, is consent required of an Israeli defendant?

Israeli jurisdiction is strikingly different. Civil jurisdiction is based, in Israel as in England, on service of process. Accordingly, Israeli courts have jurisdiction over anyone present in Israel, irrespective of his nationality, domicile, or place of residence, even with respect to acts committed outside Israel.[49] As a result, Israel does have civil jurisdiction over Palestinian residents of the Territory physically present in Israel even with respect to acts committed in the Territory, and even if the plaintiff is not Israeli. Because of the territorial limitations upon the power to serve process, people outside Israel are generally not subject to Israeli jurisdiction, except by leave of the court, which is granted on a discretionary basis.[50] Since the Territory of the Palestinian Authority is now no longer part of the territory held by Israel, its residents are not subject to Israeli jurisdiction when they are not physically in Israel. In order to serve process on them, leave must be obtained as for any person outside Israel, but the provisions on legal assistance require the Palestinian institutions to serve the summonses which will effectuate this jurisdiction.[51] Another interesting feature of these provisions is that, since the Agreement granted the Palestinian Authority the unlimited power to sue and to be sued, Israel presumably also has jurisdiction over actions against the Authority itself. And furthermore, since it is not a state, the Authority should be unable to claim sovereign immunity.

These rules clearly restrict Palestinian jurisdiction as compared with Israeli jurisdiction. While this may be understandable in the criminal law context, it is more difficult to justify in the area of civil and commercial law. The direct result of these rules is that the generous framework for cooperation in the course of legal proceedings and thereafter is of little practical significance since there will be few cases in which such cooperation will be necessary. At best, Israel will benefit from the assistance of the Palestinian Authority, but the Authority will rarely benefit from Israeli assistance.

---

49 This is because Israeli civil jurisdiction depends on service of summonses. Service by right is territorially limited. Within the territory, it has virtually no limits, and anyone served within the territory is caught in the jurisdictional net.

50 Even Israelis cannot be subjected to the civil jurisdiction of Israeli courts by service as of right outside Israel. Leave has to be obtained from the court to serve process outside Israel. Only a number of specified links can found a request for service out, and the court has discretion even with respect to these. They do include Israeli residence, but not Israeli citizenship.

51 This combination of rules has an interesting impact on the reciprocal service of documents. While Israeli summonses can be served on anyone in the Territory, the most likely addressees of Palestinian summonses and subpoenas in Israel – Israelis – are immune from Palestinian jurisdiction. Consequently, the Israeli commitment to serve Palestinian summonses is likely to remain a dead letter; Palestinian summonses will only rarely be served in Israel on Israelis.

Conclusion

The compound legal framework for economic and commercial relations looks like a framework of unification and integration. But the regulatory provisions and the jurisdictional rules are not reciprocal or even-handed. They reflect an imbalance in the relationship between Israel and the Palestinian Authority which is quite incompatible with any of the familiar types of economic union, and suggest an absence of the confidence and trust necessary for real cooperation.

This imbalance suggests that the most significant legal provision is the one appearing in the Cairo Agreement itself, granting the Authority legislative, executive, and judicial powers and the power to conclude contracts, to sue and to be sued. The Preamble to the Economic Protocol confirms this. After declaring the Parties' interest in economic cooperation, it abandons the rhetoric of aspiration and moves to the rather more pragmatic statement that:

> This Protocol lays the groundwork for strengthening the economic base of the Palestinian side and for exercising its right of economic decision-making in accordance with its own development plan and priorities.

In the light of all this, it would seem that the legal and the economic Protocols in this Agreement serve primarily political purposes which reverse their usual roles. Rather than bringing two distinct and independent legal and economic systems closer together, they separate them from one another. They are not designed to impose reciprocal limitations on the independence of each system. They are designed rather to establish a sphere of independence for a new economic entity. The focus of the legal framework is then *not* on the degree of *union* established, but rather on the degree of *independence* established. The structure of integration and union is at present little more than political optimism. Economic union, at this stage of the political process, is not the objective, but rather a very clear point of departure.[52]

---

52 It is interesting to note that the Protocol has barely changed the legal relationship between the two legal systems. Since 1967, the Territory, together with the rest of the West Bank, was under the control of the Military Government, which was in control of all legislative, executive, and judicial functions (Section 3, Proclamation Concerning Law and Administration Order (West Bank Area) (No. 2) 5727-1967). The law in force at the time Israel took control of the territories was left intact except insofar as it was amended by Military Order (id. Section 2). As a result, a large portion of the local civil (and criminal) law remained in force. The local courts continued to function in all matters which were not in the exclusive domain of the military courts. There was no formal restriction on their power to summon Israelis and to deal with matters of concern to Israel and Israelis which came within their substantive jurisdiction. Furthermore, Israeli law provided for the automatic service in Israel of documents issued by courts in the territories and for the

The imbalance can be explained by the fact that the Agreement is only an interim one, designed to postpone and delay any commitment to a permanent solution. A legal identity and full legal powers – on the governmental and the commercial level – had to be given to the Authority in order to enable it to act. But the legal framework was carefully constructed so as to avoid granting or acknowledging Palestinian statehood or sovereignty and thereby preempting a political solution. It restricted the powers of the Authority in such a way as to insulate Israelis and the Israeli economy from any of the potential effects of recognising this new economic entity.

But legal rules cannot contain and control political processes. A recent Israeli case provides graphic demonstration of this.

An Israeli oil company sought a temporary injunction against another Israeli oil company. The plaintiff wanted to prevent the defendant from

---

almost automatic enforcement in Israel of judgments issued by such courts (Emergency Order (Judea, Samaria and the Gaza Strip – Legal Assistance) (No. 2.) 5736-1976, Order Concerning Legal Assistance (No. 348) 5730-1969). These provisions were reciprocal. The rules concerning enforcement of judgments are interesting. Israeli judgments in the territories and local judgments in Israel were entitled to direct enforcement, subject to no condition at all save public policy. This situation placed judgments from the territories in a far superior position to that of other foreign judgments. This cannot be explained by the power of Israel in the territories, since Israel did not influence the local rules of jurisdiction and did not exclude Israelis from local jurisdiction. Interestingly, the Protocol rules on judgments are now more stringent, since they do require jurisdiction. But they are backed up by jurisdictional rules which exclude Israelis from local jurisdiction.

At the same time, however, a whole system of courts was established within and for the settlements, a special execution office was set up and large portions of Israeli law were extended on a personal basis to the settlers (see E. Benvenisti, *Legal Dualism, The Absorption of the Occupied Territories into Israel*, (West Bank Data Base Project, 1989); A. Rubinstein, 'Israel and the Territories: Jurisdiction of the Courts', 14 *Iyunei Mishpat* 415 (1989), (Hebrew).

It is important to note that these arrangements did not immunise the settlers from local law and its courts. It simply extended to them the umbrella of Israeli law so that their residence in the administered territories would not insulate them from Israeli prescriptive jurisdiction, and would not deprive them of the benefits of its facilitative institutions. As a purely practical matter, however, the legal lives of the two communities in the administered territories were effectively separated (Benvenisti suggests that cases involving Israelis were brought in Israeli courts because of the inefficiency of local courts, and that for this reason, even in purely local disputes, local residents tried to use Israeli courts (Benvenisti, *Legal Dualism*, p. 23)).

The formal provisions on legal assistance have been slightly expanded by the Protocol: the transfer of evidence, information, and suspects and witnesses is now reciprocal, and applies to all courts, in civil as well as in criminal matters. So too, the formal scope of Israeli jurisdiction over Israelis has been extended, and the formal scope of what is now Palestinian jurisdiction in the Territory has been constricted. In practice however, little has changed. The legal relations between the two systems before and after the Agreement are strikingly similar. Cooperation has merely been formally extended to the new authority in the Territory, and the existing jurisdictional reality has been formalised because that new authority is no longer under Israeli control.

performing a contract with the Palestinian Authority, under which, among other things, the defendant was to supply oil stations in the Jericho Area which would supply the whole of the local population. The plaintiff argued that this contract interfered with a pre-existing contract that *it* had with the three oil stations, which gave it exclusive supplying rights.

At first instance, the injunction was granted, but on appeal, a judge of the District Court in Tel Aviv revoked the injunction on the intriguing basis that Israeli courts are not authorised to intervene in matters of policy set by the Palestinian Authority in its capacity as *de facto* sovereign in the Territory under its control.[53] The reasoning behind this decision is not very clear. On the one hand, the judge suggests that Israeli courts have no jurisdiction over such matters because the Cairo Agreement does not grant them any such jurisdiction. The jurisdiction of Israeli courts is, however, determined exclusively by Israeli law. Even if the Cairo Agreement had restricted Israeli judicial jurisdiction – and as we have seen, it did not – its provisions would have to be incorporated into Israeli law in order for them to bind an Israeli court. There is no legal basis for an Israeli court to think that its jurisdiction is limited because a certain power is not granted it by an international agreement. But even if the Cairo Agreement were directly relevant, the unrestricted ability of the Palestinian Authority to sue and to be sued is probably the only provision in it that is relevant to Israeli jurisdiction, since this provides the Authority with the legal personality necessary to its status as defendant.

On the other hand, if the judge was referring to the doctrine of sovereign immunity, it clearly does not apply in this case for two separate reasons. The first is that the Palestinian Authority is not a state, and only recognised sovereign states enjoy sovereign immunity. The second reason is that, even if it were a state, the doctrine, as it is now understood in many countries including Israel, does not apply in commercial cases. Were a foreign sovereign state involved, an Israeli court could quite legitimately express an opinion on the case and even perhaps issue an injunction against the defendant foreign state or its commercial organs.[54] Furthermore, in the matter under discussion, the Authority was not even a defendant; the oil company was. The reluctance felt by the judge to interfere in this matter indicates that the political relationship between the Parties makes it in some ways more awkward to take jurisdiction over commercial matters in which

53 1726/1994 (Civil Case) (T.A.), Judge Uri Goren, 24th October 1994.

54 In England, where the doctrine of sovereign immunity is also not applied in commercial cases, the statutory regime governing this issue does not permit the court to issue injunctions against foreign sovereigns.

the non-sovereign Palestinian Authority is involved than it is to take such jurisdiction over foreign sovereigns.[55]

This decision, while clearly not required by law, reveals the powerful and inevitable political impact of recognising even the limited existence of the Palestinian Authority, and it demonstrates the futility of using legal tools to mute dynamic political issues. On a more optimistic note, it suggests that the deliberate legal imbalance between the parties cannot be maintained simply by an economic agreement, and that, once the inevitable political balance is achieved and ultimately recognised in law, the aspect of the legal framework most likely to survive may be the aspiration, and the legal basis it provides, for cooperation.

55 The Supreme Court affirmed the decision on a very narrow basis (Civil Motion for Leave to Appeal 5878/1994, 14th November 1994): as a result of the Cairo Agreement and the Palestinian Authority's decisions with respect to the supply of oil for the local population, the local oil stations are no longer able to perform their contract with the plaintiff. The balance of justice requires that the needs of the local population be preferred to the plaintiff's interest in the preservation of its contract. As a result, the discretionary remedy of an injunction is not justified in the circumstances. The court explicitly left open the door to a civil suit for compensation against the relevant party.

8. Power and Trade: The Israeli-Palestinian Economic Protocol

Sharif S. Elmusa and Mahmud El-Jaafari[1]

Economics have been so central to the Arab-Israeli accommodation effort over the last two years that there sometimes appears to be a deliberate attempt to submerge political issues. As an example of the intimate interaction between politics and economics, accommodation has been marketed as the road to regional prosperity while the prosperity – coupled with the creation of economic interdependencies – is being billed as the guarantee for the accommodation's durability. These premises are exemplified in the "Casablanca Declaration" issued on 1 November 1994 at the end of the two-day Middle East/North Africa Economic Summit that was attended by high-level official delegates, businessmen, and specialists from the two regions, Europe, the United States, and other countries.

The premises can be argued and deserve a separate analysis. Nonetheless, the "vision" of mutually reinforcing peace and prosperity has been very much in evidence in the Palestinian-Israeli accommodation process as well. It underlies, in particular, the pledge of $2.4 billion by the international community to aid in the reconstruction of Gaza and the West Bank. Where the Palestinian-Israeli case vitally differs from the others is that the web of economic links does not have to be created; unlike, say, in the Israeli-Jordanian case, it has been in existence since the beginning of the occupation.

This web, woven by Israel to serve its own economic and strategic interests, has kept the Palestinian economy in a state of underdevelopment and subordination to the Israeli economy. The Palestinians tried unsuccessfully during the *intifada* to unravel this web by boycotting Israeli goods, resisting tax payments, and encouraging local production. Subsequently, Palestinian negotiators tried to renegotiate the economic relationship between the occupied Palestinian territory (OPT) and Israel. The first of the resulting two agreements consists of the economic provisions (a statement of general principles and an outline of areas of cooperation) of the Declaration of Principles (DOP) signed by Israel and the Palestine Liberation Organization (PLO) on 13 September 1993 (Article XI, Annexes III and IV). The second agreement was the "Paris Protocol on Economic Relations between the Government of Israel and the PLO Representing the Palestinian People", signed in Paris on 29 April 1994 and subsequently

[1] An earlier version of this article appeared in the 1995 Winter issue of the *Journal of Palestine Studies.*

incorporated as Annex IV in the Gaza-Jericho agreement signed in Cairo on 4 May 1994.[2] It is this latter agreement that is the focus of this paper.

The Paris Protocol, which consists of a preamble and a dozen articles and annexes covering banking, trade, taxes, labour, insurance, tourism, and so forth, delineates the spheres of Palestinian autonomous decision making as well as the rules that will govern the economic relationship that will emerge between the self-governing Palestinian areas and Israel. It also sets the framework for and the constraints on the development of the Palestinian economy over the next few years. The extent to which the Palestinians take advantage of the opportunities and mitigate the constraints will depend on the ability of the Palestinian National Authority (PNA) to build the prerequisite institutions and legal environment and to formulate proper policies. It will also depend on the security situation, on Israel's goodwill, and on the PNA's relations with other Arab countries.

Although articles have been written about the protocol, none to our knowledge has attempted a detailed analysis of its possible impact on the Palestinian economy. The present article aims to do so by examining the conditions set out in the trade and labour articles of the protocol, the entire document being too long and complicated to be handled in a single writing. Trade and labour represent the major forms of economic transactions between the two sides and heavily influence the behaviour of the Palestinian economy. In the course of our inquiry, we will consider such questions as whether the new trade and customs union regime will reduce the OPT trade deficit with Israel, diversify the Palestinians' trading partners, lead to economic development, help integrate Gaza and the West Bank, and stabilize the job market for Palestinian workers in Israel.

I. Economic Relations on the Eve of the Protocol

Prior to its occupation by Israel in 1967, the West Bank was an integral part of Jordan both politically and economically. Gaza, on the other hand, was administered by Egypt and had economic links with Egypt and Eastern Europe, then Egypt's main trading partner. Economic ties-between the West Bank and Gaza, geographically separated by Israel, were non-existent.

The situation changed dramatically with the occupation,[3] after which both the West Bank and Gaza were enveloped in a one-sided customs

---

2 See 'Israel-PLO Protocol on Economic Relations', Paris, 29 April 1994, in *Journal of Palestine Studies* 23, No. 4, (Summer 1994), pp. 103-118.

3 Much has been written about the Palestinian economy under Israeli occupation. The following summation draws heavily on this body of writing. For more details, see, among others, George Abed, *The Economic Viability of a Palestinian State*,

union with Israel. This customs union entailed exports from Israel to the two regions and labour flows in the opposite direction. But while the economies of the West Bank and Gaza became extensively linked to Israel, they remained isolated from each other in a way reminiscent of the classical dependency syndrome in which third world countries were tied to Europe and the United States but not to one another. At the same time, the West Bank's economic ties with Jordan and Gaza's with Egypt diminished. Israel did not allow goods from Jordan to the OPT, and the rules of the Arab boycott of Israel inadvertently limited the flow of goods from the OPT to Jordan and the rest of the Arab world.[4]

An outline of the economic relationship between Israel and the West Bank and Gaza both before and under the protocol is illustrated in table 1. Before the protocol, Israel controlled banking operations in the OPT, and the Israeli currency became the main legal tender there. In fact, the banking services were minimal, and little credit was disbursed. As for trade, Israel set tariffs according to its perceived economic advantage, which was not necessarily beneficial to the OPT. The same was true of the value-added tax (VAT), the monies of which were retained by Israel together with other monies.[5] The World Bank euphemistically dubbed Israel's extraction of such economic surplus "fiscal compression".[6]

Trade between the OPT and Israel remained primarily a one-way activity. Israeli products and reexports flowed without impediment to the OPT, whereas numerous non-tariff restrictions (security, health and safety, bans on imports) were imposed on Palestinian exports to Israel, to say nothing of the significant subsidies to Israeli producers. The Palestinians, for their part, were allowed to import only through Israel. An outcome of all these practices throughout the years of occupation

---

(Washington D.C., Institute for Palestine Studies, 1990); the articles in George Abed, (ed.), *The Palestinian Economy: Studies in Development Under Prolonged Occupation*, (London, Routledge, 1988); Meron Benvenisti, *The West Bank Data Project: A Survey of Israel's Policies*, (Washington D.C., American Enterprise Institute, 1984); Osama Hamad and R. Shaban, 'One-Sided Customs and Monetary Union: The Case of the West Bank and Gaza Strip under Israeli Occupation', in S. Fischer et al, (eds.), *The Economics of the Middle East*, (Cambridge, MA, Massachusetts Institute of Technology Press, 1993), pp. 117-148; David Kahan, *Agriculture and Water Resources in the West Bank and Gaza (1967–1987)*, (West Jerusalem, The Jerusalem Post, 1987); Mahmud El-Jaafari, 'Non-Tariff Trade Barriers: The Case of the West Bank and Gaza Strip Agricultural Exports', *Journal of World Trade* 5, No. 3, (1991), pp. 15-32; Sara Roy, 'The Gaza Strip: A Case of Economic De-Development', *Journal of Palestine Studies* 17, No. 1, (Autumn 1987), pp. 56-88; World Bank, *Developing the Occupied Territories: An Investment in Peace*, 7 Vols, (Washington D.C., 1993).

4 In accordance with the Arab boycott rules, goods produced in the West Bank and Gaza using Israeli inputs or in plants established after 1967 were not permitted into Jordan. Sometimes, the rules of the Arab boycott were stretched to include other goods, especially after Jordan "disengaged" from the West Bank in 1988.

5 Other types of surplus included revenues generated from having Israel's new shekel (NIS) the main legal tender (seigniorage tax) and deductions collected from the Palestinians working in Israel.

6 World Bank, *Developing the Occupied Territories*, Vol. 2, p. 28.

was that the OPT had with Israel an extraordinary trade-partner concentration and an overwhelming chronic merchandise trade deficit (see table 2).[7]

Industrial and agricultural development was also subjected to the heavy hand of Israeli regulations and policies. Israel used its hold over licensing to stymie industrial development in the West Bank and Gaza by frequently refusing to grant permits to Palestinians wishing to establish factories. Industrialization was also impeded by the high prices resulting from extensive land expropriation and land use restrictions, the absence of a banking system providing credit, and poor infrastructure and support services.

The Palestinian domestic production thus remained service- and agriculture-based, with agriculture contributing around one-third of the GDP in the last several years (see table 2). The agricultural sector grew, thanks mainly to investment by Palestinian farmers in the high-yielding, water-saving technology of drip irrigation. Despite the presence of large tracts of land in the West Bank that could readily have been reclaimed, there was no horizontal expansion because of the restrictions on Palestinian access to land and water, as will be discussed below.[8] The public infrastructure deteriorated, investments in this sector not exceeding 3 percent of the GDP according to World Bank estimates.[9] The major part of private investment went into housing.

The overall lack of investment impeded job creation; about one-third of the labour force had to seek employment in Israel and the settlements. The export of labour to Israel helps explain both the rise of income level in the OPT, despite the marked unemployment level, and the difference between the GDP and the GNP, the former averaging less than three-quarters of the latter in 1990–92. However, since the *intifada* and particularly since the Gulf War in 1991, employment in Israel has become hostage to political winds.

Israel was able to subordinate the economies of the West Bank and Gaza Strip not only because of its military and institutional hold, but more importantly because its economy was far larger, more sophisticated, and more diversified than the Palestinian. For example, the Israeli GDP averaged eighteen times the Palestinian GDP in the period 1990–92. Israel's industry supplied a wide range of consumer

---

7 The reader ought to keep in mind that the statistics in this table rely, for the most part, on the annual editions of the *Statistical Abstract of Israel*. Though the abstracts have provided the most complete time-series data on the OPT's economy, they have been disputed by independent researchers. We use them here for illustration only. In particular, the open borders between Israel and the OPT make it difficult to have reliable trade data. Also, statistics in general since the *intifada* are believed by many analysts to be less reliable than before.

8 Sharif Elmusa, 'Dividing the Common Palestinian-Israeli Water Resources; An International Water Law Approach', *Journal of Palestine Studies* 22, No. 3, (Spring 1993), pp. 57-77.

9 World Bank, *Developing the Occupied Territories*, Vol. 2, p. 2.

goods, especially plastics and electrical appliances, whereas Palestinian small industrial output consisted of low-value-added products, mainly simple processed foods, handicrafts, and shoes.

It is against this backdrop that the impact of the protocol, and, in a way, Palestinian future economic performance, must be assessed.

II. Overview of the Protocol

The protocol covers essentially all the Palestinian economic sectors, the Palestinian and Israeli roles, and Palestinian economic relations with Israel and other countries. Its implementation is to be overseen by a Joint Economic Committee or JEC (Art. II), which will decide on disputes and review any issue at the request of either party. It will also determine the quantities of various goods that Palestinians can import and other import rules.

The protocol does not permit the Palestinians to have their own currency (which would carry with it the symbolism of sovereignty); the official legal tender remains the Israeli new shekel (NIS), although the Jordanian dinar and the dollar can still be used. In any case, the Palestinian economy is probably not in a position to support a convertible currency at present. Be that as it may, the absence of a separate currency automatically deprives the PNA of the instruments of making monetary policy, especially the determination of interest rates and currency value. Palestinian economic performance will thus be linked to the monetary conditions in Israel and, to a lesser extent, Jordan.

On the other hand, the protocol does enable the Palestinians to have significant control over banking operations, allowing them to set up for this purpose the Palestinian Monetary Authority (Art. IV.1). This authority is empowered to make a full range of fiscal policies that had been in the hands of the Israeli government: management of official reserves, bank licensing and regulation, and settlement of foreign exchange accounts with Israel and Jordan. Should a viable banking sector evolve, this could constitute one of the main missing instruments for encouraging savings and investment and facilitating trade.

The Palestinians will also be able, according to the protocol, to establish independent direct tax levels and to collect the taxes. They are much more bound when it comes to indirect taxation such as tariffs and the VAT, as will be explained below. But whereas in the past indirect tax revenues were channelled to the Israeli government, according to the protocol they will be transferred to the PNA and partly collected by it.

In the areas of trade and labour, the protocol spells out the rules governing imports and exports between the areas under the PNA and Israel, and between those areas and the rest of the world. Goods that

Palestinians may import from places other than Israel are specified in three separate lists along with restrictions concerning quantity, origin, and standards. The protocol also deals with the free movement of exports between the autonomous areas and Israel, once again after health, safety, and other standards are met. It allows for the free movement of labour, but theoretically gives the two parties the freedom to restrict entry.

III. Imports

Article II regulates the OPT's imports from countries other than Israel. Imports from Israel to the West Bank would remain, as before, unhindered, and the protocol does not address how Israel makes its own trade policy.

The protocol lists the types of goods that Palestinians may import from places other than Israel under categories A1, A2, and B (petroleum and cars are dealt with separately). Goods not included in these categories are subject to the old import restrictions. Lists A1 and A2 contain food and agricultural products (not including fresh fruits and vegetables), basic construction materials (e.g., cement, steel), fertilizers, and household electric appliances (e.g., refrigerators, washing machines). The PNA will be able to set the customs levels on these goods based on the last General Agreement on Trade and Tariffs agreement (GATT; Uruguay Round) when it takes effect in Israel.[10] Construction materials (with the exception of aluminum), fertilizers, and household appliances would have to be imported from Jordan or Egypt, and the remaining items in these categories from these two and other Arab or Islamic countries. The commodities must not be final-assembly products; the domestic Jordanian, Egyptian (or other) contribution must be 30 per cent of the exports' value. The items must also comply with specified quantitative limitations determined by the two sides "up to the Palestinian market needs". The quantities of construction materials, fertilizers, and wheat, however, were preset in the protocol at levels equivalent to an estimated 50 percent of the market needs; others were to be negotiated subsequently. The quantities would be subject to periodic reviews to take into consideration changes in demand.

List B consists of capital goods for economic development, including agricultural equipment (e.g., harvesters, threshers), heavy construction and earth moving equipment, and factory and household textile machinery and tools. No tariff, origin, or quantity restrictions apply to

---

10 Until GATT takes effect, customs levels will be based on the Brussels Definition of Valuation (BDV).

these goods as they are deemed essential for the development of the Palestinian economy.

The protocol partially frees petroleum and cars from the one-sided customs union. Under the protocol, the PNA can import gasoline from Jordan or Egypt (if it meets European and American standards) in quantities fixed by the JEC and sell it to the consumers at prices 15 percent lower than in Israel. Other petroleum products, such as heating oil, can also be imported from Jordan, and without price restrictions. The PNA would be able to determine its own rates on motor vehicles, but cars more than three years old would not be allowed in.

The goods and quantities not fixed by the JEC or covered in the protocol will continue to be subject to tariff rates, purchase taxes, levies, and other charges that are at least equal to those prevailing in Israel; the PNA is entitled to set higher levels. Also, the PNA will levy VAT on *all* imports as well as on locally produced goods. The minimum rate of the VAT is 15-16 percent, nearly equal to the Israeli rate of 17 percent.

The Palestinians could achieve two types of financial gain from the new import regulations. First, import taxes and levies on *all* goods explicitly designated for Palestinians in the areas under the jurisdiction of the PNA will accrue to the PNA even if imported via Israeli middlemen. Such revenues were conservatively estimated by the World Bank at 8 percent of the Palestinian GDP.[11] But while theoretically this should be a straightforward gain, how much of it will actually be realized will depend on the Palestinians' ability speedily to establish a sophisticated network of wholesale importers. (Purchasing on a retail basis from Israeli importers, as has hitherto been the common practice, makes it much harder to designate goods for the Palestinian areas.)

A second import-related financial benefit could come from the import of goods from cheaper sources. In the case of petroleum, motor vehicles, and the capital goods in list B, this should be straightforward. Israeli tariffs on list B's capital investment goods are 21 percent,[12] too high for the OPT's development requirements, so freeing such goods from Israeli taxation is an important gain. But list B does not cover all capital investment equipment: computers, for example, or pesticides for agriculture continue to be subject to the previous customs union rules while the price of these materials has risen sharply in the last years and the price of output has fluctuated around the same level.[13]

The array of restrictions, especially on agricultural imports and lists Al and A2, casts a long shadow on potential gains. The two sides are to

---

[11] World Bank, *Developing the Occupied Territories*, Vol. 2, p. 33.

[12] Karim Nashashibi and Oussman Kanaan, 'Which Trade Arrangements for the West Bank and Gaza?, *Finance and Development* 31, No. 3, (1994), pp. 10-13.

[13] The price index of pesticides nearly doubled between 1986 and 1992, while those of West Bank's vegetables increased by 25 percent and of Gaza's by less than 10 percent. State of Israel, Israeli Central Bureau of Statistics, *Statistical Abstract*, 1993.

refrain from importing "agricultural products" that may adversely affect the farmers of the other side, without prejudice to existing international arrangements (Art. VIII.12). As the Palestinians have no existing international arrangements, the clause is effectively a barrier to the Palestinians more than to the Israelis, especially since the Israelis can inspect Palestinian imports while the Palestinians do not have the corresponding right. The extent to which this would affect the Palestinians is difficult to ascertain without a detailed study of Israel's farm output, its international obligations, and its potential conflict with relation to Palestinian demand. Still, the fact that Israel saw the need to include such a clause indicates that it must have anticipated losses if the Palestinians purchased certain types of commodities from other sources, especially fruits and milk (still to be negotiated) but which Israel exports in large quantities to the West Bank and Gaza.

Restricting the import of household electric appliances in lists A1 and A2 to Jordan and Egypt may effectively keep the Palestinians from moving outside the customs union wall for these items. Not many such appliances are likely to be imported from Jordan or Egypt thanks to the generally low quality and the domestic-content requirements of these products. Most of these durables, then, will probably continue to come from Israel, thus earning Israel its traditional 70 percent import tariff. Israel's insistence on origin for these goods perhaps stems from the fact that such durables constitute 20 percent of its own industrial output.[14]

Further, the requirement that tariff rates on A1 and A2 be equal to the GATT rates denies the PNA the freedom to set its own tariff levels and draws it into joining the GATT whether it likes it or not. In any case, neither the PNA nor consumers are likely to gain or lose much financially from importing food and agricultural commodities from new sources, Israeli tariffs on foodstuffs being either low or non-existent.

Many questions can be raised about the quantitative limitations on the goods in lists Al and A2, which not only undermine many of the potential gains but also could illegitimately enrich wholesale merchants and induce collusion between them and PNA officials. Tying permissible import levels to "market needs" is problematic for a number of reasons, not least of which is the non-existence of reliable household consumption surveys and the unreliability, in the view of most experts, of macro statistics, especially after the *intifada*. Even the population size in the West Bank and Gaza is uncertain. It often seems that the Israelis deduce West Bank and Gaza consumption as a residual of Israel's production, consumption, and trade estimates. Also, how can consumption levels be determined when income changes and when for many goods there are no reliable estimates on income elasticity of

---

[14] The statistics are from Nashashibi and Kanaan, "Which Trade Arrangements", p. 12.

demand (which measures how demand responds to income change)? Further, the protocol's stipulation that imports cannot exceed market needs (are "up to the market needs") could encourage Israel to "err" on the lower side, to protect its own exports to the West Bank and Gaza.

Even if the quantities were commensurate with market needs, how can one guarantee, in the absence of borders, that the goods would not filter to the Israeli market where they could fetch higher prices, or, conversely, that goods from Israel would not continue to dominate the market? Merchants could reap windfall profits from the first instance, but the Palestinian consumers would lose. In the second instance, goods from Israel would enjoy a comparative advantage owing to the geographic proximity and the ease with which they can be brought in to the OPT.

The PNA is to set the allotment of quantities. Experience elsewhere suggests that giving bureaucrats such a responsibility is conducive to the creation of the "moral hazard" problem among them.[15] Indeed, charges have already been levelled against the leadership of the PNA that it has not made public auctions for the import of cement, communications equipment, and petroleum, and that it favoured particular merchants.[16]

IV. Exports

The protocol states that there is to be free movement of both agricultural produce and industrial goods between the two sides without additional customs and import taxes, subject to certain exceptions and arrangements (Arts. VIII and IX). The Palestinians would be able to export their commodities to other countries as well, presumably without the earlier barriers. Within the constraints of the protocol, the Palestinians would be able to adopt policies promoting development in the areas of credit, research, development assistance, and direct-tax benefits (the VAT, as noted, is set at 15-16 percent).

Exports from the OPT to Israel would have to meet the environmental, health, and safety standards in force in Israel. Moreover, there are quantitative restrictions on the export by Palestinians to Israel of vegetable products, poultry, and eggs. These quotas are to be phased out and would be completely eliminated by 1998 (see table 3).

The extent to which the protocol would affect Palestinian exports and the attendant trade deficit is difficult to assess. In industry, it would depend on the growth of manufacturing and the diversification of the present structure (see below). In agriculture, the quotas put in place to

15 The lists are not supposed to be made available to merchants, according to a statement by Samir Hulayli, a member of the team that negotiated the protocol, reported in *al-Quds*, 6 June 1994.

16 Julian Ozanne, *al-Hayat*, 1 November 1994, p. 10.

protect Israeli produce from Palestinian competition nearly vitiate any export advantage: Only 25 percent of the OPT's vegetable production would have unrestricted access to the Israeli market.

In addition, according to our estimates, the quotas on some produce items to be exported by the Palestinians[17] are below the level of what used to be exported illegally.[18] It is unclear to us on what basis Palestinian negotiators accepted the quotas, unless they assumed that illegal exports would continue, or why Israel would restrict the export of Palestinian melons when it exports this crop to the OPT. And while Israel clearly set quotas on eggs and poultry to protect its own producers,[19] no commensurate restrictions were placed on Israeli fruits and vegetables to protect Palestinian farmers.[20]

Palestinian industry and agriculture would also be at a disadvantage vis-à-vis their Israeli counterparts because of the generous subsidies Israel gives to both sectors. For example, Israel's support for its agriculture in the form of credit on concessionary terms, subsidies of factors of production (especially water and land), export finance, and minimum price levels for certain products, averaged 32 percent of the value of than sector's output during 1984–90.[21] By contrast, support for Palestinian agriculture has been minimal, sporadic, and mainly from non-governmental organizations. In order to give Palestinian exports a fair competitive edge, the support levels to both agricultural sectors would have had to be made even. The Palestinians can try to find other markets, but this is by no means an easy task, especially for agriculture, in light of regional production and marketing conditions.

---

17 The quotas target cucumbers, melons, potatoes, and tomatoes. Eggs and poultry are also subject to quotas.

18 The cucumbers' quota reaches 15 thousand tons in 1996, whereas our estimates using an econometric model indicate that cucumber exports between 1990–1992 averaged 19 thousand tons/year. The corresponding quota and export figures of potatoes are 15 thousand tons and 17 thousand tons.

19 Before the protocol, export of eggs and poultry to Israel was prohibited, but the quotas set today do not provide much relief. The difference between egg production over consumption in the West Bank and Gaza greatly surpasses the quotas, and there is no excess chicken (for meat) production. For example, we estimate that excess egg production the West Bank and Gaza amounted to 180-190 million eggs in 1992, or about six times the protocol's export quota for 1994 and three times of that for 1998, when the quotas would be terminated. Palestinian egg producers could switch from eggs to chickens for meat, but conversion would be relatively costly.

20 Israel sells large quantities of agricultural products (other than agricultural inputs, such as fertilizers and pesticides), especially fruits and vegetables, the value of which in 1986 was 15 percent of total Israeli agricultural exports. Estimates by Mahmud El-Jaafari, 'Agricultural Imports of the West Bank and Gaza' (in two parts), *al-Bayadir al-Siyasi*, 13 and 20 August 1988.

21 Nashabishi and Kanaan, "Which Trade Arrangements", p. 11.

V. Diversification of Trade Partners

Economic integration, or rather reintegration, with the countries of the region will not be easy. The imports provision in the protocol opens a window, albeit with the severe limitations mentioned earlier. The restriction that many goods be imported specifically from Egypt and Jordan narrows the window further. These restrictions may have been unavoidable, for, from an economic standpoint, Jordan would have insisted that its trade deficit with the West Bank and Gaza (see table 2) be addressed. From a political standpoint, Palestinians would want close trade ties with Jordan not only for geo-strategic (if not Arab nationalist) reasons, but also because much of the trade in Jordan is in the hands of the Palestinian-Jordanians and because Jordan provides a key exit to the rest of the Arab world. Trade links with Egypt would provide balance, especially given its steady ties with the PLO leadership for over a decade. Israel, for its part, would have wanted to strengthen the position of Jordan and Egypt in the OPT for their expected moderating political influence. By strengthening Jordan's economic position in the OPT, Israel may also seek to fuel competition between Jordan and the PNA.[22] Whatever the reasons, the domestic-origin and country-restrictions exclude other potential regional trade partners and even undermine the possibility of importing goods from sources beyond the customs union wall, as was argued above.

But even if the trade gates were opened, would integration take place? Inter-Arab trade usually comprises less than 5 percent of the overall value of Arab trade. Jordan, whose economy is probably the most integrated with other Arab economies, usually receives more than three-quarters of its imports from outside the Arab region,[23] largely because of the region's lack of complementarity in production and diversified industrial structure, although inter-Arab political quarrels also take their toll. Similarly for the Palestinians, imports, especially of capital and durable consumer goods, would come from the industrialized countries and from Southeast Asia, at least for the medium term. Many foodstuffs, especially wheat and rice, would also come from outside the region.

In the export domain, however, Jordan was successful in finding a large niche in the Arab markets of Saudi Arabia, the Gulf, and Iraq: Even though these were disrupted, the example shows what can happen

---

22 Israel unilaterally agreed to allow Jordan to export $30 million worth of goods to the West Bank as part of an economic agreement it signed with Jordan on 16 August 1994. (See *Qol Yisra'el*, 16 August, and *Radio Jordan Network*, 16 August, as translated in *FBIS*, 17 August 1994.) On possible Israeli motivations for strengthening Jordan's position, see, for example, David Makovsky, *Jerusalem Post*, 22 July 1994.

23 Compare the figures for imports over the years as printed in the Central Bank of Jordan's annual reports.

under normal conditions.[24] But the West Bank and Gaza would have more difficulty locating market outlets than Jordan, at least in the short term, because their production costs, greatly influenced by the Israeli cost structure, are higher than in the non-oil producing states. It would also be more difficult for the Palestinians to find the least costly materials because of the import restrictions. In order to compete, Palestinian producers would have to become highly efficient, not an easy task considering the general state of under-development in the OPT.

While integration with regional partners is vital and has been much stressed by analysts, we believe that priority should go to integrating Gaza and the West Bank, two pieces of territory separated by Israel. Such integration – neither encouraged nor discouraged by the protocol, which does not address the issue – will not be easy. It would require much planning owing to the two economies' similar production structures. It would also require lifting Gaza from its peripheral status, temporarily obscured by its position as seat of the PNA, with regard to the West Bank. Certainly, having the same currency (if it ever comes into being), banking systems, and legal and regulatory environment would help, but without the flow of goods, services, people, and information, integration cannot happen. The crucial importance of overcoming the territorial discontinuity becomes clear when one recalls that Pakistan's split in 1971 was caused by the lack of integration of the western and eastern parts of the country and the marginalization of East Pakistan (Bangladesh).

VI. Economic Growth and Diversification

Implementation of the protocol would give to the Palestinians, though not retroactively, most of the indirect tax monies (estimated conservatively by the World Bank at 8 percent of the Palestinian GDP in 1991[25]) that Israel appropriated until then. These funds can become an important source for investment. Although not part of the protocol, the money pledged by the donors, insufficient and slow in coming as it is, would also give a boost to growth.

The donor funds are largely earmarked for administrative costs and infrastructural projects. Economic growth from such outlays could occur as a result of the demands of goods and services that the projects would generate and the increased efficiency of the facilities and services on which economic activities depend. Even if the contribution to growth

---

24 For example, in 1985–1986 Jordan's exports to these countries amounted to approximately 50 percent of its total exports. However, in 1992, after the Gulf War, that figure had dropped to less than 25 percent. See the Central Bank of Jordan's annual reports for 1988 and 1992.

25 World Bank, *Developing the Occupied Territories*, Vol. 2, p. 28.

and diversification of the economic structure were small, the investment would improve the quality of roads, communications, health services, and education facilities – areas that touch the daily lives of the population.

The long-term sustainable growth would have to come from agriculture, industry, and services, especially tourism. We highlight here only the possibilities of agricultural and industrial development; tourism, though dealt with in the protocol, requires a different treatment.

Agricultural growth can come from either horizontal (land area) or vertical (intensification) expansion. Both face serious constraints in the OPT. Horizontal expansion is severely checked by land and water availability, even though there are more than 170,000 dunums of irrigable land without soil or topographic barriers in the West Bank that could be added to the present 90,000-100,000 dunums under cultivation. That they have not been reclaimed is the result of Israel's freeze on the Palestinians' irrigation water supply at 1967 levels, not to mention Israeli acquisition of parts of the land for settlements and alleged security reasons. Since land and water questions have been deferred – the former to the final status negotiations and the latter *sine die* despite the DOP's mention of water negotiations during the interim period – horizontal expansion is out.

As for vertical expansion, possibilities are seriously hampered by the uncertain access of Palestinian produce to markets. The Israeli market is protected by the protocol's quotas on Palestinian produce exports and by Israel's subsidies to its own farmers. In the regional markets, Palestinian produce would be disadvantaged by the higher production costs stemming from higher wages, import restrictions on fertilizers and pesticides, farm subsidies in the neighbouring countries, and woefully inadequate institutional support. If despite these barriers intensification was to occur, it would be on a limited scale through greenhouse cultivation, which requires large amounts of water and pesticides that could have a hazardous impact on health and groundwater resources. Thus, short of removing onerous impediments or adopting environmentally unsound practices, the agricultural sector is likely to remain close to its present position.

Industry, meanwhile, basically of the family-operated, craft type, probably contributes less than 10 percent of the GDP. Manufacturing is currently centred on food processing, textiles, and soap-making. Some small-scale subcontracting operations, especially in Gaza, have been undertaken with Israeli firms seeking cheaper labour costs.

In theory, there is room for industrial expansion. The establishment of import-substitution manufacturing (e.g., textiles, shoes, cosmetics, cigarettes, household detergents, building materials) is one avenue. But while there is a base and experience in these branches, several constraints should be noted. Modern production methods and improved quality would be essential for the output to be competitive in the domestic market, and the small size of this market would make appreciable growth in manufacturing dependent on exports. There, the potential for inroads into the Israeli market is checked by the standards requirements and by the subsidies to Israeli industry, although room may exist for the low-value-added manufacture of shoes and textiles.

The protocol gives the PNA leeway to subsidize industry. The income tax of companies may be the main avenue, since the VAT is already predetermined. Tax "holidays", however, would deprive the PNA of sorely needed tax revenues and should be conditional on achievement. Diversification into regional markets may be possible in principle, as the Jordanian example would suggest, but would require access to capital equipment and intermediate inputs from cheap sources. The protocol's list B of imports frees many items of equipment and machinery from the customs union wall. But aside from a variety of wood products, it does not include much that would be considered intermediate inputs, especially chemicals. Also, the industrial inputs would depend on the type of industry to be established, and cannot conceivably be tallied in advance. Contingencies could be negotiated, of course, but it would seem that, even assuming good faith on the part of Israel (a dubious assumption considering the fifteen months or so since the DOP), the process of negotiations and approvals would cause costly delays. These uncertainties and complications could further discourage potential investors, who have commonly gravitated toward services and real estate, thanks in part to Palestinian inexperience in manufacturing.

VII. Labour

Employment in Israel accounted for about 40 percent of the employment in the West Bank and Gaza and remained relatively stable before the *intifada*, involving some 109,000 workers in 1987.[26] Deductions from registered workers' wages to cover insurance payments and benefits to which they were entitled were retained by Israel.[27] Most of the Palestinian workers were employed in construction, agriculture, and services.

With the *intifada*, curfews and other security-related measures caused interruptions in the flow of Palestinian labour to Israel, but it was the Gulf War of 1991 that radically changed the situation. Israel sealed the West Bank and Gaza, preventing workers from crossing into Israel, and the pre-war employment levels have never even been approached since

---

26 World Bank, *Developing the Occupied Territories*, Vol. 2, p. 26.

27 Israel denies this accusation but has produced no evidence to support its claim. The deductions were estimated at $250 million, without the interest, over a 25-year period. See S. Fischer et al. (eds.), *Securing Peace in the Middle East*, (Cambridge, MA, Massachusetts Institute of Technology Press, 1994), p. 84.

then. Moreover, short-term as well as prolonged closures of the West Bank and Gaza continue sporadically, usually following either actual Palestinian attacks on Israelis inside Israel or Israeli government fears of the imminence of such attacks.[28] The result has been serious income drops for the workers and adverse impact for the Palestinian economy as a whole.

The protocol states that "both sides will attempt to maintain the normality of movement of labour between them", with the proviso that this would be subject to each side's (essentially Israel's) right to "determine from time to time the extent and conditions of the labour movement in its area" (Art. VII). It was also agreed that Israel would pay to the PNA 75 percent of the income tax deductions, but no mention is made of retroactive payments.

Palestinian labour in Israel has become a "necessary evil" for both sides, albeit less necessary for Israel than for the Palestinians. For Israel, Palestinian workers take jobs that the Israelis themselves increasingly shun. Generally dependable and hardworking, they also could be paid less and receive smaller insurance, health, and other benefits than their Israeli counterparts.[29] The fact that they have to leave Israel every day after work (although some stay the night illegally) in principle reduces social tensions. Still, many Israelis do not like to see Arabs working in their midst.

On the Palestinian side, work in Israel initially provoked controversy and sometimes armed attempts to stop it. Although lack of jobs in the West Bank and Gaza eventually reconciled many Palestinians to the realities, work in Israel was not without its social, economic, and political costs. For one thing, reliance on the Israeli markets means that decisions affecting the well-being of hundreds of thousands of people in the West Bank and Gaza are made by a government in which they have no voice. Israel appears also to have used the entry of workers to Israel for political ends, for example to pressure them to make concessions during the bilateral negotiations in Washington and to force the PNA to take tough measures against the opposition. Finally, for the Palestinians as a group, the social costs of their labour engaging in the low status jobs can be high: The psycho-social impact on the workers from this kind of relationship and the extent to which it conforms to the oppressor-oppressed distortions described by Paulo Freire and Frantz Fanon has yet to be investigated. In any case, it does not serve the goal of coexistence.

Nonetheless, the "employer-employee" relationship between Palestinians and Israelis cannot be terminated abruptly without considerable damage to the Palestinians: Israel must accept responsibility for the past benefits it reaped from Palestinian labour and for the policies it

---

28 It is interesting to note that the closures are a Labour party innovation, at odds with Likud's ideology of the OPT being integral parts of Israel.

29 See, for example, Fischer, *Securing Peace*, pp. 69-82.

implemented in the West Bank and Gaza that led to the lack of job creation there. Unfortunately, the protocol gives Israel an opening to escape this responsibility. Israel has not hesitated to use this opening, as evidenced by its repeated closures of the OPT since signing the agreement and its recent announcement that some 19,000 foreign workers, largely from Asia, would be allowed into Israel, presumably as a substitute for Palestinian workers.[30]

VIII. Assessment

Past economic relations between Israel on the one hand and the West Bank and Gaza on the other were formulated by the dictates of Israeli power to serve its own interests. Whatever benefits accrued to the Palestinians often came as unintended consequences. The protocol reflects the historical reality, the continuing occupation during the interim period, and Israel's insistence on protecting its own producers and maintaining insofar as possible its dominant share in the Palestinian market.

It would have been nearly impossible to have two highly divergent customs regimes without demarcating the political boundaries between the two sides. The attenuated one-sided customs union that emerged was therefore predetermined by the DOP: politics shaped economics.

But other parts of the protocol could have been different. The import restrictions as well as the VAT could have been relaxed much more without appreciable adverse impact on Israeli producers. The protocol could have freed the import of pesticides, for example, and all rather than half of the estimated fertilizers they need. A measure of reciprocity regarding agricultural exports could have been stipulated: free access or quotas for both sides, for example, rather than quotas for Palestinians and free access for Israel. Israel could also have made water and farmland "advances" to boost Palestinian agriculture as well as land advances to relieve the pressure on land prices for industrial sites. Handing over the tariff, VAT, deductions from workers employed in Israel, and other revenues could have been done retroactively. Israel's ability to close the labour market to Palestinians could have been handled in a way that acknowledges accommodation as a long process not lending itself to retaliation after every act of violence, and that recognizes Israel's moral responsibility toward the welfare of the Palestinian population (especially since high unemployment jeopardizes the accommodation process itself). All of these suggestions fall within the framework of the DOP, and could have imbued the protocol with the spirit of generosity and neighbourliness it sorely needs.

---

30 Clyde Haberman, *New York Times*, 31 October 1994, p. A11.

That the Palestinians were unable to obtain such concessions reflects, apart from the uneven balance of power, the uneven negotiating capability of the two sides. Israel, of course, benefitted from the mass of systematic information and analyses on the workings of its own economy as well as the economies of the West Bank and Gaza over the years. The Palestinians, by contrast, lacked detailed information and studies. They also failed to take full advantage of the available expertise because of the paralyzing centralism and preference for organizational and personal loyalties over expertise that have marred the conduct negotiations. Samir Hulayli, a member of the team that negotiated the protocol, acknowledged the lack of consultation but attributed it to lack of time.[31] Still, considering what was at stake for Israel – the peace treaty with Jordan, for example – the Palestinians could have pressed harder.

Those who judge the protocol on the extent to which it frees the Palestinian economy from Israeli political, security, and economic shackles will be disappointed, but such expectations in any case would have been unjustified considering the constraints of the DOP and the long years of dependence on the Israeli economy. A better yardstick for evaluating the protocol would be the breaches it introduces in the wall of the one-sided customs union and the possibilities for immediate financial gain – here one would be less disappointed.

Postscript

The extent to which the Palestinians are able to take advantage of the small openings offered depends, as has been stated, on two key features of the environment in which the protocol is implemented. First, is the degree to which Israel allows the free movement of goods, labour, and capital into and out of the West Bank and Gaza. Second, is the ability of the Palestinians themselves, particularly the PNA, to set up the prerequisite institutions and regulatory framework as well as to pursue appropriate economic policies.

The record on these matters, after more than a year since the signing of the protocol, has been less than encouraging. The most detrimental threat to the implementation of the protocol and to economic performance has been the security situation and delays in implementing other aspects of the Gaza-Jericho agreement. Gaza's economy in particular has been imperilled by prolonged closures following two devastating suicide bomb attacks by Islamic militants inside Israel.[32] The closures not only put out of work around one-half of the labour force in

---

31 Quoted in *al-Quds*, 6 June 1994.

32 The first was on 19 October 1994 and the second on 22 January 1995, *FBIS*, 19 October 1994 and 23 January 1995.

the strip, they also led to the interruption of the flow of materials and goods in and out of it. At one point, a merchant from Gaza needed to obtain three permits for the entry of goods into Israel: one for the truck, a second for the driver and a third for the goods themselves. Israel also severely hampered the movement of wholesale importers; to get to Israeli ports they had to use public transportation and obtain temporary permits that are typically revoked when incidents occur.[33] Such restrictions hurt not only workers, farmers, and businessmen, but also the truck owners and drivers. Inter-Palestinian clashes in December 1994 between the PNA security forces and the Islamic opposition underscored the potential for instability, not an encouraging prospect for investors.

Nor has the access of the Palestinian economy to the outside world been facilitated, thanks to Israel's failure to implement provisions in the Gaza-Jericho agreement. The four "safe" passages between Gaza and Jericho, stipulated in this agreement, were not opened. Gaza's trade with other Arab countries, a window that the protocol was supposed to open, was thus curtailed. Nor have the Palestinians been able to set up customs offices at the bridges and at Gaza's entrances; Israel remains the gatekeeper of Palestinian trade.[34] Finally, Israel has not eased the freedom of entry and residence for Palestinian expatriate entrepreneurs, thereby impeding the inflow of badly needed capital.

The institutional and regulatory sphere is also replete with obstacles. True, the PNA has established a skeletal institutional framework represented by various ministries (economics, planning, finance) and PECDAR (Palestine Economic Council for Development and Reconstruction), originally meant to act as the interface between the donors and the PNA for channelling aid money and ensuring transparency. These institutions, however, sorely need the staffing and expertise necessary to carry out their functions effectively, yet they have been given a layer of new, inexperienced personnel to preside over a bureaucracy dispirited by the occupation. Their work has been hampered by what might be described as a hybrid of hyper-centralization coupled with disorganized decentralization. On the one hand, President Arafat exercises apparently unlimited powers, approving many business deals and making appointments anywhere he wishes in the bureaucracy. On the other hand, no clear mandates have been assigned for the various ministries and departments which are often in conflict over authority and scope of work. This unruly situation is no doubt an outcome of the novelty of the job for the PNA, political and professional, if not personal, of competition among members of the

---

33 *Al-Hayat*, among others, frequently reports such events. See, for example, Susanna Tarbush, *Al-Hayat*, 13 December 1994, p. 10, citing Samir Hulayleh.

34 *Al-Hayat*, 8 June 1995, citing members of a Palestinian economic delegation in London.

Palestinian elite, and of a lack of an overall institution-building plan.[35] It has led, for example, international donors, who dispense aid to the PNA, to demand that by mid-May 1995 the PNA outline the "functional diagrams and policy responsibilities" of the main ministries in charge of economy and to name a "single point of contact" for finance, economy and trade, etc.[36]

Moreover, legal and regulatory problems may already have deterred potential investors.[37] One such problem is that the legal codes of Gaza and the West Bank need unification. Before the occupation in 1967, the West Bank's laws were those enacted by the government of Jordan after the merger of the East and West Banks in 1950 and those extant from the Ottoman and British Mandate times. In Gaza, on the other hand, most of the basic laws were inherited from the Ottoman and British Mandate periods; Egyptian laws were mostly regulatory, procedural and administrative. Israel superimposed its own laws, which typically took the form of Military Orders, and kept the legal regimes in Gaza and the West Bank separate.[38] In addition to unification, the laws need modernization to take into account environmental and health and safety concerns,[39] and the momentous transformations in global communications and trade regimes over the last three decades.

It was likely from the outset that the ability of the PNA to consolidate and update previous legislation and to unify the legal codes in Gaza and the West Bank would be complicated by the requirement that it secure Israeli approval for legal changes (DOP, Article IX, and Gaza-Jericho agreement, Article VII) and by the absence of a Palestinian legislative body owing to the delay of the elections. It is also difficult to see how commercial and investment laws, even if unified and reformed, could be

---

35 For example, according to 'Awn Shawa, the mayor of Gaza appointed by Yasir Arafat, there was a conflict over the scope of authority between PECDAR and the large municipalities, with PECDAR trying to implement municipal projects; he also cited a similar conflict between the ministry of local authority and the municipalities: see 'Awn Shawa, 'Municipalities and the Central Government', in *The Palestine National Authority: A Critical Appraisal*, (Washington, D.C., The Center for Policy Analysis on Palestine, special report, May 1995). The report includes several essays which highlight the many powers enjoyed by President Arafat and the chaotic situation of the bureaucracy; it generally paints a gloomy picture of the PNA's performance.

36 See 'Tripartite Action Plan of Revenues, Expenditures and Donor Funding for the Palestinian Authority', issued by the Ad-Hoc Liaison Committee in Paris, (27-28 April 1995). Text forthcoming in *Journal of Palestine Studies*, Vol. 24, (Summer 1995). The term "Tripartite" is used because the "action plan" was worked out by the donors, the PNA, and Israel.

37 For example, Abd Al-Majid Shuman, the head of the Arab Bank and the Jordan-Palestinian Economic Follow-up Committee, cited the need to overcome legal, administrative, and procedural problems that prohibit development, including the lack of a unified investment code, *Al-Hayat*, 1 June 1995.

38 Anis Kassim, 'Legal Systems and Development in Palestine', *The Palestine Yearbook of International Law*, (Nicosia, Cyprus, Al-Shaybani Society of International Law Ltd., 1984), pp. 19-35.

39 The World Bank, *Developing the Occupied Territories*, Vol. 3, p. 107.

effective without a simultaneous overhaul of a largely dysfunctional judicial and court system (see articles by Anis al-Qasem and Mona Rishmawi in this volume). Nonetheless, the cited donors' "tripartite action plan" set the 1st June 1996 as a target date for the completion of the unification of the laws in Gaza and Jericho (not in all of the West Bank, where the Israeli-controlled Civil Administration would not be altogether dissolved).

This is not to say that there has been no progress in any sphere. The Palestinians have begun to receive the VAT and other tariffs as well as workers' deductions in accordance with the protocol. A number of banks have opened branches in the West Bank and Gaza, and plans were announced for building societies. One of the main pillars of a modern economy is thus being erected. Several investment companies have also been formed, largely by Palestinian expatriates and, on occasion, Arabs. A Palestinian concern was awarded a contract to revamp the Gaza telephone network, the first contract of its kind.[40] There has also been a construction binge in both Gaza and the West Bank, although it has led to land speculation, reminiscent of that in many Arab countries during the 1970s oil-induced economic boom, and does not seem to offer housing to the middle- or low-income strata.[41] Saudi Arabia also has agreed to open its market to Gaza's produce, which would be shipped through Egyptian and Jordanian territory, giving respite to the strip's farmers, though inadvertently reinforcing its separation from the West Bank.[42] But overall, progress has been agonizingly slow: economics have remained hostage to politics, and the postulate of mutual reinforcement between peace and prosperity has remained just that, a postulate. Unless Israel loosens its grip on Palestinian trade and economic activity and unless governance is substantially reformed, rebuilding the devastated Palestinian economy and unravelling its web of dependence on the Israeli economy will be a long way off.

---

40 *Al-Hayat*, various issues.

41 For example, a small flat in the new highrise buildings in Gaza city, which were owned by a handful of landlords, fetched $500 per month – more than the average salary of the civil servant; Hussein Hijazi, *Al-Hayat*, 6 February 1995. A similar situation also exists in the West Bank.

42 *Al-Hayat*, 8 June 1995.

TABLE 1
Palestinian-Israeli Economic Relations
Before and According to the Protocol

Item	**Before**	**According to**
Customs Union	One-sided	Attenuated one-sided
Decision making by	Israel	JEC + PNA
Currency	NIS + JD	NIS + JD
Monetary policies set by	Israel	Israel
Fiscal policies set by	Israel	PNA
Customs		
Value determination by	Israel	Israel + PNA
Revenues to	Israel	PNA
Direct tax		
Value determination by	Israel	PNA
Revenues to	Israel	PNA
VAT		
Value	17%	15-16%
Revenues to	Israel	PNA
Agriculture exports		
From OPT to Israel	severely restricted	quotas until 1998
From Israel to OPT	free flow	free flow
From OPT to other parties	Israeli control	control lifted
Industrial exports		
From OPT to Israel	severely restricted	regulated
From Israel to OPT	free flow	free flow
From OPT to other parties	Israel sets	PNA sets
Flow of OPT workers to Israel controlled by	Israel	Israel
Land and Water effective control by		
Gaza	Israel	Joint
West Bank (excl. Jericho)	Israel	Israel

JD = Jordanian dinar; JEC = Joint Economic Committee; NIS = new Israeli shekel; OPT = occupied Palestinian territory; PNA = Palestine National Authority; VAT = value-added tax; excl. = excluding.

TABLE 2
Main Economic Indicators and Trade of West Bank and Gaza

Item	West Bank	Gaza	Total
Indicator			
GNP ($millions)[a]	2,114	844	2,958
GNP/capita ($)[a]	2,257	1,347	1,893
GDP ($millions)[a]	1,629	553	2,182
of which:			
Agriculture (%)	37	25	34
Industry (%)	7	10	8
Construction (%)	11	17	13
Services (%)			
Public (%)	9	18	11
Other (%)	36	30	34
GDP/GNP (%)[a]	77	66	74
Merchandise Trade[b]			
Imports			
Total ($millions)	731	332	1,063
of which:			
From Israel ($millions)	638	291	929
From Jordan ($millions)	10	0	10
From Israel/ total (%)	87	88	87
Exports			
Total ($millions)	187	66	253
of which:			
To Israel ($millions)	152	53	205
To Jordan ($millions)	27	14	41
To Israel/ total (%)	83	80	82
Balance			
Total ($millions)	–544	–266	–810
With Israel ($millions)	–486	–238	–724
With Jordan ($millions)	17	14	31
With Israel/ total (%)	89	89	89

(–) = deficit

Source: Based primarily on State of Israel, Central Bureau of Statistics, *Statistical Abstract of Israel*, 1991–93.

Notes:
[a] Average of two years, 1990–91. The GNP per capita is based on an average population of 9,365 thousand in the West Bank and 6,265 thousand in Gaza. Several independent studies, however, have disputed the Israeli official population estimates as undercounts; hence the GNP/capita in the table should be viewed as an upper bound [see summary on the population statistics in the World Bank, *Developing the Occupied Territories*, Vol. 6, (Washington D.C., Author, 1993), pp. 4-7]
[b] Average of three years, 1990–1992.

TABLE 3

Year	Poultry (In tons)	Eggs (In millions)	Potatoes (In tons)	Cucumbers (In tons)	Tomatoes (In tons)	Melons (In tons)
1994	5,000	30	10,000	10,000	13,000	10,000
1995	6,000	40	13,000	13,000	16,000	13,000
1996	7,000	50	15,000	15,000	19,000	15,000
1997	8,000	60	17,000	17,000	22,000	17,000
1998	unlimited	unlimited	unlimited	unlimited	unlimited	unlimited

Note:
The PNA would have to notify Israel regarding the apportionment of these quotas between the West Bank and Gaza.

V. Water and Law

9. The Jordan-Israel Water Agreement: A Model or an Exception?[1]

Sharif S. Elmusa

The waters of the Jordan River are vital for Jordan, the West Bank, Israel and the areas in Syria and Lebanon where some of the basin's rivers rise. Dividing these waters – estimated at about 1,500 million cubic meters per year (mcmy)[2] and fluctuating from one year to the next – has been a nettlesome issue from the onset of Zionist colonisation of Palestine, but especially since the creation of Israel in 1948.[3]

In 1953, the United States stepped in and sent a special ambassador, Eric Johnston, to mediate. His mediation culminated in what has become known as the Johnston Plan, which included water allocations among the four riparians as well as an integrated development plan involving all of them. The Johnston Plan's allocations were accepted by the Arab states and adhered to by Jordan and Israel until 1967, after which Israel greatly expanded its use of the basin waters. At the same time, Israel prevented Jordan from building the Maqarin dam by impounding water from the Yarmuk that had been included in the Johnston Plan. In doing so, it limited Jordan to the water it had been diverting since the early 1960s from the Yarmuk to the King Abdallah canal (running parallel to the Jordan and terminating near the Dead Sea) and to the water it impounded in the side wadis (See Table 1).[4] Israel likewise denied access to the waters of the basin altogether to the Palestinians on the West Bank and the Lebanese. Thus the conflict over the basin's waters

---

[1] I would like to thank Dr. Munthir Haddadin, a senior member of the Jordanian delegation that negotiated the Peace Treaty and head of the Jordan delegation in the water Multilaterals, as well as the Jordan Information Bureau, Washington, D.C., for providing me with timely information. An earlier version of this article has appeared in *Journal of Palestine Studies*, Vol. 24, Spring 1995.

[2] 1 mcmcy can irrigate 150 hectares (370 acres) of vegetables or provide household water for 20,000 people at Jordan's consumption level or for 10,000 people at Israel's.

[3] For the history of the water conflict, see, among others, American Friends of the Middle East, *The Jordan Water Problem* (Washington D.C., 1964); Miriam Lowi, *Water and Power: The Politics of a Scarce Resource in the Jordan River Basin* (London, 1993); Subhi Kahhaleh, *The Water Problem in Israel and Its Repercussions on the Arab-Israeli Conflict*, (Washington, D.C., Institute for Palestine Studies (IPS papers No. 9), 1981); Thomas Naff, and Ruth Matson (eds.), *Water in the Middle East: Conflict or Cooperation* (Westview Press, 1984), pp. 176 and 181-97; Samir Saliba, *The Jordan River Dispute* (The Hague, Martinus Nijhoff, 1965); Georgiana Stevens, *Jordan River Partition* (Hoover Institution on War, Revolution and Peace, 1965).

[4] Syria was able to secure its share and perhaps more by impounding the water of the numerous wadis that feed the Yarmuk from its territory.

has persisted and has been one of the main issues pending resolution in the peace talks, where it was pursued in the Bilaterals and in one of the five Multilateral groups.

The Israeli-Jordanian peace treaty signed on 26 October 1994 contains what amounts to a detailed water agreement between the two sides.[5] If all allocations materialise, the Agreement would increase Jordan's water supply by more than 25 percent of its existing total water budget, and restore to Jordan nearly all of the East Bank's allocations under the Johnston Plan. Thus, it would help that country overcome its water shortages, especially in the household sector. The Agreement does not much affect Israel's total water budget.

Besides allocation, the Agreement sets the stage for what appears to be bilateral management of segments of the basin that are common to the two states. While the Agreement apparently resolves the Jordanian-Israeli part of the dispute, it falls short of resolving the entire conflict over the basin. A comprehensive resolution would have to secure acceptable water allocations for the Lebanese, Syrians, and Palestinians. It would also have to be based on a more ecologically-sound integrated management system that treats the basin as a unit, rather than on a politically motivated series of bilateral agreements that segment the basin and put Israel, by virtue of its basin position, at the hub.

I. An Overview of the Agreement

The water provisions of the Israel-Jordan peace treaty are contained in the Preamble and the Water and Environmental Annexes (II) and (IV), in that order. In the Preamble, the articles on water are placed after those of international boundaries and security, indicating the high priority of water in the treaty. The importance of restoring Jordan's water claims was often stressed in the daily press during the negotiations, and, even before the terms of the treaty were made public, Jordanian officials were quick to emphasise what they said were the significant water gains that Jordan realised in the negotiations.[6] Israel did not stand to gain or lose much water in an accord with Jordan, so the water issue was secondary to its desire to secure a peace treaty with a second Arab state and cement it through co-operation on projects in fields such as water. These considerations greatly facilitated the conclusion of the water agreement.

[5] I am interested here only in inland water issues; but the treaty includes also agreements on maritime waters.

[6] See, for example, statements by Abd al-Salam al-Majali, Jordan's prime minister when the treaty was signed, and senior Jordanian water negotiator Munthir Haddadin, *Jordan Times,* 19 October 1994.

The Agreement is wide ranging, including provisions fixing water allocations for both parties, cooperation in the spheres of data exchange and building storage facilities, protection of the water resources and formation of a joint water committee for overseeing the implementation of the Agreement and management of the shared resources.

II. Allocations

The centrepiece of the Agreement lies in the water allocations. The Agreement employs notions such as 'rightful', 'just' and 'practical' to describe the principles on which the allocations are based (Annex I, Article 6, items 1 and 2). These notions are in the spirit of the doctrine of 'equitable apportionment' of international water law respecting joint water resources,[7] though neither international water law nor the criteria according to which principles are translated into quantities are explicitly mentioned. The Agreement gives water (1) to Israel from Wadi Araba in the south, (2) to Jordan from yet-to-be-identified source, and (3) to both Jordan and Israel from the Lower Jordan and Yarmuk (see Table 1).

A. Israel's Use in Wadi Araba

This area is Jordanian territory seized by Israel piecemeal between 1968 and 1970.[8] The Agreement restores Jordan's sovereignty to the territory but stipulates that "Israel shall retain the use" of the wells in the area, with the proviso that licenses for replacement wells would be issued by Jordan (annex II, article IV.1). The wells' total yield is presently estimated at 8 million cubic meters per year (mcmy). Moreover, Israel, "within five years" of signing the Agreement, could extract additional amounts up to 10 mcmy,[9] bringing Israel's extraction from the area to 8-18 mcmy.

The water from the Wadi Araba wells has been used in part to irrigate 130 hectares in the Al-Ghamr area, but most of it is piped into Israel across the border.[10] In establishing the modalities of the water division, article IV.2 refers only to "the period of Israel's use", but

---

[7] See, for example, Sharif Elmusa, 'Dividing the Common Palestinian-Israeli Waters: An International Water Law Approach', *Journal of Palestine Studies*, Vol. 22/3, No. 87, 1993, p. 74.

[8] The Jordan Media Group, *The Jordan-Israel Peace Treaty*, (Amman, Jordan, November, 1994), (photocopy).

[9] With the provision that the joint water committee set up under the Agreement determine that such extraction is "hydrologically feasible" and "does not harm" Jordan's existing use (annex II, article IV 3 and 4).

[10] Correspondence with Munthir Haddadin, 31 Jan 1995.

nowhere in the Agreement is the period specified. According to senior Jordanian negotiator Munthir Haddadin, the understanding is that Israel can use the water as long as Jordan receives water from across the border with Israel in the north.[11] This condition, and the absence of financial or other forms of compensation for the Wadi Araba water, creates a situation of *de facto* exchange between north and south.

Although Israel has no legal grounds for continuing to use the water in an area it occupied by force, it apparently wanted the exchange to be *de jure*, but seems to have relented in the final hours of the talks.[12] The difference between a *de facto* and a *de jure* exchange is important: in the latter case, Israel could turn off the spigot to Jordan in the north anytime it ceases to pump water from the wells of Wadi Araba for whatever reason. As it stands, the Agreement does not entitle Israel to do that. For the duration of Israeli water withdrawal from the wells, however, the *de facto* exchange in effect reduces the total amount of water available to Jordan.

As for the 130 hectares cultivated by Israeli farmers, the Agreement recognizes "Israeli private land use rights" and the Israeli farmers as "land owners" and facilitates their entry to, and use of, the land (annex I (c)).[13] The period of their land ownership extends to twenty five years and is automatically renewable, unless either of the two parties requests otherwise, at which point consultations would be held (annex I.b.6). Thus, while the Agreement restores Jordan's sovereignty over this agricultural land, it does not empower Jordan unilaterally to extend/terminate the use by Israeli farmers.

Despite the extremely small size of the Al-Ghamra area, it was the treaty's arrangements there that aroused the greatest Arab criticism, especially since Israel suggested that they could serve as a model for the Golan Heights. Much of this criticism was based on the belief that Jordan had agreed to lease the land to Israel, whereas in fact there is no mention in the Agreement of lease or rent. The incongruity lies, to my mind, in conferring on the Israeli farmers the status of "land owners." For neither international law of belligerent occupation nor Jordanian land law entitles the Israeli farmers to acquire title to a land their government occupied by force and with which Jordan was in a state of war during the period they farmed it.[14] Once Jordan found itself

---

[11] *Ibid.*

[12] *Ibid.*

[13] According to M. Haddadin (correspondence 31 January 1995), this situation was duplicated in the Baqura area in the north on an area of 83 hectares although in this area Jewish farmers and companies cultivated land since the mid-1920s. According to *Al-Hayat,* (7 November 1994), these are part of 600 hectares (ha) bought by Jews within the 70-year concession that Britain gave to Pinhas Rutenberg in 1923 for the generation of hydroelectric power. Of the 600 ha, 500 ha fell under Jordan control in the 1949 armistice and were designated "enemy property", and 100 ha in the no-man's land.

[14] The situation would be more complicated in Al-Baqura, in the north, where Jews had farmed the area during the British mandate, as mentioned above.

compelled for political or humanitarian reasons to let them stay, some other special arrangement should have been made.

B. Jordan's Allocations from Unidentified Sources

Of the estimated 215 mcmy that Jordan would get under the Agreement, 50 mcmy of drinkable water quality, or about 23 percent of the total, are to come from yet-to-be-identified sources. The Agreement states that plans for supplying this quantity will be drafted by the Jordanian-Israeli Joint Water Committee within one year of the signing of the Peace Treaty and presented to the respective governments (annex II, article I.3). In order to be counted as "additional" water that Jordan gains under the Agreement, the 50 mcmy would obviously have to be supplied from Israeli or from joint Israeli-Jordanian sources. Apart from the already-allocated water from the Jordan and Yarmuk rivers, there is not, as far as I know, much water in other joint sources left to be exploited; so the water would have to come from Israel. There is no point in speculating why the Agreement does not identify Israel as the source, but unless there is a non-public understanding between the two governments the omission raises concerns about whether Israel will consider itself bound to provide this allocation to Jordan. Final judgment about it must be deferred until the supply plan is drafted.

C. Allocations from the Yarmuk and the Jordan

The water quantities in the north are the most significant and the allocations regime more complicated than in the south. In principle, the Agreement entitles Jordan to an estimated 165 mcmy of water from the Yarmuk and the Jordan (including the saline springs), in addition to the 130 mcmy it already diverts to the King Abdallah Canal from the Yarmuk at Al-Adasiyya and the 130 it impounds from the side wadis. This brings Jordan's total share from the Yarmuk and the Jordan to 295 mcmy, and as much as it could harness from the side wadis. However, the *de facto* exchange water of 8-18 mcmy that Israel would exploit in Wadi Araba effectively reduces Jordan's total share from the Jordan and the Yarmuk sources to 277-287 mcmy, and the water it would regains from these two sources under to 147-157 mcmy. Still, even after the *de facto* exchange, the 147-157 mcmy are significant when we consider that Jordan's total water use was estimated at 730 mcmy in 1990.

Israel, on the other hand, would get a total of 39 mcmy from the Yarmuk and the Jordan and unspecified quantities from the excess flood from the two rivers, and the 8-18 mcmy from Wadi Araba. These quantities are in addition to Israel's present use from the Jordan river between its confluence with the Yarmuk and Tira't Zvi, near the Israeli-West Bank border, which is yet to be jointly determined.

Whether Israel would gain or lose depends first on how much water it has actually been diverting from the Yarmuk (see Table 2), and second, on how much it will tap from the excess flood. At any rate, the gain or loss from these sources would represent a minuscule fraction of Israel's total water budget (1,745 mcmy in 1990) and any changes that may come about from the Agreement would hardly affect it.

While Jordan, as noted, gains from the treaty in terms of overall allocations compared to the status quo ante, it is important to emphasize that its 'gain' is not the result of reallocating harnessed water but of the planned construction of storage works on the Jordan and the Yarmuk to harness the flood waters and improve the efficiency of diversion to the Abdallah canal, as well as of future desalination of the saline springs.

This is in line with Israel's long standing advocacy of increasing supply as a way of resolving the water conflict with Arab riparians rather than reallocating existing use. This approach works to a certain extent with Jordan, because Israel itself has not been using much of the water that Jordan would get but was preventing Jordan from tapping it. Duplicating the same approach would be far more difficult with Lebanon, and, especially, with the Palestinians because Israel exploits their allocations.

III. The Agreement and the Johnston Plan

The Johnston Plan, although accepted by all four riparians of the Jordan basin when it was negotiated back in 1955, was never ratified.[15] As mentioned, however, the plan's allocations were adhered to by Israel and Jordan up until the June war, and the United States conditioned aid for related development projects in both states on their compatibility with the plan.[16] As late as 1965, Israel clearly still viewed the plan as an achievement to be safeguarded,[17] and even after it began taking

---

[15] Besides allocations, the plan had a political part calling for regional cooperation, which the Arab League Council found unacceptable without first resolving the Palestinian problem.

[16] See, *Department of State Administrative History*, Vol I, Chapter 4, Section H, Part 2; Johnston Administration; declassified 6 December 1983, LBJ Library, case # NLJ 83-223; and "*Memorandum for the President*", from Robert Cutler, Special Assistant, Dwight Eisenhower papers, declassified, 001384, 1984, Case no. 80-331, document No. 1.

[17] In a press conference on 11 January 1965, for example, Israeli Prime Minister Levi Eshkol noted that: "there are commitments in the world toward us, in the wake of the Johnston Plan" and on 17 May reportedly remarked that the Plan was "regarded as agreed from an international point of view." Cited in *Department of State Administrative History*.

advantage of its control of much of the headwaters in the basin following the war to greatly increase its water extractions, it felt compelled to invoke the Johnston Plan to justify the increased volumes.[18] Although Israel subsequently downplayed the relevance of the Johnston Plan, citing changed conditions (changes based on the fait accomplis Israel itself has created),[19] the plan continues to be explicitly cited by both the Palestinians and the Lebanese as the basic terms of reference.[20] The Syrians have not made, to my knowledge, public declarations about the issue. Moreover, while the Agreement does not refer to the Johnston Plan, there is evidence suggesting that it was at the background of negotiations.[21] It is instructive to look at the present Agreement in the light of the Johnston Plan.

Overall, the new agreement gives Jordan an estimated 9-19 mcmy less than the East Bank's share in the Johnston Plan (after subtracting the *de facto* water exchange in the south) (see Table 2). The Johnston Plan spelled out fixed quantities for all the four riparians of the basin (except Israel), whose share was a residual to be harnessed after the Arab riparians took their shares. The Israeli-Jordanian Agreement, on the other hand, for the most part gives exact figures only for Israel, thereby reversing the terms of the Johnston Plan by giving Israel priority. Only a few of Jordan's allocations are stated as quantities, and what we have in Table 1 are for the most part estimates, some of the allocations (65 mcmy) being residues (that is, what is left after Israel takes its share) and others not yet known since they will be tapped via storage facilities to be built in the future. While Jordan may be able in years of plentiful rain to tap more water than estimated, it may not be able to realize those levels during droughts. Jordan is particularly vulnerable in drought periods because its limited water supply comes mainly from surface sources with practically no carryover from one year to the next owing to the high evaporation rates. In theory, special arrangements for drought years, for instance dividing the waters according to percentages of flow rather than according to fixed quantities, could be spelled out when the two sides elaborate the terms of joint water management.

Another detail worth mentioning in relation to the Johnston Plan concerns the saline springs. The Agreement gives 10 mcmy to each side after desalination, stipulating that Israel "will explore the possibility of

18 The justification was that the West Bank's share included in Jordan's total share now belonged to it. (Soffer, 'The Relevance of the Johnston Plan to the Reality of 1993 and Beyond' in J. Isaac and H. Shuval (eds.), *Water and Peace in the Middle East* (Amsterdam, Elsevier, 1994), p. 113. This claim, as the late Bashir Nijim remarked, equates occupation with sovereignty. ('Water Resources in the History of the Palestine-Israel Conflict', *Geojournal*, Vol. 21, No 4, p. 320).

19 See, for example, Soffer, 'The Relevance of the Johnston Plan', pp. 115-6.

20 For Lebanon's position, see interview with Fadi Qumayr, head of the Litani Project Commission, *Al-Hayat*, December, 1993, day unclear.

21 For example, Munthir Haddadin told the *Jordan Times* of 20 October 1994 that Israel's share in the Yarmuk was fixed at its level in the Johnston Plan.

financing" operation and maintenance costs, but not capital costs (annex II, article I.2.d.). The saline springs had originally emptied in Lake Tiberias until Israel rechannelled them into the Lower Jordan in 1964 to reduce the lake's salinity, claiming that its action was envisaged in the Johnston Plan.[22] As a result of this action, the lower Jordan was made unusable for over 30 years, so it would seem only fair that Israel as compensation should bear the costs of desalination (not just "explore the possibility of financing"), especially since Jordan would get a smaller share of the springs' water than it appears to have been allotted in the Johnston Plan whereas Israel would obtain a larger share.[23] Also, Jordan, which is heavily indebted, will need large outlays for building the other water works mentioned in the Agreement.

Concerning the allocations to Jordan and Israel from the Yarmuk, the Johnston Plan had allotted 25 mcmy to Israel, while the Agreement gives Israel 12 mcmy in summer and 13 mcmy in winter. There is some ambiguity, however, since the Agreement also stipulates that Jordan would "concede" 20 mcmy in winter in return for which Israel would concede to Jordan 20 mcmy from the Jordan in summer (annex II, article I l.a and 2.a).[24] The exchange of 20 mcmy allows for two interpretations. Jordan can say, as Munthir Haddadin told the *Jordan Times* on 20 October 1994 that Israel's share was fixed at 25 mcmy only, the same as in the Johnston Plan, and that Jordan was storing the water in Tiberias. But the exchange can also be interpreted as effectively giving Israel 45 mcmy from the Yarmuk and 20 mcmy less from the Jordan. Storing the waters of the Yarmuk in Lake Tiberias, in addition to the intended joint construction of smaller dams on the river would seem to deal the *coup de grace* to the Johnston Plan's Maqarin dam meant as a co-operative scheme between Jordan and Syria, with Jordan obtaining the bulk of the water and Syria of the hydropower.

---

[22] Commenting on this claim, the declassified *Department of State Administrative History* cited above notes that "the United States did not find that the Johnston proposals had clarified what disposition of the saline springs was considered appropriate".

[23] There is uncertainty about how the springs water was divided in the Johnston Plan. Subhi Kahhaleh, director general of the Arab League's "Authority to Exploit the Waters of the Jordan River and its Tributaries" from 1964 to 1967, mentions (in *The Water Problem in Israel*, p. 27) that 15mcmy of Jordan's total share in the Plan were to come from the saline springs, while Miriam Lowi (*Water and Power*, 1994, citing Foreign Policy Records made available under the Freedom of Information Act, FOI 7.u.684a.85322/9-1955) cites the reported minutes of the Arab Technical Committee as saying that 30 mcmy from the saline springs would be given to Jordan over and beyond the 720 mcmy representing Jordan's total allotment under the Plan. Thus according to Kahhaleh's version, Jordan received in the Agreement 5 mcmy less than its share of the Johnston Plan, while according to Lowi's 20 mcmy; at the same time, Israel received 5-10 mcmy more than its share in the Plan.

[24] The seasonal approach adopted in the Agreement is more realistic than the Johnston plan's annual approach, as it takes into consideration the seasonal variations in the flow as well as in water use.

IV. The Agreement and the Palestinians

Among all the riparians, the Palestinians face the toughest challenge from the Israelis. Their location in relation to Israel is downstream whereas Syria and Lebanon are upstream and Jordan is upstream on the Yarmuk and downstream on the Jordan. Further, the Jordan-Israel Agreement exhausts the available unused water, since most of the water Israel agreed to give back to Jordan comes, as already noted, from floodwater or from water Israel had polluted in the Lower Jordan. The Palestinians will therefore have the hard task of reclaiming from the Jordan basin their share of water that Israel is already exploiting, or "occupying." My estimate of this share is 209 mcmy (181 mcmy from the Jordan and about 35 mcmy from side wadis).[25]

Under the Johnston Plan, the 181 mcmy were to be transported via a "West Ghor Canal." The canal was never built, although Palestinian farmers pumped water directly from the Jordan until Israel seized the West Bank and declared large segments of the Jordan Valley closed military areas, destroying a reported 140 of their water pumps.

Another complication for the Palestinians is the fact that the two sides have another major water conflict over the groundwater resources recharged primarily from the West Bank but exploited for the most part by Israel.[26] Finally, the Palestinians, unlike other Arab countries, have to wrestle with Israel over other formidable issues, such as the settlements, Jerusalem, and the refugees. To have a reasonable chance of securing equitable allocations from the Jordan basin, the Palestinians would have to work hard for an Arab consensus on the Johnston Plan as terms of reference.

The Agreement contains several elements that could prove helpful for the Palestinians water negotiators. The first is Israel's consent to joint verification of its own water by the joint water committee, as in the case of the Lower Jordan (annex II, article 1.2.c.). This is important for Palestinians, whose information on Israeli uses of the common groundwater comes from Israeli sources. The second is the structure of the joint water committee, which consists of a main committee with two

---

[25] The Johnston Plan did not spell out allocations for the West Bank as it involved only states. But since the plan estimated the irrigable area in the western Valley at about 30 percent of the total irrigable area (51,9846 hectares), one can infer that the West Bank's water share would be 30 percent of Jordan's total water allotment of 720 mcmy. (The East Bank share would be 504 mcmy of which 296 mcmy from the Yarmuk and the Jordan and 208 from the side wadis.). (American Friends of the Middle East, *The Jordan Water,* p. 79.) Jordan's share in the Johnston Plan was allotted on the basis of estimates made in 1955 by Baker-Harza, a Chicago-based engineering firm. An alternative estimate by a PLO report puts the West Bank's share as being 290 (250 from the Yarmuk and 70 from the Jordan) mcmy, but does not specify how it reached this conclusion, Department of Economics and Planning, *Water* (in Arabic), (Tunis, 1992), p. 69 (photocopy).

[26] See, for example, Elmusa, 'Dividing the Common.Palestinian-Israeli Waters'.

sub-committees, one for the north and the other for the south. The Palestinians would be wise to cite this precedent and press for a similar structure, with the two subcommittees to deal with groundwater sources and the Jordan basin.

Informal Israeli-Palestinian talks on water currently underway, in which Palestinians with official capacities have been participating, have been confined at Israeli insistence solely to the economics of water management and joint management of the common groundwater sources (which Israel wants because the headwaters of these sources are in the West Bank). If the Palestinians agree to joint management of the groundwater without first securing Israeli reciprocity in the basin, it is likely that they would forfeit a management role there. Similarly, none of the Israeli-Palestinian water discussions have addressed the question of water allocations. In the Jordan-Israeli Agreement, the allocations have been settled while the joint management format is to be defined later. Reversal of this sequence for the Palestinians or making allocations a water management function, could compromise their negotiating position on allocations.

V. The Agreement and the Management of the Jordan Basin

Contemporary river management thought and international water law both advocate, for ecological reasons, that rivers be managed in an integrated fashion as a single unit rather than in segments dictated by political boundaries. Integrated management that would include all the parties of the Jordan basin was an essential feature of the Johnston Plan, and was even proposed by Israel itself before Johnston was dispatched to the region.[27]

The integrated, basin-wide approach, however, has apparently been superseded by the bilateral approach in the Israel-Jordan Agreement. While the Agreement does not exclude the kind of integrated basin management foreseen by the Johnston Plan, nowhere does it raise the possibility. Further, the articles on joint Israeli-Jordanian management of the Jordan and the Yarmuk refer only to those segments of the rivers that would be exploited by the two parties. It would appear, though, that Israel's goal is to segment the river and conclude bilateral treaties with each of the Arab riparians, which would place it at the hub of the river management system, instead of being one of the parties in an integrated management system. Undoubtedly, Israel's basin position encourages it to pursue such a goal, as it holds segments of the river in common with each Arab riparian (except the Palestinians); none of the Arab parties enjoys such a hydrostrategic position.

[27] Miriam Lowi, *Water and Power,* pp. 82-3, citing U.S. National Archives.

That Jordan consented to the segmented management is, of course, a consequence of the current fragmented Arab position that sharply contrasts with the unified position at the time the Johnston Plan was negotiated forty years ago. The situation may not be irreversible, especially if the Jordanian-Israeli joint management provisions could be incorporated within a wider, multilateral accord.

TABLE 1
Water Allocations of Israel and Jordan under Water Agreement, 1994
(in million cubic meters per year)

Source and State	Amount	Priority	Season	Due Date and Notes
Jordan				
Yarmuk River				
King Abdallah Canal (KAC)	130[a]			Existing – no mention in treaty
Stream	8[a]	Residue	Summer	Immediate
Stream	17[a]	Residue	Winter	Immediate
Flood	50[a]			Future (into KAC)
TOTAL	205[a]			
Lower Jordan River				
Side Wadis	130[a]			Existing – no mention in treaty
Stream (exchange)	20[b]		Summer	Immediate
Flood	20		Winter	Future
Additional	40[a]	Residue		Future (storage & rehabilitation)
TOTAL	40 + 40[a]			
Saline springs	10		non-Summer	Immediate[c]
To-be-identified	50			
TOTAL	245 + 100			
Israel				
Yarmuk				
Stream	12		Summer	Immediate
Stream	13		Winter	Immediate
Stream (exchange)	20[b]		Winter	Immediate
Flood	?			

Lower Jordan		
Stream	?	Existing (to be assessed jointly)
Flood	?	Future
Additional	3	
Saline springs	10	Future
Israeli use in Wadi Araba		
Groundwater	8[a]	Existing (to be assessed jointly)
Groundwater	≤10	Future (by mutual agreement)

Summer = 15 May–15 Oct Winter = 16 Oct–14 May

Sources: Based on "Peace Treaty Between The State of Israel and The Hashemite Kingdom of Jordan"; *Jordan Times*, October 20, 1994. For the text of the treaty, see *Journal of Palestine Studies*, Vol. 23, Winter, 1995, pp. 133-139.

Notes:

[a]The figures are not specified in the water Annex (II), they are estimates by Munthir Haddadin. All, except those of the use in wadi Araba, appeared in the above issue of the *Jordan Times*. The use in the Wadi Araba was to be assessed jointly by December 31, 1994; based on the information that Jordan has received from Israel, Haddadin made the preliminary estimate of 8 mcm/year, personal correspondence, January 26, 1995; he also confirmed the accuracy of the estimates that appeared in the JT.

[b]Jordan "concedes" in winter 20 mcm/year winter water from the Yarmuk to Israel, while Israel "concedes" 20 mcm/y of summer water to Jordan from the lower Jordan River at Deganya, south of Lake Tiberias (annex II, article I.l.b and I.2.a).

[c]The saline springs are earmarked for desalination within four years; meanwhile, Jordan will get the 10 mcm/y from Lake Tiberias (*JT*).

TABLE 2
Actual Use Versus Quotas under the Johnston Plan in the Jordan River Basin

State	Johnston Plan Quota		Actual Use	
	(mcmy)	% of total	(mcmy)	% of total
Lebanon[a]	35	3	0	0
Syria[b]	132	10	130-170	13-15
Israel[c]	400	31	620-700	61-62
Jordan[d]	720	56		
East Bank[e]	511	40	260	23-26
West Bank[f]	209	16	0	0
Total	1287	100	1010-1130	100

Sources: Based on sources in footnote 4 and Abu Taleb, Maher, et al, *The Jordan River Basin* (presented at World Bank workshop on comprehensive water management, Washington, D.C., 24 June–8 July 1991); Thomas Naff, *Jordan River Average Flows* (photocopy, 1991); Tahal Consulting Engineers Ltd., *Israel Water Sector Review: Past Achievements, Current Problems and Future Options*", (Tel-Aviv - Washington D.C., report submitted to the World Bank, 1990), p. 21.

Notes:
[a]All from the Hasibani.
[b]Quotas: 90 from the Yarmuk, 22 the Jordan, and 20 the Banyas; actual use is all from the Yarmuk.
[c]Quotas: 375 from the Jordan, 25 the Yarmuk; actual use: 550 the Jordan and 700-100 the Yarmuk.
[d]Quotas: 100 from the Jordan, 377 from the Yarmuk, and 243 western and eastern side wadis.
[e]Quotas: 302 from the Jordan and the Yarmuk and 209 the side wadis; actual use: 130 from the Yarmuk and 120 from the side wadis.
[f]Quotas: 175 from the Jordan and the Yarmuk and 34 from the side wadis.

10. Joint Management of Groundwater Resources: Its Need and Implications[1]

Eran Feitelson

Introduction

Conflicts over water issues arise from spatial discrepancies between water sources, water users and administrative (or national) spheres of control. Moreover, political boundaries often separate between locations where problems are felt and locations where the most effective and efficient solutions can be applied.[2] As this is the case especially in arid and semi-arid regions, where water sources are few and often far apart, conflicts over water have erupted in the Middle East since early times.[3]

However, water need not be only a source of conflict. Due to the scarcity and temporal variance of water in such semi-arid regions, the full utilization of water requires cooperation.[4] Thus water works and institutions have long been central elements of societal organization in this region.[5]

Today the water picture is further complicated by the extensive externalities it involves. Water withdrawals or waste water disposal at one point may affect water quality and quantity at other points downstream. Moreover, seemingly unrelated actions by one party (such

---

[1] This paper is based on an ongoing study conducted jointly by the Truman Institute of the Hebrew University and the Palestine Consultancy Group. This study is funded by IDRC and the CRB Foundation. All views expressed in this paper, however, are only those of the author, and do not necessarily reflect those of anyone else involved in the project.

[2] H. Ingram, L. Milich and R. Varady, 'Managing Transboundary Resources: Lessons from Ambos Nogales', *Environment* 36(4) (1994), p. 9.

[3] P. Gleick, 'Water Wars and Peace in the Middle East', *Environment* 36(3) (1994), pp. 6-15, 35-42.

[4] This has been recognized in Annex III of the Israeli-Palestinian Liberation Organisation Declaration of Principles on Interim Self Government Arrangements, signed in Washington D.C., 13 September 1993. However, the level of cooperation in the subsequent agreement on the Gaza Strip and the Jericho area, signed in Cairo, 4 May 1994, is quite minimal. Several concrete steps toward cooperation are included in the Israel-Jordan Treaty of Peace, signed in Arava, 26 October 1994. Yet none of these agreements provide for a true joint management structure.

[5] K. Wittfogel, *Oriental Despotism: A Comparative Study of Total Power*, (1957).

as industrial or urban development projects) may affect water quality available to other parties.

In this paper I discuss the implications of the water situation in the Middle East, and especially as regards Israelis and Palestinians, for the direction that negotiations should take. In doing so I argue that the water situation between Israel and her neighbours requires that they embark on joint management schemes of their shared resources. In particular it is essential that the mountain aquifers shared by Israelis and Palestinians be managed jointly. The directions and issues involved in such joint management schemes are discussed and the implications for the ongoing negotiations noted.

I. Background: The Complexity of the Israeli Water System

The Israeli water system is composed of three major storages; Lake Kinneret, the mountain aquifers and the coastal aquifers. In addition there are several smaller aquifers. The three major storages are connected by a national system that allows Israel to transport water from the water rich north to the arid south.[6] The national system, depicted in Map 1, is composed of the national water carrier and secondary regional systems that distribute water to jurisdictions and tap local aquifers. These systems also augment the water supply systems of the territories.

The national water carrier connects all the main water basins in Israel, from the Jordan River through the coastal basins down to the south. This system allows water to be transferred among the three major reservoirs of Israel; Lake Kinneret, the mountain aquifer and the coastal aquifer. Indeed, the national water carrier is used in winter to transport water from the Jordan basin for recharging the coastal aquifer. The aquifers are the main multi-year storage, while the Kinneret serves as an annual storage.

In arid and semi-arid regions the main problem in water supply is overcoming the temporal variance in water recharge between seasons and between years of plenty and droughts. Thus water storage is the crucial element in any comprehensive water supply system in such regions. A major problem in storing water in such a semi-arid climate is the water loss in storage due to evaporation.[7] Aquifers serve thus as

---

[6] J. Schwartz, 'Management of Israel's Water Resources', in J. Isaac and H. Shuval (eds.), *Water and Peace in the Middle East*, (Kluwer, 1994), pp. 69-71; E. Feitelson, *Water Use Patterns in Israel: Evolution, Issues and Forecasts*, (unpublished manuscript, 1994).

[7] R. Cummings, *Water Resource Management in Northern Mexico*, (Johns Hopkins University Press, 1972).

ideal storages, as there is no water loss to evaporation and as their capacity is very large.

Over-pumping in the thirties and fifties has led to the draw down of the coastal aquifer. Moreover, as this aquifer underlies the locus of most human activity in Israel, parts of it have been polluted by anthropogenic sources.[8] Thus the major storage of high quality water is the mountain aquifer, shared by Israel with the West Bank.[9]

The mountain aquifer actually consists of three separate aquifers. The western and northeastern, whose recharge areas lie mostly in the West Bank, but whose natural outlets are mostly within pre-1967 Israel, and the eastern aquifer, located mostly in the West Bank. This aquifer, most importantly its western part, is a karstic aquifer, and is thus highly susceptible to pollution.[10] Moreover, despite much research, many features of this aquifer are unknown.[11]

The intricacy of the system has increased in recent years as Israel has developed a wider network of recycled water schemes (also depicted in Map 1). Currently the Tel Aviv metropolitan area's wastewater is treated near Rishon Lezion, pumped to and stored in the coastal aquifer and then pumped out and transported to the western Negev.[12] Conceptual schemes currently under discussion foresee the increase of inter-regional and inter-basin transfers of treated wastewater.[13]

From a legal and institutional perspective, the Israeli system is a highly centralized one, whereby almost all water sources have been nationalized. Thus all drilling and pumping is strictly controlled by a permit and quota system. Moreover, all use is determined by a combination of a quota and price system. Historically this system was used to subsidize the agricultural sector, and especially in peripheral areas.[14]

---

[8] Israel State Comptroller, *Report on the Management of the Water Market in Israel*, (Jerusalem, 1990), (in Hebrew).

[9] Y. Bargur, 'The Israeli Water Market – Trends and Resource Development under Scarcity Conditions' in *Israel 2020: Master Plan for Israel in the 21st Century*, (Final Report Stage A, Vol. 2, Technion Research and Development Foundation, Haifa, 1993), (in Hebrew); Schwartz, *Management of Israel's Water Resources*.

[10] H. Gvirtzman, 'Groundwater Allocation in Judea and Samaria' in Isaac and Shuval (eds.), *Water and Peace in the Middle East*.

[11] E. Mazor, *Groundwater Management*, (position paper, Weitzman Institute, 1993), (in Hebrew).

[12] Dan Reqion Sewaqe Treatment and Reclamation Proiect, Dan Region Association of Towns (Sewerage) and Mekorot Water Company, September 1991.

[13] J. Harrosh, 'Recycling Wastewater for Environmental Protection and Farm Water Supply', *International Water & Irrigation Review* 13 (3) (1993), pp. 9-13; G. Shelef and Y. Azov, *Municipal Wastewater Treatment and Re-use in Israel*, (paper presented at the conference on Agriculture and the Environment, Rehovoth, 3–6 October 1994).

[14] Feitelson, *Water Use Patterns in Israel*; Israel State Comptroller, *Report on the Management of the Water Market.*

II. The Need for Joint Management

Discussions of international water agreements usually focus on the apportionment of water within a shared basin. A second category, less often discussed, is the promotion of joint management or exploitation of a river basin.[15] Very few studies discuss groundwater issues. Almost none address situations where the basin concept has lost much of its meaning due to extensive inter-basin transfers of water, combining all basins in a unitary system.[16]

The geographic centrality of the Israeli water system in the Israeli-Palestinian, and Israeli-Arab arena, and of aquifers within this system, suggest that the issue of shared aquifers is of paramount importance in addressing Israeli-Arab water issues.

As noted above, cooperative arrangements usually focus either on equitable apportionment of water or on joint management of water resources. Most of the discussions of the Israeli-Palestinian or Israeli-Arab water issues have focused on equitable apportionment issues.[17] However, in order to be able to divide a water resource, it is necessary to control either water flows or water extractions. Control of water flows can be readily accomplished in the case of surface water, as can be seen in the Indus River case.[18] It is much more difficult to divide groundwater, as flows are often not fully understood, and usually cannot be controlled.[19] Also the control of groundwater extractions is complicated as it requires the monitoring of all wells and regulated pumping. Moreover, as the costs of pumping vary widely, and as

---

15 E. Benvenisti, *The Law's Challenge: Creating Incentives for Regional Cooperation*, (paper presented at the second workshop on Joint Management of Shared Aquifers, Jerusalem, 27 November – 1 December 1994).

16 On the problem of spatial scope of joint management institutions, see E. Feitelson, 'Pertinent Issues in Joint Management of Aquifers: An Overview of Recent Reviews' in Feitelson and Haddad (eds.), *Joint Management of Shared Aquifers: The First Workshop*, (The Palestine Consultancy Group and the Truman Institute for Advancement of Peace, Jerusalem, 1994).

17 For example: N. Kliot, *Water Scarcity and Conflict in the Middle East*, (Routledge, 1994); E. Benvenisti and H. Gvirtzman, 'Harnessing International Law to Determine Israeli-Palestinian Water Rights: The Mountain Aquifer', *Natural Resources Journal* 33 (1993), pp. 543-567; S. Elmusa, 'Towards an Equitable Distribution of the Common Israeli-Palestinian Waters: An International Water Law Framework' in Isaac and Shuval (eds.), *Water and Peace in the Middle East*.

18 For summaries of this case see: M. Ferenz and S. Sylvan, *The Design of a Palestinian-Israeli Water Commission: A Best-Practice Approach*, (paper prepared for the CRB Foundation, John F. Kennedy School of Government, Harvard University, 1994); D. Housen-Couriel, *Some Examples of Cooperation in the Management and Use of International Water Resources*, (The Armand Hammer Fund for Economic Cooperation in the Middle East, Tel Aviv University and The Truman Institute for the Advancement of Peace, The Hebrew University of Jerusalem, 1994).

19 D. Grey, 'The Development of Water Resources in the Occupied Palestinian Territories: Some Key Issues' in Isaac and Shuval (eds.), *Water and Peace in the Middle East*.

pumpage locations also need to take account of quality considerations, extraction points have to be carefully located.

In the case of the mountain aquifer, the existence of saline water bodies requires a careful pumpage regime. Also, pumping is cheaper at the foothill area, much of it in the confined aquifer area within pre-1967 Israel.[20] Thus Israel pumps the water for Jerusalem in the coastal plain. This water will also supplant Ramallah's water supply through the new Motsa-Bitounia pipeline. Another factor complicating the apportionment issue are the fluctuations in recharge. To address this problem, Dudley suggests that storage capacities, rather than water flows, be shared.[21] However in the case of the mountain aquifer there is some uncertainty as to storage capacity. Moreover, this capacity is constrained by quality considerations which have to be jointly agreed upon and monitored. Consequently Dudley suggests the need for a management body to operate any capacity sharing regime.[22]

All aspects of the Israeli-Palestinian case discussed above suggest that a one-time division of water is unfeasible in the groundwater case. In addition, the susceptibility to pollution and the inability or high cost of cleaning aquifers require that both sides cooperate to maintain the aquifers' water quality. Yet preventive action for protection of aquifer water quality is not a one-time decision. Rather, it requires continual monitoring and plans of action. In other words, a joint management regime is essential both to administer the apportionment rules that will be agreed upon and to ensure the protection of the aquifer.

Joint management requires an institutional structure. Currently there are a only few examples of joint management of aquifers.[23] To facilitate the development of such joint management structures, a draft treaty was proposed, which was based mainly on the Mexican-American case.[24] Still, the actual experience in joint management of aquifers is scant and most of it does not encourage emulation.[25] Israel and the Palestinians would thus need to form their own management structures. In the next section an approach to identifying possible structures for joint management of shared aquifers is outlined.

---

20 This is due to higher static pressures.

21 N. Dudley, *Sustaining of International Water Resource Allocation Agreements through Capacity Sharing*, (Proceedings of the International Symposium on Water Resources in the Middle East: Policy and Institutional Aspects, International Water Resources Association, Urbana Illinois, 24-27 October 1993).

22 N. Dudley, 'An Innovative Institutional Arrangement with Potential for Improving the Management of International Water Resources' in Isaac and Shuval (eds.), *Water and Peace in the Middle East*.

23 Housen-Couriel, *Some Examples of Cooperation*.

24 R. Hayton and A. Utton, 'Transboundary Groundwaters: The Bellagio Draft Treaty', *Natural Resources Journal* 29 (1989), pp. 663-722.

25 D. Eaton and J. Eaton, 'Joint Management of Aquifers between the Jordan River Basin and the Mediterranean Sea by Israelis and Palestinians: An International Perspective' in Feitelson and Haddad (eds.), *Joint Management of Shared Aquifers*.

III. The Identification of Joint Management Structures

Several approaches can be identified in studies addressing cross-boundary water issues. The first approach is to learn and adapt practices and principles designed elsewhere to the Israeli-Arab case. An example of this approach can be seen in the attempts to apply international law principles to the Middle East situation,[26] or to identify the best elements in other cases as a basis for proposing an Israeli-Palestinian joint management structure.[27] A second approach is to try to identify an 'ideal' structure. This approach can be discerned in the Bellagio draft treaty and in theoretical studies of desirable structures and practices.[28] A third approach is to advance new concepts and ideas that may address some aspects of the water issues.[29]

In an ongoing study regarding possible structures for joint Israeli-Palestinian management of shared aquifers, the second and third approaches are combined. The existing literature was reviewed to identify the issues that needed to be addressed in joint management schemes and expert opinion regarding such experience was elicited.[30] The purpose of this effort is to identify possible structures for the joint management of shared aquifers. As the international experience regarding these issues is limited, it is expected that some of the structures that will be identified may be novel. It is hoped that the identification of a slew of possible structures for joint management will facilitate discussion of their pros and cons, thus raising the awareness of important long term issues.

In the next section the issues identified in this study are summarized, followed by a brief account of an initial set of such possible structures.

---

26 Kliot, *Water Scarcity and Conflict*; Benvenisti and Gvirtzman, *Harnessing International Law*; Elmusa, *Towards and Equitable Distribution.*

27 Ferenz and Sylvan, *The Design of a Palestinian-Israeli Water Commission.*

28 Examples of such theoretical studies are: J. Moore, 'An Israeli-Palestinian Water-Sharing Regime' in Isaac and Shuval (eds.), *Water and Peace in the Middle East*; and N. Zeitouni et al., 'Water Sharing through Trade in Markets for Market Rights: An Illustrative Application to the Middle East' in Isaac and Shuval (eds.), *Water and Peace in the Middle East.*

29 D. Brooks, 'Adjusting the Flow: Two Comments on the Middle East Water Crisis', *Water International* 18 (1993), pp. 35-39; H. Zarour and J. Isaac, 'Nature's Apportionment and the Open Market: A Promising Solution to the Arab-Israeli Water Conflict', *Water International* 18 (1993), pp.40-53.

30 The methodology of this study is described in E. Feitelson and M. Haddad, 'Possible Structures for Joint Israeli-Palestinian Management of Shared Aquifers: An Introduction' in Feitelson and Haddad, *Joint Management of Shared Aquifers.*

IV. The Issues of Joint Management

In an overview of recent reviews of joint management structures in different parts of the world, several issues that need to be addressed when thinking about such structures were identified.[31] These issues are:

A. Goals for Joint Management and Level of Cooperation

Joint management structures can address a single issue or multiple issues as part of an integrated resource management approach. They can also vary in the level of cooperation between the parties. The parties can cooperate on data collection and dissemination or have joint decision making on certain issues. The level of cooperation can also vary according to issue. For example, it is possible that parties will routinely exchange data, but agree that if certain thresholds are crossed (such as pollution levels reached or lack of rains up to a certain date) they will jointly declare a drought or pollution emergency whereby the joint management structure would assume temporary emergency decision making functions.

B. Financing

Any structure involves some actions that need to be funded. The extent and type of funding necessary is a function of the goals of the joint management structure. However, even when the role is limited, there may be cross boundary externalities that will require action by the parties, and an agreement on the funding for such action. External funding, if appropriately structured can have an important facilitating role.[32] Actually, most previous agreements were facilitated by financial incentives.[33]

C. Conflict Resolution Mechanisms

It is almost inevitable that differences will arise over time. Thus any joint management structure needs to include some conflict resolution mechanism. It is possible to involve external parties in this mechanism

---

[31] E. Feitelson, 'Pertinent Issues in Joint Management of Aquifers: An Overview of Recent Reviews' in Feitelson and Haddad, *Joint Management of Shared Aquifers*.

[32] For an interesting recent proposition on these lines, see M. Caswell and G. Frisvold, *Transboundary Water Quality Trading: Implications for Overseas Development Assistance*, (paper presented at the international conference on coordination and decentralization in water resources management, Rehovot, 3-6 October 1994).

[33] Eaton and Eaton, *Joint Management of Aquifers*.

but the greater the reliance on external involvement the lesser the incentive for the parties to resolve their differences directly with each other.[34]

D. Independence of the Joint Management Structure and its Decision Making Processes

The joint management structure can be a meeting of representatives, or an autonomous body. It can also involve two layers, whereby technical decisions are taken by an autonomous body but policy decisions are raised to a political level of representatives. The degree of autonomy will also be a function of whether the joint management structure is provided with its own resources and staff or whether it needs to rely on the staff and resources of the existing institutions of the parties.

E. Spatial Scope

The common spatial definition of joint management structures is the river basin. However, in the Israeli-Arab case, ground water is a major issue: the spatial extent of aquifers is less well defined than that of rivers and there are many inter-basin water transfers within Israel. Thus defining the spatial scope of any joint management structure may not be straightforward.

F. Public Participation or Scrutiny

The transparency of a joint management structure may affect the public support for it, but may also compromise its decision making abilities. Today water decision making in Israel is mostly done behind closed doors, with no significant public input.

G. Implementation Sequence

A joint management structure need not be formed instantaneously: in many cases the goals and authority of such structures have evolved over time.[35] The development of the joint management structure can be

[34] E. Benvenisti, 'Legal Aspects of International Institutions for the Management of Shared Water Resources' in Feitelson and Haddad, *Joint Management of Shared Aquifers*.

[35] This was the case with the Nile River. See B. Grover, 'Remarks on Interjurisdictional Water Management' in Feitelson and Haddad, *Joint Management of Shared Aquifers*.

planned: it may be helpful, for instance, to develop the trust in the capabilities of such a structure by having it first deal with verification and relatively non-confrontational technical issues, prior to assuming more difficult or contentious decision making roles.

In addition to the issues involved in designing joint management structures, consideration needs to be given to issues that may affect their acceptance. Perhaps the most important of these is the degree to which a proposed structure infringes upon the sovereignty of the parties, or upon the work of existing institutions. The greater the degree of infringement, the higher the probability that significant opposition will arise as to the proposed structure.

Another issue that needs to be recognized are the economic implications of the proposed structure. Such implications have two facets. One, an efficiency facet: whether the structure can facilitate efficient use of water by the parties and thus allow the best use of water to be made to the potential benefit of all. Two, the distributive facet: it is important to recognize in advance any sector that may be adversely affected by the proposed structure. Otherwise the structure may face significant internal opposition.

A third issue of relevance is the compatibility of proposed structures with the existing water laws of the various parties. Unless they are compatible, the ratification of the proposed structures may require special legislative processes by the parties, processes that may impede the implementation of these proposed structures.

V. Some Possible Joint Management Structures

The possibilities for joint management structures vary widely. Eaton has suggested twelve possibilities ranging from incremental problem resolutions, through agreement to talk, to talk and monitor, to coordinate, to limits on action, all the way to joint management and agreement to super-jurisdictional control.[36] In the second stage of the study, seventeen possible structures were described.[37] These possible structures are briefly summarized in Table 1 (not reproduced here). This summary shows that the structures vary in function, level of cooperation, financing, staffing requirements, decision making options, and issues they address.

At the bottom part of the scale, joint management structures can focus on a single issue that does not require action or political decisions in itself, such as monitoring apportionment or water quality, research or

---

[36] Eaton and Eaton, *Joint Management of Aquifers*.

[37] The structures are detailed in a draft working paper, S Sylvan, *Institutional Models for a Palestinian-Israeli Joint Management Body*, (11 September 1994).

training. Further up the scale, the structure can focus on a single issue that requires decisions such as arbitration, managing emergency situations or a forum for updating apportionment rules. Structures can also deal with multifacet issues such as pollution control, coordination of water resource development projects or the administration of water markets. At the top end of the scale are comprehensive structures. These can take the form of commissions responsible for resource management,[38] or regulated utilities. Such utilities may allow both sides to surrender authority in a politically palatable way, and to provide a more discrete and ideologically acceptable way of encouraging external involvement and investment.

Following an initial evaluation of these structures, detailed elsewhere,[39] a tentative typology of these structures was advanced. This typology divides the structures in Table 1 into five groups:

A Structures whose primary focus is resource protection;

B Structures whose primary focus is on the efficient and flexible use of the resource;

C Structures necessary to sustain any agreement regarding the resource, including structures that help mitigate potential conflicts;

D Integrative structures, encompassing all or most of the desired functions;

E Supplementary structures (such as training).

Elements of the first three types of structures can be combined into various loosely structured, yet comprehensive, set-ups.[40] Such set-ups can be developed over time to suit the Israeli-Palestinian peculiarities. A major dilemma that emerged from this analysis was whether negotiators should aim to construct such loose structures that could be developed incrementally in a fairly straightforward manner, or whether full integrative structures such as those proposed in the Bellagio draft treaty should be preferred.[41] To this end it is necessary to analyze at this stage the implications of the need for the joint management of aquifers.

---

[38] One of the options for such a committee is detailed in the Bellagio draft treaty.

[39] E. Feitelson and S. Sylvan, *Possible Institutional Models for a Joint Aquifer Management Body*, (paper presented at the second workshop on joint management of shared aquifers, Jerusalem, 27 November - 1 December 1994).

[40] Various elements of the fifth group can be added to these structures. For an example, see Feitelson and Sylvan, *Possible Institutional Models*.

[41] Hayton and Utton, *Transboundary Groundwaters*.

VI. Some Implications of Joint Management for Negotiations

The brief description of possible joint management structures, as well as the initial attempt to evaluate them, focus attention on a number of questions that need to be addressed within the negotiations process.

Perhaps the most poignant issue raised by the discussion of joint management, and especially of aquifers, is the importance of current agreements for the quality of water resources and the close relationship between water quality and the cost of water that will be available to future generations. Thus the question of how to assure sustainable development and the use of existing resources should be at the centre of negotiations.

A closely related question is how to deal with fluctuations, uncertainty and emergencies. This question requires that water rights be defined in a way that will not compromise the ability to adjust in a timely manner to fluctuations in recharge, new discoveries (both in terms of options for better management and the use of and threats to resources), or to respond to droughts or pollution emergencies. A rigid quantitative definition of water rights does not allow for such necessary and rapid adjustments.

One way of introducing flexibility into the water rights question is to change attitudes towards water. In particular it is important to discuss the possibilities for water trading.[42] Such trading is not possible without an adequate institutional and legal infrastructure.[43] The nature and specifics of this infrastructure, as well as the rules of trade, should be part of the negotiations.

Another method for introducing flexibility is through the privatization of various elements of the water supply and treatment infrastructure. This can perhaps be accomplished by establishing cross-border utilities. Such utilities are also a means for addressing the touchy and important question of how to fund the joint management of water resources. In almost all scenarios the parties will need to undertake actions in response to or in conjunction with the actions and activities of other parties. Such actions cost money and to prevent these issues from becoming a basis for contention, compensatory or complementary financing mechanisms would be necessary.

Who should pay whom and when is only a part of the potential sources for disagreement over time between the parties. Another question that needs careful attention at this stage is how are the two sides

---

42 H. Shuval, *The Strategy of the Market Approach as a Basis for Joint Water Management*, (paper presented at the second workshop on joint management of shared aquifers, Jerusalem, 27 November - 1 December 1994).

43 On this issue, see the various papers presented at a seminar on transferability of water entitlements in J. Pigram and B. Hooper (eds.), *Transferability of Water Entitlements*, (Center for Water Policy Research, University of New England, Armidale, Australia, November 1990).

to settle future differences in a peaceful manner. This question requires that the parties also discuss and agree on the extent to which they would like to put such issues in the hands of external bodies.[44] The answer to this question is closely interlinked with another touchy issue – the question of the extent to which the different parties are willing to forego elements of their sovereignty.[45]

Many of the optional structures impinge on the sovereignty of the two sides. However, there is a large degree of latitude as to the degree to which each structure would impinge on the sovereignty of different parties. Thus, there is an urgent need to discuss the degree to which parties are willing to forego various aspects of their sovereignty for the better management of their shared water resources.

Finally, the two sides should pay close attention to the implications of specific provisions in the agreements for the various sectors within each community. Unless the concerns of interest groups within each entity are addressed, the parties may find it difficult to ratify the agreement, due to effective local opposition. In the case of water, particular attention should be given to the agricultural sector. It may be possible to mitigate adverse effects on this sector by financial compensation mechanisms. Their details should be worked out by each side, as well as between the two sides, with possible external support.

Conclusions

This paper does not review the current water negotiations. Rather it highlights some of the issues that should be discussed in these negotiations. In particular it suggests that the long term issues regarding the requirements for sustaining the water resources to the benefit of all inhabitants should take precedence. If this is the case it will become obvious that there is an unavoidable need to identify structures for joint management of the region's water resources. This is especially crucial in the Israeli-Palestinian case due to the geo–hydrological interdependence of the two sides and their heavy reliance on the aquifers they share.

The paper suggests several possible structures for joint management of water resources. The wide variety of such options shows that the identification of a 'best' structure will be a difficult task. It is thus pertinent that all parties devote the necessary time and resources to the identification of such structures, in both the formal negotiations efforts.

---

[44] E. Benvenisti, 'Legal Aspects of International Institutions for the Management of Shared Aquifers' in Feitelson and Haddad (eds.), *Joint Management of Shared Aquifers.*

[45] On this issue, see K. Piddington, 'Sovereignty and the Environment: Part of the Solution or Part of the Problem', *Environment* 31 (7) (1989), pp. 18-20, 35-39.

After all, the decision making and conflict resolution mechanisms embedded in such structures, rather than the specific decisions regarding water allocations, are the most important element in assuring that the water agreements, when reached, will be sustainable.

MAP 1
Israel's Water and Wastewater Supply Systems

WATER SUPPLY SYSTEM WASTEWATER SYSTEMS AND PLANS

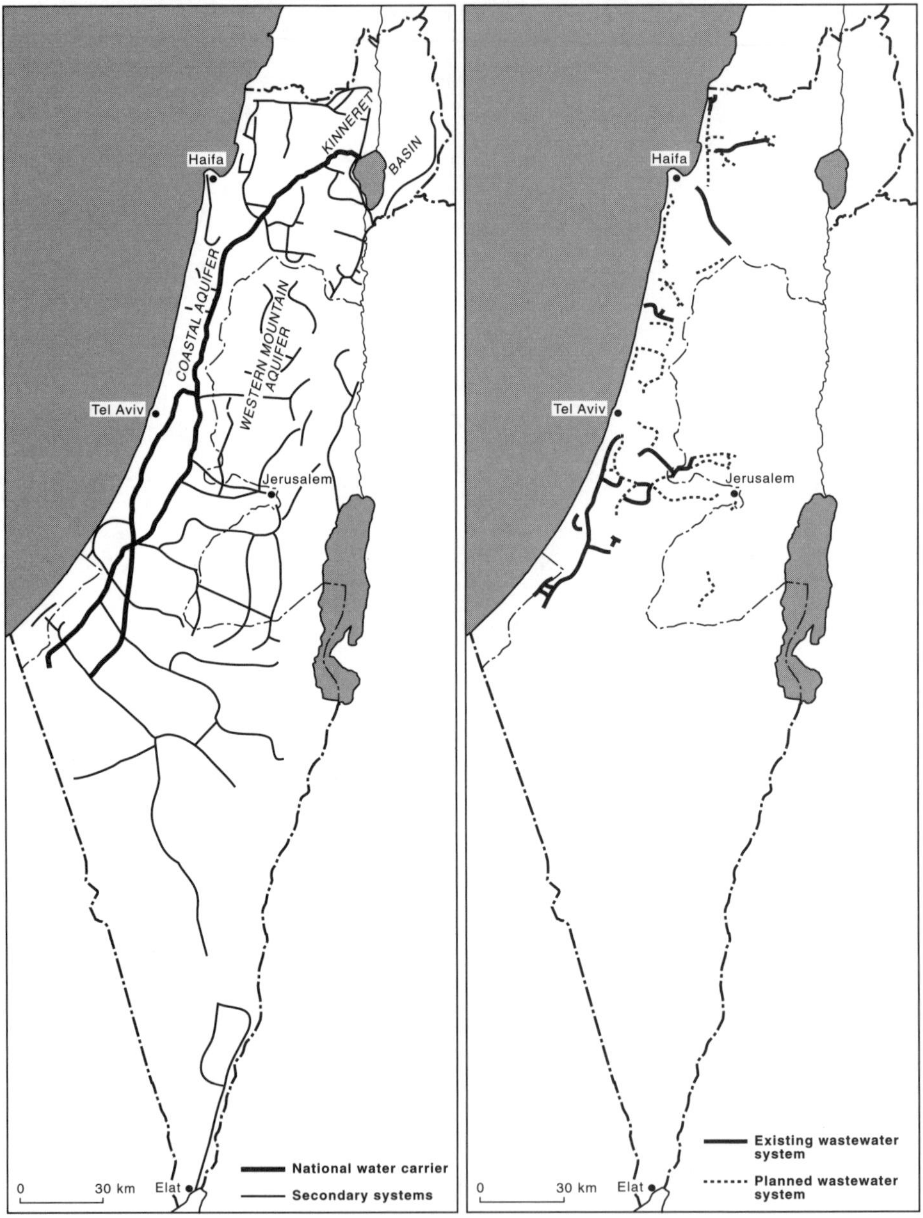

VI. Creating Legal Institutions

11. Creating Legal Institutions: The Effectiveness of the Israeli Legal System

Ruth Levush

Introduction

In accordance with the Declaration of Principles on Interim Self-Government Arrangements (hereafter the DOP),[1] and the Agreement on the Gaza Strip and the Jericho Area,[2] the Palestinian Authority was empowered, among others, with legislative powers. It was also empowered to administer justice through an independent judiciary. In exercising these functions under the current interim agreements and in anticipation of the permanent settlement envisaged by the DOP, Palestinians should engage in the development of their own legal system. The following article discusses the creation of legal institutions and the efficiency of the Israeli legal system. The Israeli system is not offered here as a model to be applied by the Palestinians. There are obviously various differences which will make such application non-workable. On the other hand, there are numerous similarities originating from mutual historical and cultural background. Therefore it may be of value to examine the development of the Israeli legal system which evolved in the same land and under similar conditions.

Discussion of the effectiveness of any legal system focuses on means. For an individual, effectiveness may be perceived in a number of ways, such as the degree of protection from arbitrary actions of the government and the availability of protection from adverse actions by fellow citizens. Efficiency may be determined also by responses to a series of questions: If the citizen is a victim of illegal actions, is redress readily available? How quickly can justice be had? What is the certainty of the offender being identified, apprehended and punished? The sense of some stability, prevention and punishment of anti-social behaviour, as well as resolution of disputes by judicial means rather than by force, are some of the factors and examples stemming from the existence of the "rule of law" in a society.

In a democracy, the legitimacy of public actions is premised on the rule of law. The idea that all governmental actions must be authorized by law is the residue of the long, historical struggle against tyrannical rule. In this sense, legitimacy presupposes legality: the existence of a legal system and of the power to issue orders according to its rules. The

1 Washington, D.C., 13 September 1993 (Government of Israel, Ministry of Foreign Affairs).
2 Cairo, 4 May 1994 (Government of Israel, Ministry of Foreign Affairs).

rule of law "means that government in all its actions is bound by rules fixed and announced beforehand – rules which make it possible to foresee with a fair degree of certainty how the authority will use its coercive powers in given circumstances and to plan one's individual affairs on the basis of this knowledge".[3] The rule of law is a hedge against arbitrary, ad hoc governmental action which is potentially tyrannical.[4]

Legal systems in democratic countries search for the proper balance between governmental authority and civil rights. Conflicts may arise when government actions to protect the rights of the public at large affect individual rights. In the West, particularly in the U.S., the balance at times tilts towards individual rights. Some view this situation as a major contribution to the high rate of crime. Efficiency, according to this view, should be measured by the system's success in deterrence of criminal activity, as may be indicated by a low crime rate, a high rate of convictions, and the degree of protection innocent civilians enjoy.[5]

The discussion of Israeli legal institutions and the efficiency of the system might best be focused on the development of a modern democratic centralized system in general. Such a system is of utmost importance in the process of the establishment of sovereignty. Israel is a young democracy which grew out of the British Mandatory power over Palestine. The new independent state had to build new legal institutions. To establish its sovereignty, it was necessary to establish a system based on the rule of law. Sovereignty depends, among other things, on the respect people have for the legal institutions of the state. Such respect should not rely on political orientation. Sovereignty in this light means that the citizen obeys the laws of the state, even if he disagrees with any particular concept embodied in them. The opportunity to change the law is through popular elections. All branches of government, on their part, should, likewise, obey the law.

The rule of law in a society does not mean a permanent fixed set of rules. Meir Shamgar, President of the Supreme Court of Israel stated his opinion on this subject:[6]

---

3 Hayek, *The Road to Serfdom*, (1944), p. 72 , as cited in M. Edelman, *Courts, Politics, and Law in Israel*, (1994), p. 33.

4 Edelman, *id.*

5 Such trends in the U.S. advocate limitations on the scope of rights of the accused. Interestingly, one of the issues before some U.S. voters in the 8 November 1994 general election was whether a constitutional amendment should be passed establishing the rights of the victims of crime throughout the criminal justice process. The proposed amendment as it appeared in the ballot in Maryland read: "Victim Rights – Established that crime victims have a right to be treated with respect and sensitivity throughout the criminal justice process; a right under certain circumstances to be notified of, to attend, and to be heard at, a criminal justice proceeding; and a right to be notified of these rights. No money claim or right to stay proceedings arises from this article." Copied from the official sample ballot of the general election, 8 November 1994.

6 M. Shamgar, 'The Supreme Court of Israel: Present Trends and Concepts', 20(2-3) *Israel Law Review* 175 (1985) (Hereafter I.L.R.).

> If our concepts and values are to be protected, law must develop permanently; this is especially true in our modern constantly-changing world. The law of the ancient Medes and Persians, as we remember, "altereth not"' and formally, our divine laws are also not subject to change as we learn in Deuteronomy 4:2 and 13:1:... But we know by now that even the divine norms were not only open to hermeneutics but were significantly developed through the Jewish oral law.

According to Shamgar, there are two alternative avenues of development of the law: the legislature, on the one hand, and the court, concurrently or consecutively, on the other hand.

The following analysis will centre on the efficiency of the Israeli legal system in applying the doctrine of the rule of law.

I. Historical Overview

The independent State of Israel came into being on 14 May 1948, on the eve of the British evacuation from Palestine. According to the U.N. Resolution of 29 November 1947,[7] the British Mandate was supposed to come to an end no later than 1 August 1948. Accordingly, the British should have submitted their power to a U.N. special commission to serve as an interim government to assure the passing of power to two states, a Jewish state and an Arab state which would be democratic and respect certain basic human rights.[8] The U.N. Commission was to

> instruct the Provisional Councils of Government of both the Arab and Jewish States, after their formation, to proceed to the establishment of administrative organs of government, central and local... The Provisional Council of Government of each State shall, not later than two months after the withdrawal of the armed forces of the mandatory Power, hold elections to the Constituent Assembly which shall be conducted on democratic lines....

The British government refused to cooperate in the carrying out of the U.N. plan, claiming that it was not mutually agreed upon by the Jews and the Arabs.[9] They caused the U.N. commission to stumble by letting it enter Palestine only shortly prior to termination of the Mandate, and by further pulling out their military force without submitting power to their successors in an orderly manner. On 29 April 1948 the British Parliament passed the Palestine Act according to which

---

7 U.N. General Assembly Resolution 181(II) on the Future Government of Palestine [the Partition Plan], 29 November 1947, in R. Lapidoth & M. Hirsh (eds.), *The Arab-Israel Conflict and its Resolution: Selected Documents*, (1992), p. 33.

8 Plan of Partition with Economic Union, *id.* at p. 35.

9 A. Rubinstein, 1 *Hamishpat Hakonstitutsioni Shel Medinat Israel* [The Constitutional Law of the State of Israel] 37, 4th edn, (Jerusalem & Tel-Aviv, 1991).

His Majesty's Parliament's power over Palestine would cease to exist on 15 May 1948.

In the absence of any contribution to the establishment of a new regime the natural outcome could have been a political and legal vacuum. This situation was prevented because of two major reasons: the initiative of the leaders of the Jewish population of Palestine; and the receptiveness of the Jewish community of Palestine to the creation of legal institutions.

A. Initiative of the Leaders of the Jewish Population of Palestine

Even before the Partition Resolution, the National Council (of the Jewish Community in Palestine) had appointed a Committee on Constitutional Questions. That Committee prepared several memoranda. After the UN Resolution, the Jewish Agency for Palestine (of the World Zionist Organization) had Dr. Lio Kohn prepare a draft constitution.[10] According to the U.N. Resolution of 29 November 1947, the British mandate would come to an end no later than 1 August 1948. The U.N. recommended before Britain and other members of the organization the acceptance and carrying out of "the partition plan under economic union". According to the plan, Britain was supposed to gradually pull out its forces from Palestine and complete this process by 1 August 1948. Within two months of the pull-out and not later than 1 October 1948, two states would be established – one Arab and one Jewish, and an international regime of the U.N. would apply to Jerusalem. These three bodies were supposed to be economically united. The resolution provided for the transfer of power from Britain to a U.N. committee which would establish by 1 April 1948 a provisional council in the Jewish and the Arab state. Each such provisional council would then conduct democratic elections for the Constituent assembly.

The British did not act in accordance with the Resolution or the plan. This, however, did not result in prevention of the establishment of legal institutions in the State of Israel. In March 1948 the Jewish national committee, with the agreement of the management of the Palestine section Jewish Agency, decided to form the provisional council of the future Jewish state. On 14 May 1948, the day preceding the end of British rule, the Jewish People's Council, elected earlier, convened in Tel-Aviv Museum[11] and approved the Proclamation of Independence, which declared as follows:

---

10 Edelman, *Supra* note 3, at p. 7.

11 See Statement by D. Ben-Gurion, first Prime Minister in Israel, 13 December 1949, Lapidoth & Hirsh, *The Arab-Israel Conflict*, at p. 106, concerning the temporary location of the first government in Tel-Aviv rather than in Jerusalem. The actions taken by the Jewish People's Council, despite unfavourable conditions, illustrate their pragmatic approach.

> We declare that, with effect from the moment of the termination of the Mandate, being tonight, the eve of Sabbath, the 6th Iyar, 5708 (15th May, 1948), until the establishment of the elected, regular authorities of the State in accordance with the Constitution which shall be adopted by the Elected Constituent Assembly not later than the 1st October 1948, the People's Council shall act as a Provisional Council of State, and its executive organ, the People's Administration, shall be the Provisional Government of the Jewish State, to be called "Israel".[12]

Immediately following the proclamation, the Provisional Council of State declared that

> The provisional Council of State is the legislative authority. The Provisional Council of State is entitled to delegate some of its legislative power to the Provisional Government for the purpose of urgent legislation.[13]

The proclamation further defined the procedure to be followed by the Provisional Council in legislation, and replaced the powers vested under law in the King of England or his designees in the Provisional Council of State. English was replaced by Hebrew and the word "Palestine", when appearing in the law, was replaced by "Israel". The Council declared that the laws existing in Palestine on 14 May 1948 should be in force as would be consistent with the provisions of the proclamation, with any future laws passed by or with the authority of the Provisional Council of the State, and with the modifications emanating from the establishment of the state and its authorities.

The Declaration of the Establishment of the State of Israel mentioned a draft constitution to be adopted by an elected constituent assembly not later than 1 October 1948. Until this day, no constitution has ever been adopted. After convening on 14 February 1949, the Constituent Assembly, instead of drafting a constitution, converted itself on February 16 into a legislative body (the first Knesset) and enacted the Transition Law, commonly referred to as the "small constitution." The Constituent Assembly could not agree on a comprehensive written constitution, primarily for fear that a constitution would unleash a divisive conflict between religious and state authorities, a fear that continues to date.

In June 1950, the Knesset passed a compromise resolution, known as the "Harari decision", approving a constitution in principle but postponing its enactment until a future date. The resolution stated that the constitution would be evolved "chapter by chapter in such a way that each chapter will by itself constitute a fundamental law". It stipulated:

---

[12] Declaration of the Establishment of the State of Israel, 1 Laws of the State of Israel (hereafter LSI) 4 (5708–1948).

[13] Proclamation of 14 May 1948, 1 LSI 6 (5708–1948).

> The chapters will be submitted to the Knesset to the extent to which the Committee [for Constitution, Law, and Justice of the Knesset] completed its work, and the chapters will be incorporated in the constitution of the State.

To date, eleven Basic Laws have been enacted.[14] There has been great progress, particularly in recent years towards completing the task of writing a comprehensive constitution. In fact, Israel functions without a formal written constitution. Its governing arrangements are an outgrowth of the decision of the Provisional Government and the 1949 Transition Law. The stable pattern which has emerged makes it possible to describe the operative constitution: Israel is a secular republic, with a theoretically sovereign parliament (the Knesset), a politically powerful cabinet (the Government), an independent secular judiciary,[15] and a largely ceremonial President.[16]

B. The Receptiveness towards the Creation of Legal Institutions in Pre-State and Independent Israel

The Jewish community in Palestine was ready for the establishment of independent legal institutions. This readiness may be expressed with the desire for an independent state, and the will to prepare judges and lawyers to operate its legal institutions. During the Ottoman rule there were very few qualified judges or lawyers among the Arabs or the Jews of Palestine. According to Gad Frumkin, who served as a Justice of the Supreme Court during the entire period of the British Mandate (1920 to 1948), there were only three certified attorneys in Palestine in 1918.[17]

During the British Mandate period, more effort was made to provide the residents of Palestine with legal education. The British laid the foundation for legal education in Israel by opening a law school in 1920, under the name of "Law Courses" which functioned throughout the entire period of British rule in Palestine, that is until 1948.[18] Separate law education institutes were established by the Jewish

---

14 Basic Law – the Knesset (1958); Basic Law: Israel Lands (1960); Basic Law: the President of the State (1974); Basic Law: the Government (1968); Basic Law: The State Economy (1976); Basic Law: The Army (1976); Basic Law: Jerusalem, the Capital of Israel (1980); Basic Law: the Judiciary (1984); Basic Law: the State Comptroller (1988); Basic Law: Freedom of Occupation (1992); and Basic Law: Human Dignity and Freedom (1992).

15 Religious law applies in Israel only in matters of marriage and divorce. Continuing the tradition of the "millet" system, religious courts have jurisdiction over such matters.

16 Edelman, *Courts, Politics, and Law in Israel*, p. 9.

17 One Moslem and two Jews, see G. Frumkin, *Derech Shofet Bi-Yerushaliam* [A Way of a Judge in Jerusalem] 1 (Tel-Aviv, 1954) [in Hebrew].

18 See R. Levush, 'The Reception of Legal Systems – Implantation and Destiny in Israel' in *Réception des Systèmes Juridiques – Implantation et Destin* (Brussels, Bruilant, 1994), p. 427.

community with the motivation of promoting its national aspirations. The Hebrew University was established in Jerusalem in 1925, with the support of Jews and non-Jews from all over the world. A special institute for advanced legal studies had been established before the law faculty started operating.[19] This institute was designed to unify some of the legal bases for Jewish lawyers, many coming from various countries, with different legal backgrounds.[20]

Legal education of the elite, however, is not sufficient to successfully apply a legal system. In a 1962 law review article,[21] Justice Alfred Vitkon[22] analyzed the problems facing a developing country, as Israel was at that time. According to Vitkon, society creates law, but at the same time, law creates society. For law to be able to influence the image of society, there should exist proper conditions, which include its receptiveness by the society and its leaders. Receptiveness of central law was traditionally lacking in many Jewish communities in Palestine and in the diaspora. For generations, Jews in the diaspora fulfilled their religious law. At the same time, that law decreed that they obey the state rule.[23] This was a policy that supported the survival of both Jews and their culture. The law of the state, however, was often discriminatory to Jews. This complicated relationship created mistrust towards state-centralized law. Similarly, the British Mandatory law, which was perceived as unfair and biased against national aspirations of the Jewish community in Palestine, did not instil in the community a sense of respect for law. Therefore, unlike other newly independent countries, the new independent State of Israel found it hard to continue the legal system which was operated by the previous regime. Original Israeli law became under these circumstances part of the national renaissance, just like the resurrection of the Hebrew language.

The wish to establish a state was very strong at the time. But that wish was not sufficient for the creation of a central legal system. The forces behind the national goals originated in romance, some in pioneer, Jewish, religious or social idealism. The idealistic spirit promoted first

19 Frumkin, *Derech Shofet Bi-Yerushaliam.*

20 Levush, 'The Reception of Legal Systems', p.426.

21 A. Vitkon, 'The Theory of Law, Law in a Developing Country', *Mishpat Ve-Shiput* (Law and Adjudication) (Tel-Aviv, 1988).

22 Born in Berlin before World War 1, he studied in one of the best high schools in the short bloom of the humanistic culture of the twenties, a period which fertilized the illusions of the majority of German Jews. Vitkon benefited from that period by obtaining a wide education, including that of law in the university. With the rise of Hitler, Vitkon left Germany on his way to England, to complete his legal education in anticipation of immigrating to Israel. Vitkon, thus, enjoyed both the knowledge of continental law with its analytical traits, as well as the British law, with its elegant pragmatism. Vitkon is regarded as the forefather of Israeli tax law. See M. Landoi, 'In Memorandum', *Mishpat Ve-Shiput* (Tel-Aviv, 1988).

23 *Dina demalchuta dina* = the law of the king is the law.

and foremost agricultural settlement; the legal profession, commonly held by Jews in the diaspora, was therefore disliked.

An added difficulty with regard to adherence to a centralized legal system in the State of Israel was the heterogeneous nature of society. The Jewish community of Israel, in the late forties, was composed of people from various ethnic and cultural groups. The differences between these groups included differences in customs, educational level, material and spiritual wishes. Law performed special roles in such a society. Among roles played by the legal system was that of uniting this diverse society. Another was education. Education was achieved sometimes by the introduction of legal norms by legislation. A variety of laws were introduced by the legislature, affecting personal rights. Examples are Age of Marriage Law, 5710–1950, as amended,[24] which prohibited the marriage of minors, and Women's Equal Rights law, 5711–1951, as amended,[25] which abrogated permission by personal law as a defence in polygamy cases, and prohibited the divorce of a woman against her will. Although some of the new legal norms were opposed at first by segments of the Israeli society, Jewish or Arab, the passing of time, and the new social and educational conditions that the State provided, have assisted in better acceptance and respect of these legal norms.[26]

The general adherence of the public, as well as the government, to central law, reflects the efficiency of the system. The present system which is composed of all branches of government, operating within clearly established jurisdictional borders and according to law, testifies to the success in the creation and maintaining of a legal system which adheres to the rule of law. Acceptance and respect of the State's legal norms and its courts by the Israeli public do not derive out of fear of punishment by the government for non-compliance; rather out of conviction of the correctness of these norms. The Israeli system, however, is not immune to future dangers. Stability and general respect for the rule of law should not be taken for granted. The recent statements of Prime Minister Rabin, expressing contempt for the legal profession, and the personal attacks on Justice Barak, following the Supreme Court decision of *Danilovitz v. El-Al Airline*, regarding homosexual rights, are certainly worrisome.[27]

---

24 6 Dinim (Laws) 3425 (1986–) [in Hebrew].

25 5 LSI 172 (5711–1950/51).

26 On the application of state secular law by Moslem courts in Israel, see A. Layish, *Women and Islamic Law in a Non Muslim State*, (1975)

27 See articles such as 'Independence of the Law', and '*Bib v. Barak*', *Ha'aretz* daily, 9 December 1994; See also, 'Who is afraid of Barak?', *Yediot Acharonot Musaf*, 16 December 1994.

II. Israeli Courts as the Guardians of the Rule of Law

Whilst codification of Israeli private and administrative law has steadily developed, it was always accompanied by a strong affirmation by the judges as law interpreters (and makers). The heavy case load before Israeli courts is an indication of the public trust in the judiciary. That in itself is a great achievement if compared to trust and respect owed to the judicial branch before independence. In 1989, more than 740,000, and in 1992 almost 800,000 cases were heard in Israeli courts, approxi mately half of them in civil courts. Comparative figures show that the proportion of civil cases per person in Israel is one of the highest in the world, and indeed, most of the increase in the case-load of the courts is in civil proceedings. In the last twenty years the number of criminal cases has remained steady in relation to the growth in population,[28] while the number of civil cases has increased, in real terms, by 79 per cent. The tendency for increased case-load is also apparent in other tribunals, such as labour and religious courts. The significant growth in the case-load of the courts has not been accompanied by a parallel increase in the manpower resources of the judicial system. The result of this situation has been a delay in the judicial process. Among other factors contributing to court delays and overburdening are the following: increase of population; industrialization and greater sophistication of the economy; legislative reforms which call for adjudication of questions of statutory interpretation; introduction of regulatory schemes in more areas; and certainly, the high measure of litigiousness in Israeli society. A legislative proposal for a consolidation of the courts in order to minimize the delay in the judicial process has so far failed, mainly because of the strong opposition of district court judges, who saw the proposed reform as an attempt to undermine their status.

Among all branches of government the judiciary in Israel enjoys the most respect. This respect was earned by the judges appointed since the establishment of the State. As noted before, there has been an atmosphere of distrust in the judiciary during the British Mandate. The nationalistic, ideological fervour of the early days was certainly not sufficient for the building of a respected judiciary. In Professor Shetreet's words,

> it is by respect and public confidence that a judicial system gains for itself the power to ensure that its judgments are enforced by the executive if need be, and to acquire the trust necessary for persons to resort to it when the need arises. This is particularly so when the citizen requires the assistance of the judiciary for obtaining remedies against the executive.[29]

---

28 S. Shetreet, *Justice in Israel: A Study of the Israeli Judiciary*, (1994), p. 108.
29 *Id*. at p. 64.

Various factors contributed to the creation of public trust in the Israeli judiciary. First is the separation of the judges from any political affiliation. The second important factor is the decision in the early days of independence that one of the tasks of the Supreme Court was to act as a buffer between the State and the individual, to protect the individual and his rights against excessive State intervention.[30] Another important factor in creating public trust was the insistence of the Supreme Court from the start on complete independence. Thus, in its first decision the High Court of Justice began to assert its authority when it ruled that it had jurisdiction to determine whether or not a given person is subject to military law, rejecting the State's claim that the court had no authority to intervene in any matter relating to the armed forces, and that any question on this subject was in the domain of the security services.[31]

Although independent from the start, the legal framework under which the courts operated, was codified in one document in 1984. Basic Law: Judicature[32] specifies the jurisdiction of courts, appointment of judges, condition of employment for judges and other related issues. Basic Law: Judicature clearly provides for the independence of the Judiciary: "A person vested with judicial power shall not, in judicial matters, be subject to any authority but that of the Law".[33] It also guarantees publicity of proceedings.[34] The law further establishes the procedure for appointment of judges. Compared with that of the U.S., the Israeli process of appointment of judges is much less political and affords better chances of finding qualified appointees. According to the law,

> 4(a) A judge shall be appointed by the President of the State upon election by a Judges' Election Committee.
>
> (b) The Committee shall consist of nine members, namely, the President of the Supreme Court, two other judges of the Supreme Court elected by the body of judges thereof, the Minister of Justice and another Minister designated by the Government, two members of the Knesset elected by the Knesset and two representatives of the Chamber of Advocates elected by the National Council of the Chamber. The Minister of Justice shall chair the Committee.

Another important contribution of the law is the detailed description of the areas of jurisdiction of the Supreme Court, particularly with regard to the jurisdiction of the High Court of Justice. The incorporation of this provision was considered extremely important, as

---

30 *Bejerano v. Minister of Police* 2 P.D. 80, *Kol Ha'am v. Minister of the Interior*, 1 Selected Judgments of the Supreme Court of Israel 90.

31 See the first decision of *Neiman v. Military Governor* 1 P.D. 50 (1948).

32 38 L.S.I. 101 (5744–1983/84).

33 *Id.* § 2.

34 In the absence of a written constitution the law provides as an exception, instances where "otherwise provided by Law or unless the court otherwise directs under Law."

the procedure constituted an essential guarantee for the protection of the rights of the individual.[35]

An independent judiciary is an essential element of the rule of law and a precondition for the existence of a democratic society.[36] For the court to be able to carry out its duties, it has to enjoy judicial independence. The real aim of judicial independence is the creation of a separation which enables a balanced relationship between the arms of government and assures the existence of a system of adjudication which acts without political accountability and carries in its heart and mind only the search for a just and right solution of each and every legal problem brought before it.[37] Independence of the judiciary in Israel is achieved through five factors: (1) appointment of judges by a balanced committee; (2) the endowment by law of the above committee of Judicial Appointments with the sole power to promote judges and to appoint the Chief Justice; (3) life tenure; (4) public sensitivity to the safeguarding of judicial independence; (5) judicial tradition of ancient and of recent times which regards the search for justice as the guiding genius of the profession.

There is a feeling amongst the general public in Israel that the independence of the judiciary, having been consolidated and established in law, is not under any risk. This is not the case. In fact, the independence of Israeli judiciary has constantly been tested. Deviations from the proper norms of judicial independence are to be found in every period of the State's history and in every aspect of the relationship between the judiciary and the executive.

Indeed, there have been numerous cases of executive interventions in the judicial process, either by the carrying out of executive acts designed to pre-empt a judicial determination, or by the frustration of judicial decisions, caused by the executive preventing their implementation. According to Shetreet, the pattern of executive intervention in the judicial process is certainly far from being frequent. Nevertheless, it is alarming.

The strengthening of the status of the courts in Israel, and particularly of the Supreme Court was vital to the development of Israeli constitutional law in a country which does not have a written constitution. According to the rule of *stare decisis* applicable in Israel, decisions by the Supreme Court bind all lower courts. In the absence of a valid constitution, the courts must enforce any ruling of the Knesset (the legislature). Nevertheless, the Supreme Court sitting as a High Court of Justice has managed to develop fundamental constitutional principles which in other Western democracies are protected by

35 *Supra* note 33, § 15.

36 Shetreet, *Justice in Israel*, at p. 3.

37 *Id.* at 179-80.

constitutions. This is done by interpretation.[38] The Court has been active in the development of several fields of law, mainly public law and human rights. There has been a systematic increase of the power of the Supreme Court by enlarging the scope and depth of judicial review.[39] The increase of the power of the Supreme Court as will be explained further could not have taken place without the confidence of the public in the Court.

By way of example, the following is a discussion of case law developed in Israel in three important areas: general human rights, public law, and security related issues. As will be further demonstrated these areas are vital to maintaining the democratic character of the State and the political awareness of its citizens.

A. General Human Rights

In the absence of a written constitution, the Supreme Court relied on the Declaration of Independence as a document incorporating the wishes and the intent of the founding fathers of the reborn state. The declaration, thus, served as a tool for the interpretation of laws enacted by the Knesset rather than as a constitutional document by itself.

Based on interpretation of the declaration of independence and other general principles, the Supreme Court sitting as a High Court of Justice was able to create legal norms which were not expressly provided by legislation. This was done with the understanding that when the Administration is granted powers which may injure human rights, the courts will usually interpret the enabling provisions restrictively, so that the injury will be as limited as possible. One area in which the Supreme Court was greatly influential in the creation of legal norms is that concerning freedom of speech. In the absence of a clear constitutional provision, like the 1st Amendment in the U.S., theoretically the Executive could act freely, while not respecting this unprescribed right. The Legislature could likewise enact laws which disregard it. Several decisions of the Supreme Court established that there is a constitutional right in Israel of freedom of speech. Therefore, the application of any provisions of law which allow for violation or limitation of this right should be made in the most restrictive way. In the celebrated case of *Kol Ha'Am,* Justice Agranat stated clearly:[40]

> The system of laws under which the political institutions in Israel have been established and function are witness to the fact that this is indeed a state founded

---

[38] See A. Shapira, 'The Supreme Court as a Defender of Basic Rights of the Individual in Israel – A Shielded Castle or a Paper Tiger?', 3 *Iyune Mishpat* 625 (1973) [in Hebrew].

[39] D. Kretzmer, 'Forty Years of Public Law', 24(3-4) I.L.R. 342 (1990).

[40] *Kol Ha'am v. Minister of the Interior*, 7 PD 871 (1953).

> on democracy. Moreover, the matters set forth in the Declaration of Independence, especially as regards the basing of the State "on the foundations of freedom" and the securing of freedom of conscience, mean that Israel is a freedom-loving State. It is true that the Declaration "does not consist of any constitutional law laying down in fact any rule regarding the maintaining or repeal of any ordinances or laws" but insofar as it "expresses the vision of the people and its faith", we are bound to pay attention to the matters set forth in it when we come to interpret and give meaning to the laws of the State... for it is a well-known axiom that the law of a people must be studied in the light of its national way of life.

Sitting as a High Court of Justice, the Supreme Court established the parameters of freedom of expression as recognized by the Israeli system. It held that the right is not absolute. It could however be limited only in rare cases, where a severe danger is expected as a result of the speech. The danger, according to the Israeli test is not "clear and present" as in the American test; rather it is "near certainty". In the circumstances of the case, two communist newspapers published articles containing material which, in the opinion of the Minister of the Interior, was likely to endanger the public peace. Acting under section 19(2) of the Press Ordinance the Minister suspended the newspapers for periods of ten and fifteen days respectively. The owners of the newspapers petitioned the High Court of Justice to have the orders reversed. Justice Agranat, for the Court, held that in exercising his power of suspension under law, the guiding principle is that the Minister must consider whether it is probable that as a consequence of the publication a danger to the public peace has been disclosed. A mere tendency to endanger the public peace will not suffice to fulfil that requirement. Even if he is satisfied that the public peace is likely to be endangered by the publication, the Minister must nevertheless consider whether that danger is so grave as to justify the use of so drastic a power as suspension of a newspaper. Justice Agranat held that although the court would not interfere with the discretion of the Minister when properly exercised, the Minister in this case had not considered the probability of the public peace being endangered, but had acted in the belief that a mere tendency in this direction was sufficient. Based on the above, the suspension of publication of both newspapers was set aside.

Based on the "near certainty test" established in *Kol Ha'Am v. Minister of the Interior*, the Court ruled that a decision made by the Film and Theatre Censorship Board to exclude a publication of a certain photograph in a cinema news bulletin was based on illegal grounds.[41] The respondent Board had withheld authority for the exhibition of part of a newsreel made by the Petitioner which depicted the forcible eviction by the police in execution of a court order of the tenants of a poor neighbourhood, in the course of which a woman was dragged

---

41 *Israel Film Studios LTD. v. Levi Geri and the Film and Theatre Censorship Board, Ministry of the Interior*, 17 PD 208 (1962).

along and a portion of her body exposed. The Board based itself upon the ground that the extract did not reflect the problem in its entirety and was liable to mislead public opinion and exert an undesirable educational influence. The majority opinion, by Justice Landau, held that

> the principle of freedom of information is so vital to the regime prevailing in our country that it is to be maintained also in the area of cinema news bulletins, unless some overriding reason exists for departing therefrom. The decision of the Board and its reply to the petition before us do not reveal that it took into account this vital principle. Had it done so, it could not have decided as it did.

The doctrine was applied again in the case concerning the play "Efrayim Returns to the Army",[42] where a refusal of the Film and Play Supervisory Board to grant permission for performance of the play was in question. The refusal was based on the decision of the Board that the play presented the Israeli Military Government in the West Bank "in a false, distorted, wicked and malicious way, even comparing it to the Nazi regime". Justice Barak recognizes the authority of the Board to grant or deny a permit to a play, based on the Public Performances (Censorship) Ordinance. Although the ordinance does not provide for considerations for such a decision, clearly "the Board's power is limited, as is the power of any government authority". Based on analysis of the scope of the purpose of the enactment, Justice Barak concluded that

> its purpose was to grant the Board authority to prevent beforehand the performance of a play which injures the public order... 'Public order' is a broad concept, whose definition is difficult and varies by context. In the present context it includes injury to the existence of the state, its democratic regime, public peace, morals, religious sentiments, personal reputation, ... and other such matters pertaining to the public order...The question is not whether or not the play has an adequate artistic value....The question is whether performing the play, whatever its value, will injure the public order.

After stating that the existence of Israel as a democracy depends on maintaining a delicate balance between freedom of expression and public order, Justice Barak holds that "the proper balancing formula is that freedom of expression yields only when the injury to the public order is harsh, serious and severe". Evaluation of the circumstances of that case convinced the Justice that it could not be said that the injury to feeling, which undoubtedly existed, was so severe as to justify limiting the freedom of expression. Justice Barak stated that "[t]he force of democracy lies not in acknowledging my right to hear what pleases my ear. It lies in recognizing the right of the other to utter words that hurt my ears and cause pain in my heart". Since the Board's decision did not

---

[42] *Laor et al. v. Film and Play Supervisory Board*, 40 PD 64 (1986).

pass the normative test of "near certainty danger" it acted outside of the limits of its authority. The decision was therefore overruled.

In the 1985 *Kahane* case,[43] Justice Barak analysed the legality of the decision of Israel's semi-governmental Broadcasting Authority to ban broadcasting of Rabbi Kahane's speeches. Kahane was the leader of a one person party which advocated racist ideas and the transfer of Arab Israelis to Arab countries.[44] Kahane and his followers argued that the ban violated their own as well as the public's freedom of speech and information. In his analysis, Justice Barak recognizes the existence of conflicting rights involved in the issue of racist speech: freedom of speech versus the democratic character of the state, public security and peace, human dignity and public feelings. In the clash between freedom of speech and "public order" the latter may prevail. Accordingly, for the speech to be limited it has to fulfil two tests: first, it has to cause serious and severe injury to the public order; secondly, there should be enough certainty that it will be followed by deeds that will palpably injure public order, peace or the foundation of democracy. Since no consideration was made in this case by the Broadcasting Authorities to the impact of Kahane's words on public order, the petitioner won.

B. Public Law

In recent years the Israeli judiciary has become a significant branch of government. Significantly, the Supreme Court has contributed to the greater judicialization of Israeli society by its substantial liberalization of the rules of standing and of the principles of justiciability.[45] This, in contrast to the weakening role of the political branches, has made the Israeli Supreme Court a significant participant in the government of the country. The process of increasing judicialization has brought about increasing involvement of the judiciary in the adjudication of politically charged cases.

The process of constant development in the area of administrative law, started immediately with independence. The early judges, even though most of them were devoid of any experience whatsoever in adjudication or administration, succeeded quickly to establish an independent position for themselves, to impose their authority on the government, and to inculcate public servants with the awareness that the law applies to all public authorities and obligates all ministers and public officials. They established that an excess of power was likely to

---

43 H.C. 399/85, *Kahane et al. v. Executive Board, Israel Broadcasting Authority et al.*, 41(3) P.D (1987).

44 The Israeli law of elections has since been amended to exclude such parties from the election process. Kahane himself was murdered by an Arab in New York, in front of a large crowd.

45 See e.g. H.C. 910/86 *Rasler v. Minister of Defense*, 42(2) P.D 441 (1988).

invalidate any decision, even in the sensitive area of national security. They placed restrictions on administrative discretion, even when the statute refrained from doing so, and required the authority to take account of human rights, proclaimed as natural rights, in order to balance public and private interests. The Supreme Court, which in the Mandatory period seemed closely identified with and inordinately influenced by the government, was now perceived by all as the bastion of the citizen against the government.[46]

The Supreme Court has constantly been enlarging the scope of its review, to the point that the net of judicial review is cast today over all arms of government, and over almost all types of activities.[47] The variety of governmental actions over which judicial review has been exercised in recent years includes a decision of the President of the State to pardon criminals,[48] a decision of the Presidium of the Knesset not to table proposed legislation,[49] a decision of the Knesset plenary to remove the immunity of a Knesset Member,[50] a decision of the Minister of Justice not to extradite a man pronounced extraditable by a court,[51] and a decision of the Minister of Defence to postpone the enlistment of Yeshiva students.[52]

An interesting trend is found in recent years whereby the Supreme Court extended its jurisdiction and applied its judicial review to actions and proceedings of the Knesset. For the Court to review Knesset actions it must overcome three substantial hurdles:

(1) Jurisdictional: According to the system of government in the State of Israel the Knesset stands at the "top of the pyramid of governmental authorities".[53] It creates the law and it is within its power to change it. In order to establish its jurisdiction to review the actions of the legislature, the court is required to establish that the Knesset, despite the fact that it is the law-maker, is subordinate to the rule of law;[54]

(2) Justiciability: Considering that the legislature represents the sovereignty of the nation and reflects its free will, there is a principal

---

46 I. Zamir, 'Administrative Law: Revolution or Evolution', 24(3-4) I.L.R. 358 (1990).

47 Kretzmer, 'Forty Years of Public Law', at 342.

48 *Barzilai v. Government of Israel*, 40(3) P.D. 505. (1986). This case concerns the pardon granted by the President to head of the General Security Service and three of his employees, for offences they were charged with, but not yet convicted of, regarding the "Bus No. 300" incident, when the Palestinian bus hijackers were executed after being arrested. The decision focuses on interpretation of presidential powers in Israel.

49 See 39(4) P.D. (1985); *Kahane v. Speaker of the Knesset*, 40(4) P.D. 393 (1986).

50 See *Mi'ari v. Speaker of the Knesset*, 41(2) P.D. 169 (1987).

51 *Aloni v. Minister of Justice*, 41(2) P.D. 1 (1987).

52 *Ressler v. Minister of Defense*, 42(2)441 (1988).

53 *Flatto-Sharon v. Knesset Committee*, 35(4) P.D. 118, 135.

54 See S. Shetreet, *Justice in Israel*, at p. 426; See also, *Miari v. Speaker of the Knesset*, 41(4) P.D. 169.

question as to whether the court should adjudicate questions that are within the jurisdiction of the legislature; and

(3) Standing: If the Knesset has allegedly acted unlawfully, should the petitioner be required to point to a right of his that has been infringed ?

A review of court decisions on parliamentary issues shows that the Court avoided discussion of these pre-conditions, usually based on the fact that the parties themselves did not raise them.[55]

Based on the rule of supremacy of the law, in the absence of a written constitution, attempts to attack the validity of statutes merely because of their content never succeeded. The only argument against the validity of a law that the court has been prepared to consider is the argument that the law was not passed by a required majority as the legislature itself had required. A leading case on this issue is *Bergman v. Minister of Finance and State Comptroller.*[56] The decision centred on the denial of public campaign funds to the new list of candidates for the Knesset, as provided by the Knesset and Local Authorities Elections (Financing, Limitation of Expenses & Audit) Law, 1969 [hereafter the financing law]. The Court held that the latter denial of funds to new lists constituted a substantial violation of the lists' equality of opportunity, provided by section 4 of Basic Law: the Knesset, which by itself, according to section 46, could not have been amended without a resolution of a plenary meeting of the Knesset at every stage of the legislation. Since no such majority was obtained during the enactment of the financing law, the Minister of Finance was ordered to refrain from acting upon it until either the Knesset passed it again with the required majority, or the inequality in it was removed.

The second time the High Court of Justice set aside a Knesset statute was in 1981, in the case of *Derech Eretz Association et al v. Broadcasting Authority et al.*[57] The background was again a breach of the equality principle of section 4 of Basic Law: the Knesset, this time by the Election (Means of Propaganda) (Amendment no. 6) Law 1981, which had not been enacted by the necessary special majority. Due to the approaching date of the pending elections to the Knesset, the law was simply passed with the required special majority, marking the end of the affair. The same issue came up again in *Rubinstein v. Speaker of the Knesset,*[58] where the Court accepted the claim that the enactment of an

---

55 S. Shetreet, an expert on Israeli judiciary, is of the opinion that these issues should not be left in the hands of the parties to the petition. Determination of the issue of justiciability, e.g., demands the review of considerations which are beyond the interests of the parties but of which the court itself must take account. Shetreet states as example the danger of politicization of the judiciary, the danger that the dismissal of a petition on its facts may grant validity to acts, which, although they are lawful, may not be proper, and so forth. See Shetreet at p. 430.

56 23(1) P.D. 693 (1969).

57 35(4) P.D. 1 (1981).

58 37(3) P.D. 141 (1983).

amendment to the Financing of Political Parties Law, aiming at increasing retrospectively the financing unit granted to each party, constituted a breach of equality, and was therefore invalid.

The Court reached a similar conclusion in *Laor et al. v. Chairman of the Knesset*,[59] where it held that the retroactive increase of the amount of a financing unit, after completion of the campaign and the elections, constituted a breach of the equality rule, since it retroactively changed the relative rights of those claiming for a share in party financing, and therefore affected their equality of opportunities.[60] The Petitioners' claim, that the special majority necessitated by section 46 of Basic Law: The Knesset, applied to all three readings of the bill, as well as the preliminary reading, was accepted. Accordingly, the Court held that the amendment was not appropriately passed, and therefore held that the respondents should return to the state treasury the sums of money they received based on the latter amendment. Interestingly, the Knesset responded by amending section 46 retrospectively to the day it was enacted,[61] providing that the special majority was required only in the three readings and not in the preliminary reading. The amendment nullified the outcome of the decision in the *Laor* case.

The Court was willing to entertain various cases in which Knesset internal proceedings were in dispute. Member of Knesset[62] Kahane's controversial actions provided fertile grounds for judicial law-making. It may be of benefit to review some of these decisions to illustrate the efficiency of the Court in establishing legal norms. In the first of Kahane's petitions,[63] it was decided that according to the proper interpretation of the Knesset rules, the presidium of the Knesset is not authorized to refuse to table a bill because of its racist character. Following the refusal of the Speaker to abide by the Court's ruling, Kahane petitioned the Court again, referring to the Contempt of Court Ordinance. As Shetreet states, apparently in order to avoid an open confrontation with the Knesset, the Court gave a technical and narrow interpretation to the Ordinance, and to its ruling in a previous case, holding that its first decision had not amounted to an operative injunction, but rather to a "normative injunction" interpreting the powers of the Speaker of the Knesset and his deputies. In November 1985 the Knesset passed a bill to amend section 134 of the Knesset rules, according to which "the Speaker of the Knesset and his deputies shall not approve proposed legislation which in their opinion, is of racist character or negates the existence of the State of Israel as the State of

59 44(3) P.D. 529 (5751–1990).

60 For general information on campaign finance in Israel, See R. Levush (coordinator), *Campaign Financing of National Elections in Foreign Countries*, (Law Library of Congress, 1995), p.110.

61 Basic Law: The Knesset (Amendment No. 11) 1990, Sefer Hachukim 196.

62 Hereafter MK.

63 *Kahane v. Speaker of the Knesset,* 39(4) P.D. 485.

the Jewish People".[64] Following this amendment, MK Kahane's third petition was rejected, this time on substantive grounds.

It is worth noting that the Court also entertained petitions the subject of which could be characterized as purely political. Such petitions were the ones submitted in 1990 concerning the legality of coalition agreements. In 1990, each of the two major parties tried over a long period to form a government, following the fall of the unity government. Owing to the almost equal number of seats of the right and the left blocks, the dependence of the major parties (Likud and Ma'arach) on the small parties, and sometimes even individual MKs, intensified greatly. This fact created opportunities for extracting exaggerated conditions and promises by those small parties, with the leaders of both major parties forced to compete as to who would offer more to one MK or another. As a result, the coalition agreements reached intensified the public's mistrust of the political system. Public pressure resulted in three petitions to the High Court of Justice in 1990. The *Shalit v. Peres*[65] decision analyses the duty to disclose the agreements between all parties of the Knesset. In *Levy v. The Prime Minister of Israel*[66] the Court analyzed the legality of a request for a monetary guarantee to secure future obligations arising from a coalition agreement.[67]

The Supreme Court sitting as a High Court of Justice held that the inclusion of a monetary obligation in a public contract illegally harms the statutory discretion; furthermore, it constitutes a harmful grant of a financial benefit in the area of political relationship. The harm to the democratic process is therefore evident. The 1990 coalition agreement was the subject of another decision of the High Court of Justice. *Zerzevsky v. Prime Minister*[68] centred on the legality of a political agreement guaranteeing special positions in the government, the nomination of an arbitrator to arbitrate any future disagreements and the creation of monetary guarantees for execution of the agreement. The Court held that the issue of political agreement is justiciable. The fact that the obligations arising from such an agreement are basically political, in that they concern the establishment of a government institution, cannot prevent judicial review of issues for which judicial criteria exist. The Court held that provisions of a political agreement which contradict or negatively affect statutory discretion are void.

The trend, which is evident in "political" decisions, offers an indication of not only enlargement of the substantive scope of jurisdiction of the court and easing, or avoiding the issue of

---

64 103 Divre Haknesset 444 (1985), section 134(c) of the Knesset Code.

65 *Shalit v. Peres*, 44(3) P.D. 353 (1990).

66 *Levy v. The Prime Minister of Israel*, 44(2) P.D. 213 (1990).

67 Between MK Modai and the Likud party.

68 *Zerzevsky v. Prime Minister*, 45(1) P.D. 793 (1991).

justiciability altogether, but also, of opening the doors to the public, without insisting on standing.[69]

C. Security-Related Issues

1. Emergency Powers

The State of Israel was born in the midst of a war. One hopes that the peace treaties with Egypt and Jordan and the peace accords with the P.L.O. signal the end of that era. However, the continuing state of war was not only one of the predominant features of Israeli society and culture, it also had an obvious and strong effect on the legal system. This was possible through the passing of emergency regulations.

The legislative authorization for passing emergency regulations is found in the Law and Administration Ordinance, 5708–1948.[70] According to section 9:[71]

> (a) If the Provisional Council of State deems it expedient so to do, it may declare that a state of emergency exists in the State, and upon such declaration being published in the Official Gazette, the Provisional Government may authorize the Prime Minister or any other Minister to make such emergency regulations as may seem to him expedient in the interests of the defense of the State, public security and the maintenance of supplies and essential services.
>
> (b) An emergency regulation may alter any law, suspend its effect or modify it, and may also impose or increase taxes or other obligatory payments.
>
> (c) An emergency regulation shall expire three months after it is made, unless it is extended, or revoked at an earlier date, by an Ordinance of the Provisional Council of State, or revoked by the regulation-making authority.
>
> (d) Whenever the Provisional Council of State thinks fit, it shall declare that the State of emergency has ceased to exist, and upon such declaration being published in the Official Gazette, the emergency regulations shall expire on the date or dates prescribed in such declaration.

On 19 May 1948 the Provisional Council declared the existence of a state of emergency. This declaration is still valid.[72]

For many years, it seemed that the Court did not exercise judicial review over the usage of the emergency powers authorities. In *General Attorney v. Ostraicher*,[73] the Court rejected the petitioner's claim that

---

69 In *Zerzevsky*, e.g., all the petitions were filed by ordinary citizens.
70 1 L.S.I. 9 (5708–1948).
71 Repealed by § 59 of Basic Law: The Government. The effect of the repeal is from the day the Prime Minister elected in the elections to the next Knesset, expected in 1996.
72 See also Basic Law: The Government, § 64(a), Sefer Hachukim No. 1396, 5752–1992, p. 214, which extends the declaration of state of emergency to the time when the law becomes applicable.
73 17 P.D. 2088 (1963).

the passing of a decree requiring the transportation of bread only in closed, dry and clean boxes, was *ultra vires*, because it had nothing to do with an emergency situation. Justice Agranat held that the viewing of a certain action as necessary in time of peace does not contradict it being necessary in time of emergency, but that the purpose of the emergency powers was to speed up legislation only in time of emergency. In the 90's a new trend developed with regard to the willingness of the Court to review the discretion of the minister who issues emergency regulations under section 9 of the Law and Administration Ordinance.

In *Poraz v. State of Israel,*[74] Justice Shlomo Levin held that the passing of emergency regulations in order to speed up regular legislative proceedings was illegal. There is indeed no logic in currently utilizing emergency powers by the government to ease the procedures of zoning and planning bodies due to the urgent need of preparing housing for the immigration of the Jews from the U.S.S.R.[75] Justice Shlomo Levin adopted Justice Barak's test[76] for the application of the authorization law. The test is three fold: first there should be a specific necessary legal goal, then there should be a legal means-authority; and last, the discretion in the relationship between the goal and the mean should be legal. In *Poraz*, the Court recognized that absorption of immigrants is a necessary legal goal, and that the passing of emergency regulations in order to overcome bureaucratic problems and prepare in an efficient and speedy way constituted a responsive means. The Court held, however, that the third element was not fulfilled in that case: the minister did not consider the possibility of reaching the same goal with regular legislation. Therefore, the regulations were declared void. This decision greatly strengthened the principle of the rule of law in Israel.

This brief review of the developments in the scope of judicial review of the application of emergency regulations illustrates the important role of the Supreme Court in Israel sitting as a High Court of Justice. In the absence of a written constitution, the Court utilizes the tool of interpretation. Recognizing the inherent dangers emergency regulations pose to the rule of law, the Court used a strict test for their application.

Concern over the negative implications of maintaining a special system based on an almost permanent state of emergency was shared by Israeli jurists and scholars. Prof. Rubinstein has warned that the situation according to which the Knesset could actually relieve itself from the burden of legislation, did not coincide with the principles of the rule of law.[77] Prof. Shetreet and Prof. Gavison[78] expressed support for the repeal of such regulations as the Defence (Emergency)

---

74 *Id.*

75 *Poraz v. Minister of Construction and Housing*, 44(3) P.D. 317.

76 *Rozen v. Minister of Trade Industry and Tourism*, 33 P.D. 281 (1979).

77 A. Rubinstein, 2 *The Constitutional Law of the State of Israel* 612, (4th edition, 1991) [in Hebrew].

78 24(3-4) I.L.R. (1990).

Regulations, 1945. Instead, they advocated their replacement by modern legislation which would be more sensitive to civil rights, as had already been done in respect of administrative detention[79] and wire tapping.[80]

Recognizing the potential damage to the society when the normal course of application of law in the country is not followed, the Knesset finally repealed section 9 of the Law and Administration Ordinance, 5708–1948.

Basic Law: The Government[81] which will come into effect from the election to the 14th Knesset in 1996, largely limits the scope of application of emergency regulations. According to section 49:[82]

> a. In the event the Knesset saw that an emergency situation exists in the State, it may, upon its initiative or upon a suggestion by the government, declare a state of emergency.
>
> b. The period in which the declaration is valid will be as provided by the declaration, but will not exceed one year; The Knesset may repeat and declare a state of emergency.
>
> c. In the event the government saw that a state of emergency exists in the State and because of the urgency of the matter it is necessary to declare a state of emergency before the Knesset convenes, it may declare a state of emergency; Such declaration will become invalid within 7 days from the time when it was made, unless approved or repealed earlier by the Knesset by a resolution of the majority of its members. If the Knesset has not convened, the government may repeat the declaration of state of emergency.
>
> d. Declarations by the Knesset or the government of state of emergency will be published in Rashumot. If it is impossible, the declaration will be published in a different proper way, as long as it will be published in Rashumot as soon as possible.
>
> e. The Knesset may, at any time, repeal a declaration of state of emergency; A notice of repeal will be published in Rashumot.

The important changes in the new law include limitations on the purpose and possible applications of emergency regulations. According to section 50:

> a. In a state of emergency the government may pass emergency regulations to protect the State, public safety and maintenance of supply of necessary goods and services. Emergency regulations will be tabled with the Knesset committee of foreign affairs and national security as soon as possible after being passed.
>
> b. The Prime Minister may pass or authorize a minister of the government to pass emergency regulations if convinced that it is impossible to convene the government and there is an urgent crucial need for passing the regulations.

---

79 Emergency Powers (Detention) Law, 1979, 33 L.S.I. 89 (1978–79).

80 Secret Monitoring Law, 1979, 33 L.S.I. 141 (1978–79).

81 15 Dinim 9985 (1992–); Sefer Hachukim no. 1396 of 4.14.92.

82 Translation by author.

c. Emergency regulations may change, temporarily void, or condition the application of any law, impose or increase taxes or other duties, unless otherwise prescribed by law.

d. Emergency regulations cannot prevent petition to the courts, and cannot determine retroactive punishment, or permit the inflicting of damage to a person's dignity.

e. Emergency regulations will not be passed, nor will any arrangement based on them be carried out except for the extent necessary due to the state of emergency.

f. Emergency regulations will become void within three months from the time they passed unless extended by law, or voided by the Knesset in a law, or by resolution by the majority of the Knesset members.

g. Emergency regulations will come into effect following publication in Rashumot. If publication is impossible, they will be published in another suitable way, as long as published in Rashumot when possible.

h. Emergency regulations will be in effect no more then 60 days from the cessation of state of emergency, unless extended by law.

Requirements such as the tabling regulations with the appropriate Knesset committee, the publication in the official gazette and the prohibition of retroactive punishment, are clearly associated with demands stemming from adherence to the rule of law. The express negation of power of emergency regulations to prevent petitioners from reaching the court system grants legislative ground for the existing situation, whereby the Supreme Court sitting as a High Court of Justice entertains petitions of persons harmed by such regulations. The "revolutionary" reform, provided by section 50(d) is the prohibition of application of emergency regulations in a way that will inflict harm to a person's dignity.

The principle of protection of "a person's life, body and dignity" was established a month earlier in Basic Law: Human Dignity and Freedom.[83] According to Justice Barak,[84] the passing of this law, as well as Basic Law: Occupation, formed a constitutional revolution, in that these two laws "bind not only the citizens and residents, and not only the administrative authorities,... (but the Knesset itself)." The enactment of section 50(d) of Basic Law: The Government, according to Barak, supports this revolution. The guarantees provided by Basic Law: Human Dignity and Freedom includes the rights to safeguarding life, body and dignity, property, personal liberty, exit and entry from and into Israel, privacy and personal confidentiality. Section 12 of the law addresses the issue of emergency regulations while providing that:

---

83 *Sefer Hachukim* of 17 March 1992.

84 Remarks of the Honorable Justice Aharon Barak upon Receiving the Degree of Doctor Honoris Causa from the University of Haifa, 18 May 1992.

> Emergency Regulations shall not have the power to change this Basic Law, to suspend its force temporarily, or to set conditions upon it, however, when there exists a state of emergency in the State by virtue of a proclamation... Emergency regulations may be promulgated... which deny or restrict rights according to this Basic Law, provided that the denial or the restriction are for a worthy purpose, and for a period and to an extent that shall not exceed what is necessary.

The recent developments in the Middle East towards peace raise hopes that normalcy will replace the state of emergency in effect since 1948. Indeed, a state of war has been recognized in the past as a justification for circumventing normal legal procedures by other democratic countries, such as England[85] and the U.S.[86] The logic behind enabling the executive to circumvent the legislature is that in time of emergency there may be reasons obliging the creation of "speedy legislation". This may occur when the legislative body is unable "to pass in the necessary speed, or preventing it to operate, either in a proper way or at all".[87]

On the other hand, and while there may be justification for allowing passing of emergency regulations, concern has been raised as to the extent of such authorization. Some scholars call for the termination of the general declaration of state of emergency in Israel. Unlike in England and in the U.S., the state of emergency in the Middle East is no longer temporary. It had almost become permanent. Shetreet suggested long before the new conditions in the Middle East that the permanent state of emergency in force since 1948 should have been terminated and a different arrangement should have been introduced, distinguishing between special emergency situations that would allow the exercise of only limited powers. In my opinion, it may still be premature to dispense with the declaration altogether. Peace treaties are still not concluded between Syria, Lebanon and Israel. Iran still sees itself as an enemy of the Jewish State. Terrorism and extremism may be on the rise. The new legislation, Basic Law: The Government, and Basic Law: Human Dignity and Freedom represents a compromise between security and democratic concerns. It is evident, however, that these basic laws will facilitate the task of the courts in protecting human rights. The basic constitutional principles are now written in basic laws, which have more weight then regular laws. These basic laws, particularly Basic

---

85 See *Liversidge v. Anderson* [1942] A.C. 206, as cited by Rubinstein, *The Constitutional Law,* at p. 618, where the House of Lords refused to intervene in the discretion of the Minister of Interior in arresting a person during World War II under emergency regulations authorizing the arrest of a person who is likely to be of a hostile origin or with connections to hostile countries.

86 See W. Brennan, Jr., 'The Quest to Develop a Jurisprudence of Civil Liberties in Times of Security Crises', 18 *Israel Yearbook on Human Rights* (hereafter I.Y.H.R.) 11 (1988).

87 Klinghoffer, 'On Emergency Regulations in Israel', in *Jubilee Book for Pinchas Rozen*, (1962), p. 86, cited by Justice Levin.

Law: Human Dignity and Freedom, provide the Court with the power of repeal of regular laws.[88]

2. Security Considerations

The method often used by the Court in reviewing actions, claimed to be based on security considerations, was to exercise judicial review on the issue of whether or not the executive operated within its jurisdiction. Already in the early days of the State, the Supreme Court annulled security decisions where it was proven that the public office holder exceeded his authority or did not fulfil the procedural requirements laid down by law.[89] Various decisions since 1970 indicate an extension of scope of intervention of the Court in security considerations. In these cases the Court was willing to go into the merits of these considerations, and not only evaluate the propriety of their procedure.[90] In the case of *Elon Moreh*,[91] the Court reviewed the security considerations of the Cabinet and the Chief of Staff, when taking possession of private land in the West Bank. The Court found that the decision was not based on "military needs", which are not sanctioned by conventional international law, and thus part of Israeli domestic law. Officers of the State of Israel must respect Israeli law even when they act outside the territorial boundaries of the State.[92] The Court held that it had power of review of such actions conducted by the military under section 7 of the Courts Law, 1957. The reason for this is that the Military Commander and his subordinates are public officials who exercise a public function by virtue of law.[93] Based on the latter, in *Samara v. Commander of Judea and Samaria*[94] the Court intervened to reverse the decision of the Commander, who had applied pre-established criteria on security grounds to the question of whether the petitioner, a resident of Germany, could reunite with his wife and children in the West Bank. In

88 See A. Barak, 'The Constitutional Revolution: Protected Basic Rights', pre-print given to author, published in 3 *Interpretation at Law* (1994).

89 See *Al-Karbuteli v. Minister of Defense*, 2 P.D. 5 (1949–50); *Aslan v. Military Governor*, 5 P.D. 1480 (1951); *Al-Khouri v. Chief of Staff*, 4 P.D. 34 (1950); and *Alrahman v. Minister of Interior*, 6 P.D. 364 (1952)

90 See S. Shetreet, 'The Scope of Judicial Review of National Security Considerations in Free Speech and other Areas: The Israeli Perspective', 18 I.Y.H.R. 35 (1988).

91 *Dweikat v. Government of Israel*, 34(1) P.D. 1 (1980).

92 The Israeli Supreme Court sitting as a High Court of Justice extended its jurisdiction to apply to petitions of residents of the West Bank and Gaza against the Military. This is based on the view that the Military is authorized to act based on law – Basic Law: the Army; The Court has *in personam* jurisdiction over Israeli military personnel, but does not have territorial jurisdiction. By petitioning to the Court the petitioners agree to adjudication of their cases against the military.

93 *Jamayat Askan Alm'Almun v. Commander of IDF Forces in the Judea and Samaria Region*, 37(4) PD (1983).

94 34(4) P.D. 1 (1980).

Asly v. Jerusalem District Commissioner,[95] it was held that a decision for the withdrawal of a newspaper licence due to security considerations must be backed by sufficient evidence and should prove to be a reasonable conclusion from such evidence.

The willingness of the Supreme Court sitting as a High Court of Justice to exercise judicial review of security considerations taken by the military was expressed by Justice Barak in a 1988 case concerning the military censor's decision banning publication of sections of an article about the Mossad, Israel's intelligence agency. According to Justice Barak:

> The security character of administrative discretion hampered judicial review in the past. Judges are not members of the security establishment and they should refrain from intervening in security considerations. Over the years it has been explained that security considerations are not unique insofar as judicial review is concerned. Judges are not administrators, yet the principle of separation of powers requires that they review the lawfulness of administrative decisions. In this regard, security considerations enjoy no special status. They, too, must be applied in accordance with the law and they, too, must be subject to judicial review. Just as judges are capable and obliged to examine the reasonableness of professional discretion in each and every sphere, so they are capable and obliged to examine security-related discretion. This is the basis for the approach that there are no special limits to the scope of judicial review over administrative discretion in matters of state security.[96]

The lawfulness of actions by the military was reviewed in a variety of cases during the Palestinian *Intifada*. Thus, in *The Inash El Asra Association v. The Commander of IDF Forces in the Judea and Samaria Area*,[97] the Court ordered the shortening by one year of the period of closure by Order of the Military Commander of a social club, in which subversive activities had been occurring, notwithstanding warnings from the military administration. The Military Commander argued that the need arose specifically to close the club for two years during the *Intifada*. The Court rejected the argument and held:

> One of the compelling basic principles which must direct the policy of the government in Administered Territory is the wish to facilitate, to the greatest extent possible, the regular continuation of normal life, and the maintenance of educational and charitable institutions such as those for the promotion of which the Association [the petitioner] was created, and will naturally be able to contribute to the attainment of this object. And also, conversely, the closure of such institutions, which have existed and operated for an extensive period of time, is likely to cause traumas and the increase of tension, which do not contribute in any way to the imposition of normal life.

---

95 37(4) P.D. 837 (1983).

96 *Schnitzer v. Chief Military Censor*, 42(4) P.D. 617 (1988).

97 43(3) P.D. 673 (1989).

Similarly, in *Tamimi v. The Minister of Defense,*[98] the High Court of Justice rejected the refusal of the Commander of IDF Forces in Judea and Samaria (West Bank) to enable lawyers there to establish a Bar Association for the coordination and administration of their professional affairs. The Court held that it was the duty of the Military Commander to respect the laws in force in the territory and to restore normal life, as required by Article 43 of the Hague Regulations. Accordingly, the Military Commander must maintain a proper balance between this duty and the security requirements. An infringement upon that duty is permitted only when it is absolutely unavoidable as a result of the security requirements.

The situation whereby the highest court of the land provides protection to residents of a territory subject to belligerent occupation by exercising judicial control over actions of State officials is unique. The Israeli Supreme Court found itself in a position that required it to act. This is because of two reasons: first – human – and second – practical. The human reason is the conditions a million and a half Palestinians found themselves under for a long period of time due to military occupation. The practical one is defending the rule of law in Israel itself. The territories, no matter who controls them are an integral part of reality in Israel. One can only drive on the road to Jerusalem, to Raanana and Kfar Saba, or to Lod, and realize that it is impossible to disregard realities in adjacent communities. The situation whereby Israeli officials, and soldiers, in fact control such areas poses a danger to the trust these people have in the rule of law generally. Limits should be imposed on their behaviour. Whereas the decision whether to control areas, how and for how long are strategic or political decisions, the abnormal legal situation in areas which were so much connected to Israel itself was a cause for concern for the Court responsible for the administration of the rule of law in Israel.

In evaluating the degree of intervention of the Supreme Court in cases where security considerations were used in justification of violations of human rights, two conflicting views may be found. One, held by Shetreet, according to whom the Supreme Court has responsibly performed the task of safeguarding human rights against security powers;[99] the other is held by Prof. Gavison, for whom the Court has intervened only in isolated instances.[100] She notes that deportations,

98 41(4) P.D. 57 (1987).

99 I.L.R. p. 421; See also U. Amit-Kohen, R. Jarach, C. Glick, N. Biton, *The "Intifada" and the Rule of Law* , (Israel Ministry of Defense Publications, 1993), p. 81.

100 I.L.R at 448. A similar view is held by George E. Bisharat, who states that "the efficacy of the Supreme Court's supervision of the military government (in the West Bank and Gaza) is questionable". While noting that during the first eighteen years of occupation, only five of the sixty-five petitions from the territories that reached adjudication were resolved in favour of the petitioners, Mr. Bisharat recognizes the influence of the Court by saying: "The military government, however, has had to consider the possibility of Supreme Court intervention in formulating its policies." See

sealing and demolition of houses, administrative detention on the basis of privileged evidence, have all been approved by the Court. According to Gavison,

> our Supreme Court does not protect human rights during emergencies any less effectively than courts in the most civilized and democratic of countries have done… at the same time, when it is examined… whether the Court managed to prevent unjustifiable infringements of human rights, the answer is often in the negative.[101]

Conclusion

Israel has achieved great progress in developing an independent and democratic legal system. There were numerous major problems throughout the period since independence. In the early days, the system had to overcome the lack of respect for the judiciary, or to a central legal system, as evolved from the British Mandate period, and the time when Jews formed a minority in foreign countries, prior to immigration to Israel. Lack of experienced judges might have been another problem.[102] Another problem might have been the heterogeneous nature of Israeli society, the Jewish majority of which originated from such diverse areas as East and West Europe, Asia, the Middle East, Africa, etc. In addition there were the non-Jewish communities with their own customs. The finding of common ground, or rather the successful application of a central legal system in such a diverse society, was not an easy task by itself.

Law has served in Israel as a catalyzer for sovereignty, the development of the sense of community, and education. It imposed new norms on societies that were reluctant to follow them at first. Such are the laws prohibiting the marriage of minors,[103] polygamy,[104] the prohibition of dissolution of marriage against the will of the wife,[105] etc. Law, together with the new socio-economic conditions in the new

---

G. E. Bisharat, 'Land, Law, and Legitimacy in Israel and the Occupied Territories', 43(2) *The American University Law Review* 529–30 (1994). For an opinion totally negating any significance to the Israeli High Court of Justice decisions with regard to protection of property and other civil rights of Palestinians, see R. Shehadeh, *Occupier's Law, Israel and the West Bank*, (Institute for Palestine Studies, 1985), p. 22.

101 For more on the issue of protection of human rights in time of emergency see William J. Brennan, 'The Quest to Develop a Jurisprudence of Civil Liberties in Times of Security Crises', 18 I.Y.H.R. 11 (1988).

102 In Kenya, e.g., British judges continued to reside even after independence.

103 Age of Marriage Law, 5710–1950, 5 Dinim [Laws] 1801 (1986–) [in Hebrew].

104 Women's Equal Rights Law, 5711–1951, § 8(a), 5 LSI (5711–1950/51).

105 *Id.*, § 8.

state influenced the changes in customs as well as perceptions of the public.

The greatest accomplishment achieved in Israel in the field of law has been the establishment of a system which adheres to the rule of law. Accordingly, the government, like the ordinary citizen, is bound to the same rules, thus enabling the citizen to foresee with a fair degree of certainty how the authority will use its coercive powers. This is done through legislation, which must be made public. Of utmost importance is the feeling of the citizen that if his rights are violated there is redress. This feeling of trust was obtained to a great extent by the judiciary and particularly the Supreme Court's activity in the field of protection of general human rights. Based on this trust, the Court expressed its willingness to exercise judicial review over improper political activities. As noted by Prof. Shetreet, the increase of judicial review of parliamentary activities is an outcome of the process of the weakening of the political institutions, a lack of public confidence in them, together with an inability to determine certain political matters by the political bodies. The willingness of the Court to entertain political petitions might have contributed to the increase in the public's respect. At the same time, systematic intervention might have the opposite reaction of damaging the Court's reputation as an apolitical body.[106]

Examination of efficiency of the system in dealing with security-related issues reveals some important changes in public perceptions and attitudes of judges. These changes might have been influenced by the erosion of the status and image of the defence establishment as a result of the Yom Kippur and Lebanon Wars. The absolute trust placed in the executive and security establishment before these wars was further damaged following the findings of the Agranat Inquiry Commission on the Yom Kippur War and the Kahan Commission set up to investigate the events at Sabra and Shatila. Both Commission reports revealed that at times the security authorities were not innocent of faults and grave mistakes. According to Shetreet, this trend was further deepened by the Pollard affair,[107] as well as the "Bus No. 300" affair. These developments, together with the judicial review the Court extended to actions of the military, have increased the trust of the public in the legal system. Nobody is above the law, even the army.

The existence of emergency powers in the system is undoubtedly a cause for concern. The three new basic laws which were passed in 1992 indicate a new, some say, revolutionary way in the constitutional law of Israel. While maintaining the ability to pass such emergency regulations, these laws largely limit the scope and implications of such regulations. The Supreme Court will now be able to continue the path it took in

106 Shetreet, *Justice in Israel*, p. 446.

107 Pollard is an American Jew who spied for Israel, was caught and is currently serving a life sentence in a U.S. jail.

narrowly interpreting application of emergency regulations; only this time, such an approach will be based on constitutional laws, rather than on vague ideas.

The state of belligerent occupation over the West Bank and Gaza raised severe problems in the administration of justice. Since those territories were never annexed to Israel, Israeli law did not apply to them. The Israeli Supreme Court, therefore, had no territorial jurisdiction over activities taking place in the territories. The concern over the far reaching implications a long period of abnormal reality such as belligerent occupation could leave on Israeli society convinced the Court to open its gates to petitions of their residents. The level of the Court's involvement in protection of the rights of these residents may be in dispute. It was said that it follows from the fact that courts can hardly act differently, and never in history have they acted differently whenever a period of real emergency prevailed in their country. Their role in society does not enable them to review strictly the security considerations of those in charge of security in genuine states of emergency. As Prof. Gavison stated "the Court cannot rescue society from itself…".[108] Some solutions should be brought about by the executive. In signing the Peace Accords with the P.L.O., the executive responded to such a call for action.

In evaluating the efficiency of the Israeli legal system, it must be recognized that great achievements have been reached in all aspects of law. Whereas law is subject to constant changes, the fundamentals necessary for the application of a stable legal system have been positively planted in the system. Much work still has to be done. Although the judicial and recent legislative developments are generally positive, a written constitution would be of major benefit. This would offer the power to repeal laws which may affect fundamental rights. Most importantly, it would strengthen a Court empowered to review constitutional questions and guarantee its independence. Peace will further contribute to the stability and normalization of the system.

---

108 R. Gavison, 'Forty Years of Israeli Law: Constitutional Law', 24(3-4) I.L.R. 448 (1990).

12. Judicial Independence under Palestinian Rule

Mona Rishmawi

Introduction

Israel and the Palestine Liberation Organisation (PLO) signed the Declaration of Principles on Interim Self-Government Arrangements on 13 September 1993. The Declaration envisaged three phases for the resolution of the Israeli/Palestinian problem.

The first phase was implemented following the signing of the Agreement on the Gaza Strip and the Jericho Area on 4 May 1994, according to which, the powers that have been vested in the Israeli military government in Gaza and Jericho were transferred to the Palestinian Authority which is a quasi-government led by Mr. Yasser Arafat, and composed of 24 ministers from the Palestinian community from exile and the Occupied Territories. Certain matters related to external security, settlements, Israelis, and foreign relations, however, remained under the jurisdiction of Israel.

The second phase consists of an interim period of five years during which a gradual transfer of certain responsibilities that were under the jurisdiction of Israel is to take place. These responsibilities are education, culture, health, social welfare, direct taxation and tourism. Jurisdiction over Jerusalem, Israeli settlements, foreign relations, border control, are not to be transferred during this phase.

The final phase deals with the permanent status of the West Bank and Gaza. Negotiations on the permanent status, according to the agreements, are to start no later than the beginning of the third year of the interim period.

The limitations of the agreements affect the prospects for proper independent judiciary under the Palestinian rule. This paper will first outline some conceptual challenges relating to the questions of laws and courts in the Palestinian areas. It will then briefly describe the existing legal system there. Some features of the Palestinian actions in Gaza and Jericho will then be examined. The paper will conclude by proposing some concrete action.

I. Conceptual Challenges

Most societies accept that there is a need for laws to govern human and social interaction. While generally accepting this premise, the

Palestinians of the West Bank and Gaza view "law" in the negative. Throughout recent Palestinian history, "law" has been used as an instrument for oppression. During the last three decades, "law" has been associated with Israeli Military Orders which gave sweeping powers to the military, affecting all aspects of life of the Palestinian population. As the Military Orders have been forcefully applied, "law" has a negative connotation in the Palestinian context. Much of the Israeli human rights violations have been justified as necessary for "maintaining law and order".

In a society ruled by law, "maintaining law and order" should be interpreted as not the mere application of legal rules irrespective of their content and method of enforcement. If law is to be just, its objective should be to preserve human rights. Law, therefore, becomes a positive tool to allow for the healthy growth of each individual within society and to guarantee the respect of her civil, political, social, cultural, and economic rights.

Also, law should positively respond to social needs. In the West Bank and Gaza, laws which govern civil behaviour were mainly kept as they were in 1967. Only rules that advance Israeli goals were added. As a result, and although a nucleus for a civil law system exists in the West Bank and Gaza, the majority of the civil law rules are dated and need to be modernised. In addition, during the occupation, the civilian judicial structures in the West Bank and Gaza have been severely undermined.

To transform the Palestinian image of "law", there is a need not only to delete the oppressive nature of many of the legal rules applied in the West Bank and Gaza, but also to create new structures. In general, confidence in the legal and judicial institutions should be enhanced. A proactive approach is needed to make law respond to the needs of the population to ensure that its human rights are preserved.

Such an approach necessitates more than a slogan committing the Palestinian political bodies to the principles of democracy. It requires a detailed understanding of the objectives, concepts and mechanisms of democratic institutions. It also requires that those who are in power are themselves examples of how to respect the Rule of Law and human rights. Is the current Palestinian Authority willing and capable of playing such a role?

At first glimpse, the PLO appears to be a democratic liberation movement. It has accepted multi-partisan representation, and has divided its ruling organs into executive and legislative powers. Various factors, however, have led to aborting the democratic character of the organisation. In reality, power is centred in the hands of the Head of the Executive Committee who often manipulates rules and procedures. Such centralisation and manipulation severely undermine the democratic character of the PLO. The detailed knowledge of the goals and functions of democratic institutions is conspicuously lacking in the official Palestinian political context.

There is more hope for democracy at the popular level. Regular elections of student councils at universities, trade-unions, and professional organisations have allowed the Palestinians to taste some flavours of democracy, although on a small scale. Also many non-governmental organisations (NGOs) emerged during recent years, mainly to challenge Israeli policies in the West Bank and Gaza and to respond to societal needs. The NGOs address matters ranging from health care, women's issues and human rights to agriculture, land and water. While these organisations highlight the important role of the civil society, this concept is not developed adequately.

A strong civil society with a developed human rights culture is essential for democracy. During the occupation, the Palestinian human rights organisations have been challenging Israeli violations in the West Bank and Gaza. Since Palestinian autonomy, these organisations have been equally challenging Palestinian violations of human rights. These organisations have been paving the way for creating a human rights culture within the society. This task, however, is far from being completed.

In this context, it should be noted that there is a difference between Palestinians who came from outside and those who normally live inside the Occupied Territories. Although they cannot be blamed for their forced exile, most of those who returned to the Occupied Territories are persons with a dominant military background. They are now members of either the police force or the security service. In addition, there are several professionals who quit their professions to join the revolution. When they returned, they were placed at the head of civic institutions. The high-level professional exiled Palestinians are still in exile.

The centralised PLO, which is trying to transform itself from a revolutionary to a State apparatus, is ruling a population that has been oppressed and occupied for many years. To complicate matters even further, this population is not convinced by or content with the deal that was constructed in Oslo on 13 September 1993. The lack of democratic process to ensure the participation of this population in decision-making, aggravates the situation.

Of special concern is that matters within the PLO, and therefore within the Palestinian Authority, are highly personalised. Mr. Yasser Arafat rules on every aspect of life: he enters into agreements with Israel, other foreign governments and the World Bank; he appoints ministers, civil servants and judges; he orders the cleaning of streets and the arrest of individuals; he arbitrates family disputes, etc.

Under such circumstances, there is little appreciation for details or technical advice. In contrast with Israel which had large technical teams to study the Accords, the Oslo agreement was signed without being reviewed by any Palestinian lawyer. Also, the Cairo Agreement on

Gaza and Jericho was, for instance, signed with a provision that kept the Israeli Military Orders in force in Gaza and Jericho.

Palestinian State institutions are given the importance that Mr. Arafat (or Israel) decides to give them, not the importance that they deserve in a proper entity based on the Rule of Law. As will be demonstrated below, under such circumstances, amending the prevailing legal rules is not considered a priority; judges and prosecutors are appointed not necessarily on merit; arrests are made without adequate legal procedure; and, court jurisdiction is flouted by security forces.

II. The Prevailing Legal System

According to the Israeli/Palestinian Agreements, the laws that were in force in the Gaza Strip and Jericho before the implementation of the Agreements continue to apply, unless repealed in accordance with the provisions of the Agreements. As a result, the following laws are still in force in the two areas: British Mandate Laws (applicable in the Gaza Strip), Jordanian Law (applicable in Jericho), and Israeli-imposed Military Orders. Additionally, while existing laws, especially the Israeli Military Orders, grant wide powers to the military apparatus in these areas, the newly installed Palestinian authorities have frequently invoked the PLO Revolutionary Criminal Procedures. In addition to being harsh, these laws are not part of the laws of the land.

The May 1994 Agreement on the Gaza Strip and the Jericho Area includes a provision that kept the Israeli Military Orders in force in the Gaza Strip and Jericho. Military Orders have been issued since June 1967 by Israeli occupation authorities and cover all aspects of life in the West Bank and the Gaza Strip. Totalling almost 1400 in the West Bank and 1100 in the Gaza Strip, many of these Orders were issued as amendments to existing laws and have severely undermined the Rule of Law and the functioning of the judicial system in both areas. The Palestinian power to enact new rules is governed by long and cumbersome procedures which were spelled out in Article 7 of the Gaza/Jericho Agreement. Accordingly, the Palestinians are required to notify Israel of every proposed piece of legislation. Israel may, within 30 days, request that the joint committee decide whether the proposed legislation conforms to the Israeli/Palestinian Agreements. Should the joint committee fail to reach an agreement, joint appeals committees are formed. Months can pass before the proposed legislation goes into effect. Israel reserves the right to veto the legislation if it sees that it threatens a "significant Israeli interest".

III. Some Features of Palestinian Actions in Gaza and Jericho

The Palestinian legal and judicial institutions have suffered during the years of occupation. In addition to Military Orders and decrees, a stage of litigation has been cancelled and many matters falling within the jurisdiction of the Palestinian courts have been seized in favour of the Israeli military courts and tribunals; access to justice has been obstructed through imposing high fees on litigation; files have been closed; and, judges have been appointed by a military committee, and not always on merit. These problems and others have made the public lose confidence in the judicial process.

If Palestine is to be based on the Rule of Law, public confidence in the judiciary must be restored. The judiciary should be empowered to became a separate and equal state power. Only then, can it fulfil its role as the main protector of human rights and justice. Bearing these principles in mind, the following is a brief discussion of some Palestinian actions concerning the administration of justice.[1]

A. The Applicable Laws

As mentioned above, according to the Israeli/Palestinian Agreements, the laws which were in force before the implementation of the Agreements continue to be in force unless repealed in accordance with the provisions of the Agreements. As a result, the following laws are still in force in Gaza and Jericho: British Mandate laws (which are applicable in Gaza), Jordanian law (which is applicable in Jericho), and Israeli-imposed Military Orders. The Palestinian power to change these laws is governed by long and cumbersome procedures which were spelled out in article 7 of the Gaza/Jericho Agreements.

While these laws, especially the Israeli Military Orders, grant wide power to the security apparatus in these areas, the Palestinian authorities still invoke the PLO Revolutionary Criminal Procedures. The reason for this might be that the Palestinian authorities wish to grant wide powers to the Palestinian Police and other security forces, while being embarrassed to use the laws of occupation. In addition to being harsh, these laws are not part of the laws of the land. Furthermore, very few Palestinians, if any (including those who invoke them), have copies of such procedures.

Clarifying such confusion does not seem to be a priority for the Palestinian Authority. Answering a question last summer on the adoption of the Basic Laws which commit the Palestinian authorities to

---

[1] The discussion below is based on a visit to the West Bank and Gaza in September/October 1994, and information received from there since then. The information is valid until December 1994.

human rights, the Minister of Justice said that their priority is to work on investment laws.

B. Appointing Judges to the Gaza and Jericho Courts

Without clarifying the legal rules on who has the authority to appoint, dismiss and promote judges, several controversial judicial appointments were made in Gaza and Jericho. A jurisdiction was also added in Jericho.

A former Gazan lawyer who returned from forced exile after the implementation of the Gaza/Jericho Agreement was appointed by Mr. Arafat as the Chief Justice of Gaza. One of his first actions was an attempt to dismiss women judges in Gaza. Upon an intervention by Mr. Arafat, he retreated. Mr. Arafat also appointed an Attorney-General who does not possess a high reputation amongst the Gazan lawyers.

During the occupation, Jericho had a magistrate court. Under Palestinian rule, a district court has been established in Jericho. A legally trained Palestinian from outside the Occupied Territories was appointed as its head. Contrary to accepted judicial practice, the appointment was made by the Minister of Municipal Affairs. The judge does not possess adequate knowledge of the existing laws in the area. His decisions are commonly based on personal views rather than on the letter of the law. As a result, he has already committed several legal mishaps. Such errors render the question of appeal even more pressing.

In the past, the decisions of the Jericho court were subject to appeal before the Ramallah Court of Appeal. Since the Ramallah court is still under Israeli rule, there is a confusion on how to appeal the decisions of the Jericho courts. Despite the difference in the legal system, it seems that a decision was made that appeals should be made before the Gaza High Court sitting as a court of appeal. The court, however, has been returning the cases to the Jericho court without examining them. Appeals of the decisions of the Jericho courts have consequently been frozen.

C. The Jericho Prosecutor

In Jericho a new prosecutor has been appointed. He is also a Palestinian from outside the area and does not have adequate knowledge of the legal systems prevailing in the West Bank and Gaza. The most important are questions of criminal proceedings. As one Palestinian judge correctly puts it, "the law of criminal procedure is the main law which preserves the rights of the accused. If it is not understood, and clearly and systematically applied, the rights of the accused will be in jeopardy."

In practice, the legal basis for arresting or detaining a person is made without respect to criminal procedures. The authorities do not identify themselves when making the arrest and they use civilian cars. The arresting authorities do not notify the arrested person of his legal status, and they do not inform the family of the place of detention.

As a result, a number of persons have been arrested for long periods without their cases being submitted to court. Lawyers also face difficulty when trying to examine the prosecution file. Complaints to the Minister of Justice have been in vain.

D. The Role of the Palestinian Security Forces

There are at least five Palestinian security forces which operate in the West Bank and Gaza. These forces play a significant role in undermining the judiciary and conduct arrests without warrants or legal ground.

In addition they are involved in conflict resolution in so-called arbitration agreements. Several cases, either while undergoing court examination or after verdict, have been arbitrated by the Palestinian Authority. The arbitrators, who normally do not possess legal training, may reach conclusions which differ from those of the court. The question becomes that of enforcement. Contrary to the requirements of the Jordanian Law on Arbitration, the arbitration agreement often states that the arbitration decision is binding on the parties, that appeals can only be made to the Palestinian Authority, and that only Palestinian authorities can execute the decision.

The Jericho Intelligence Services sometimes act as the arbitrator. This sheds serious doubt over the question of consent of the parties, a fundamental requirement in arbitration.

E. Treatment of Prisoners

Amongst the main problems facing the Palestinian prisoners is the inadequacy of the review procedure of their cases. In Gaza, political prisoners are commonly detained without legal basis. Suspects are not informed about the reasons for detention. The only reason that is commonly given is that the arrest is taking place by order of the president.

Detainees remain in prison for a long time. In Jericho, release on bail is subject to the whim of the prosecutor. While the majority of political prisoners are generally well-treated, those suspected of common crimes are beaten at random. In July 1994, Farid Jarbu‘ was the first Palestinian to die in Palestinian Police custody.

A positive matter, however, is that human rights groups are allowed to visit places of detention in Jericho without complicated procedures.

IV. Recommended Concrete Action

A few months after the Oslo agreement was signed, the International Commission of Jurists (ICJ) and its Centre for the Independence of Judges and Lawyers (CIJL) sent a mission to the West Bank and Gaza Strip in December 1993, to study the status of the Palestinian civilian courts.[2]

The Mission reviewed the status of the civilian courts under Israeli rule. Then it offered a number of recommendations aimed at making the civil nucleus for a proper civil judiciary under a Palestinian self-governing authority. These recommendations remain valid and they are reiterated here. They include that:

the Palestinian authorities incorporate international human rights norms within the new legal system;

the widest possible consultation of all sectors of society be exercised at every stage when drafting various Palestinian legal instruments, including basic laws, without discrimination;

judges and lawyers be fully consulted about questions relating to the judiciary and the legal profession;

the establishment of an independent legal profession be encouraged in view of its centrality to the principles of the Rule of Law;

the development of legal competence in the areas of the West Bank and the Gaza Strip be strengthened and encouraged through initiating and carrying out appropriate measures such as programmes for applied legal studies;

there be strict separation between the executive, legislative and judicial powers in the future Palestinian authority;

the independence of the judiciary be guaranteed and enshrined in the constitution and different laws;

---

[2] In June this year, the ICJ/CIJL published the Mission's report. *The Civilian Court System in the West Bank and Gaza: Present and Future* is available from the ICJ Secretariat in Geneva, or from al-Haq in Ramallah.

the judiciary be given full powers over all matters of a judicial nature, especially those relevant to human rights;

a High Council of Judiciary be established with the power to appoint, promote and dismiss judges;

the power of judicial review on civil, administrative and constitutional matters be exercised by the highest judicial authority, either by establishing a Court of Cassation or a Supreme Court;

the Palestinian police force be required to follow the Code of Conduct of Law Enforcement Officials and to respect human rights norms;

the independence of Palestinian human rights NGOs be respected and that they be allowed to function without the interference of the authorities.

This is a vast and challenging agenda.

Appendix

Appendix
Israeli-Palestinian Interim Agreement on the West Bank and the Gaza Strip

Washington, September 28, 1995

The Government of the State of Israel and the Palestine Liberation Organization (hereinafter "the PLO"), the representative of the Palestinian people;

PREAMBLE

Within the framework of the Middle East peace process initiated at Madrid in October 1991;

Reaffirming their determination to put an end to decades of confrontation and to live in peaceful co-existence, mutual dignity and security, while recognizing their mutual legitimate and political rights;

Reaffirming their desire to achieve a just, lasting and comprehensive peace settlement and historic reconciliation through the agreed political process;

Recognizing that the peace process and the new era that it has created, as well as the new relationship established between the two Parties as described above, are irreversible, and the determination of the two Parties to maintain, sustain and continue the peace process;

Recognizing that the aim of the Israeli-Palestinian negotiations within the current Middle East peace process is, among other things, to establish a Palestinian Interim Self-Government Authority, i.e. the elected Council (hereinafter "the Council" or "the Palestinian Council"), and the elected Ra'ees of the Executive Authority, for the Palestinian people in the West Bank and the Gaza Strip, for a transitional period not exceeding five years from the date of signing the Agreement on the Gaza Strip and the Jericho Area (hereinafter "the Gaza-Jericho Agreement") on May 4, 1994, leading to a permanent settlement based on Security Council Resolutions 242 and 338;

Reaffirming their understanding that the interim self-government arrangements contained in this Agreement are an integral part of the whole peace process, that the negotiations on the permanent status, that will start as soon as possible but not later than May 4, 1996, will lead to the implementation of Security Council Resolutions 242 and 318, and that the Interim Agreement shall settle all the issues of the interim period and that no such issues will be deferred to the agenda of the permanent status negotiations;

Reaffirming their adherence to the mutual recognition and commitments expressed in the letters dated September 9, 1993, signed by and exchanged between the Prime Minister of Israel and the Chairman of the PLO;

Desirous of putting into effect the Declaration of Principles on Interim Self-Government Arrangements signed at Washington, DC on September 13, 1993, and the Agreed Minutes thereto (hereinafter "the DOP") and in particular Article III and Annex I concerning the holding of direct, free and general political elections for the Council and the Ra'ees of the Executive Authority in order that the Palestinian people in the West Bank, Jerusalem and the Gaza Strip may democratically elect accountable representatives;

Recognizing that these elections will constitute a significant interim preparatory step toward the realisation of the legitimate rights of the Palestinian people and their just requirements and will provide a democratic basis for the establishment of Palestinian institutions;

Reaffirming their mutual commitment to act, in accordance with this Agreement, immediately, efficiently and effectively against acts or threats of terrorism, violence or incitement, whether committed by Palestinians or Israelis;

Following the Gaza-Jericho Agreement; the Agreement on Preparatory Transfer of Powers and Responsibilities signed at Erez on August 29, 1994 (hereinafter "the Preparatory Transfer Agreement"); and the Protocol on Further Transfer of Powers and Responsibilities signed at Cairo on August 27, 1995 (hereinafter "the Further Transfer Protocol"); which three agreements will be superseded by this Agreement;

Hereby agree as follows:

CHAPTER 1: THE COUNCIL

TRANSFER OF AUTHORITY

ARTICLE I

1. Israel shall transfer powers and responsibilities as specified in this Agreement from the Israeli military government and its Civil Administration to the Council in accordance with this Agreement. Israel shall continue to exercise powers and responsibilities not so transferred.

2. Pending the inauguration of the Council, the powers and responsibilities transferred to the Council shall be exercised by the Palestinian Authority established in accordance with the Gaza-Jericho Agreement, which shall also have all the rights, liabilities and obligations to be assumed by the Council in this regard. Accordingly, the term "Council" throughout this Agreement shall, pending the inauguration of the Council, be construed as meaning the Palestinian Authority.

3. The transfer of powers and responsibilities to the police force established by the Palestinian Council in accordance with Article XIV below (hereinafter "the Palestinian Police") shall be accomplished in a phased manner, as detailed in this Agreement and in the Protocol Concerning Redeployment and Security Arrangements attached as Annex I to this Agreement (hereinafter "Annex I").

4. As regards the transfer and assumption of authority in civil spheres, powers and responsibilities shall be transferred and assumed as set out in the Protocol Concerning Civil Affairs attached as Annex III to this Agreement (hereinafter "Annex III").

5. After the inauguration of the Council, the Civil Administration in the West Bank will be dissolved, and the Israeli military government shall be withdrawn. The withdrawal of the military government shall not prevent it from exercising the powers and responsibilities not transferred to the Council.

6. A Joint Civil Affairs Co-ordination and Cooperation Committee (hereinafter "the CAC"), Joint Regional Civil Affairs Subcommittees, one for the Gaza Strip and the other for the West Bank, and District Civil Liaison Offices in the West Bank shall be established in order to

provide for co-ordination and cooperation in civil affairs between the Council and Israel, as detailed in Annex III.

7. The offices of the Council, and the offices of its Ra'ees and its Executive Authority and other committees, shall be located in areas under Palestinian territorial jurisdiction in the West Bank and the Gaza Strip.

ELECTIONS

ARTICLE II

1. In order that the Palestinian people of the West Bank and the Gaza Strip may govern themselves according to democratic principles, direct, free and general political elections will be held for the Council and the Ra'ees of the Executive Authority of the Council in accordance with the provisions set out in the Protocol Concerning Elections attached as Annex II to this Agreement (hereinafter "Annex II").

2. These elections will constitute a significant interim preparatory step towards the realisation of the legitimate rights of the Palestinian people and their just requirements and will provide a democratic basis for the establishment of Palestinian institutions.

3. Palestinians of Jerusalem who live there may participate in the election process in accordance with the provisions contained in this Article and in Article VI of Annex II (Election Arrangements Concerning Jerusalem).

4. The elections shall be called by the Chairman of the Palestinian Authority immediately following the signing of this Agreement to take place at the earliest practicable date following the redeployment of Israeli forces in accordance with Annex I, and consistent with the requirements of the election timetable as provided in Annex II, the Election Law and the Election Regulations, as defined in Article I of Annex II.

STRUCTURE OF THE PALESTINIAN COUNCIL

ARTICLE III

1. The Palestinian Council and the Ra'ees of the Executive Authority of the Council constitute the Palestinian Interim Self-Government

Authority, which will be elected by the Palestinian people of the West Bank, Jerusalem and the Gaza Strip for the transitional period agreed in Article I of the DOP.

2. The Council shall possess both legislative power and executive power, in accordance with Articles VII and IX of the DOP. The Council shall carry out and be responsible for all the legislative and executive powers and responsibilities transferred to it under this Agreement. The exercise of legislative powers shall be in accordance with Article XVIII of this Agreement (Legislative Powers of the Council).

3. The Council and the Ra'ees of the Executive Authority of the Council shall be directly and simultaneously elected by the Palestinian people of the West Bank, Jerusalem and the Gaza Strip, in accordance with the provisions of this Agreement and the Election Law and Regulations, which shall not be contrary to the provisions of this Agreement.

4. The Council and the Ra'ees of the Executive Authority of the Council shall be elected for a transitional period not exceeding five years from the signing of the Gaza-Jericho Agreement on May 4, 1994.

5. Immediately upon its inauguration the Council will elect from among its members a Speaker. The Speaker will preside over the meetings of the Council, administer the Council and its committees, decide on the agenda of each meeting, and lay before the Council proposals for voting and declare their results.

6. The jurisdiction of the Council shall be as determined in Article XVII of this Agreement (Jurisdiction).

7. The organisation, structure and functioning of the Council shall be in accordance with this Agreement and the Basic Law of the Palestinian Interim Self- Government Authority, which Law shall be adopted by the Council. The Basic Law and any regulations made under it shall not be contrary to the provisions of this Agreement.

8. The Council shall be responsible under its executive powers for the offices, services and departments transferred to it and may establish, within its jurisdiction, ministries and subordinate bodies, as necessary for the fulfilment of its responsibilities.

9. The Speaker will present for the Council's approval proposed internal procedures that will regulate, among other things, the decision-making processes of the Council.

SIZE OF THE COUNCIL
ARTICLE IV

The Palestinian Council shall be composed of 82 representatives and the Ra'ees of the Executive Authority, who will be directly and simultaneously elected by the Palestinian people of the West Bank, Jerusalem and the Gaza Strip.

THE EXECUTIVE AUTHORITY OF THE COUNCIL
ARTICLE V

1. The Council will have a committee that will exercise the executive authority of the Council, formed in accordance with paragraph 4 below (hereinafter "the Executive Authority").

2. The Executive Authority shall be bestowed with the executive authority of the Council and will exercise it on behalf of the Council. It shall determine its own internal procedures and decision-making processes.

3. The Council will publish the names of the members of the Executive Authority immediately upon their initial appointment and subsequent to any changes.

4a. The Ra'ees of the Executive Authority shall be an *ex officio* member of the Executive Authority.

b. All of the other members of the Executive Authority, except as provided in subparagraph c. below, shall be members of the Council chosen and proposed to the Council by the Ra'ees of the Executive Authority and approved by the Council.

c. The Ra'ees of the Executive Authority shall have the right to appoint some persons, in number not exceeding twenty percent of the total membership of the Executive Authority, who are not members of the Council, to exercise executive authority and participate in government tasks. Such appointed members may not vote in meetings of the Council.

d. Non-elected members of the Executive Authority must have a valid address in an area under the jurisdiction of the Council.

OTHER COMMITTEES OF THE COUNCIL

ARTICLE VI

1. The Council may form small committees to simplify the proceedings of the Council and to assist in controlling the activity of its Executive Authority.

2. Each committee shall establish its own decision-making processes within the general framework of the organization and structure of the Council.

OPEN GOVERNMENT

ARTICLE VII

1. All meetings of the Council and of its committees, other than the Executive Authority, shall be open to the public, except upon a resolution of the Council or the relevant committee on the grounds of security, or commercial or personal confidentiality.

2. Participation in the deliberations of the Council, its committees and the Executive Authority shall be limited to their respective members only.

Experts may be invited to such meetings to address specific issues on an ad hoc basis.

JUDICIAL REVIEW

ARTICLE VIII

Any person or organization affected by any act or decision of the Ra'ees of the Executive Authority of the Council or of any member of the Executive Authority, who believes that such act or decision exceeds the authority of the Ra'ees or of such member, or is otherwise incorrect in law or procedure, may apply to the relevant Palestinian Court of Justice for a review of such activity or decision.

POWERS AND RESPONSIBILITIES OF THE COUNCIL

ARTICLE IX

1. Subject to the provisions of this Agreement, the Council will, within its jurisdiction, have legislative powers as set out in Article XVIII of this Agreement, as well as executive powers.

2. The executive power of the Palestinian Council shall extend to all matters within its jurisdiction under this Agreement or any future agreement that may be reached between the two Parties during the interim period. It shall include the power to formulate and conduct Palestinian policies and to supervise their implementation, to issue any rule or regulation under powers given in approved legislation and administrative decisions necessary for the realisation of Palestinian self-government, the power to employ staff, sue and be sued and conclude contracts, and the power to keep and administer registers and records of the population, and issue certificates, licenses and documents.

3. The Palestinian Council's executive decisions and acts shall be consistent with the provisions of this Agreement.

4. The Palestinian Council may adopt all necessary measures in order to enforce the law and any of its decisions, and bring proceedings before the Palestinian courts and tribunals.

5a. In accordance with the DOP, the Council will not have powers and responsibilities in the sphere of foreign relations, which sphere includes the establishment abroad of embassies, consulates or other types of foreign missions and posts or permitting their establishment in the West Bank or the Gaza Strip, the appointment of or admission of diplomatic and consular staff, and the exercise of diplomatic functions.

b. Notwithstanding the provisions of this paragraph, the PLO may conduct negotiations and sign agreements with states or international organizations for the benefit of the Council in the following cases only:

(1) economic agreements, as specifically provided in Annex V of this Agreement;

(2) agreements with donor countries for the purpose of implementing arrangements for the provision of assistance to the Council;

(3) agreements for the purpose of implementing the regional development plans detailed in Annex IV of the DOP or in agreements entered into in the framework of the multilateral negotiations; and

(4) cultural, scientific and educational agreements.

c. Dealings between the Council and representatives of foreign states and international organizations, as well as the establishment in the West Bank and the Gaza Strip of representative offices other than those described in subparagraph 5.a above, for the purpose of implementing the agreements referred to in subparagraph 5.b above, shall not be considered foreign relations.

6. Subject to the provisions of this Agreement, the Council shall, within its jurisdiction, have an independent judicial system composed of independent Palestinian courts and tribunals.

CHAPTER 2: REDEPLOYMENT AND SECURITY ARRANGEMENTS

REDEPLOYMENT OF ISRAELI MILITARY FORCES

ARTICLE X

1. The first phase of the Israeli military forces redeployment will cover populated areas in the West Bank – cities, towns, villages, refugee camps and hamlets – as set out in Annex I, and will be completed prior to the eve of the Palestinian elections, i.e., 27 days before the day of the actions.

2. Further redeployments of Israeli military forces to specified military locations will commence after the inauguration of the Council and will be gradually implemented commensurate with the assumption of responsibility for public order and internal security by the Palestinian Police, to be completed within 18 months from the date of the inauguration of the Council as detailed in Articles XI (Land) and XIII (Security), below and in Annex I.

3. The Palestinian Police shall be deployed and shall assume responsibility for public order and internal security for Palestinians in a phased manner in accordance with Article XIII (Security) below and Annex I.

4. Israel shall continue to carry the responsibility for external security, as well as the responsibility for overall security of Israelis for the purpose of safeguarding their internal security and public order.

5. For the purpose of this Agreement, "Israeli military forces" includes Israel Police and other Israeli security forces.

LAND

ARTICLE XI

1. The two sides view the West Bank and the Gaza Strip as a single territorial unit, the integrity and status of which will be preserved during the interim period.

2. The two sides agree that West Bank and Gaza strip territory, except for issues that will be negotiated in the permanent status negotiations, will come under the jurisdiction of the Palestinian Council in a phased manner, to be completed within 18 months from the date of the inauguration of the Council, as specified below:

a. Land in populated areas (Areas A and B), including government and Al Waqf land, will come under the jurisdiction of the Council during the first phase of redeployment.

b. All civil powers and responsibilities, including planning and zoning, in Areas A and B, set out in Annex III, will be transferred to and assumed by the Council during the first phase of redeployment.

c. In Area C, during the first phase of redeployment Israel will transfer to the Council civil powers and responsibilities not relating to territory, as set out in Annex III.

d. The further redeployments of Israeli military forces to specified military locations will be gradually implemented in accordance with the DOP in three phases, each to take place after an interval of six months, after the inauguration of the Council, to be completed within 18 months from the date of the inauguration of the Council.

e. During the further redeployment phases to be completed within 18 months from the date of the inauguration of the Council, powers and responsibilities relating to territory will be transferred gradually to Palestinian jurisdiction that will cover West Bank and Gaza Strip territory, except for the issues that will be negotiated in the permanent status negotiations.

f. The specified military locations referred to in Article X, paragraph 2 above will be determined in the further redeployment phases, within the specified time-frame ending not later than 18 months from the date of the inauguration of the Council, and will be negotiated in the permanent status negotiations.

3. For the purpose of this Agreement and until the completion of the first phase of the further redeployments:

a. "Area A" means the populated areas delineated by a red line and shaded in brown on attached map No. 1;

b. "Area B" means the populated areas delineated by a red line and shaded in yellow on attached map No. 1, and the built-up area of the hamlets listed in Appendix 6 to Annex I; and

c. "Area C" means areas of the West Bank outside Areas A and B, which, except for the issues that will be negotiated in the permanent status negotiations, will be gradually transferred to Palestinian jurisdiction in accordance with this Agreement.

ARRANGEMENTS FOR SECURITY AND PUBLIC ORDER

ARTICLE XII

1. In order to guarantee public order and internal security for the Palestinians of the West Bank and the Gaza Strip, the Council shall establish a strong police force as set out in Article XIV below. Israel shall continue to carry the responsibility for defense against external threats, including the responsibility for protecting the Egyptian and Jordanian borders, and for defense against external threats from the sea and from the air, as well as the responsibility for overall security of Israelis and Settlements, for the purpose of safeguarding their internal security and public order, and will have all the powers to take the steps necessary to meet this responsibility.

2. Agreed security arrangements and co-ordination mechanisms are specified in Annex I.

3. A Joint Co-ordination and Cooperation Committee for Mutual Security Purposes (hereinafter "the JSC"), as well as Joint Regional Security Committees (hereinafter "RSCs") and Joint District Co-ordination Offices (hereinafter "DCOs"), are hereby established as provided for in Annex I.

4. The security arrangements provided for in this Agreement and in Annex I may be reviewed at the request of either Party and may be amended by mutual agreement of the Parties. Specific review arrangements are included in Annex I.

5. For the purpose of this Agreement, "the Settlements" means, in the West Bank – the settlements in Area C; and in the Gaza Strip – the Gush Katif and Erez settlement areas, as well as the other settlements in the Gaza Strip, as shown on attached map No. 2.

SECURITY

ARTICLE XIII

1. The Council will, upon completion of the redeployment of Israeli military forces in each district, as set out in Appendix 1 to Annex I, assume the powers and responsibilities for internal security and public order in Area A in that district.

2a. There will be a complete redeployment of Israeli military forces from Area B. Israel will transfer to the Council and the Council will assume responsibility for public order for Palestinians. Israel shall have the overriding responsibility for security for the purpose of protecting Israelis and confronting the threat of terrorism.

b. In Area B the Palestinian Police shall assume the responsibility for public order for Palestinians and shall be deployed in order to accommodate the Palestinian needs and requirements in the following manner:

(1) The Palestinian Police shall establish 25 police stations and posts in towns, villages, and other places listed in Appendix 2 to Annex I and as delineated on map No. 3. The West Bank RSC may agree on the establishment of additional police stations and posts, if required.

(2) The Palestinian Police shall be responsible for handling public order incidents in which only Palestinians are involved.

(3) The Palestinian Police shall operate freely in populated places where police stations and posts are located, as set out in paragraph b.(1) above.

(4) While the movement of uniformed Palestinian policemen in Area B outside places where there is a Palestinian police station or post will be carried out after co-ordination and confirmation through the relevant DCO, three months after the completion of redeployment from Area B, the DCOs may decide that movement of Palestinian policemen from the police stations in Area B to Palestinian towns and villages in Area B on roads that are used only by Palestinian traffic will take place after notifying the DCO.

(5) The co-ordination of such planned movement prior to confirmation through the relevant DCO shall include a scheduled plan, including the number of policemen, as well as the type and number of weapons and vehicles intended to take part. It shall also include details of arrangements for ensuring continued co-ordination through appropriate communication links, the exact schedule of movement to the area of the planned operation, including the destination and routes thereto, its proposed duration and the schedule for returning to the police station or post. The Israeli side of the DCO will provide the Palestinian side with its response, following a request for movement of policemen in accordance with this paragraph, in normal or routine cases within one day and in emergency cases no later than 2 hours.

(6) The Palestinian Police and the Israeli military forces will conduct joint security activities on the main roads as set out in Annex 1.

(7) The Palestinian Police will notify the West Bank RSC of the names of the policemen, number plates of police vehicles and serial numbers of weapons, with respect to each police station and post in Area B.

(8) Further redeployment is from Area C and transfer of internal security responsibility to the Palestinian Police in Areas B and C will be carried out in three phases, each to take place after an interval of six months, to be completed 18 months after the inauguration of the Council, except for the issues of permanent status negotiations and of Israel's overall responsibility for Israelis and borders.

(9) The procedures detailed in this paragraph will be reviewed within six months of the completion of the first phase of redeployment.

THE PALESTINIAN POLICE

ARTICLE XIV

1. The Council shall establish a strong police force. The duties, functions, structure, deployment and composition of the Palestinian Police, together with provisions regarding its equipment and operation, as well as rules of conduct, are set out in Annex I.

2. The Palestinian police force established under the Gaza-Jericho Agreement will be fully integrated into the Palestinian Police and will be subject to the provisions of this Agreement.

3. Except for the Palestinian Police and the Israeli military forces, no other armed forces shall be established or operate in the West Bank and the Gaza Strip.

4. Except for the arms, ammunition and equipment of the Palestinian Police described in Annex I, and those of the Israeli military forces, no organization, group or individual in the West Bank and the Gaza Strip shall manufacture, sell, acquire, possess, import or otherwise introduce into the West Bank or the Gaza Strip any firearms, ammunition, weapons, explosives, gunpowder or any related equipment, unless otherwise provided for in Annex I.

PREVENTION OF HOSTILE ACTS

ARTICLE XV

1. Both sides shall take all measures necessary in order to prevent acts of terrorism, crime and hostilities directed against each other, against individuals falling under the other's authority and against their property, and shall take legal measures against offenders.

2. Specific provisions for the implementation of this Article are set out in Annex I.

CONFIDENCE BUILDING MEASURES

ARTICLE XVI

With a view to fostering a positive and supportive public atmosphere to accompany the implementation of this Agreement, to establish a solid basis of mutual trust and good faith, and in order to facilitate the anticipated cooperation and new relations between the two peoples, both Parties agree to carry out confidence building measures as detailed herewith:

1. Israel will release or turn over to the Palestinian side, Palestinian detainees and prisoners, residents of the West Bank and the Gaza Strip. The first stage of release of these prisoners and detainees will take place on the signing of this Agreement and the second stage will take place prior to the date of the elections. There will be a third stage of release of detainees and prisoners. Detainees and prisoners will be released from among categories detailed in Annex VII (Release of Palestinian Prisoners and Detainees). Those released will be free to return to their homes in the West Bank and the Gaza Strip.

2. Palestinians who have maintained contact with the Israeli authorities will not be subjected to acts of harassment, violence, retribution or prosecution. Appropriate ongoing measures will be taken, in co-ordination with Israel, in order to ensure their protection.

3. Palestinians from abroad whose entry into the West Bank and the Gaza Strip is approved pursuant to this Agreement, and to whom the provisions of this Article are applicable, will not be prosecuted for offences committed prior to September 13, 1993.

CHAPTER 3: LEGAL AFFAIRS

JURISDICTION

ARTICLE XVII

1. In accordance with the DOP, the jurisdiction of the Council will cover West Bank and Gaza Strip territory as a single territorial unit, except for:

a. issues that will be negotiated in the permanent status negotiations: Jerusalem, settlements, specified military locations, Palestinian refugees, borders, foreign relations and Israelis; and

b. powers and responsibilities not transferred to the Council.

2. Accordingly, the authority of the Council encompasses all matters that fall within its territorial, functional and personal jurisdiction, as follows:

a. The territorial jurisdiction of the Council shall encompass Gaza Strip territory, except for the Settlements and the Military Installation Area shown on map No. 2, and West Bank territory, except for Area C which, except for the issues that will be negotiated in the permanent status negotiations, will be gradually transferred to Palestinian jurisdiction in three phases, each to take place after an interval of six months, to be completed 18 months after the inauguration of the Council. At this time, the jurisdiction of the Council will cover West Bank and Gaza Strip territory, except for the issues that will be negotiated in the permanent status negotiations. Territorial jurisdiction includes land, subsoil and territorial waters, in accordance with the provisions of this Agreement.

b. The functional jurisdiction of the Council extends to all powers and responsibilities transferred to the Council, as specified in this Agreement or in any future agreements that may be reached between the Parties during the interim period.

c. The territorial and functional jurisdiction of the Council will apply to all persons, except for Israelis, unless otherwise provided in this Agreement.

d. Notwithstanding subparagraph a. above, the Council shall have functional jurisdiction in Area C, as detailed in Article IV of Annex III.

3. The Council has, within its authority, legislative, executive and judicial powers and responsibilities, as provided for in this Agreement.

4a. Israel, through its military government, has the authority over areas that are not under the territorial jurisdiction of the Council, powers and responsibilities not transferred to the Council and Israelis.

b. To this end, the Israeli military government shall retain the necessary legislative, judicial and executive powers and responsibilities, in accordance with international law. This provision shall not derogate from Israel's applicable legislation over Israelis in personam.

5. The exercise of authority with regard to the electromagnetic sphere and air space shall be in accordance with the provisions of this Agreement.

6. Without derogating from the provisions of this Article, legal arrangements detailed in the Protocol Concerning Legal Matters attached as Annex IV to this Agreement (hereinafter "Annex IV") shall be observed. Israel and the Council may negotiate further legal arrangements.

7. Israel and the Council shall cooperate on matters of legal assistance in criminal and civil matters through a legal committee (hereinafter "the Legal Committee"), hereby established.

8. The Council's jurisdiction will extend gradually to cover West Bank and Gaza Strip territory, except for the issues to be negotiated in the permanent status negotiations, through a series of redeployments of the Israeli military forces. The first phase of the redeployment of Israeli military forces will cover populated areas in the West Bank – cities, towns, refugee camps and hamlets, as set out in Annex I – and will be completed prior to the eve of the Palestinian elections, i.e. 22 days before the day of the elections. Further redeployments of Israeli military forces to specified military locations will commence immediately upon the inauguration of the Council and will be effected in three phases, each to take place after an interval of six months, to be concluded no later than eighteen months from the date of the inauguration of the Council.

LEGISLATIVE POWERS OF THE COUNCIL

ARTICLE XVIII

1. For the purposes of this Article, legislation shall mean any primary and secondary legislation, including basic laws, laws, regulations and other legislative acts.

2. The Council has the power, within its jurisdiction as defined in Article XVII of this Agreement, to adopt legislation.

3. While the primary legislative power shall lie in the hands of the Council as a whole, the Ra'ees of the Executive Authority of the Council shall have the following legislative powers:

a. the power to initiate legislation or to present proposed legislation to the Council;

b. the power to promulgate legislation adopted by the Council; and

c. the power to issue secondary legislation, including regulations, relating to any matters specified and within the scope laid down in any primary legislation adopted by the Council.

4a. Legislation, including legislation which amends or abrogates existing laws or military orders, which exceeds the jurisdiction of the Council or which is otherwise inconsistent with the provisions of the DOP, this Agreement, or of any other agreement that may be reached between the two sides during the interim period, shall have no effect and shall be void ab initio.

b. The Ra'ees of the Executive Authority of the Council shall not promulgate legislation adopted by the Council if such legislation falls under the provisions of this paragraph.

5. All legislation shall be communicated to the Israeli side of the Legal Committee.

6. Without derogating from the provisions of paragraph 4 above, the Israeli side of the Legal Committee may refer for the attention of the Committee any legislation regarding which Israel considers the provisions of paragraph 4 apply, in order to discuss issues arising from such legislation. The Legal Committee will consider the legislation referred to it at the earliest opportunity.

HUMAN RIGHTS AND THE RULE OF LAW

ARTICLE XIX

Israel and the Council shall exercise their powers and responsibilities pursuant to this Agreement with due regard to internationally-accepted norms and principles of human rights and the rule of law.

RIGHTS, LIABILITIES AND OBLIGATIONS

ARTICLE XX

1a. The transfer of powers and responsibilities from the Israeli military government and its civil administration to the Council, as detailed in Annex III, includes all related rights, liabilities and obligations arising with regard to acts or omissions which occurred prior to such transfer. Israel will cease to bear any financial responsibility regarding such acts or omissions and the Council will bear all financial responsibility for these and for its own functioning.

b. Any financial claim made in this regard against Israel will be referred to the Council.

c. Israel shall provide the Council with the information it has regarding pending and anticipated claims brought before any court or tribunal against Israel in this regard.

d. Where legal proceedings are brought in respect of such a claim, Israel will notify the Council and enable it to participate in defending the claim and raise any arguments on its behalf.

e. In the event that an award is made against Israel by any court or tribunal in respect of such a claim, the Council shall immediately reimburse Israel the full amount of the award.

f. Without prejudice to the above, where a court or tribunal hearing such a claim finds that liability rests solely with an employee or agent who acted beyond the scope of the powers assigned to him or her, unlawfully or with wilful malfeasance, the Council shall not bear financial responsibility.

2a. Notwithstanding the provisions of paragraphs 1.d through 1.f above, each side may take the necessary measures, including promulgation of legislation, in order to ensure that such claims by Palestinians, including pending claims in which the hearing of evidence has not yet begun, are brought only before Palestinian courts or tribunals in the West Bank and the Gaza Strip, and are not brought before or heard by Israeli courts or tribunals.

b. Where a new claim has been brought before a Palestinian court or tribunal subsequent to the dismissal of the claim pursuant to subparagraph a. above, the Council shall defend it and, in accordance with subparagraph 1a. above, in the event that an award is made for the plaintiff, shall pay the amount of the award.

The Legal Committee shall agree on arrangements for the transfer of all materials and information needed to enable the Palestinian courts or tribunals to hear such claims as referred to in subparagraph b. above, and, when necessary, for the provision of legal assistance by Israel to the Council in defending such claims.

3. The transfer of authority in itself shall not affect rights, liabilities and obligations of any person or legal entity, in existence at the date of signing of this Agreement.

4. The Council, upon its inauguration, will assume all the rights, liabilities and obligations of the Palestinian Authority.

5. For the purpose of this Agreement, "Israelis" also includes Israeli statutory agencies and corporations registered in Israel.

SETTLEMENT OF DIFFERENCES AND DISPUTES

ARTICLE XXI

Any difference relating to the application of this Agreement shall be referred to the appropriate co-ordination and cooperation mechanism established under this Agreement. The provisions of Article XV of the DOP shall apply to any such difference which is not settled through the appropriate co-ordination and cooperation mechanism, namely:

1. Disputes arising out of the application or interpretation of this Agreement or any related agreements pertaining to the interim period shall be settled through the Liaison Committee.

2. Disputes which cannot be settled by negotiations may be settled by a mechanism of conciliation to be agreed between the Parties.

3. The Parties may agree to submit to arbitration disputes relating to the interim period, which cannot be settled through conciliation. To this end, upon the agreement of both Parties, the Parties will establish an Arbitration Committee.

CHAPTER 4: COOPERATION

RELATIONS BETWEEN ISRAEL AND THE COUNCIL

ARTICLE XXII

1. Israel and the Council shall seek to foster mutual understanding and tolerance and shall accordingly abstain from incitement, including hostile propaganda, against each other and, without derogating from the principle of freedom of expression, shall take legal measures to prevent such incitement by any organizations, groups or individuals within their jurisdiction.

2. Israel and the Council will ensure that their respective educational systems contribute to the peace between the Israeli and Palestinian peoples and to peace in the entire region, and will refrain from the introduction of any motifs that could adversely affect the process of reconciliation.

3. Without derogating from the other provisions of this Agreement, Israel and the Council shall co-operate in combating criminal activity which may affect both sides, including offences related to trafficking in illegal drugs and psychotropic substances, smuggling, and offences against property, including offences related to vehicles.

COOPERATION WITH REGARD TO TRANSFER OF POWERS AND RESPONSIBILITIES

ARTICLE XXIII

In order to ensure a smooth, peaceful and orderly transfer of powers and responsibilities, the two sides will cooperate with regard to the transfer of security powers and responsibilities in accordance with the provisions of Annex I, and the transfer of civil powers and responsibilities in accordance with the provisions of Annex III.

ECONOMIC RELATIONS

ARTICLE XXIV

The economic relations between the two sides are set out in the Protocol on Economic Relations, signed in Paris on April 29, 1994, and the

Appendices thereto, and the supplement to the Protocol on Economic Relations, all attached as Annex V, and will be governed by the relevant provisions of this Agreement and its Annexes.

COOPERATION PROGRAMS

ARTICLE XXV

1. The Parties agree to establish a mechanism to develop programs of cooperation between them. Details of such co-operation are set out in Annex VI.

2. A Standing Co-operation Committee to deal with issues arising in the context of this cooperation is hereby established as provided for in Annex VI.

THE JOINT ISRAELI-PALESTINIAN LIAISON COMMITTEE

ARTICLE XXVI

1. The Liaison Committee established pursuant to Article X of the DOP shall ensure the smooth implementation of this Agreement. It shall deal with issues requiring co-ordination, other issues of common interest and disputes.

2. The Liaison Committee shall be composed of an equal number of members from each Party. It may add other technicians and experts as necessary.

3. The Liaison Committee shall adopt its rules of procedures, including the frequency and place or places of its meetings.

4. The Liaison Committee shall reach its decisions by agreement.

5. The Liaison Committee shall establish a subcommittee that will monitor and steer the implementation of this Agreement (hereinafter "the Monitoring and Steering Committee"). It will function as follows:

a. The Monitoring and Steering Committee will, on an ongoing basis, monitor the implementation of this Agreement, with a view to enhancing the cooperation and fostering the peaceful relations between the two sides.

b. The Monitoring and Steering Committee will steer the activities of the various joint committees established in this Agreement (the JSC, the CAC, the Legal Committee, the Joint Economic Committee and the Standing Cooperation Committee) concerning the ongoing implementation of the Agreement, and will report to the Liaison Committee.

c. The Monitoring and Steering Committee will be composed of the heads of the various committees mentioned above.

d. The two heads of the Monitoring and Steering Committee will establish its rules of procedures, including the frequency and places of its meetings.

LIAISON AND COOPERATION WITH JORDAN AND EGYPT

ARTICLE XXVII

1. Pursuant to Article XII of the DOP, the two Parties have invited the Governments of Jordan and Egypt to participate in establishing further liaison and cooperation arrangements between the Government of Israel and the Palestinian representatives on the one hand, and the Governments of Jordan and Egypt on the other hand, to promote co-operation between them. As part of these arrangements a Continuing Committee has been constituted and has commenced its deliberations.

2. The Continuing Committee shall decide by agreement on the modalities of admission of persons displaced from the West Bank and the Gaza Strip in 1967, together with necessary measures to prevent disruption and disorder.

3. The Continuing Committee shall also deal with other matters of common concern.

MISSING PERSONS

ARTICLE XXVIII

1. Israel and the Council shall cooperate by providing each other with all necessary assistance in the conduct of searches for missing persons and bodies of persons which have not been recovered, as well as by providing information about missing persons.

2. The PLO undertakes to co-operate with Israel and to assist it in its efforts to locate and to return to Israel Israeli soldiers who are missing in action and the bodies of soldiers which have not been recovered.

CHAPTER 5: MISCELLANEOUS PROVISIONS

SAFE PASSAGE BETWEEN THE WEST BANK AND THE GAZA STRIP

ARTICLE XXIX

Arrangements for safe passage of persons and transportation between the West Bank and the Gaza Strip are set out in Annex I.

PASSAGES

ARTICLE XXX

Arrangements for co-ordination between Israel and the Council regarding passage to and from Egypt and Jordan, as well as any other agreed international crossings, are set out in Annex I.

FINAL CLAUSES

ARTICLE XXXI

1. This Agreement shall enter into force on the date of its signing.

2. The Gaza-Jericho Agreement, the Preparatory Transfer Agreement and the Further Transfer Protocol will be superseded by this Agreement.

3. The Council, upon its inauguration, shall replace the Palestinian Authority and shall assume all the undertakings and obligations of the Palestinian Authority under the Gaza-Jericho Agreement, the Preparatory Transfer Agreement, and the Further Transfer Protocol.

4. The two sides shall pass all necessary legislation to implement this Agreement.

5. Permanent status negotiations will commence as soon as possible, but not later than May 4, 1996 between the Parties. It is understood that these negotiations shall cover remaining issues, including: Jerusalem, refugees, settlements, security arrangements, borders, relations and co-operation with other neighbours, and other issues of common interest.

6. Nothing in this Agreement shall prejudice or preempt the outcome of the negotiations on the permanent status to be conducted pursuant to the DOP. Neither Party shall be deemed, by virtue of having entered into this Agreement, to have renounced or waived any of its existing rights, claims or positions.

7. Neither side shall initiate or take any step that will change the status of the West Bank and the Gaza Strip pending the outcome of the permanent status negotiations.

8. The two Parties view the West Bank and the Gaza Strip as a single territorial unit, the integrity and status of which will be preserved during the interim period.

9. The PLO undertakes that, within two months of the date of the inauguration of the Council, the Palestinian National Council will convene and formally approve the necessary changes in regard to the Palestinian Covenant, as undertaken in the letters signed by the Chairman of the PLO and addressed to the Prime Minister of Israel, dated September 9, 1993 and May 4, 1994.

10. Pursuant to Annex I, Article VII of this Agreement, Israel confirms that the permanent checkpoints on the roads leading to and from the Jericho Area (except those related to the access road leading from Mousa Alami to the Allenby Bridge) will be removed upon the completion of the first phase of redeployment.

11. Prisoners who, pursuant to the Gaza-Jericho Agreement, were turned over to the Palestinian Authority on the condition that they remain in the Jericho Area for the remainder of their sentence, will be free to return to their homes in the West Bank and the Gaza Strip upon the completion of the first phase of redeployment.

12. As regards relations between Israel and the PLO, and without derogating from the commitments contained in the letters signed by and exchanged between the Prime Minister of Israel and the Chairman of the PLO, dated September 9, 1993 and May 4, 1994, the two sides will

apply between them the provisions contained in Article XXII, paragraph 1, with the necessary changes.

13a. The Preamble to this Agreement, and all Annexes, Appendices and maps attached hereto, shall constitute an integral part hereof.

b. The Parties agree that the maps attached to the Gaza-Jericho Agreement as:

a. Map No. 1 (The Gaza Strip), an exact copy of which is attached to this Agreement as map No. 2 (in this Agreement "map No. 2");

b. Map No. 3 (Deployment of Palestinian Police in the Gaza Strip), an exact copy of which is attached to this Agreement as map No. 5 (in this Agreement "map No. 5"); and

c. Map No. 6 (Maritime Activity Zones), an exact copy of which is attached to this Agreement as map No. 8 (in this Agreement "map No. 8");

are an integral part hereof and will remain in effect for the duration of this Agreement.

14. While the Jeftlik area will come under the functional and personal jurisdiction of the Council in the first phase of redeployment, the area's transfer to the territorial jurisdiction of the Council will be considered by the Israeli side in the first phase of the further redeployment phases.

Done at Washington DC, this 28th day of September, 1995.

For the Government of the State of Israel	For the PLO

Witnessed by:

The United States of America	The Russian Federation
The Arab Republic of Egypt	The European Union

INTERIM AGREEMENT

INDEX

INDEX

Note: The Annexes, Exchange of Letters and Maps are not reproduced here.

Index